Seeing Black and White

SEEING
BLACK AND WHITE

Alan Gilchrist

OXFORD

UNIVERSITY PRESS
OCM 64688840
2006

OXFORD

UNIVERSITY PRESS

Oxford University Press, Inc., publishes works that further
Oxford University's objective of excellence
in research, scholarship, and education.

Oxford   New York
Auckland   Cape Town   Dar es Salaam   Hong Kong   Karachi
Kuala Lumpur   Madrid   Melbourne   Mexico City   Nairobi
New Delhi   Shanghai   Taipei   Toronto

With offices in
Argentina   Austria   Brazil   Chile   Czech Republic   France   Greece
Guatemala   Hungary   Italy   Japan   Poland   Portugal   Singapore
South Korea   Switzerland   Thailand   Turkey   Ukraine   Vietnam

Published by Oxford University Press, Inc.
198 Madison Avenue, New York, New York 10016

www.oup.com

Oxford is a registered trademark of Oxford University Press

Library of Congress Cataloging-in-Publication Data
Gilchrist, Alan.
Seeing black and white / by Alan Gilchrist.
p.   cm. (Oxford psychology series; no. 40)
Includes bibliographical references and index.
ISBN 0-19-518716-4
ISBN-13 978-0-19-518716-8
1. Imagery (Psychology).   I. Title.   II. Series.
BF241.L54   2006
153—dc22   2006006283

9 8 7 6 5 4 3 2 1

Printed in the United States of America
on acid-free paper

*This book is dedicated to the
memory of Irvin Rock,
my wonderful mentor
and warm friend.*

Foreword

And God said let Gilchrist be and all was light.
—V. S. Ramachandran

I feel honored to be asked to write this foreword for Professor Alan Gilchrist's book, as I have followed his work on perception with keen interest over the years.

The study of perception has a long and venerable history dating back to the great 19th-century German physicist, physiologist, and ophthalmologist Hermann Von Helmholtz, who more than anyone else pointed out that the visual image is inherently ambiguous. A circular image in the retina can be produced by an infinity of oval objects of different widths, each tilted by a certain amount. Black print in sunlight reflects more light than a white page seen in artificial light at night, yet it looks black. The only way the brain *could* solve such a problem, Helmholtz realized, was by using certain built-in knowledge or "assumptions" about the statistics of the natural world ("built in" can either mean built in by learning or by genes; Helmholtz emphasized the former, and Hering, the latter). These assumptions are used by the visual system to eliminate an infinity of improbable solutions and home in effortlessly on the correct solution. Since these mechanisms are unconscious—on autopitot, as it were—Helmholtz called them "unconscious inferences," a phrase that has never been improved on. The study of perception, then, is the study of these assumptions and of their implementation in the neural hardware of the brain.

One approach to perception is to study visual illusions, which have the same effect on psychologists as the smell of burning rubber on an engineer: an irresistible urge to find the cause (as Peter Medawar once said of philosophers). Illusions are not mere curiosities; they are cleverly contrived stimuli that reveal the hidden assumptions that drive perception and allow us to discover underlying rules of operation. This book is full of lovely new examples of illusions of brightness and lightness, many of which were discovered by the author.

In the last century the experimental study of perception went through three distinct stages. First, in the early 20th century the Gestalt psychologists (including Wertheimer, Koffka, Köhler, and Anstis) used astonishingly simple displays to uncover what they called the "laws" of perception, reminding us that great science is driven mainly by ingenuity and experimental cunning rather than fancy equipment. Unfortunately, some of them—although not the best among them—had the habit of calling every observation a "law," with the air of having actually explained something. (Such explanations, as Peter Medawar might have said, are "mere analgesics that dull the ache of incomprehension without removing the cause.") It is to Gilchrist's credit that he doesn't fall into this trap.

But at least the Gestaltists discovered and studied perceptually compelling phenomena; what they did was *interesting*. The same cannot be said of the next big movement, called (ironically) "classical psychophysics," which was championed by Stevens at Harvard. This movement, which completely eclipsed Gestalt psychology, was partly the result of the pernicious effects of behaviorism and a general suspicion of "introspective" psychology. It became unfashionable, for several decades, to *ask* the subject what he or she was actually seeing in a visual display. Which is ironic, given that that's why most of us study perception in the first place! The emphasis was placed, instead, on obtaining detailed quantitative measurements of small second-order effects, in order to plot what are pompously referred to as "psychometric functions" (i.e., graphs). A time will come when this whole movement will be seen as a curious anomaly in the history of psychology, a manifestation of "physics envy" and the accompanying belief that the *mere* act of measuring something makes it scientific (what I call "researchmanship" rather than research).

When I was a graduate student in Cambridge, in the late seventies, the use of any perceptual stimuli, other than blurred stripes, was considered taboo. (To be sure, sine wave gratings *were* useful stimuli for providing more complete and accurate descriptions of visual performance than two-point discrimination, resulting in the use of modulation-transfer functions. But it's fair to say people got a bit carried away.) Giles Brindley told us there are two types of experiments: Class A (obtaining "psychometric functions") and Class B (simply observing carefully what you see—for example, the work of Bela Julesz or Edwin Land). He warned us not to trust Class B "because they are no better than dreams." (It's a good thing he wasn't around when Newton passed white light through a prism, Galileo saw the moons of Jupiter, or Faraday moved a magnet to and fro within a coil. He might have tapped them on the shoulder and said, "This isn't science until you have obtained a graph," thereby aborting the birth of physics.) And as for biology, David Hubel once reminded me that the most important book ever published—Darwin's *Origin of Species*—doesn't have a single graph in it!

This desire to "ape" physics is especially ironic given that physics itself had to initially go through a qualitative "Faraday" stage before it reached a mature quantitative "Maxwell" stage. Psychology has to—and will—pass through the same stages, and there is simply no point in trying to jump ahead.

Fortunately, this obsession with blurred stripes turned out to be a temporary aberration. In the last three decades there has been a tremendous resurgence of interest in those phenomena that drew us all to the study of perception in the first place. This was spearheaded by Irvin Rock, Richard Gregory, J. J. Gibson, George Sperling, Bela Julesz, Julie Hochberg, Gaetano Kanizsa, and Donald MacKay in the generation previous to mine. Although their work was initially ignored by the "classical psychophysics" types, (remember Kenneth Ogle's dismissal of Julesz and Leo Hurvich's contempt for Edwin Land?), it has now become part of "mainstream" research in perception. The study of perception became *interesting* once again. When I tell younger colleagues about the Ogle/Julesz debate, the usual reaction I get is, "Who's Ogle?" Exactly my point.

Following this, there was a sort of "neo-gestalt" revolution—a movement that owes its existence largely to a handful of contemporary researchers: Ken Nakayama, Pat Cavanagh, Randy Blake, Chris Tyler, Ted Adelson, Lothar Spillman, and, now, Alan Gilchrist, Dale Purves, and Pawan Sinha. Thanks to all these researchers (and many whose names I've left out) there has been a renaissance of interest in such phenomena as illusory contours, occlusion, shape-from-shading, binocular rivalry, apparent motion, and perceptual "constancies"—intrinsically fascinating phenomena that were eclipsed by "Class A" psychophysics for nearly three decades. (But to be fair to Brindley, Class A research has had its victories, especially in the study of color vision. The discovery of the detailed laws of Trichromacy is one of the great triumphs of visual science, although—as David Hubel noted—its practitioners study it with a passion that seems grossly out of proportion to its evolutionary importance.) But it's the revival of interest in what used to be called "illusions" that has fired the imagination of physiologists (no mean feat!) and AI researchers.

If you look at the big picture, these last two decades have been heady times for perceptual psychologists. The neo-gestalt revolution is here!

One of the foremost among these revolutionaries is the author of this book. What I especially like about his work is that, unlike many of us who jump around from topic to topic, he has devoted his whole life to the single-minded pursuit of the laws that govern our perception of lightness/brightness. Anyone acquainted with Gilchrist knows that he doesn't merely *study* lightness; he *lives* it. (I remember driving around Manhattan with him. Any advertisement or newly painted or oddly illuminated wall becomes an "experiment" for him as he jumps out of the car excitedly, oblivious to the traffic; high on science, high on life, and just high!) The result of his lifelong obsession is this book, the most comprehensive and thorough monograph on this topic that has ever been published, a tome that Helmholtz and Hering would have taken great delight reading in their bathrooms. The book is full of dazzling insights and beautiful new visual effects that the author has accumulated over a lifetime—truly a labor of love.

But the book isn't merely a catalog of illusions. Theories of lightness perception receive extensive analysis. A central and recurring theme is that what Gilchrist calls structure-blind theories are bound to fail. That is, any viable lightness theory must be sensitive to the perceptual structure of the image. This includes the critical role of depth perception in lightness and the distinction between reflectance and illumination edges. Particularly vulnerable here are spatial filtering models, because they lack any mechanism that can distinguish edges in the image that result from a change of illumination from those caused by a change of reflectance.

As a Gestaltist, Gilchrist invokes the principle of pragnanz, or simplicity, to explain many perceptual outcomes. But he acknowledges that these could be accounted for equally well by Bayesian theory. A good illustration of what I would call Bayesian logic and Gilchrist would call simplicity is provided by a lovely demonstration by Bergström. Imagine you have a sheet of paper with a Land-style black/white/shades of gray Mondrian painted on it, with sharp edges and different random shades of gray (see Figure 7.6). Now using an old-fashioned slide projector, project a square wave grating (sharp-edged gray stripes) on a plain sheet of white paper. Of course, that's what you see, gray stripes as on a zebra, but no depth (even though the same stimulus could be produced by venetian blinds). But now project the same stripes on the *Mondrian*. Astonishingly the stripes now magically spring to depth! They look like slanted rooftops. Why?

It's because the Mondrian squares' luminance varies *randomly*, but along the edge of each stripe the *sign* and *magnitude* of luminance *covary* as we traverse the randomly varying Mondrian checks, parallel to the stripes, in a manner that could *only* have been produced by venetian blinds illuminated by a single light source. The brain prefers this parsimonious interpretation (venetian blinds in 3D) to the highly improbable alternative of the luminances covarying in this manner simply by chance.

Midway through his career, Gilchrist experienced an important theoretical shift as his empirical work began to suggest that visual processing is less intellectually consistent and more quick-and-dirty. His newer thinking, seen in his recent proposal called anchoring theory, is somewhat reminiscent of my earlier claims that perception is a "bag of tricks." Contrary to AI researchers, the solution to even any single perceptual problem—say, motion correspondence or shape-from-shading—proceeds not by the use of a single sophisticated algorithm but by the simultaneous deployment of multiple heuristics or short-cuts. One reason for this is that evolution has no foresight, so it's much easier to *evolve* multiple shortcuts rather than a single sophisticated algorithm. Contrary to AI researchers' views, you cannot figure out perceptual mechanisms by "reverse engineering" because, as Francis Crick said, "God is a hacker," not an engineer, and there is no such thing as "reverse hacking" (it's an oxymoron). The second reason for using multiple parallel heuristics is that it buys you tolerance for noisy images. It's a bit like two drunks striving to reach a goal. Each will stumble if he tries on his own ("illusions"), but by leaning on each other they can stagger toward the goal. That's perception in a nutshell. And a good example can be seen in Gilchrist's resurrection of the Kardos principle of co-determination: lightness is not computed ex-clusively within each framework of illumination, but involves a com-promise between local and global frames of reference.

Like Gilchrist, Crick was a devout atheist and formidable opponent of creationists, although he was equally opposed to pop evolutionary psychology (the view that every quirk of the mind must have evolved as a specific result of selection and must have a function). The story is told about what happened when he reached the gates of heaven. "Introduce me to God, if he exists," said Francis. "Why, of course, Francis," said St Peter. "Just follow me." Crick was then escorted to a filthy old shack around which were scattered rusty old nuts and bolts and bits and pieces of hundreds of different machines. A wizened old man emerged, wiping the sweat off his hand with a filthy rag covered with oil and soot; God was apparently a mechanic! "God, I have only one question for you," said Crick. "One that has been troubling me for years."

"What's that? I'd be happy to answer it, Francis."

"Why do insect embryos have imaginal discs?"

"Well, Francis, frankly, I don't know. But I've been using it for 200 million years and so far no one has complained."

This story encapsulates what I once called the "utilitarian theory" (or bag-of-tricks theory) of perception.

To say that perception is a bag of tricks doesn't imply that it's cha-otic and completely unlawful. The human body is a bag of tricks, but Starling's laws of cardiac function are still taught to medical students and still useful in clinical assessment. The same holds for many of the rules that govern perception. We must be wary of overarching theo-ries, but the laws themselves have an internal logic dictated by the statistics of the environment.

For example, Gilchrist proposes a model of lightness whereby the retinal image is decomposed into overlapping illuminance and reflectance images by classifying edges (and he emphasizes the presence of illumination edges and points out the need for edge classification). He also identifies what he calls the "anchoring problem." Prior to his work, lightness theories were mainly preoccupied with—and could only predict—*relative* lightness values perceived in the display. Gilchrist's approach helps provide an answer to a question many a bright undergraduate asks (but most professors brush aside because they can't answer): if most cells in the visual pathway are sensitive only to edges and contrast, how do we ever perceive the *level of surface lightness*?

Gilchrist also devotes some pages to the so-called nature-nurture debate in the context of perception. To what extent are the mechanisms of perception innately specified by the genome (acquired through natural selection) and to what extent by learning? Personally I don't see what all the fuss is about. The more important agenda, surely, is to answer the question of what the potential sources of information are, which of these sources are actually exploited by the visual system, and how this is actually achieved ("how" answered both in terms of the steps involved and in terms of implementation in neurons). The question of what the rules are—specified in functional terms—and how these rules incorporate the statistics of the natural world is interesting in itself. And it's *orthogonal* to the question of whether the rules are acquired through evolution or through learning.

By way of analogy consider stereopsis. Our two eyes look at the world from two slightly different vantage points. This gives rise to differences between the images that, for any given angle of fixation, are proportional to the relative distances between objects in the world. The fact that this information (retinal disparity) is *available* was first noticed by Leonardo Da Vinci, who realized that because of this principle you could never fully depict realistic depth on a canvas. But it remained for Wheatstone to show that the information is not only available but is actually used by the brain. He did this by stripping pictures of all other depth cues (using skeleton outline drawings) and showing that depth was seen when the pictures in the two eyes were slightly different (a Brindley Class B experiment). It's truly amazing that people had been wandering around the planet for thousands of years probably thinking that the only reason we had two eyes was that if you lost one you would still have the other to spare. (The real selection pressure for frontal vision in nocturnal primates came from the need to be more sensitive to light, but once that happened, additional selection came from the utility of stereopsis.) It's only after Wheatstone's discovery that we really understood stereopsis. Now my point in reviewing this bit of arcane history is to show that Wheatstone's discovery—that disparity is a powerful source of information which the brain actually *uses*—is important in itself. The question of whether this mechanism is hardwired through natural selection (creatures with genes that accidentally specify disparity-detecting mechanisms survived and were transmitted at the expense of those that didn't) or acquired through repeated exposure to disparate images in infancy (and perhaps calibrated through feedback) is equally interesting but logically distinct from the question of what the mechanism (disparity detection) actually is. A failure to recognize this has resulted in considerable confusion. While on the subject of disparity, I might mention that my own physiological experiments (published with Peter Clarke and David Whitteridge in *Nature* in the 1970s) showed clearly that disparity-detecting neurons were indeed "hardwired" and present at birth, thereby settling a debate between Helmoltz and Hering that lasted for two decades over this very issue, i.e., the question of whether the correspondence between disparate retinal points is innate or acquired. (Helmholtz enjoyed such immense prestige that he blocked Hering's appointment to a chair at Leipzig for daring to suggest that disparity detection was innate; ironically, our experiments suggest that Hering was right all along!)

It's unfortunate that in most areas of psychology this whole question of nature versus nurture (it should really be nature *via* nurture, as Matt Ridley says) has become transformed into a theoretical debate when it should really be an empirical one. Some aspects of vision (such as basic laws of trichromacy, disparity detection) will surely turn out to be largely hardwired, whereas others, such as the "qualia" of *fluorescence* or binocular *lustre* will turn out to be mainly learned. I doubt very much that people who detected fluorescence (based on noticing marked deviations from anchoring that cannot be explained either by the illumination or reflectance or a luminous light source) survived and left babies, whereas those didn't died out! Like the philosopher's fictitious example of Mary suddenly being exposed to (and experiencing the quale?) of color for the first time, the existence of fluorescence proves that genuinely new qualia can emerge when your brain "flags" or labels new stimulus contingencies.

Gilchrist, like his distinguished teacher Irvin Rock (and *his* equally brilliant teacher Hans Wallach), doesn't devote a lot of attention to physiological mechanisms that might underlie the phenomena of lightness perception, but he is not to blame for this. Indeed over the decades more visual physiologists could be faulted for ignoring psychophysics rather than vice versa (although they were mesmerized by sine wave gratings for a while). Which is ironic, for, as Horace Barlow once said, "a physiologist trying to study vision without a thorough knowledge of psychophysics, is like a parthenogenetic, asexual martian trying to understand the functions of the testicles by studying their detailed anatomy alone without knowing anything about sex." If he saw sperms wriggling in the testes he might regard them as parasites!

Gilchrist's book is a rich compendium of mysteries analogous to the wriggling parasites that will keep physiologists busy for a long time and send AI researchers—with their simple-minded algorithms—back to the drawing board. None of these algorithms can explain even as simple an observation as the one made by Ernst Mach. If you look at a folded white card standing upright on a table illuminated from one direction, and if you flip its depth mentally, you suddenly see the side in shadow as being painted pitch black. This is because you can no longer attribute the low luminance on the shadow side to the depth; so you attribute it to reflectance instead. How neurons in the visual pathways achieve this is still largely a mystery.

But psychophysicists are as much to blame for ignoring physiology as physiologists for ignoring function. My reply to Barlow would be as follows: Imagine trying to figure out the functions of the digestive system without ever having dissected the liver, the pancreas, the stomach, the salivary glands, etc., and by simply looking at its "output" (feces). Yet this is precisely what most psychologists do when they practice black-box psychophysics (Stuart Sutherland once described black-boxology as "an ostentatious display of flow diagrams as a substitute for thought").

Fortunately Gilchrist's book is more than just a catalog of visual illusions and phenomenological musings. He makes a gallant attempt, throughout the book, to develop unifying principles. A recurring theme is the importance of depth cues in the interpretation of lightness. Even more important are principles such as "articulation" of the scene or "anchoring," two laws that Gilchrist was the first to explore carefully. Some of these principles lead to testable conjectures. The result is an illuminating monograph, anchored firmly in empiricism, that articulates an in-depth analysis of the problems in the field. And at the same time, the author points to new directions for research that will keep the younger generation busy for generations to come.

V. S. Ramachandran

Preface

I don't remember when I started writing this book, but I think it was about twenty years ago. Several factors have slowed down the project, in addition to the more trivial factors that one can imagine. I was never willing to work on the book at the expense of raising our son Johan. Then, halfway through the writing, my theoretical perspective underwent a major shift with the recognition that the concept of co-determination (a kind of interaction between frames of reference) allows one to explain a vast range of lightness errors—including both failures of lightness constancy and what are called illusions. Without this shift the book would have been more exclusively about veridical lightness perception. At one point I felt the book was complete except for the history chapter. My work on this benefited enormously from the translation by Dejan Todorović of the important but unknown book *Ding und Schatten* (*Object and Shadow*) by the Hungarian Gestaltist Lajos Kardos. I am greatly indebted to Dejan for his important contribution to this book and to the field. Being able to read Kardos in English influenced both my thinking and this book. First, I discovered that Kardos had long ago proposed virtually the same theoretical construction to which I had arrived independently through my own empirical work. Second, the work of Kardos made me realize just how coherent, and I would say, fascinating, had been the development of lightness theory prior to World War II. In the end, the history chapter took over much of the book, as the historical approach solved many of my organizational puzzles.

But I found it impossible to present each topic in a coherent way and at the same time, portray the historical flow. In the resulting compromise, much of the book is organized chronologically, whereas some of the later chapters are organized by topic.

I am grateful to those who have contributed to this book in various ways. In addition to translating Kardos, Dejan Todorović provided extensive and knowledgeable feedback on an earlier draft. John McCann and Fred Kingdom also read the draft and gave me valuable suggestions. My thinking has benefited greatly from discussions with Ted Adelson, Tiziano Agostini, Bart Anderson, David Brainard, Paola Bressan, Patrick Cavanagh, Piers Howe, Anya Hurlbert, Jan Koenderink, Sasha Logvinenko, Mark McCourt, Ennio Mingolla, Ken Nakayama, Luiz Pessoa, V. S. Ramachandran, Hal Sedgwick, Manish Singh, Pawan Sinha, Jim Todd, and Daniele Zavagno.

I thank my former students for the research collaboration we have shared, which always included valuable discussions: Alan Jacobsen, James Schubert, Joseph Cataliotti, Fred Bonato, Branka Spehar, Xiaojun Li, Vidal Annan, Elias Economou, and Suncica Zdravković. A special thanks to my newest student, Ana Radonjić. I thank my good colleagues Larry Arend, Sten Sture Bergström, Walter Gerbino, and Paul Whittle, otherwise known as the Trieste Group. We met annually for many years to discuss lightness. Those discussions were unparalleled for their depth and insight. And I thank Katja Doerschner for creating the image of the Kardos lab shown in Figure 4.3. Thanks also to Tara Schweighardt for her efficiency in securing permission to reproduce over 75 figures. And thanks to the various authors and publishers for their kind permission to use these figures.

Finally, let me acknowledge the many years of support from the National Science Foundation: BNS 7702655, BNS 8909182, DBS 9222104, SBR 9514679, BCS 9906747, BCS 0236701, and the Public Health Service: 1 R25 GM 60826-02, S06 GM08 223.

Contents

Seeing Black and White

1

Introduction

Most people are surprised to learn that seeing has not yet been explained by science. Incredibly, we cannot even explain why some surfaces appear black while others appear white. Take machine vision. No computer program exists that can merely identify the color of objects in a picture. What is the problem?

Let's start with the physics of black and white. What is the physical difference between a surface that appears black and one that appears white? The relevant physical dimension is called *reflectance*. All surfaces absorb some of the light that illuminates them and reflect the rest. The percentage of light reflected is called reflectance. White surfaces reflect approximately 90% of the light they receive, while black surfaces reflect approximately 3%. Thus, if a white surface and a black surface lie next to each other on a tabletop, the white surface will reflect 30 times as much light into the eye as the black surface. We know that this reflected light is focused into an image that is projected onto the inner rear surface of the eye, called the retina, which consists of a dense carpet of photoreceptor cells known as rods and cones. So again, assuming that these photoreceptors create neural signals in proportion to the light striking them, what is the problem?

The main problem stems from variations in the illumination,[1] both over time and over space. If the white paper lies within a shadow that falls across the tabletop, it can easily reflect the same absolute amount of light as the black paper lying outside the shadow. This happens when the illumination outside the shadow is 30 times greater than the illumination inside the shadow. In this case the light reflected from the white paper is completely identical to that reflected from the black paper. The light reflected from either paper, considered in iso-

Figure 1.1. Adelson's checkered shadow. Squares A and B have identical luminance, though they appear different (http://web.mit.edu/persci/people/adelson/checkershadow_illusion.html). Reprinted with permission.

lation, contains no hint of the surface gray shade from which it was reflected.

An astonishing example of this can be seen in Adelson's checkered shadow display, shown in Figure 1.1. The light intensity coming from the two identified squares is equal, yet one appears dark gray and one appears light gray.

In short, the amount of light reflected by a surface into the eye is a product of both the reflectance of that surface and the intensity of illumination it receives. The formula is $L = R \times E$, where L is luminance, R is reflectance, and E is the intensity of the illumination. The problem gets worse. While reflectance typically varies by a factor of no more than 30, illumination can easily vary by a factor of 100 million. The illumination levels of a starlit night and a sunny day span just such a range.

Thus, there is no correlation between the amount of light reflected by a surface and its physical shade of gray, or reflectance. Light of any intensity can appear as any shade of gray!

It's a great mystery story! A black paper in bright light and a white paper in shadow reflect identical light to the eye. Still the black paper appears black and the white paper appears white. How can this be? Human perception is the only existing proof that it can be done at all (Arend, 1994). Somehow the visual system must use the surrounding context. But what program or algorithm does it use?

Thinkers have struggled with this problem for over a thousand years, and the most recent period of 150 years has witnessed a sustained assault on the problem. Some have proposed that the intensity of illumination is somehow estimated and discounted. Others have tried to solve the problem using known physiological mechanisms. Still others claim to solve the problem by learning, or by probabilities computed from past experience. None of these has shown success beyond a limited domain of sub-problems. Computational theorists have proposed that the retinal image is systematically decomposed into its constituent parts by processes that invert the initial optical synthesis of the image. These models are good—too good in fact! They fail to capture the errors and illusions present in human perception. Indeed, such errors may contain the crucial clues. A key message of this book is that the overall pattern of errors is the signature of the human visual software. Models driven by this logic have recently shown encouraging results.

ESSENTIAL TERMS AND CONCEPTS

Armed with some tools, and an awareness of prior work, anyone can participate in the unraveling of this great mystery. The basic terms may be confusing at first but can soon be mastered. Worse, however, is the rampant abuse of terms that has so often characterized this field. Writers have repeatedly invented new terms for existing concepts, and a given term has been used for different concepts, sometimes even by the same writer. Here, then, is a somewhat simplified review of the basic terms as defined mainly by current consensus. More thorough definitions can be found in the glossary.

It is customary in visual perception to distinguish three domains: (1) the distal stimulus, (2) the proximal stimulus, and (3) the percept. These roughly correspond to the object, the image, and the appearance. Failure to make sharp distinctions among these will guarantee confusion.

Distal Stimulus

The term *distal stimulus* refers to the physical environment, without reference to the observer.

We have already mentioned reflectance, the overall percentage of incident light reflected by a surface. The reflectance of a surface is determined by its molecular structure and is a stable feature of the surface. Neutral or achromatic surfaces reflect the same percentage of light at all wavelengths. A perfectly matte (or Lambertian) surface reflects equal amounts of light in all directions, whereas a glossy surface reflects light primarily at an angle to the surface that is equal to the angle of the incident light. A perfectly glossy surface is a mirror. Work in this field often assumes that all surfaces are matte.

Illuminance, or the strength of the illumination, is measured as the intensity of light per unit of area on the surface, such as lumens per square meter.

Proximal Stimulus

Here is where the physical environment makes contact with the organism, where the pattern of light reflected by the environment makes contact with the light-sensitive cells that populate the retina. We refer to this pattern as the *retinal image*, and the intensity at each point in the image is usually called *luminance*. Luminance, as we have seen, refers to the amount or intensity of light reflected by a surface and includes the combined effect of reflectance plus illuminance. The amount of light reflected by a surface is an absolute value that requires a unit of measurement such as candles per square meter. It should not be confused with reflectance, which is a percentage.

Strictly speaking, luminance refers to the intensity of light just before it reaches the lens, and is thus a property of the distal stimulus. The intensity of light actually reaching the rods and cones, measured in Trolands, is somewhat less, owing to the imperfections in the eye as an optical device. However, in practice luminance is treated as a property of the proximal stimulus.

Percept

What we see does not always correspond to the object seen. The moon, for example, appears white, although its reflectance is closer to that of black. We refer to the perceived black, gray, or white value of a surface by the term *lightness*. Lightness is perceived reflectance. I will sometimes use the term *perceived lightness*, even though it is redundant, to emphasize the perceptual nature of the term.

Lightness versus Brightness

A related term, called *brightness*, has caused no end of confusion. Essentially, brightness is perceived luminance. While both lightness and brightness are perceptual terms, only lightness refers to the perception of an objective property of a surface—its reflectance. Brightness refers to the perception of a proximal quantity—the raw intensity of some part of the image. The distinction between lightness and brightness is analogous to the distinction between the perceived size of an object and the perception of its visual angle (or size in the image).

It is sometimes said that lightness and brightness apply to different domains, lightness to opaque surfaces from black to white, and brightness to self-luminous regions. But this is not current usage. While self-luminous regions have brightness but not lightness, opaque surfaces have both lightness and brightness. Brightness, when applied to an opaque surface, involves a special, non-natural mode of seeing, sometimes called the proximal mode, such as is used by painters.

Arend and his colleagues (Arend & Goldstein, 1987b, p. 2283) use an excellent operational definition for lightness and brightness matches. For lightness matches, observers are asked to make a test patch "look as if it were cut from the same piece of paper." For brightness matches, observers are asked to make a test patch "have the same brightness as the corresponding patch in the standard, disregarding, as much as possible, other areas of the display."

In addition to this now-correct usage, the term *brightness* has been used in two distinctly different ways. First, it has sometimes been used in place of lightness, and strangely, some writers continue to use the term *brightness* for both perceived reflectance and perceived luminance, without distinction. Second, the term *brightness* has been used to refer to the perceived brightness of the illumination, perhaps because there is no special term for perceived illumination, although it is an essential concept. The perceived illumination level does not always correspond to the physical illumination level, but illumination is usually perceived with rough accuracy.

Lightness Constancy

Lightness constancy, the central topic of this book, refers to the fact that the perceived lightness of a surface remains roughly constant even though the illumination, and thus the luminance of the surface, changes. Lightness is not 100% constant under a change of illumination, but typically fails by some modest percentage. The lightness of a surface is approximately constant in the face of other challenges as well. Only several decades ago did it become recognized that there is a second, major kind of lightness constancy. The perceived lightness of a surface remains just as constant when those surfaces neighboring or surrounding the surface are changed (as in Fig. 1.2), as when the

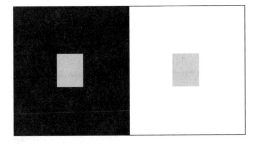

Figure 1.2. Simultaneous lightness contrast. The two gray squares are identical but appear different.

illumination changes. Nowadays it is common to distinguish two basic kinds of constancy: the classic form of constancy, now called illumination-independent or type I constancy, and the more recent background-independent or type II constancy.

Contrast

Perhaps no term has been more abused than the term *contrast*. At least three different uses can be described.

Contrast as a Definition of the Stimulus

Contrast often refers merely to the ratio (sometimes difference) between the luminance on one side of an edge (or gradient) and the luminance on the other side. Thus, we might speak of the contrast between a figure and its background or the contrast in a photographic print, where the term *contrast* is synonymous with the term *luminance ratio*. Notice that this use of the term, by itself, is theoretically neutral. Even Gestalt theory, with its emphasis on stimulus relations, relies on contrast in this sense, though completely rejecting contrast as a theoretical mechanism. There are two commonly used formulae for calculating contrast, Weber contrast ($\Delta L/L_b$, where ΔL is the luminance difference between a target and its background and L_b is background luminance) and Michelson contrast (Lmax $-$ Lmin/Lmax $+$ Lmin, where Lmax is the higher of two luminances at an edge and Lmin is the lower of the two). Although there may be some disagreement as to which of these definitions is more appropriate, the term *contrast*, when defined by either of these formulae, has a very clear meaning.

Contrast as an Illusory Phenomenon

The term *contrast* is sometimes shorthand for simultaneous lightness contrast, a familiar illusion, often found in textbooks, and shown in Figure 1.2. Here two identical patches of gray are made to appear different by placing one on a white background and the other on a black background. The term *contrast*, when used in this way, is also neutral, referring only to the perceptual outcome, not to the underlying mechanism.

Additional confusion has been created by using the term *simultaneous contrast* to refer to a very different stimulus: a disk with a surrounding annulus seen against a dark background. In this case a disk of constant luminance will appear to darken as the luminance of the annulus increases. This illusory darkening goes in the same direction as the textbook illusion, but it is qualitatively different from it and more appropriately treated as an example of lightness constancy. Changes in annulus luminance are perceived as changes in illumination level, and correspondingly the effect is many times stronger than that of the textbook illusion. The term *simultaneous contrast* is best reserved for the latter.

Contrast as a Theory

The perceived darkening of a surface when it is placed on a brighter surround has long suggested a mechanism of suppression of a lower luminance by a nearby higher luminance. Hering (1874/1964) spoke of "lateral interactions in the somatic visual field," anticipating the discovery of lateral inhibition. Heinemann (1972) refers to brightness "induction." Cornsweet (1970) has applied the idea to a kind of edge theory. In this context the notion of contrast becomes one of enhancing or exaggerating the brightness difference at an edge or gradient. Jameson and Hurvich (1964) explain all these phenomena as the net result of an excitation process and an inhibition process.

Due to historical confusion, the term *contrast* should be avoided or at least used sparingly. I will not use the term in the first sense, but rather the term *luminance ratio*. For the third sense I will use the term *contrast theory*. Whenever I use the term *contrast* by itself, it will be shorthand for the simultaneous lightness contrast illusion.

SCOPE OF THE BOOK

Color perception concerns both chromatic colors and achromatic colors. These are funny terms: the first is redundant, the second is an oxymoron—colored colors and non-colored colors. Should black, gray, and white be called colors? Every painter needs them on the palette and every box of crayons includes them. On the other hand, if you tried to sell a black-and-white television set as a "color" television, it would be considered fraudulent.

This book is about the perception of achromatic colors, sometimes called neutral colors or nonselective colors. By extension our topic includes the achromatic dimension of chromatic colors. For example, pink differs from maroon only on this dimension. Otherwise chromatic color perception will not be treated, apart from some isolated references. Yet I believe that all the important problems can be found within the achromatic domain. Certainly, that most central problem— the constancy problem—is found fully formed in the lightness dimension. And this has always seemed to me a good place to start.

Second, this book is about the perception of surface color, which is the property of an object. It is not about the perception of light. This is implied by the word "black" in the title. Only a surface can be black; light is not black. We will be considering the perception of objective properties of the real, everyday world, not isolated patches of light in a dark laboratory. This doesn't mean that we will not be talking about vision per se. There is a significant prejudice in this field that surface color perception under complex conditions is a matter of high-level cognition, of interpretation of what is seen. I do not share this view. We will talk about lightness as seen by humans and goldfish alike.

Very little treatment will be given to brightness perception, except when the term *brightness* has been used to refer to lightness. Brightness refers to our perception of the intensity of light associated with a given portion of the visual field. The visual system needs to know about object properties, including lightness; it has little use for values of raw light intensity. Thus, a theory of brightness is no more needed than a theory of perceived visual angle.

Third, the book is about human perception, as opposed to machine vision: how black and white *are* computed, not how they might be. Still, I believe the book will be of interest to students of machine vision. The problems of human and machine vision are strikingly similar. And we in human vision have had 150 years to discover, partly through experimentation, aspects of the problem that might not readily emerge in a machine vision context. We will review crucial obstacles, some scarcely mentioned elsewhere, to an adequate model, human or machine, of surface lightness. An important example of this is the anchoring problem, discussed in Chapter 9. No model can begin to account for perception of surface colors without a solution, either explicit or implicit, to the anchoring problem.

Historical Approach

Although I have tried to make a complete survey of current work in lightness, this book is primarily organized along historical lines. There are compelling reasons for this. Every era has its blinders. Ideas can be adequately evaluated only when they are properly placed in historical context. Much of the power of modern science lies in its social dimension—it is a collective effort. This effort is impoverished when the work of other people and other times is neglected. In the field of lightness, the neglect of history has cost us dearly. Long-discredited ideas have been unwittingly recycled. Important experiments and theories have been forgotten. The wheel has been unnecessarily invented too many times.[2] I believe the reader will find that the history of lightness research forms a coherent story of scientific evolution. And I hope that by the concluding chapter it will be clear that when the chain of continuity has been broken, as it was most notably in the shift that followed World War II, our field has suffered serious setbacks.

Finally, the reader may notice a relative absence of physiology and mathematics, both of which I consider somewhat premature in lightness. Until we achieve a better grasp of the qualitative principles that characterize the computation of lightness, the physiologist will not know what to look for, or how to interpret the physiological data. As for mathematics, some detailed formulae are given in Chapter 11. I believe that mathematics will prove more useful as concepts are increasingly refined. If progress in lightness theory is slow, this is due to a lack of consensus and perhaps a lack of ideas, not a lack of precision.

What Lies Ahead

The story that is told in these pages is the story of the scientific development of lightness theory that has unfolded in the West, with rough continuity, from the 19th century until the present. These developments fall roughly into five periods of time. During the first, or classic, period, extending though much of the 19th century, great thinkers such as Mach, Helmholtz, and Hering defined the basic problem of lightness constancy and staked out opposing solutions. During the second period, covering roughly the first quarter of the 20th century, scores of scientists joined the study of lightness, led by David Katz (Katz, 1935), who established basic methods and published an influential book called *The World of Colour*. The third period saw the arrival of the Gestalt psychologists, with their penetrating insights and dramatic experiments. Rejecting the clumsy two-stage conception of raw sensations and cognitive interpretation, they proposed a single perceptual process that was parsimonious and elegant. This period was cut short by the tragic events surrounding World War II. The period following the war was dominated by the behaviorists, who placed their bets on the physiological mechanism of lateral inhibition. This "contrast" period saw little headway and forgot many of the earlier advances. These four periods are covered in Chapters 2 through 5, respectively.

Excitement returned to the study of lightness perception roughly around 1970 with the computer revolution. The challenge of machine vision led to a more complete description of the problem and to more sophisticated models. This computational period is covered in Chapters 6 and 7. Chapter 8 steps out of the historical story line to survey theoretical positions on the closely related question of perception of the illumination.

Chapter 9 deals with the essential but only lately recognized problem of anchoring. Prior to that recognition, lightness theories had no anchoring rules and thus could predict only relative lightness values, not specific values.

In Chapter 10 I argue that the overall pattern of errors in human lightness perception offers a powerful way to identify the kind of software used by the lightness system. In a systematic survey of lightness errors, I show that many of the errors predicted by lightness theories do not occur, and many of the errors that do occur are not predicted by the theories. I note that the computational models fail to account for errors, and I argue for error-driven models. In Chapter 11 I offer a specific error-driven theory of lightness framed in terms of the rules of anchoring. In Chapter 12, I outline and critique all the main theories of lightness. I try to lay out the strengths and weaknesses of each model, including my own. In the final chapter, Chapter 13, I try to draw conclusions from the evidence reviewed. I argue that the twin assumptions of raw sensations and their cognitive interpretation have undermined progress and should be discarded. I describe three sources of motivation for theories of lightness: physiology, veridicality, and error. I analyze the strengths and weaknesses of each, and I summarize where matters now stand and suggest what I believe are the current challenges for lightness theory.

2

The Classic Period

Prior to the 19th century one can find references to the problem of lightness and color constancy, but no sustained experimental program. Most notable in this regard are the insightful writings of the Arab scholar Alhazen, a writer of astonishing modernity, though he lived a thousand years ago.

ALHAZEN

Although Alhazen was unclear about the location in the eye at which the optical image is formed, he recognized many of the basic problems of perceptual constancy simply by considering the pattern of light entering the eye. Of color constancy he wrote (Alhazen, 1083/1989, p. 141, "Neither the form of the light nor that of the colour existing in the coloured object can pass except as mingled together, and the last sentient can only perceive them as mingled together. Nevertheless, the sentient perceives that the visible object is luminous and that the light seen in the object is other than the colour and that these are two properties." The same logic applies to changes in illumination level: "the light on one and the same object may vary by increase or decrease while the object's colour remains the same; and though the radiation of colour varies with the lights falling upon it, the colour does not change in kind."

But only the light mixture is directly sensed (p. 142): "that which light perceives by pure sensation is light *qua* light and colour *qua* colour. But nothing of what is visible, apart from light and colour, can be perceived by pure sensation, but only by discernment, inference, and recognition, in addition to sensation" and (p. 141) "the faculty of judgement perceives that the colours in these objects are not the same as the lights that supervene upon them." Here Alhazen anticipates Helmholtz's notion of unconscious inference. He also anticipated Hering's concept of memory color (p. 142): "colour is originally perceived by pure sensation; when it has been repeatedly seen, sight will then perceive what colour it is by recognition."

EUROPEAN SENSORY PHYSIOLOGY

Our main story begins during the 19th century with the insight that our visual experience corresponds, not with proximal stimulation, but with the distal properties of the objects we see. Hering (1874/1964, p. 23) wrote, "Seeing is not a matter of looking at light-waves as such, but of looking at external things mediated by these waves; the eye has to instruct us, not about the intensity or quality of the light coming from external objects at any one time, but about these objects themselves." Helmholtz (1866/1924, p. 286) wrote, "Colours have their greatest significance for us in so far as they are properties of bodies and can be used as marks of identification of bodies." Mach (1922/1959, p. 208) wrote, "We generally perceive, not light and shadow, but objects in space. The shading of bodies is scarcely noticed."

To appreciate the importance of this insight at that time, it is necessary to understand the theoretical context in which it occurred. The sustained scientific assault on vision that continues to the present day was given its initial impetus by the discovery of the retinal image in the early 17th century. Kepler correctly identified the retina as the point at which light penetrating the eye first makes contact with the sensorium. "At this point," noted Helmholtz (1868, p. 118), "the older physiologists thought they had solved the problem, so far as it appeared to them to be capable of solution. External light fell directly upon a sensitive nervous structure in the retina, and was, as it seemed, directly felt there." It was only natural to assume a one-to-one relationship between visual experience and local stimulation, and by the time of Helmholtz, this assumption, later called the constancy hypothesis by the Gestalt psychologists, had become deeply embedded in thinking about sensory processes. I will call this the *doctrine of local determination*.

The effects of light upon the retina were treated as subjective phenomena. Weber and Fechner studied the brightness sensations produced by illuminations of different intensity. Their use of illuminations rather than white or gray objects obscured the distinction between the subjective and the objective reference in visual experience. This distinction was revealed by Hemholtz, Hering, and Mach. By considering instead our experience of surfaces and objects, they exposed a paradox that created the field of lightness research. This paradox has continued to frustrate theorists until today.

MACH

Ernst Mach (1865/1965, p. 270) wrote, "we are never in doubt whether we have before us a white or gray paper even under quite different conditions of illumination: in bright sunshine, overcast sky, in twilight, or by candle light, we have always almost the same sensation." He attributed this constancy of the appearance of the paper to the fact that "the relation of the quantity of light on the entire retina and the image of the paper remains constant under otherwise equal conditions."

Mach investigated the brightness experiences produced by various luminance gradients, especially the ramp-like luminance profiles that occur in penumbrae. He discovered what are now called Mach bands, soft bright bands seen at the high end of the ramp and dark bands at the low end. One of the first to anticipate the discovery of lateral inhibition, he ascribed these bands to "a reciprocal action of neighboring areas of the retina."

HELMHOLTZ

The most important figure of this period was clearly Hermann von Helmholtz, the great physicist and sensory physiologist. Helmholtz accepted the doctrine of local determination—sensations correspond directly to local stimulation—so firmly embedded in the zeitgeist of that time. Yet he nevertheless formulated the most serious challenge to that doctrine. He was the first in the modern era to clearly state the lightness constancy problem. He noted that a white paper in shadow and a black paper in bright light might have the same luminance. But even under such circumstances, we easily recognize the white paper as white and the black paper as black, even though the two papers must produce identical sensations. This implies that what we see corresponds not to the local stimulation, but to the distal property of the object we are looking at.

Speaking of color in addition to lightness, he wrote (1866/1924, p. 287), "in our observations with the sense of vision we always start out by forming a judgment about the colours of bodies, eliminating the differences of illumination by which a body is revealed to us." We do this by means of past experience with objects in different illuminations: "There is plenty of opportunity of investigating these same corporeal colours in sunshine outdoors, in the blue light of the clear sky, in the weak white light of the overcast sky, in the red-yellow light of the setting sun, and by red-yellow candle light. And besides all this there are the coloured reflections of surrounding bodies. In a shady forest the illumination is predominantly green. In rooms with coloured walls, it is the same colour as the walls. We are never distinctly conscious of these latter variations of illumination, and yet they can be demonstrated often enough by the coloured shadows. By seeing objects of the same colour under these various illuminations, in spite of the difference of illumination, we learn to form a correct idea of the colours of bodies, that is, to judge how such a body would look in white light; and since we are interested only in the colour that the body retains permanently, we are not conscious at all of the separate sensations which contribute to form our judgment."

Helmholtz was able to accommodate the facts of lightness constancy without rejecting the direct linkage of sensation and local stimulation by dividing the visual response to stimulation into two levels, as Thomas Reid and the British empiricists had done. The first level is the level of raw sensations, which correspond directly to local stimulation. The second level, called perception, corresponds to the distal stimulus, to the environmental situation that produces the local stimulation. The first level accounts for the subjective quality in vision, the second level for the objective quality.

Apart from its lack of parsimony, dividing the visual response into two parts, one faithful to the proximal stimulus and one faithful to the distal stimulus, seemed to meet the challenge of lightness constancy without rejecting the doctrine of local determination.[1] His problem was to explain how the raw sensations are transformed into percepts, and how a percept can come to represent the object of vision when it is built out of sensations keyed to the local stimulus.

Helmholtz argued that we are able to eliminate the illumination by means of associations formed out of prior experience. For example, imagine you are looking at a white object in reddish illumination. The local stimulation is reddish, even though you perceive a white surface. This perceptual substitution is possible because in the past you have seen the same paper successively in illuminations of different color. Thus, we know that a paper that makes a white sensation in white light will make a reddish sensation in reddish light, a greenish sensation in greenish light, and so forth. In other words, a whole cluster of associations has been formed, representing the set of different sensations produced by the same white object in different illuminations. When we obtain a reddish sensation in viewing the white paper in reddish light, we are able, through the cluster of associations, to retrieve the sensation made by the same paper in white light and correctly identify the paper as white.

But there is a logical problem with this account. The same reddish sensation could be produced by a red paper in white light. Thus, the same sensation is also associated with an entirely separate cluster of sensations corresponding to the red paper in illuminations of various colors. How is it that one cluster of associations is activated and not the other cluster?

To solve this problem, the visual system must be able to correctly identify the color of the illumination in which the target surface appears. Ironically, however, if the visual system were able to identify the color of the illumination, it could solve the basic equation $L = R \times E$ for reflectance (that is, it could deduce that $R = L/E$, where L and E would now both be given) without recourse to memory or associative processes. Thus, it is not clear how learning and association make any substantive contribution to color constancy in Helmholtz's theory. The critical question is how the color and the intensity of the illumination are identified, and to this question Helmholtz fails to provide a clear answer. He does seem to acknowledge the importance of the question when he writes (Helmholtz, 1868, p. 144), "What is constant in the colour of an object is not the brightness and colour of the light which it reflects, but the relation between the intensity of the different coloured constituents of this light, on the one hand, and that of the corresponding constituents of the light which illuminates it on the other. This proportion alone is the expression of a constant property of the object in question."

In the following passage, Helmholtz (1866/1924, p. 276) hints that mean chromaticity can be used to represent the color of the illumination: "when a large variety of objects can be freely compared, the white of sunlight is the mean colour, from which the deviations of the other colours in the various directions of the colour chart are estimated. But if another colour A is predominant, so that the average of all colours seen at the same time resembles A, we are inclined to use this average as the starting point of our temporary colour discrimination and to identify it with white." Although this suggestion is made in the context of color constancy, it is analogous to the use of mean luminance to represent illumination level for computation of lightness.

As for contrast effects, Helmholtz made a sharp distinction between successive contrast, which he attributed to physiological causes, and simultaneous contrast, which, like lightness and color constancy, he attributed to psychological processes. He claims that simultaneous contrast results from an error in judgment, but his account is not very explicit. He suggests that when a difference is distinctly seen, as when two papers are immediately adjacent, we perceive a larger difference between them than otherwise. But he also claims that small differences are overestimated. And he notes that we overestimate the difference when it is unidimensional; that is, when the difference is either purely one of color or purely one of luminance, but not both.

It has been said (Logvinenko & Ross, 2004) that Helmholtz attributed the standard simultaneous lightness contrast illusion to a mistake in taking the illumination into account; due to the difference in the average luminance surrounding the two targets, they are treated as lying within fields of slightly different levels of illumination. But I have been unable to find this claim in Helmholtz.

HERING

Ewald Hering, the powerful antagonist of Helmholtz, took pains to emphasize his differences with the great man. Their disputes have so dominated the discourse on lightness that until this day the two perspectives they represent, called sensory and cognitive, are seen by many as defining the main poles of perceptual theory (Turner, 1994).

While Helmholtz stressed the psychological side of perception, Hering stressed the physiological side, and he anticipated the discovery of lateral inhibition. While Helmholtz had been more concerned with constancy and veridicality, Hering was more concerned with contrast illusions, and he emphasized the failures of constancy.

At a time when psychology was struggling to free itself from the earlier mentalistic views, Hering (1874/1964) found Helmholtz's cognitive account unnecessarily mystical. Hering was especially critical of Helmholtz's attribution of the simultaneous contrast illusion to cognitive factors, finding it much more economical to attribute this illusion to what he called "reciprocal interaction in the somatic visual field."

Simultaneous Lightness Contrast

Hering featured the simultaneous contrast illusion (see Fig. 1.2), which had been given wide attention earlier by Chevreul (1839), because it seemed to clearly reveal the operation of opponent peripheral processes. The neural excitation produced at the retinal locations corresponding to the two gray targets must be equal due to their equal luminance values. But the excitation corresponding to the target on the white background is strongly inhibited due to the much higher excitation of the surrounding retinal tissue that receives light from the white background. This strong inhibition does not occur for the target on the black background. What we experience as the different lightness level of the two targets is really our experience of the net effect of excitation and inhibition on each target (Hering, 1874/1964, p. 141).

Hering's Paradox

On the matter of lightness constancy, Hering not only attacked Helmholtz's theory as vague and overly cognitive, but he also claimed that Helmholtz's account of unconscious inferences concerning the illumination level is logically incoherent. Given that the luminance coming to the eye from a given surface is a joint product of its reflectance and its illuminance, then its reflectance could be determined if its illuminance were known, as in Helmholtz's formulation. But the illuminance can be determined only if the reflectance is known. "Since it is only on the basis of the colors in which we see things that we could acquire knowledge of the illumination intensity as the alleged measuring unit for our estimations, and yet these colors are themselves said to be originally the result of the same estimations, the view just described moves in a fruitless circle" (Hering, 1874/1964, p. 21).

This argument has come to be known as *Hering's paradox*. Of course, if the paradox were truly binding, lightness constancy could not exist. Escape from the paradox lies in the fact that we receive light from many surfaces simultaneously, as noted by Woodworth (1938, p. 599). As in the solution of simultaneous equations, the various luminance relationships in the image form higher-order variables that are not necessarily subject to the paradox. The paradox is problematic only when applied to a single target surface at a time. And, indeed, when only a single homogeneous surface is visible, as in a ganzfeld, we are unable to determine either the lightness or the illumination.

Hering's Account of Constancy

Still, Hering's larger point was that the stimulus basis for taking the illumination into account had never been spelled out by Helmholtz. He felt that much of the achievement of lightness constancy could be attributed to peripheral sensory mechanisms, namely pupil size, adaptation, and lateral inhibition.

Physiological Factors

When the illumination is increased, so also is the luminance of a given object in the scene. But the intensity of light reaching the retina does not increase as much as the luminance of the object because the eye responds to the brighter illumination by reducing its pupil size, thus decreasing the amount of light let into the eye. To this must be added the fact that in brighter illumination, the photoreceptors in the eye become less sensitive, so that the neural response corresponding to the object increases by even less than the light intensity at the retina. And finally, even this increase in the neural response is limited by the fact that the luminance in the image region that surrounds the object is also increased, increasing its ability to inhibit the neural response produced by light from the object itself.

These factors working in concert provide a rough constancy of lightness despite changing illumination, according to Hering.

The Mismatch of Excitation and Inhibition

In Hering's view, most surfaces in a scene change in lightness when the illumination changes, but now and then one finds a surface that shows complete constancy. "One individual area in the visible field can always be imagined or will actually exist which does not change its color in spite of a change of total illumination, for whose changed light intensity the eye is thus instantaneously adjusted by simultaneous contrast in such a way that the color continues to look the same as it did before the change in illumination" (Hering, 1874/1964, p. 141).

"We should therefore have here an example of object-color constancy in spite of different total illumination of the visible field . . . this consists in the fact that the ratio of the light intensities of the surround and the infield is by chance precisely that by which the darkening action of the surround on the field, which increases with their common illumination, is continuously compensated for by the similarly increasing light intensity of the infield" (Hering, 1874/1964, p. 140).

Memory Color

The factors he invoked to explain constancy are not limited to physiological factors. Although he scoffed at Helmholtz's notion of unconscious inferences, Hering, true to the zeitgeist of the day, also invoked past experience in his account of color constancy. In Hering's view, memory color reinforces the trend towards constancy, taking up where the physiological factors leave off, further limiting the error in our color percepts:

> By the cooperation of the regulating mechanisms we have discussed or by self-regulation the color changes in the visual field are kept within much narrower limits than those established by the intensity changes of illumination. The color in which an object appears, disregarding the limiting cases, acquires a certain stability and becomes in our memory an enduring, integrated constituent part of the object. If memory colors of objects have been formed in this way, then they are a further influence on the way we see, and in addition to the physiological factors just described, which combine with the effective radiations to determine the color of seen things, there is still another, which one could designate according to usual terminology as "psychological," since it depends on individual experiences already established in the nervous substance. (Hering, 1874/1964, p. 20)

Approximate Constancy

Hering was aware that these factors, both physiological and psychological, even acting in concert, would not produce complete constancy, but he noted that constancy is not complete in any case. He preferred to use the expression "the approximate constancy of seen things." Hering did not claim, as did Cornsweet (1970) later, that when the illumination level changes, both the excitation at the target location and the inhibition (produced by the surround) acting on the same location change by the same proportion, leaving target excitation essentially constant. Hering believed that, depending on a variety of factors, the change in neural inhibition produced by the surround might be less than, greater than, or equal to the change in target excitation. Complete constancy, according to Hering, occurs almost by accident, when variables such as target luminance, surround luminance, and adaptive state fall into just the right relationship to one another.

Other Contributions

Hering established the reduction screen as a fundamental tool in lightness work. A large card containing a small hole near its center is held, somewhat short of arm's length, so that the hole falls completely within a homogeneous target surface while the card itself occludes the surrounding context. Two such holes can be used to equate the luminance of two separate targets, the eye performing as a very sensitive photometer under these conditions.

Hering (1874/1964, p. 8) demonstrated the role of penumbra, or blurred contours, in his well-known shadow/spot experiment: "If I suspend a bit of paper from a thread before a lamp in such a way that a faint shadow is cast upon my writing-pad, I see the shadow then as a casual dark spot lying on the white of the paper. If however, I now draw a broad black line about the shadow, so as to cover the penumbra completely, what I see within the black line is a grey spot, which looks exactly as if the white paper had been coloured with grey paint or a grey paper with a black border had been pasted on the white."

Critique of Hering

The critique of Hering's theory of simultaneous contrast will be deferred to Chapter 5, following a description of the more detailed contemporary theories based on Hering. Here we consider Hering's treatment of constancy.

Constancy not Explained

As for Hering's theory of constancy, a later experiment by Jaensch and Müller (1920), described in Chapter 3, showed that constancy remains even when all of Hering's factors, both physiological and psychological, are excluded. Unfortunately, this important experiment has been neglected.

Indeed, both Katz and MacLeod have pointed out that the adaptive mechanisms in his theory are as likely to threaten constancy as to provide for it. Katz (1935, p. 265) noted, "in certain cases the interaction of retinal elements is actually a *hindrance* to the recognition of colours. Against a bright sky a white flag-pole or a white windowframe will appear gray or black." MacLeod (1932, p. 35) made the same point: "Local adaptation can in fact be effective in a direction opposite to that of colour constancy, so that under certain circumstances one can speak of a constancy of colour in spite of the operation of antagonistic adaptive mechanisms." Pointing to yet another problem, Katz (1935, p. 434) wrote, "Paradoxical as it may at first sound, a thoroughly efficient set of external adaptive mechanisms, such as Hering postulates, could not even be considered as desirable. For it would compensate completely or almost completely for changes in illumination, and thereby render them imperceptible."

Black and White as Opponent Processes

An important phenomenological observation by Hering has long provided appeal for his opponent process theory of chromatic color. Hering observed that while we often see reddish blues, reddish yellows, greenish blues, and greenish yellows, we do not experience reddish greens or bluish yellows. To Hering, this observation strongly supports his claim that red and green are opponent colors, as are yellow and blue. But Hering's claim that black and white are also opponent colors runs into problems on just this point (see Heggelund, 1974, p. 1072). As Mach (1922/1959, p. 68) remarked, "The only point that still dissatisfies me in Hering's theory is that it is difficult to perceive why the two opposed processes of black and white may be simultaneously produced and simultaneously felt, while such is not the case with red-green and blue-yellow." Indeed, Hering himself agreed with Mach's observation, writing (Hering, 1874/1964, p31). "every gray is at the same time whitish and blackish, now it is more of the one, and now more of the other."

Predicts Wrong Pattern of Errors

The accidental nature of constancy in Hering's account appears incommensurate with the robust constancy shown in later experiments (Arend & Goldstein, 1987; Arend & Spehar, 1993; Burzlaff, 1931; Wallach, 1948).[2] But in addition to the question of the scope of constancy failures, there is the question of their form. Hering claims that constancy failures take the form of overconstancy as well as underconstancy; when the illumination is increased, for example, some surfaces retain a constant appearance, some appear to become lighter, and some even appear to become darker. This claim, echoed by Jameson and Hurvich (1961), has not been supported by data (for a thorough treatment of this issue, see Chapter 5). Empirical results from scores of studies reveal a qualitatively different pattern of errors. The signature form of lightness constancy failures, with exceptions only in special circumstances, is expressed as an error in lightness in the direction of the illuminant change. Thus, when the illumination is increased, any failure is seen as a lightening of all surfaces.

   Hering got the pattern of constancy failures wrong because, at least after 1894, he modeled his concept of reciprocal interaction heavily on data from the extensive set of contrast experiments conducted by his students, Hess and Pretori. Those experiments were impressive both for their scope and for the ingenious apparatus employed, but the rampant failures of constancy they obtained have since been shown to be artifactual (Gilchrist & Jacobsen, 1989; Heinemann, 1989; Jacobsen & Gilchrist, 1988a, 1988b).

Hess and Pretori

Hess and Pretori's display consisted of an adjacent pair of square panels, each with a square infield embedded in its center. By means of the apparatus illustrated in Figure 2.1, each of the four regions of the display (two infields and two surrounds) could be varied in luminance independently of the others. Each region was coated with magnesium, slanted diagonally to the line of sight, and illuminated by a light bulb that was movable along a tunnel oriented at right angles to the line of sight. Moving the lamp along the tunnel changed the luminance of the stimulus region according to the inverse-square law of illumination,[3] allowing excellent control of luminance at a time before the existence of photometers. All four stimulus regions appeared coplanar because each was seen through an aperture that projected a rectangular image to the retina.

This method of creating the stimulus was and still is ingenious. Even today it would be hard to improve upon the apparatus. The use of occlusion edges to define the boundaries of each field guarantees a crisp sharp edge between retinally adjacent fields. Although the form of the display could be easily created on a computer, a typical CRT screen would not approach the large dynamic range (over 5,000:1) afforded by Hess and Pretori's method.

Beyond the clever apparatus and the size of the data set produced, however, the Hess and Pretori study broke little new ground theoretically. Hess and Pretori found that any change in brightness caused by a change of infield luminance could be nullified by an appropriate change in surround luminance. However, they did not discover the

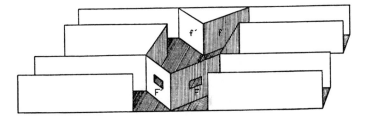

Figure 2.1. Hess and Pretori apparatus. The luminance values of the two test fields (in rear) and the two surround fields were controlled by moving light bulbs along corresponding tunnels.

ratio principle that Wallach later reported. Under the ratio principle, a change in infield luminance would be nullified by a proportionately equal change in surround luminance. Hess and Pretori found that, depending on conditions, the change in surround luminance required to nullify the effect of the infield change must be greater than, less than, or by chance equal to the infield change. Hess and Pretori failed to discover the ratio principle later revealed by Wallach for reasons that are described in Chapter 5.

DEPTH PERCEPTION AND LIGHTNESS

Common sense leads us to expect that the perception of surface lightness must be closely related to the perception of depth and three-dimensional arrangement. The particular pattern of light that reaches the eye is totally dependent upon the spatial arrangement among the object, the light source, and the observing eye. Move any one of these, and the retinal image changes.

Helmholtz, Hering, and Mach had all observed effects of depth on lightness, but none of them gave depth the central role it would later be given by the Gestaltists. Helmholtz's theory could more easily accommodate a role for depth than Hering's. A sense of three-dimensional relations is clearly implied by Helmholtz's proposal that lightness is derived by taking the illumination into account. Yet Hering (1874/1964, p. 11) himself had noted a role of depth: "Here therefore, with the different localization there is also a difference in apparent color, in spite of the identical light intensities of the two

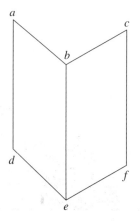

Figure 2.2. Mach's bent card. The convex corner is illuminated from one side. When perceptually reversed to form a concave corner, the shadowed side appears as a painted gray.

surfaces and unchanged tuning of the eyes." But neither Hering nor his descendents have explained how this can be reconciled with the retinotopic focus of his theory.

Perhaps the clearest early demonstration of the role of depth is found in Mach's now-famous bent-card illusion (Fig. 2.2). Mach (1922/1959, p. 209) wrote, "We place a visiting-card, bent crosswise before us on the desk, so that its bent edge *be* is towards us. Let the light fall from the left. The half *abde* is then much lighter, the half *bcef* much darker—a fact which is, however scarcely perceived in an unprejudiced observation. We now close one eye. Hereupon, part of the space-sensations disappear. Still we see the bent card spatially and nothing noticeable in the illumination. But as soon as we succeed in seeing the bent edge depressed instead of raised, the light and the shade stand out as if painted thereon."

SUMMARY

During the Renaissance, as thinking began to move away from mysticism toward a more concrete understanding of everything, including the human body, an important question arose: What is the relationship between physical stimulation impinging upon the organism and the resulting experience? The field of psychophysics was born of this question. It is not surprising that the initial conception was a rather simple one: visual experience directly corresponds to the stimulation at each point on the receptor surface. I have called this view the *doctrine of local determination*. The Gestalt psychologists called it the *constancy hypothesis*, although that term is confusing in today's language. Like many assumptions, this doctrine was not always explicitly acknowledged. It was implicit, for example, in the quest of Weber and Fechner to find the mathematical relationship between the physical intensity of light and its perceived brightness.

Helmholtz, Mach, and Hering, however, recognized that our experience of surface lightness presents a serious challenge to the doctrine of local determination. The lightness we see correlates far more highly with the reflectance of the object itself than with the proximal stimulation we receive from that object. This insight did not lead to a rejection of the doctrine of local determination; rather, that doctrine was held to characterize only the first stage in a two-stage process, the second stage involving the cognitive interpretation of the raw sensations, and this included bringing to bear the results of prior visual experience. Helmholtz emphasized central factors, while Hering emphasized peripheral factors. But this debate took place within a shared conceptual framework that featured raw sensations and their cognitive interpretation. This basic two-stage model has continued to hold enormous influence on people's thinking, even down to the present day.

3

The Katz Period

The second distinct period of lightness work took place between 1911 and 1930. In the 35 years following Hering's *Outlines of a Theory of the Light Sense*, no important theoretical developments in lightness took place until the publication in 1911 of Katz's book (translated into English in 1935 as *The World of Colour*). Koffka (1935, p. 241) wrote of Katz's book, "Its importance at the time of its publication can hardly be overrated." For the next two decades, Katz dominated the field of lightness.

Katz himself was not a Gestalt psychologist, nor was he a theorist of any note. His theoretical ideas did not deviate substantially from those of Helmholtz and Hering. But Katz broke new ground in phenomenology and experimentation, and he was respected by the Gestaltists on both counts.

KATZ ON PHENOMENOLOGY

Katz approached color perception from a phenomenological perspective, taking pains to make a complete description of the visual experience of colors before turning to the task of explanation. He took careful note of the various modes in which colors make their visual appearance, emphasizing especially the distinction between surface colors and film colors, but he also described volume colors, luminosity, and luster.

Surface Colors and Film Colors

Surface colors belong to objects. We experience them as opaque and hard; they resist the gaze, in Katz's apt phrase. Surface colors have a definite location in space. Film colors, such as the blue of the sky or the color of an afterimage, have a more ethereal quality. They do not have a clear location in space and they give the feeling that one is looking through them.

Unlike film colors, surface colors always appear together with a sense of the illumination. Katz (1935, p. 51) wrote, "a complete impression of illumination is had only where objects are perceived, and ... wherever objects are perceived an impression of illumination is always produced." According to Katz, surface colors can be turned into film colors using Hering's reduction screen (see p. 10 in Katz). Most of Katz's book deals with surface colors. and most of this work deals with lightness, not chromatic surfaces.

Other Dimensions of Surface Colors

According to Katz, two additional qualities can be found in our phenomenal experience of surface color: insistence and pronouncedness. *Insistence* refers to our experience of the raw intensity of light emanating from a surface, our experience of the product of both reflectance and illumination. Today this would be called brightness. Thus, a white surface has a higher insistence than a black surface standing in the same illumination, and a white surface in bright illumination has a higher insistence than a white surface in shadow. Insistence cannot be equated with perceived illumination, except in the special case in which target reflectance is held constant.

Katz's distinction between surface color and insistence is equivalent to the modern distinction between lightness and brightness. The first refers to the visual experience of reflectance, while the second refers to the visual experience of luminance.

Katz's term *pronouncedness* has no current equivalent. Whites and light grays gain in pronouncedness as the illumination is increased, while blacks and dark grays gain in pronouncedness as the illumination is reduced. Thus, for example, as the illumination increases, a black surface becomes more insistent but less pronounced. A white surface gains in both insistence and pronouncedness as the illumination increases.

KATZ'S EXPERIMENTAL WORK

Methods of Studying Constancy

Because Katz is best known as a phenomenologist, his extensive experimental work is sometimes forgotten. He was a pioneer in the experimental study of lightness and color constancy, especially in the application of psychophysical methods to object properties like lightness. He conducted many experiments collecting perceptual data using a variety of techniques including various matching and nulling tasks, and he invented the first measures of the degree of constancy.

Katz studied perceptual constancy using four separate methods to vary the amount of illumination.

Method of Illumination Perspective

A single light source is suspended above the head of an observer within a windowless room. Target gray samples are placed in two locations: near the observer (and the light source) in bright illumination and far from the observer in dim illumination. Either a single gray surface or a card containing several samples of gray is mounted at one or both of these locations. When a single surface is used, it can either be a simple piece of gray paper or a color wheel (Maxwell disk). His color wheel consisted of a disk containing both black and white sectors mounted on the shaft of a motor. Spinning the disk at high speed produces a homogeneous surface with a gray shade corresponding to the proportions of white and black on the disk. When the card containing gray samples is used, the observer's task is to select a gray sample on the brightly illuminated near card that matches in lightness a gray paper in the far, dimly illuminated position. When the color wheel is used, the observer's task is to adjust the relative proportions of white and black on one of the color wheels to match the lightness of the other color wheel. Thanks to the sophistication of German mechanical engineering, Katz was able to use an episcotister, a mechanical device that allows the relative proportions of the black and white sectors to be varied while the blade is spinning at high speed.

Episcotister Method

By replacing the white and black sectors with opaque and open sectors, the episcotister can also be used as a variable neutral density filter, equivalent to a pair of today's counter-rotating neutral density wedges. Such a rotating episcotister blade is positioned immediately behind one of two small viewing holes, horizontally displaced from each other near the center of a large screen. Through one of the holes, a color wheel can be seen standing in front of a background 1 or 2 meters away; through the other hole, another color wheel and background are seen. Varying the size of the open sector of the episcotister is equivalent to varying the level of illumination seen through the hole. The observer sits in front of the screen and looks alternately through each of the two viewing holes while the gray level of one of the two disks is varied until the observer reports that the two disks appear equal in lightness.

Method of Anomalous Orientation

Here the observer makes a match between two disks that stand at different angles with respect to the light source (see Woodworth, 1938, p. 608).

Light/Shadow Method

Katz's best-known method for studying constancy, shown in Figure 3.1, has become a standard in the field. A dividing screen is placed in the middle of a region of space that is illuminated from one side by either a window or a light source, separating it into two regions of illumination: a lighted region and a shadowed region. In the center of each region a color wheel containing black and white sectors is mounted immediately in front of a gray background.

In Katz's standard experiment, the lighted color wheel and the shadowed color wheel are first adjusted to the same luminance value using Hering's reduction screen method. A large cardboard containing two holes is positioned so that a patch of the lighted wheel is seen through one hole and a patch of the shadowed wheel is simultaneously seen through the other. The holes are not perceived as such; they are perceived as spots of color on the cardboard. The experi-

Figure 3.1. Apparatus used by Katz to study lightness constancy (Katz, 1935, Figure 8, p. 132). Reprinted with permission.

menter adjusts the gray level of one of the two wheels until the observer reports that the color of the spots is equal.

When the reduction screen is removed, the wheel in shadow appears much lighter than the wheel in full illumination. Now the observer proceeds to make a lightness match. The gray level of one of the two wheels is varied until the observer reports that the two wheels appear the same in lightness.

Results

Katz's experiments in lightness constancy revealed several important facts. First, the data Katz collected corroborate what Helmholtz and Hering had recognized informally: that lightness correlates more highly with object reflectance than with retinal luminance. Nevertheless, constancy is not complete; substantial failures can occur. A lightness match typically lies somewhere between a reflectance match and a luminance match, though closer to the former.

Katz also emphasized that when the observer makes a lightness equation, the two disks do not appear equal in all respects, as would be true of a metameric[1] match. They appear equal only in surface lightness; they do not appear equally illuminated. Katz maintained that whenever colors are seen in the surface mode, they are always accompanied by a simultaneous experience of the illumination. Katz (1935, p. 434) suggested that Hering had been led into error by his failure to recognize this duality in the visual experience.

Katz made tremendous progress in identifying the stimulus conditions that lead to high degrees of constancy versus those in which constancy fails. This work, of course, required a means of measuring the degree of constancy in a given experiment. His basic light/shadow method was ideally suited for measuring the strength of constancy, even without a photometer.

Measures of Constancy

Katz chose a very simple measure of lightness constancy. His measure was simply the ratio between the size of the white sector on the standard disk and the size of the white sector on the comparison disk once the two disks had been set to perceptual equality. He called this measure the *B-quotient* (for brightness-quotient). It allowed Katz to compare the amount of constancy under various stimulus conditions, but only as long as the difference in illumination was held constant. A more general formula for measuring constancy was needed, one that would measure the degree of constancy relative to the amount the illumination had been changed. Katz created such a measure and called it the Q-quotient.[2]

But it was Egon Brunswik's (1929) formula that became the standard for measuring the strength of constancy, especially as it could be applied to all kinds of constancies:

$$BR = (R\text{-}S)/(A\text{-}S)$$

For a lightness constancy experiment, A stands for the actual reflectance of the standard target, R stands for the reflectance of a comparison target located in an adjacent field of illumination and adjusted by the observer to match the standard, and S stands for the reflectance of the comparison target at which the standard and comparison targets have equal luminance. The Brunswik ratio (BR) shows where the observer's performance lies, between perfect or 100% constancy at one end (for R = A), and complete failure, or 0% constancy, at the other end (for R = S). In Katz's light/shadow method, 100% constancy means that none of the illumination difference is attributed to reflectance. A target of a given reflectance in the shadowed field appears identical to a target of the same reflectance in the lighted field. Zero constancy means that the entire illumination difference is attributed to surface lightness. Thus, for example, the same white surface that might be seen correctly in the lighted field would appear black in a shadowed field with 30 times less illumination.

Katz gives sufficient detail of his experimental conditions so that it is possible to calculate Brunswik ratios. Doing this, one often finds his constancy to be dismally poor. For example, in Katz's basic light/shadow experiments, he obtained Brunswik ratios of 29% to 39%. In the episcotister experiments, he obtained values of 12% to 23%. Do these values fairly represent the degree of constancy we typically experience? No, not for several reasons. Thouless (1931) pointed out that the Brunswik ratio understates the degree of constancy by using differences rather than ratios. Thouless proposed that the values in Brunswik's formula be converted to log values. In other words, while Brunswik used a ratio of two differences, Thouless used the ratio of two ratios (the ratio of differences of two logs):

$$TR = (\log R\text{-}\log S)/(\log A\text{-}\log S)$$

Thouless' use of ratios rather than differences is consistent with a wide range of data (Weber, Fechner, etc.) showing that the visual system responds primarily to luminance ratios. When Thouless ratios are calculated for the Katz results, we find ratios in the range of 35% to 75% (episcotister experiments: 21% to 70%).

Conditions for Good Constancy

But these Thouless ratios, even though higher than the Brunswik ratios, still fail to represent the degree of constancy we experience in everyday life because the conditions of Katz's experiments were not favorable to good lightness constancy. Ironically, we know this largely because of Katz's own work. Armed with both his experimental methods and the means to measure the strength of constancy, Katz was in an ideal position to study the conditions necessary for good constancy. Two important factors emerged from his extensive research program: articulation and field size.

Articulation

Katz observed that lightness constancy is best in highly complex scenes. More specifically, he found that the degree of lightness constancy within a given field of illumination varies with the degree of articulation within that field. Katz did not offer a formal definition of articulation, but in his experiments demonstrating it, he varied the number of different elements within a given field of illumination. In Katz's basic light/shadow experiment, the level of articulation in each of the two fields is extremely low, consisting of only two or three elements. The modest constancy Katz obtained can be mainly attributed to this factor. But, in what must be the earliest use of what is now called a Mondrian display, Katz replaced the disk in bright illumination with a chart consisting of 48 small chips, ranging from black to white, each 6 mm square, mounted on a large cardboard tableau. This produced Thouless ratios of up to 95%.

Katz's student Burzlaff (1931) extended this work. Using Katz's method of illumination perspective, Burzlaff tested constancy by asking observers to match a single disk in dim illumination with a second disk in bright illumination. Poor constancy was obtained. In a comparison experiment, Burzlaff used the chart of 48 chips. The chips on the chart placed in the bright illumination near the observer were arranged in a haphazard order, while those of the chart placed in the dim illumination were ordered from lightest to darkest. Observers selected the chip from the ordered chart that matched a target chip on the other chart. Under these conditions, virtually perfect lightness constancy was obtained.

Katona (1929) projected a round spotlight onto a wall and mounted a gray square on the wall within the spotlight. Observers viewed the target square through a reduction screen that revealed (1) only a portion of the gray square, (2) the gray square plus a portion of the spotlighted wall surrounding it, or (3) the gray square plus the entire spotlight plus a portion of the non-spotlighted wall. In the first condition Katona obtained almost zero constancy, but as more regions were seen constancy increased dramatically.

Henneman (1935) conducted a constancy experiment using two target disks presented in Katz's light/shadow arrangement. His configurations are shown in Figure 3.2. When the background surrounding each target disk was homogeneous, he obtained 29% constancy (Thouless ratio). When a single small gray disk was placed on the back-

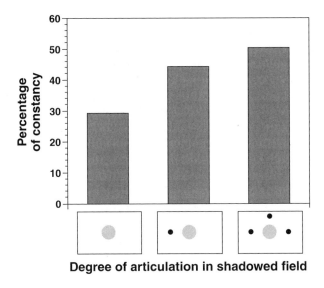

Degree of articulation in shadowed field

Figure 3.2. Results of Henneman's (1935) study of the effect of articulation on lightness constancy. Reprinted with permission from Gilchrist and Annan, 2002.

ground near each target disk, constancy jumped to 42%. With three small black disks placed near the target disk, constancy reached 50%. He concluded (1935, p. 52), "Apparently the more complicated the constitution of the field of observation in the sense of presenting a number of surfaces of different reflectivity, regions of different illumination, and objects set in different planes (tri-dimensionality), the more in accord with its actual albedo-color will a test object be perceived."

For a fuller discussion of the articulation concept, including more recent evidence, see Gilchrist and Annan (2002).

Laws of Field Size

Katz found that the degree of lightness constancy within a given field of illumination depends on the size of the field: the greater the size of a region of illumination, the greater the constancy within it. Surfaces in a small shadow appear darker than they would if the global illumination were homogeneous, but they lighten toward that value as the shadow gets larger. Likewise, surfaces illuminated by a small spotlight appear too light and darken as the spotlight gets larger. Both MacLeod (1932) and Kardos (1934) showed that a gray disk in shadow appears lighter as the shadow gets larger.

But as Rock (1975; Rock & Brosgole, 1964; Rock & Ebenholtz, 1962) has shown so often for other factors in perception, size too can be defined in either retinal terms or in phenomenal terms. Katz believed that both of these meanings of size are effective in lightness constancy, and hence he offered two Laws of Field Size. The first law holds that the degree of constancy varies with the retinal size of a field. He supported it with the observation that if one looks though a neutral-density filter held at arm's length, distant surfaces seen through the filter appear darker than they would without the filter. But as the filter is brought slowly closer to the eye such that a larger and larger area of the visual environment is seen through the filter, these surfaces now appear lighter, more veridical.

The second law holds that constancy varies with perceived size. Here Katz alters the observation. Starting again with a neutral-density filter held at arm's length, the observer begins to walk backward away from the scene while continuing to hold the filter at arm's length. Again, a larger and larger region of the environment is seen through the filter, even though retinal size is now held constant. And again surfaces seen through the filter appear lighter.

Although his second demonstration establishes the effectiveness of perceived size with retinal size held constant, Fred Bonato pointed out to me that Katz's first demonstration does not establish retinal size with perceived size held constant. When the filter is drawn closer to the observer's eye, the total area of the surfaces seen through the filter grows both in retinal and perceived size. MacLeod (1932) varied the size of a shadow surrounding an object. He reported only a limited effect when retinal size was varied by varying observer distance. And that limited effect could be due merely to a failure of size constancy—that is, phenomenal size may not remain completely constant. Subsequent work with a spotlight (Gilchrist & Cataliotti, 1994) suggests that it is perceived size of the illumination field, not retinal size, that affects the degree of constancy.

Of course, as field size is increased, articulation is likely to increase as well, but Kardos (1934) later showed that field size increases constancy even when articulation is held constant.

Impact of Katz's Findings

A measure of Katz's influence can be seen in the following sample of quotations testifying to the role of field size and articulation:

> Katz has often emphasized that for the highest possible degree of color constancy it is very important that the field of view appear filled with numerous objects readily distinguishable from each other . . . The more homogeneously the visual field is filled, the more the phenomena of colour-constancy recede . . . (Burzlaff, 1931, p. 25)

> When, for instance a section of one's surroundings is seen as shadowed it is of consequence whether or not the shadow occupies a large

visual angle and whether the shadowed sector includes a variety of objects. (MacLeod, 1932, p. 32)

> ... colour constancy was manifested only when an adequate and uninterrupted survey of the existing illumination was permitted. Anything hindering such a survey (e.g. the reduction screen, minimal observation time, etc.) either destroyed or reduced the phenomenon. One of the most important conditions is that the visual angle be large and the field richly articulated. (Gelb, quoted in Ellis, 1938, p. 201)

> The phenomenon of colour constancy cannot occur unless the visual field is articulated, and this is possible only when at least two surfaces of different albedo are simultaneously present in this field. (Gelb, quoted in Ellis, 1938, p. 207)

> I have found that constancy effects are mainly furthered by enrichment of the perception through better organization, more contours, more form and object-characters, movement, etc. (Katona, 1935, p. 61)

> Koffka would agree with Gelb in insisting upon one total perceptual process and in attributing the coloring of the visual field primarily to its articulation. (Henneman, 1935, p. 18)

> Apparently the more complicated the constitution of the field of observation in the sense of presenting a number of surfaces of different reflectivity, regions of different illumination, and objects set in different planes (tri-dimensionality), the more in accord with its actual albedo-color will a test object be perceived. (Henneman, 1935, p. 52)

> "Articulation of the visual field" has become recognized as an essential condition for the appearance of "constancy" phenomena, though this rather vague term is badly in need of clearer definition and explanation. (Henneman, 1935, p. 23)

> Some psychologists are doubtful about "correction for illumination" and inclined to explain the results by reference to complexity and "articulation" of the field. (Woodworth, 1938, p. 614)

THEORETICAL ISSUES: 1911–1930

The first third of the 20th century was an active and fruitful period in the history of lightness. Until the work of the Gestaltists beginning around 1930, the field was dominated by Katz, although debate centered on the dispute between Helmholtz and Hering.

Contrast and Constancy: Same or Different?

As we have seen, two phenomena have been central to the study of lightness perception from the beginning: lightness constancy and lightness contrast. Each theory of lightness has been primarily inspired by one or the other, yet every theory has had something to say about both of these phenomena and the relationship between them.

Musatti (1953, p. 562; translated by T. Agostini) has discussed the historical difficulty in describing the relationship between contrast and constancy: "I think that the difficulties arose from the initial plan in which they tried to compare directly the two groups of phenomena. Some of these theorists were looking for a bridge that could connect both phenomena, the other theorists were looking for an abyss that could part both phenomena but each of them tried to find in that bridge or in that abyss the explanation for both phenomena."

The Bridge

The parallels between lightness constancy and simultaneous lightness contrast are indeed striking. Both demonstrate the non-equivalence of luminance and lightness. In contrast, targets of equal luminance do not appear equal in lightness. In constancy, targets of equal lightness do not have equal luminance. Both phenomena demonstrate that context plays an important role in lightness perception. Moreover, both context effects work in the same direction (though with different magnitudes). For example, if the luminance of a target is held constant, increasing the luminance of its surround will make the target appear darker, regardless of whether that is achieved by increasing surround reflectance (as in contrast) or by increasing surround illumination (as in constancy).[3]

These parallels have led to theoretical constructions in which contrast and constancy are as closely related as possible. For Helmholtz, both constancy and contrast result from high-level cognitive processes. Hering invoked lateral inhibition in his explanation of both contrast and constancy, although in the case of constancy it was only one of several factors.

Jaensch and the Parallel Laws

Jaensch (1919, quoted in Katz, 1935, p. 239), using the term *transformation* for constancy,[4] stated the parallelism explicitly, in his "parallel laws of transformation and contrast": "Laws of contrast become laws of transformation when in the laws of contrast the term 'circumfield' is replaced by the term 'illuminated space.' " "The infield in contrast experiments is the field which undergoes contrast; in transformation experiments it is the field which undergoes transformation, i.e., the disc which is exposed to abnormal illumination (shadow, chromatic illumination). The contrast inducer is the circumfield, the transformation inducer the illuminated space."

The Abyss: Contrast and Constancy as Different

G. E. Müller, a towering figure in visual perception generally during this period of time, attacked Jaensch's claims, writing (Müller, 1923, quoted in Katz, 1935, p. 239), "Far from having here two parallel laws, we have rather two laws which are absolutely opposed to each other," and he pointed out that even Jaensch had confirmed Katz's finding that constancy is weaker in indirect than in direct vision, whereas "it is a long-established fact that contrast effects are stronger in indirect than in direct vision." Müller also noted that Jaensch's laws ignored the interesting fact that contrast is reciprocal; the infield also exerts a contrast effect on the surround, a fact that has no parallel in constancy. Others pointed to differences regarding the effects of prolonged viewing and differences in relative ease of making matches. Katz, who attributed contrast to lower, "purely physiological" processes and constancy to "higher," psychical functions, noted that large individual differences are found in constancy judgments but not in contrast judgments, a serious problem for Helmholtz's account of contrast. Henneman (1935, p. 75) gives a list of differences between constancy and contrast.

Perhaps the single most important difference between contrast and constancy is the different magnitudes of their effects. Kroh (1921, p. 214) wrote, "An infield is always more strongly influenced by a coloured illumination than by a coloured surrounding field of equal retinal value." And Wolff (1933, p. 96) observed, "as we know, transformation-appearances are generally much stronger than contrast-appearances." As reported by Musatti (1953), "Terstenjak showed experimentally that constancy phenomena are more intense than contrast phenomena, and for this reason he said that the two phenomena cannot be explained by the same principle." The difference in size of these effects has not always been obvious because contrast experiments and constancy experiments have been done under differing conditions. Gelb (1929, p. 666, translated by D. Todorović) in fact complained that Jaensch's contrast experiments "are not directly comparable with any colour-constancy experiments hitherto reported." To make a fair comparison, one must be sure that both the stimulus conditions and the measure of the effect are comparable. An experiment (Gilchrist, 1988) that meets these requirements is described in Chapter 6.

Psychological versus Physiological Explanations

Vigorous debate also centered on whether contrast and constancy are best explained in terms of psychological or physiological processes, as if psychological processes have no physiological basis and as if peripheral physiological events are registered at the highest levels.

Katz criticized Helmholtz's cognitive theory of constancy as overly intellectual: "Helmholtz's theory is difficult to reconcile not only with the rich phenomenology of human colour-perception but also with the results which animal experiments have yielded" (Katz, 1935, p. 262).

Experiments with Animals and Children

If lightness and color constancy involve high-level cognitive functioning, as suggested by Helmholtz and others, one would expect children and animals to exhibit poor constancy. The first to test lightness constancy in animals was Köhler (1917), who conducted experiments with chimpanzees and hens. He trained hens to peck grains lying on a light-gray paper, but not those lying on a dark-gray paper. Then he placed the dark-gray paper in direct sunlight so that it reflected more light that the light-gray paper. The hens still pecked at the light-gray paper. His experiment with chimpanzees was analogous, using food baskets with lighter- and darker-gray papers attached to their front side. The result, of course, was the same.

Katz and Révész (1921) exploited the fact that hens prefer white grains of rice to highly colored grains. This fact made it easy to train them to reject highly colored grains altogether. In the test phase, white grains were presented under strongly chromatic illumination so that the light they reflected was at least as colored as the light from the grains they had been taught to reject. They ate these grains in colored illumination without any hesitation. Katz noted that this colored illumination, unlike that used by Köhler, would not be at all familiar to the hens.

Burkamp (1923) demonstrated both lightness and color constancy in fish (Cyprinidae). Locke (1935) tested lightness constancy on five rhesus monkeys and five humans, finding markedly higher degrees of constancy for the monkeys than for the humans. Locke suggested that the monkeys have a greater predisposition to perceive object qualities as opposed to isolated color qualities.

Both Burzlaff (1931) and Brunswik (1929) tested lightness constancy with children of different ages. Both found relatively high degrees of constancy even in the youngest subjects tested (4 and 3 years old, respectively). Burzlaff found no general developmental trend. However, both Burzlaff and Brunswik obtained a weak developmental trend when using quite impoverished stimuli.

Taken as a whole, experiments with animals and children fail to support a highly cognitive view of the constancy process.

Countershaded Backgrounds: A Crucial Experiment

We now encounter an experiment that occupies a very strange position in lightness. It has a crucial status for not one but several issues. The experiment has been conducted many times by different researchers. Yet most of these experiments are relatively unknown, even by those who themselves have reported such an experiment. Even today this important finding is scarcely known. In addition to the general amnesia for the early European work, there is a factor that I hope to remedy: this experiment has not had a name. I propose to call it the countershaded backgrounds experiment.

Countershading is a technique applied to Katz's light/shadow method whereby a white surface in low illumination serves as the background for one side while a black (or dark-gray) surface in bright illumination serves as the background for the other side. Values are chosen so that the two backgrounds are equal in luminance. Essentially this allows a test of whether the role of the background depends merely on its physical luminance or on its perceived lightness. Such a test is relevant to several theoretical claims.

Katz (1906)

Katz used countershaded backgrounds to test Helmholtz's claim that simultaneous lightness contrast was the result of cognitive processes. If Katz found Helmholtz's theory of constancy too psychological, he found Helmholtz's psychological account of contrast unacceptable, noting that the lability that characterizes the appearance of targets in a constancy task is absent in the simultaneous contrast display. Helmholtz had not specified clearly the cognitive processes that produce the contrast illusion, but Katz inferred that, according to Helmholtz, the contrast illusion must depend on the perceived lightness of the backgrounds, rather than on their physical luminance.

To create countershaded backgrounds of equal luminance, Katz, using his light/shadow configuration, set up a large dark-gray disk in the lighted region and a large light-gray disk in the shadowed region. Smaller targets of equal luminance were created by mounting them in front of the apparatus so that, although they received equal illumination, each target was nevertheless viewed against the background of one of the large disks.

If contrast depends on the perceived lightness of the backgrounds, one would expect the target in front of the black background to appear lighter than the other target. But if contrast depends solely on the physical luminance of the background the two targets should appear equal, and this is what he obtained. Katz (1935, p. 236) concluded, "when figural conditions are held constant, contrast effects are dependent solely on the intensity and quality of retinal excitation." He argued that while this finding is consistent with Hering's peripheral explanation of contrast, it undermines Helmholtz's cognitive theory of contrast. As we will see, Katz was apparently wrong on both counts.

Countershaded backgrounds do not provide a good test of Helmholtz's account of simultaneous contrast. Helmholtz never claimed that the two sides of the simultaneous contrast display appear to be differently illuminated. They certainly do not. But they could plausibly be treated that way if illumination level is signaled by mean local luminance, as Helmholtz did suggest. By this interpretation, however, Katz's results support Helmholtz. The two targets have equal local mean luminance and thus no lightness difference would be expected, just as Katz found.

Testing a Contrast Theory of Constancy

The countershaded backgrounds experiment has another, more important use: as a test of Hering's contrast theory of constancy. Hering's theory would rely mainly on lateral inhibition to account for constancy in a Katz constancy experiment. The strong inhibition created by the illuminated background is held to offset the higher luminance of the illuminated target. Countershaded backgrounds allow a difference in perceived illumination while excluding any difference in surround luminance.

Here the Katz result seems to support Hering. Kravkov and Paulsen-Baschmakova (1929) obtained the same results as Katz in a countershading experiment that differed from Katz in only one essential respect: their backgrounds had a chromatic component. But other countershading experiments have produced the opposite results.

Jaensch and Müller (1920)

In 1920, Jaensch and Müller reported a countershading experiment with results contradicting those of Katz and of Kravkov and Paulsen-Baschmakova. Jaensch and Müller created their countershaded backgrounds as Katz had done, but they created targets of equal luminance using countershading as well. They used a target of low reflectance in the lighted region and a target of high reflectance in the shadowed region. They obtained a substantial degree of constancy (Thouless ratio 58%); observers perceived the target in the lighted region to be much darker gray than the target in the shadowed region.

The remarkable feature of this experiment is that every one of Hering's factors, both psychological and physiological, was ruled out, yet constancy survived. The two targets appeared equal in lightness even though the one in brighter illumination had a higher luminance. Hering had argued that when looking at the target in brighter illumination, its higher luminance was offset by the effect of its bright background in reducing pupil size, reducing photoreceptor sensitivity, and producing stronger lateral inhibition. But in the Jaensch and Müller experiment, none of these three could occur because the countershading produces backgrounds of equal luminance. His fourth factor—memory color—was ruled out by the abstract shape of the disk.

Figure 3.3. Apparatus used in Gelb's countershaded backgrounds experiment. The observer viewed the apparatus from directly above. Luminances were varied by adjusting the slant of the panels.

Gelb (1932)

Gelb (1932) also conducted a countershading experiment using the apparatus shown in Figure 3.3. Looking down through the open top of the apparatus, the observer sees two rectangular panels of equal luminance: a white one slanted away from the illumination, and a black one slanted toward the illumination. Each rectangle appears to have a round gray disk lying on it, although this disk is really a round aperture that reveals a portion of a larger rectangle below. His results simulated constancy in that the two equi-luminant targets (on equi-luminant backgrounds) appeared different in lightness, the target seen in the higher illumination appearing darker.

Results consistent with those of Gelb and of Jaensch and Müller were also reported by MacLeod (1932), Henneman (1935), Kardos (1934), and Koffka and Harrower (1932, also described in Koffka, 1935, p. 249). Katona (1935) replicated Katz's experiment and reported, though with some reservations, results supporting Katz.

Gelb put his finger on the factor responsible for the contradictory results. In Katz's experiment, as well as those by Kravkov and Paulsen-Baschmakova and by Katona, the targets did not lie in the same depth plane as the countershaded backgrounds. To obtain an effect on the target of background lightness, it is necessary that the target and background appear to belong to the same field of illumination.

Wolff's Resolution

The crucial role of belongingness suggested by Gelb was demonstrated by his Gestalt colleague, Wolff (1933). Wolff placed two equal gray targets at some distance in front of two backgrounds. The right-hand background was both a darker gray and more brightly illuminated compared to the left-hand background. Nevertheless, his subjects reported the two targets to be equal. Yet when he placed targets of the same gray on coplanar backgrounds equated for luminance to the original backgrounds, he obtained the usual contrast effect. His reports suggest that the lack of contrast effect found by Katz and by Kravkov and Paulsen-Baschmakova are due not to background luminance, but to the depth separation between each target and its background. Wolff (1933, p. 97) concluded, "contrast is strongest when both fields lie in the same plane and there is no contrast at all when the fields are phenomenally situated at a large distance from each other."[5] Ironically, Katz (1935, p. 237) had noted that Helmholtz "mentions for instance, the fact that contrast effects are reduced when the contrasting fields are apprehended as independent, spatially separated objects."

Implications for Contrast

Although Gelb's targets appeared different from each other while those of Katz did not, Gelb noted that his results are consistent with those of Katz in showing that contrast does not depend on background lightness. The effect of background lightness obtained by Gelb and by Jaensch and Müller is opposite to what contrast would produce. The target on the lighter-appearing background did not appear darker than the other target, as it would by contrast; it appeared lighter. In fact, the experiment makes more sense in terms of constancy than in terms of contrast. Target lightness depends on perceived illumination level: the target in higher illumination appears darker.

Background Luminance versus Background Lightness: A Summary

The results of all 10 countershading studies we have just reviewed can be summarized by two conclusions:

1. Target lightness depends on background lightness, but contrast does not. The effect is opposite to that of contrast and is perhaps better described as an effect on target lightness of perceived background illumination.

2. Target lightness depends strongly on background lightness only when the target appears to belong to (appears coplanar with) the background.

These findings deal a heavy blow to any hope that constancy can be reduced to contrast, and they undermine purely retinal theories of contrast.

Perception of the Illumination

Perhaps the first experiments done explicitly on illumination perception were conducted by Krüger (1924). Two episcotisters (rotating disks with open sectors of variable size) were set up side by side. Looking through either episcotister, the observer saw a room with a landscape visible through one window. Since virtually no light was reflected off the front black surface of the solid sector, the spinning blades of the episcotister were the equivalent of a neutral-density filter, which in turn closely simulates a reduction in overall illumination level. Krüger wanted to determine the threshold for perceiving differences in illumination and to compare this for the corresponding threshold for perceived lightness. Having the observer look through the two episcotisters successively, and using the method of limits, the obtained threshold value was about 8.7%. The corresponding threshold for perceived lightness, using a pair of Maxwell disks in equal illumination, was found to be 4.7%.

The study could be criticized in various ways. Perhaps the most important issue is whether lightness and perceived illumination were compared fairly. It is not entirely clear what would constitute a fair comparison. Probably the best approach is simply to measure the threshold under a variety of conditions. For example, it would probably be the case that the threshold for a small region of illumination, say a shadow or a projected patch of light, would be much lower than Krüger's threshold for overall illumination.

Katz's Theory of Lightness

Despite the heated arguments of this period, the debate took place within a theoretical framework that featured the dualistic assumptions of raw sensations and their cognitive interpretation. These assumptions were shared by all, and they can be seen in Katz's own theory. Although Katz marshaled strong logical and empirical challenges to the ideas of Helmholtz and Hering, he himself could not escape those same habits of thought; he merely rearranged them.

Katz's account of constancy featured the concept, given earlier by Hering, of normal illumination. Normal illumination is chromatically neutral and bright enough to allow surface microstructure to be clearly seen, but not so bright as to be dazzling. Surfaces seen in normal illumination appear in their genuine or real colors.

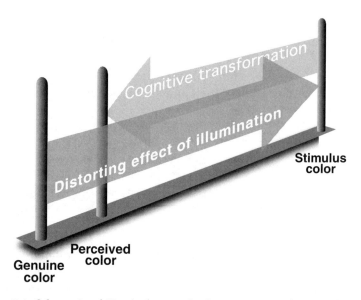

Figure 3.4. Schematic of Katz's theory of color constancy. The stimulus color produced by abnormal illumination is cognitively transformed in the direction of its genuine color.

However, when a surface lies in abnormal illumination, such as a spotlight or a shadow, the stimulus color it produces is displaced away from its genuine color (the color it would appear in normal illumination) in the direction of the abnormal illumination. In that case a central transformation process, rooted in the observer's past experience but triggered by the visual context, modifies the stimulus color back toward its genuine color, resulting in the percept. This transformation process is not engaged when the object appears in normal illumination. These components are illustrated in Figure 3.4.

Four terms are essential to Katz's account of constancy: normal illumination, genuine color, stimulus color, and transformation. Ironically, with the possible exception of genuine color, these concepts were not revealed to Katz through phenomenology. They were merely the available tools of the day. Perhaps in an effort to ground these concepts in phenomenology, Katz suggested that both the stimulus color and the transformation process were revealed by the use of the reduction screen in his basic light/shadow constancy experiment. The reduction screen, by occluding the visual context, reveals the stimulus color of a target surface: "the various procedures of reduction, however, give us some information concerning whether the retinal processes corresponding to various impressions are alike or not" (Katz, 1935, p. 83). Thus, when a target in the lighted region and a target in the shadowed region are viewed through a reduction screen and adjusted to appear identical, we can say they produce equal local stimulus and have equal stimulus colors. When the reduction screen is removed, the two targets appear different. But, as Katz notes, only one of the two targets appears to change, and that is the target in the abnormal illumination. This change reveals the transformation process in action, and it further reveals that only the target in the abnormal illumination is transformed.

Katz did not reject the duality between local peripheral stimulation and central interpretation, shared by Helmholtz and Hering. He rejected only the claim that both contrast and constancy could be explained by a single approach, either sensory or cognitive. As Gelb wrote (1929, quoted in Ellis, 1955, p. 203), "The principal difference between Katz and his predecessors is his claim that colour contrast and colour constancy require essentially different explanatory principles." Von Fieandt (1966, p. 217) has written, "Already in his first edition Katz aimed at a synthesis of the dualistic view shared by both Hering and Helmholtz. Just as Hering included both physiological and 'higher-order' psychological (memory colors and learning) among his explanatory principles, so Helmholtz too referred both to traditional physiological determinants and to something reminiscent of cognition and reasoning, his famous 'unconscious inferences.' "

Katz's influence in the prewar period was so great that his term *transformation* came to be used as a virtual synonym for the phenomenon of constancy, even though Katz himself used it to refer to the psychic process that produces constancy. MacLeod (1932, p. 37) objected, "Inasmuch, however, as the transformation of experience implies the pre-existence of a specific untransformed experience, it is best to use the term only in the discussion of a point of view which postulates a transformation process, as was the case in Katz's original work."

Katz's Failure to Escape the Zeitgeist

Katz criticized Helmholtz's theory of constancy as overly intellectual, yet it is difficult to see how his own theory is different. Transformation, like unconscious inference, is seen as a central process and depends on the observer's past experience. Both concepts are vague and speculative, and both run into the same difficulties. More concretely, neither concept is workable unless the illumination level can be determined.

Indeed, Katz's theory is undermined by his own experimental work. It is not clear how Katz's theory of constancy can be reconciled with his own research showing strong constancy in animals. And his findings on the importance of articulation and field size for constancy have no comfortable place in his theory. No explanation is given for why high articulation or large field size should produce a more successful transformation process or allow a better determination of the illumination level. Ironically, it was Kardos who later found a place in lightness theory for these two concepts.

But the biggest problem for Katz's theory came from an experiment by Gelb that, while disarmingly simple, was devastating to Katz's theoretical edifice: Gelb's paradoxical experiment.

SUMMARY

The publication of Katz's book on color in 1911 launched a 25-year period of vigorous research in lightness. Katz took a phenomenological approach, describing the various modes in which colors appear. In particular, he drew a sharp distinction between surface colors and film colors. He also noted that lightness and brightness are separate phenomenal dimensions of surface colors. Most importantly, though not widely appreciated, it was Katz who gave us our basic psychophysical methods for the study of lightness, including asymmetrical matching in side-by-side fields of illumination and shadow. Using these methods he demonstrated that lightness constancy is not complete. He created the first measures of the strength of constancy, measures that were later improved upon by Brunswik and Thouless. Katz found that the degree of lightness constancy correlates with both the size of a field of illumination and with its degree of articulation.

Katz himself did not break new ground theoretically. The work he inspired grappled with several issues disputed by Helmholtz and Hering, such as the role of central and peripheral factors and whether constancy can be reduced to contrast. To this end, many lightness constancy experiments were conducted with animals. Lightness constancy in the absence of contrast factors was tested (and found) using a method I have called countershaded backgrounds: targets in high illumination were presented in front of dark-gray backgrounds while targets in low illumination were presented in front of equi-luminant light-gray backgrounds.

4

The Gestalt Period

The emergence of Gestalt theory is often tied to the 1912 publication of Wertheimer's paper on apparent motion. But the Gestaltists did not turn their attention to lightness until the early 1930s. When they did, they turned the field upside down. In the short space of 5 years, under a darkening political sky, they published a series of devastating crucial experiments. By the time the sky blackened completely, Katz, who represented the standard view of lightness, was in retreat on every issue on which Gestalt theory challenged him.

GELB'S PARADOXICAL EXPERIMENT

Gelb (1929) replicated Katz's light/shadow experiment with only a single change: he merely seated the observer and the reduction screen within the abnormal illumination rather than within the normal illumination, as Katz and others had always done. Under these conditions when the reduction screen is removed, it is the target surface in the normal illumination that appears to change. The result is paradoxical because according to Katz, surfaces in normal illumination are not transformed. Gelb pressed the challenge. Lightness perception in normal illumination, he argued, is neither more nor less of a problem than lightness perception in abnormal illumination. The reduction screen does not reveal any raw stimulus color. Gelb wrote (1929, quoted in Ellis, 1938, p. 208), "it is to be noted that *only unification*—not a reduction to a "more retinal" seeing—has occurred. It is quite obvious that when the reduction screen is used the two disks will be seen as equal, because *now* the impression of illumination is the same for both." The whole concept of untransformed colors was cast into doubt.

In the face of Gelb's compelling challenge, Katz capitulated. In the extensively revised second edition of his book he declares, "I am in thorough agreement with Gelb's anti-empiristic arguments. I no longer use the concept of transformation in its earlier sense, and I share Gelb's view that 'the perception of surface colours in normal illumination is no less and no more a problem than is their perception in non-normal illumination'" (Katz, 1935, p. 276).

Rarely does the publication of a single experiment critical to a particular theory cause the holder of that theory to give up the core concepts of the theory and embrace the critic's point of view (see Katz, 1935, pp. 127–128). This extraordinary exchange stands as a tribute both to Katz's honesty and to Gelb's brilliance.

Katz's Error

Why did Gelb's paradoxical experiment catch Katz by surprise? I would argue that this happened because Katz, in an effort to make the conventional ideas of his day work, strayed from the phenomenological method that had served him so well. Neither the concept of the stimulus color nor the transformation concept is revealed by phenomenology. They were merely part of the intellectual baggage of the time.

But Katz allowed himself to believe that the reduction screen furnished the phenomenological foundation for his ideas, first that the film colors seen in the holes of the reduction screen are the visual experience of the raw, untransformed sensations, and second that the transformation process itself is experienced at the moment the reduction screen is removed in his constancy experiment and the appearance changes.

To hold this collection of ideas together, Katz had to ignore several nagging contradictions. This can be seen in his confusion regarding the role of the reduction screen. The key issue is whether surfaces seen in the hole of the reduction screen appear in the film color mode or the surface color mode. This issue is crucial for Katz's theory. Katz could claim that the reduction screen reveals the raw sensory color only if it creates the appearance of film color.

Katz (1935) repeatedly contradicted himself on this matter. At times he suggested that the reduction screen reveals surfaces in the film mode: "The surface colour-impression normally given by an object can easily be supplanted by the impression of film colour if a screen, containing a single aperture, is so placed before the object as to conceal it completely, except for the part appearing through the aperture" (p. 10).

Yet by Katz's own criteria, colors seen in the reduction screen fail two key tests of film color. First, according to Katz (1935), "film colour always possesses an essentially frontal-parallel character" (p. 11), and second, they appear stripped of any sense of the illumination: "The severance of illumination and illuminated object vanishes in the case of an individual film color" (p. 92). Yet elsewhere he concedes that when a color is seen in the reduction screen, it takes on both the planarity and the perceived illumination of the screen itself: "The definitely localized surface colour of the cardboard thus manifests a tendency to draw the film colour into its own plane" (p. 72). "The film colour appearing behind the hole then also tends to turn in the direction in which the cardboard is turned" (p. 72). "Looking through the reduction screen causes the film colours seen to appear in a visual field of the same illumination—that of the reduction screen" (p. 94).

What are the facts, by the way? In general the reduction screen creates the appearance of surface color. For example, most decrements appear as surface colors. But there are several exceptions. Strong decrements appear as black holes, although Katz might not have considered this to be a film color. Increments strong enough to exceed the threshold of self-luminosity (see Chapter 9) can be said to appear in the film mode.

These conclusions are consistent with Katz's reported observations, although curiously Katz seems to have ignored the increment/decrement distinction. When Katz introduces the concept of film color in his 1935 book, he speaks of the color seen when looking through the eyepiece of a spectroscope. Note that here we have a strong increment, because the region surrounding the target color is totally dark. But when the reduction screen is used in Katz's light/shadow experiment, the conditions will almost always produce surface color.

How could phenomenology have saved Katz? Had Katz paid more attention to the fact that the reduction screen usually produces surface color rather than film color, it would have been obvious why one target and not the other changes when the reduction screen is removed. The target that appears to change when the screen is removed is simply the one that appears to stand in a different level of illumination from that of the screen. The appearance of the targets in the reduction screen is determined by the level of illumination on the screen itself.[1]

Normal versus Prevailing Illumination

Katona (1929) concluded from his empirical work that, as other Gestaltists had suggested, the concept of normal illumination should be replaced by the concept of prevailing illumination. Katz himself struggled with the two concepts (Katz, 1935, p. 126): "If one particular illumination does not prevail throughout most of the visual field, we cannot have the impression of shadowing at the points of the visual field which are emitting less light. If the intensity of the illumination is reduced throughout almost the entire visual field and only a small part is illuminated *normally,* we do not have the impression that the smaller part is normally illuminated and the rest of the field is in shadow. On the contrary, the total illumination of the visual field seems lower, whereas another spot of light seems superimposed at the normally illuminated point."

Here Katz clearly acknowledges that it is the prevailing illumination that *appears* normal. But there is another test. According to Katz's theory, errors in perceived lightness occur in the abnormal illumination, not the normal. Yet the empirical work that led to his laws of field size shows that errors are greatest in small (that is, non-prevailing) regions of illumination, not abnormal regions. The concept of prevailing illumination is closely related to the notion of field size. And it has the further advantage that it can be specified by relationships within the proximal stimulus, whereas normal illumination depends on past experience. It is unfortunate that Katz did not allow greater influence of his own empirical findings on his theory.

GESTALT THEORY

Until the arrival of Gestalt theory, it was universally accepted that the two extreme poles of lightness theory were to be found in Helmholtz's cognitive theory and Hering's sensory theory, respectively. The departure offered by Gestalt theory was bold enough to make the theories of Helmholtz and Hering seem remarkably similar.

Rejection of Sensory/Cognitive Dualism

Gestalt theory rejected what Koffka called the network of traditional hypotheses. Central to this network are the twin ideas of raw sensations and central transformation. The study of lightness and color perception had been energized by the mid-19th-century recognition that perceived color corresponds most closely to distal color, not proximal color. Yet this insight had not led to a rejection of the doctrine of local determination (sensory experience equals local stimulation), but rather was assimilated into the existing concepts by the creation of an awkward mind–body dualism. According to Gelb (1929, excerpted in Ellis, 1938, p. 206), "The essentially problematic aspect of the phenomenon has invariably been taken to be the discrepancy between the 'stimulus' and 'colour' reaction. Assuming that retinal stimuli and colour-vision stood in a more or less direct correspondence with one another, any departure from this primitive and self-evident relationship—i.e. any 'discrepancy'—was explained on empiristic grounds. Thus if the discrepancy would not be rendered comprehensible by reference to 'physiological' (peripheral) factors alone, 'psychological' factors would also be invoked. In this way the phenomena of colour constancy were classified as the *product* of central processes operating upon and reorganizing genetically simpler colour-processes."

Koffka (1935, p. 243) described the dualism in this way: "The theory of brightness- and colour-constancy found itself suspended between two poles. On the one hand there were attempts to explain it by factors which in themselves had nothing to do with constancy, on the other hand, the result itself, i.e., constancy, entered the explanation. Both poles were already inherent in Hering's discussion, the first in his attempt to explain the facts by adaptation, pupillary reaction, and contrast (in Hering's sense), the second in his concept of *memory* colour."

Gestalt theory rejected this dualism, arguing that the projection of a pattern of light on the retina engages a single unified process that culminates in the percept. That process translates relationships in the retinal pattern into perceived variables such as perceived size, perceived motion, and lightness. As Köhler (1947, p. 103) wrote, "Our view will be that, instead of reacting to local stimuli by local and mutually independent events, the organism responds to the pattern of stimuli to which it is exposed; and that this answer is a unitary process, a functional whole which gives, in experience, a sensory scene rather than a mosaic of local sensations. Only from this point of view can we explain the fact that, with a constant local stimulus, local experience is found to vary when the surrounding stimulation is changed." Gelb (1929, excerpted in Ellis, 1938, p. 207) proclaimed the new monism: "Our visual world is not constructed by 'accessory' higher (central, psychological) processes from a stimulus-conditioned raw material of 'primary sensations' and sensation-complexes; rather from the very beginning, the functioning of our sensory apparatus depends upon conditions in such a way that, in accordance with external stimulus constellations and internal attitudes we find ourselves confronted by a world of 'things,' thus or thus, now more poorly, now more richly articulated and organized."

Rejection of Sensations

According to Gestalt theory, the concept of sensations was required by a need to preserve certain traditional ideas. Sensations are not found in our direct experience of the world. This does not mean that we cannot experience proximal qualities of a surface, such as its luminance or visual angle. But, as Köhler observed, just because we have some ability[2] to observe the brightness of a given surface by perceptually isolating it from its context does not mean that that brightness is an elementary sensation out of which the normal percept is built. Likewise, just because we have some ability to perceptually flatten a visual scene does not mean that our experience of a three-dimensional world is based on an early two-dimensional representation.

Emphasis on Phenomenology

Apart from their views on Katz's theoretical ideas, the Gestaltists strongly endorsed his emphasis on careful phenomenal description. Köhler had observed that all science begins with careful observation. This is even truer in visual perception, where the very data that must be explained are ultimately phenomenological—"Why do things look as they do?" in Koffka's famous phrase. One can scarcely approach this question without also considering exactly how things do look.

Koffka largely accepted Katz's description of visual experience in the lightness domain, especially the observation that surface colors make their appearance accompanied by an impression of the illumination (although he was not convinced that the illumination level is perceived in all cases).

Emphasis on Perceptual Structure

The Gestaltists observed that the units of our perceptual experience are objects, not sensations. As Wertheimer (excerpted in Ellis, 1938, p. 71) observed, "I stand at the window and see a house, trees, sky. And I could, then, on theoretical grounds, try to sum up: there are 327 brightnesses (and tones of color). (Have I '327'? No: sky, house, trees; and no one can realize the having of the '327' as such.)"

The segregation of the light entering the eye into discrete objects presents a fundamental challenge to theory. The Gestalt account of this achievement in terms of grouping principles represents the only serious attempt to grapple with this problem. Other theories have ignored this problem. For example, although past experience theories have offered explanations of many perceptual phenomena, including the constancies, we have not seen a past experience account of object segregation. The Gestalt theorists argued that such an account is logically impossible. As a result, the existence of organized wholes within the visual field is generally taken for granted, representing what Köhler (1929, p. 176) called the *experience error*.

The emphasis on perceptual structure is reflected in Gestalt attention to the powerful effects of context and frames of reference.

Emphasis on Relative Luminance

Lightness is not a property of light. It is the property of a surface, and the necessary conditions for surface perception are intimately related to those of lightness. Perhaps the fundamental condition for the perception of a surface is the presence of at least two luminance values (Gelb, 1929, p. 674). Light per se does not create surface lightness.

Emphasis on Depth Perception

The crucial role of depth was noted by virtually all of the Gestalt theorists who studied lightness. As described in Chapter 3, Wolff (1933) demonstrated experimentally that the conflicting data that had been reported in the various studies of countershaded backgrounds stemmed from differences in depth appearances. The key is whether or not the targets appear in the same plane as the countershaded backgrounds. Koffka placed great emphasis on coplanarity as a grouping principle, as we will see. Kardos (1934) demonstrated the commanding role of depth perception in a series of experiments. Katona (1929) also demonstrated depth effects in lightness.

Impact on the Theoretical Landscape

Gelb's paradoxical experiment was not a problem merely for Katz. After all, Katz had borrowed the concept of normal illumination from Hering. Gelb's experiment amounted to a serious attack on both the concept of a raw sensation and the concept of a cognitive transformation, radically undermining the dualistic framework common to all prior work. The radical break of the Gestaltists from the conventional ideas of a cognitive transformation of raw sensations was far more significant than the nuances separating Hering and Helmholtz.

KOFFKA

Of the three founders of Gestalt, it was Koffka who gave the greatest attention to the specific problems of lightness perception. Koffka praised the work of his Gestalt colleagues such as Gelb, Kardos, and Wolff, borrowing heavily from them. But although his discussion on the topic has been available in English and is thus better known, it is, in the words of Osgood (1953, p. 283) "not notable for its clarity." Koffka never achieved the coherence that he sought in his account of lightness. Yet he made enormous headway, exposing false solutions and turning theoretical discussion onto novel paths.

Koffka advanced several new concepts, notably belongingness and strength of gradient, that are scarcely remembered, although, as we will see, the loss has been ours. Other parts of Koffka's thinking have remained both relevant and known, such as his concept of frames of reference and his emphasis on the role of relative luminance in lightness.

Relative Luminance

"Our theory of whiteness constancy," Koffka wrote (1935, p. 245), "will be based on this characteristic of colours, which we found confirmed in so many passages, that perceived qualities depend upon stimulus gradients." The ambiguity of absolute luminance values had formed the central challenge to lightness theory from the beginning. Yet absolute luminance values had never been discarded on this ground. Rather, psychological processes were sought with which to supplement them. Rejecting the awkward dualism of this conventional thinking, Koffka made relative luminance central to his theory.

Koffka cited Metzger's (1930) work showing that when a homogeneous surface fills the observer's entire visual field and no microtexture is visible, no value of lightness is seen. Indeed, no surface is seen. The observer feels as if he or she is immersed in an infinite three-dimensional fog.[3] There is no lightness constancy under these conditions. If two surfaces, one black and one white, each fill the whole visual field and they are equated in luminance (by applying greater illumination to the black surface), they must be indistinguishable because they produce identical retinal stimulation. Only when a luminance step (which Koffka calls a gradient) is introduced into the field is a surface seen. And with that surface appear both a sense of lightness and a sense of illumination level.

Koffka (1935) also correctly predicted (p. 121) that a homogeneous chromatic ganzfeld would lose its color over time. This has since been confirmed by Hochberg, Triebel and Seaman (1951), and Weintraub (1964).

From our modern vantage point, the boldness of Koffka's position may not be appreciated. For example, Marr (1982, p. 259) has written, "It is a widespread and time-honored view, going back at least to Ernst Mach, that object color depends upon the ratios of light reflected from the various parts of the visual field rather than on the absolute amount of light reflected." But despite references to the value of relative luminance, a close look shows that virtually all the non-Gestalt theories are ultimately rooted in absolute luminance values. For example, Helmholtz may have alluded to the role of relative luminance, but according to his theory, lightness is attributed not to luminance ratios within the retinal image, but to another proportion: the ratio between the light reflected by a surface (absolute luminance) and the perceived intensity of light illuminating it.

It would be equally misleading to say that Hering viewed lightness as a product of relative luminance. Beyond the recognition of a role for context, contrast theories have little in common with Koffka's relational thinking. Of Hering, Koffka wrote (1935, p. 245), "since his theory has to be abandoned, as we have shown before, the term contrast is no more than a name which we prefer to avoid since it implies an explanation not in terms of gradient, but in terms of absolute amounts of light." For a discussion of the difference between contrast and gradient theories, see Gilchrist (1994, Chapter 1).

Relative Luminance not Enough

Koffka recognized that lightness cannot be based simply on relative luminance and that luminance ratios are ambiguous in several ways. First, a luminance ratio can produce lightness values only once it has been anchored: "In this formulation we explain the appearance of one object by the gradient of stimulation which connects it with another and by the appearance of the latter" (Koffka, 1935, p. 250). Second, Koffka distinguishes between a luminance ratio produced by an albedo (reflectance) change and one produced by a change of illumination, such as the border of a shadow.

Koffka sought luminance relationships within the proximal stimulus that correlate with perceived lightness. If this brings to mind J.J. Gibson's later claim that perceived properties are based on higher-order variables, it must be remembered that Gibson worked very closely with Koffka for a number of years at Smith College. "[M]y debt to him is very great," Gibson (1971, p. 9) wrote.

Two Invariance Theorems

Among the systematic relationships he finds among proximal and perceived variables, Koffka identifies two invariance theorems.

Lightness and Perceived Illumination

Having argued that that we perceive not just shape and size but also shape-at-a-slant and size-at-a-distance, Koffka readily affirmed Katz's claim that surface colors make their appearance accompanied by an impression of the illumination. And he underlined the observation made earlier by Katz that when targets standing in different fields of illumination are matched for lightness, they appear equal only on the lightness dimension. Their difference in luminance is also perceived, but attributed to the illumination.

Indeed, Koffka (1935, p. 244) gave in effect a formal invariance theorem by suggesting "the possibility that a combination of whiteness and [perceived illumination], possibly their product, is an invariant for a given local stimulation under a definite set of total conditions. If two equal proximal stimulations produce two surfaces of different whiteness, then these surfaces will also have different [perceived illuminations], the whiter one will be less, the blacker one more [brightly illuminated]." (Koffka used the term *brightness* to refer to perceived illumination. For clarity I have substituted the latter term for the former.) Empirical evidence bearing on this invariance theorem is considered in Chapter 8.

But though he tied lightness and perceived illumination closely together, Koffka (1932) rejected Katz's position (following Helmholtz)

that perceived illumination is primary and genetically prior to lightness (p. 349): "I cannot find that Katz has *proved* the impression of
the illumination to be the primary event, the constancy of colors secondary. As far as our empirical knowledge goes the two might as well
be concomitant effects of a common cause."

Principle of the Shift of Level

Koffka did not claim (as Wallach later would) that a given luminance
ratio specifies a lightness value. But he claimed (1932, p. 335) that it
specifies a difference on the lightness scale:[4] "If two parts of the retina
are differently stimulated, no constant relationship will exist between
each part of the phenomenal field and its local stimulation, but under
certain conditions there will be a constant relationship between the
gradient in the phenomenal field and the stimulus *difference*. I.e. the
two field parts may, under different conditions, look very differently
coloured, but their relation one to the other or the phenomenal 'gap'
between them will be the same if the stimulus difference is kept constant. The condition mentioned above is that the two parts of the field
belong to the same level." He illustrates the concept (Koffka, 1932,
p. 332) by comparing "(1) . . . a small gray patch on a yellow background and (2) . . . a small area reflecting neutral light within a room
under yellow illumination." Common to the two cases is the color and
luminance relationship between the target and its background.

   Though this relationship is preserved in perception, its location in
surface color space is different for the two cases, as illustrated in Figure 4.1a. In case 1 the surround is seen as yellow and the target as
gray with a slight tinge of blue. In case 2 the surround is seen as white
(in surface color) and the target as a more saturated blue. Others,
including Feyerabend (1924), had used the same comparison to show
that a loss of color in the surround is accompanied by a gain of color
in the target.

   This invariance theorem holds only when the two regions are seen
as part of the same framework of illumination, but they need not be
retinally adjacent. Koffka also gives the following example. Two target
disks are seen within a room illuminated by reddish[5] light. One disk,
d_1, reflects the same reddish light as the illumination (as any neutral
gray would) and it appears neutral in color. The other disk, d_2, reflects
objectively neutral light, causing it to appear greenish. When the disks
are now observed through two holes in a neutral reduction screen
(neutrally illuminated), both undergo a change of appearance of the
same direction and magnitude. d_1 now appears reddish, while d_2 now
appears neutral. Figure 4.1b shows this shift of level. In Koffka's
words (1935, p. 255), "we may assume that the stimulus gradient
d_1-d_2 gives rise to an equal apparent colour gradient with and without
the reduction screen, but this gradient alone does not determine the

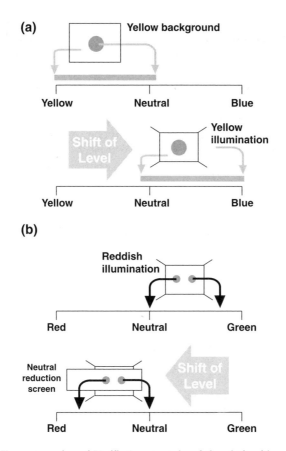

Figure 4.1. Two examples of Koffka's principle of the shift of level. Although perceived colors change, the perceived color relationships are preserved.

absolute position of this apparent gradient. . . . This whole manifold of colours may be considered as a fixed scale, on which the two colours produced by the two stimulations . . . keeping the same distance from each other, may slide, according to the general conditions. I have called this the principle of the shift of level."

"Thus 'level' means the general framework in which every single part of our phenomenal world receives its place" (Koffka, 1932, p. 336). Koffka applies to lightness the same concept of frame of reference so indispensable in motion and orientation, a striking example of which he gives on the same page: "On the west side of Lake Cayuga, a couple of hundred feet or so above its level, stands a public building on a wide lawn that slants slightly towards the lake. To everyone this building seems to be tilted in a direction away from the lake in the most striking manner." The invariance is seen in the angle formed between the building and the lawn. Physically the building is vertical and the lawn is tilted slightly toward the lake. As the lawn perceptually normalizes toward the horizontal, the building duly tilts away from the lake by the same amount, maintaining the integrity of the building–lawn angle. Here we see a foreshadowing of the anchoring problem (Gilchrist et al., 1999).

Foster (Foster & Nascimento, 1994) has conducted a series of experiments testing what he calls relative color constancy, which is directly implied by Koffka's invariance principle, finding higher degrees of constancy than typically obtained in standard color constancy experiments.

Two regions can be retinally adjacent and yet not belong to the same framework. Such was the case, as shown by Wolff (1933), in Katz's countershading experiment, described earlier. In general the theorem would not apply either at an occlusion boundary or at a cast illumination edge. In both cases the regions bordering the boundary lie in different regions of illumination.

Constancy Not Explained by Contrast

Koffka completely rejected the proposal that constancy phenomena can be reduced to contrast. He noted the very different strengths of the two phenomena and he emphasized the different kinds of backgrounds in contrast and constancy displays. In a contrast display, the backgrounds differ in lightness, while in a typical constancy display, the backgrounds differ in illumination level. He illustrated this point with a stunning experiment on colored shadows.

Koffka's Colored Shadow Experiment

In a room illuminated with diffuse daylight, Koffka (1935, p. 258) used a yellowish incandescent light to cast the shadow of an object onto a white sheet of paper. As we would expect, the shadow appeared bluish even though it reflected physically neutral light. Koffka then used yellow paper to cover the entire white paper except for the region of the shadow, presumably by cutting out of the yellow paper a region that coincided with the shadow. This modification made the region surrounding the shadow reflect more yellow light but left the shadow unaltered. Based on contrast alone, one would expect the shadow to now appear even more bluish than before. But instead, Koffka found that the shadow actually lost its bluish appearance.

This outcome makes it clear that the phenomenon of colored shadows cannot be reduced to simply a contrast effect. Kardos (1934, p. 32) serendipitously found the same result in the achromatic domain. These results suggest a qualitative difference between contrast and constancy. As Koffka (1935, p. 259) observed (using the term *transformation* to mean constancy), "Experiments like the one described last tend to make the problem of the relation between contrast and 'transformation' a very pressing one."

Shift of Level versus Difference Increase

Koffka concluded that the phenomenon of colored shadows is a phenomenon of color constancy, not a contrast phenomenon. And his explanation of colored shadows, like his explanation of constancy in general, was based on his concept of the shift of level. In Koffka's colored shadow experiment, the paper surrounding the shadow appeared as white paper, even though it reflected yellow light; "therefore a surface within this area which reflects neutral light must look blue" (Koffka, 1932, p. 342). In other words, the stimulus light that represents neutrality in the local context has shifted from physically neutral to physically yellow. Both the target and its surround now take their perceived color from the relationship between the physical light they reflect and the newly established neutral level.

Simultaneous contrast, according to Koffka, requires a different explanation. He spoke of a difference increase. The difference between the perceived color of the target and the perceived color of the surround becomes greater than the difference between their physical colors. Koffka never felt that he had resolved these issues. He was unable to explain the contrast effect in terms of the shift of level principle, and he acknowledged that the difference increase appears to violate his invariance principle.

DETERMINING THE ILLUMINATION LEVEL

Certain theories are especially obligated to explain how the illumination level is determined, because they hold lightness hostage to such a determination. And yet, every theory must deal with the question of illumination in the broader sense. Every theory must provide an account of how reflectance and illumination are disentangled and thus, by implication, how illumination level is determined. The treatment of illumination thus provides a story line that runs throughout the history of lightness work.

On the question of how the illumination level is determined, Helmholtz (1866/1924, p. 276), along with Mach (1865/1965, p. 270) and Hering (1874), got no further than indirect suggestions that mean luminance is the cue for illumination level. Helmholtz seemed to place more emphasis on past experience and associations. But, as we saw in Chapter 2, these ideas work only if the illumination can be determined. And ironically, if the illumination can be determined, these ideas are not even needed.

Like Helmholtz's association theory, Katz's transformation theory also runs afoul of the illumination issue. Katz claimed that when the target surface lies within abnormal illumination, the stimulus color is transformed in the direction of its genuine color. But unless the illumination level is known, the visual system cannot know in which direction the stimulus color should be transformed. To use a graphic example from the chromatic domain, imagine a greenish object that under reddish illumination reflects neutral light. Theoretically this neutral stimulus color could be transformed in any direction of color space. The correct direction of transformation cannot be determined without knowing the color of the illumination. The same logic applies to the achromatic domain, where level of illumination becomes the issue.

By arguing with Helmholtz over whether the transformation of stimulus color into perceived color is more or less intellectual, Katz was quibbling over nuances while avoiding the pressing concrete issue of how the level of illumination is determined.

Bühler and the Concept of Air-Light

Although the idea that illumination level is taken into account has long had an intuitive appeal, it has proven very difficult to explain how that could be done. Taking distance into account, in the domain of space perception, is more plausible because there are distance cues that lie outside the retinal image, but this cannot be said of illumination cues. The almost desperate need to find a stimulus basis for perceived illumination can be seen in Bühler's (1922) air-light (*luftlicht*) hypothesis. Bühler proposed that tiny particles of dust in the air reflect light and furnish us with a sense of the illumination level. Bühler suggested a dramatic test of the air-light concept. As MacLeod (1932, p. 49) describes it, "Bühler had proposed as crucial an hypothetical experiment with two hollow spheres. The inner surface of one sphere was to be painted black and that of the other white, and the illumination so controlled that the amount of light reflected by each would be equal. The respective surfaces were also to be so smooth that no traces of microstructure were to be discernible. Bühler contended that because of the visibility of the air a hypothetical observer with access to both spheres would be able to distinguish the black surface in strong illumination from the white surface in weak illumination."

Empirical work has not supported Bühler's claim. Katz (1935, p. 268) found no evidence that air layers as thick as 45 meters could produce an above-threshold impression of illumination. And Bocksch (1927) actually carried out Bühler's spheres experiment, with negative results.

Katz and the Total Insistence of the Visual Field

What did Katz himself say about how illumination level is determined? He flirted with the idea that illumination level is determined

by the visibility of microstructure but found the idea to be undermined by a lack of monotonicity between visibility of microstructure
and illumination level. Visibility of microstructure increases with increasing illumination only until an optimal illumination level is
reached. At that point, Katz claimed, further increases in illumination
strength actually reduce visibility of microstructure.[6]

Katz (1935) promised to reveal his proposed solution to the illumination problem by the end of his book. There he attributed perceived illumination level to what he called the "total insistence of the
visual field." "If, other conditions being equal, a high total insistence
is present, we have the impression of strong illumination; it is low,
the illumination we see is weak" (1935, p. 279). Katz's use of the term
insistence is equivalent to the modern usage of the term *brightness* (as
perceived luminance). Thus, total insistence is equivalent to the modern expression *average brightness*, and roughly equivalent to the expression *average luminance*.

So despite his critiques of Helmholtz, Katz returns to the tired idea
of mean luminance.[7] The more compelling question for theory concerns the domain over which the average is taken, and here Katz's
contribution was very limited.

Spatial versus Temporal Change of Illumination

In general, theories of lightness constancy have been driven by the
case in which the overall illumination level changes from one moment
of time to another. But illumination varies over space as well as time.
Real-world scenes are rarely uniformly illuminated; most scenes contain adjacent fields of differing illumination level. Mean luminance
works fairly well for changes in time of the overall level of illumination. But spatial variations in illumination present a much greater challenge to theory, as we will see.

Katz's basic light/shadow method is based on spatial differences
in illumination, not temporal. And even though Katz himself was unable to extend his theory to accommodate this challenge, we are indebted to him for bringing the problem of spatial changes in illumination to center stage.

Subordinate Totalities: Fields of Illumination

Acknowledging the challenge such spatial fields posed for his total
insistence concept, Katz (1935) wrote, "It is easy to determine total
insistence when the whole visual field is artificially illuminated in a
uniform way, but more difficult when the illumination is irregular"
(p. 280). At this point, however, Katz's tone becomes tentative. He
offers only a suggested direction before dropping the matter, noting
that "within the totality of the visual field there are subordinate totalities which follow their own laws" (p. 286). It appears Katz is sug-

gesting that the illumination level within a subordinate totality might be determined by the average luminance within that subordinate totality. This idea, though plausible, is not a mere extension of the idea of total insistence of the visual field. While simple processes could in principle compute average luminance throughout the visual field, average luminance can be computed for subordinate totalities only after they are perceptually segmented. The segmentation of the visual field into illumination frameworks presents a major theoretical challenge, one that has been confronted directly only by the Gestaltists.

When Katz spoke of illumination frameworks, or fields as he called them, he spoke mainly as a phenomenologist and experimentalist, not as a theorist. He had said almost nothing about the organizational factors that underlie the experience of frameworks, as if they were available to the visual system already segmented. His laws of field size came from his light/shadow experiments, but these laws had never been integrated into his larger theory of constancy. For Gestaltist theory, however, the idea that perceived qualities are determined relative to frames of reference was central.

It is ironic that Katz came face to face with the problem of perceptual organization because this is the only topic on which he had taken a stand against Gelb, having declared, "The most important place in which I have disagreed with Gelb is . . . where the significance of the articulation of the visual field for colour-constancy is discussed. There I drew attention to the fact that the articulation of the visual field cannot in itself provide a basis for the apprehension of the quality and intensity of the illumination in the visual field" (Katz, 1935, p. 278). It appears that Gelb and Katz were using the term *articulation* in different ways. Katz took the concept to refer to something like the number of elements in a framework,[8] whereas Gelb was undoubtedly using the term in a broader way, referring to the organization of the whole visual field into frameworks.[9]

The Gelb Effect

Gelb offered his now-classic illusion as an example of articulation in this broader sense. He described the illusion in this way (Gelb, 1929, quoted from Ellis, 1938, p. 207): "In a semi-darkened room a homogeneous black disk revolves upon a colour wheel. The beam of a strong projection lantern is focused upon the disk so that the entire disk and nothing else receives the light from this lamp. When set in motion the disk is seen as a white or very light-grey object appearing in a faintly illuminated room. This impression of white is absolutely compulsory. It does not matter how one thinks about the illumination; it is impossible to see 'an intensely illuminated black' instead of 'white' . . . *Now* we bring a small bit of really white paper into the light a few centimetres in front of the disk. *Instantly* the disk is 'black'."

Illumination Frames of Reference

Koffka on the Gelb Effect

Koffka used the Gelb effect to illustrate the operation of gradients and frames of reference. First, he observed that when the disk is presented alone in the spotlight, its luminance relative to the dark surround is roughly equal to that between white and black. Because the disk stands at the top of this ratio, it appears white. When the true white paper is introduced into the spotlight next to the disk, an additional luminance ratio is formed between the disk and the white paper, but the disk stands at the bottom of this ratio. How should its lightness now be computed? Should the disk appear (1) black, (relative to the white paper), (2) white (relative to the dark surround) or (3) middle gray because its luminance stands halfway between the high luminance of the white paper and the low luminance of the dark environment? Koffka ruled out choice (3), noting that the overall luminance range in the display is much greater than what is possible with reflectance variation alone. This range must be segmented into sub-ranges, each of which does not exceed the range of typical reflectances.[10] But once the two sub-ranges are segmented, a problem arises: should the lightness of the disk be derived in relation to the upper sub-range or the lower sub-range?

Appurtenance (Belongingness)

Here Koffka (1935) supplied a uniquely Gestalt answer: appurtenance, or belongingness: "a field part x is determined in its appearance by its 'appurtenance' to other field parts. The more x belongs to the field part y, the more will its *whiteness* be determined by the gradient xy, and the less it belongs to the part z, the less will its whiteness depend on the gradient xz" (p. 246).

Coplanarity

What, then, determines the degree of appurtenance between the target disk and its two potential partners? Koffka (1935) emphasized the factor of coplanarity: "Which field parts belong together, and how strong the degree of this belonging together is, depends upon factors of space organization. Clearly, two parts at the same apparent distance will, *ceteris paribus*, belong more closely together than field parts organized in different planes" (p. 246).[11] In short, the disk is grouped more strongly with the coplanar white paper than with the non-coplanar dark background.

Belongingness: Graded or All-or-None?

In these passages, Koffka presents appurtenance not as an all-or-none factor, but as a graded variable that can become stronger or weaker.

This can also be seen in a subsequent passage in which Koffka summarizes his theory in two propositions (1935, p. 248): "(a) the qualities of perceived objects depend upon *gradients* of stimulation, (b) not all gradients are equally effective as regards the appearance of a particular field part; rather will the effectiveness of a gradient vary with the degree of appurtenance obtaining between the two terms of this gradient."

Together with the role of coplanarity, this leads to two conclusions about the appearance of the disk. First, it should appear neither completely white nor completely black because both luminance ratios should influence its lightness. Second, disk lightness should be closer to black than to white due to coplanarity. The disk should appear dark gray.

But Koffka is not entirely consistent. Like Gelb himself, Koffka describes the disk as turning completely black[12] when the white paper is placed beside it, as if the disk belongs exclusively with the white paper. This implies that appurtenance is all-or-none. Perhaps Koffka is merely exaggerating. But this all-or-none construction appears in other comments as well. He says (Koffka,1935, p. 260) that the disk shares its lightness with the dark background but its illumination with the white paper. This implies an exclusivity: that the border between the disk and the white paper is perceived as a reflectance border, while that between the disk and the dark background is seen as an illuminance border. Koffka does make a strong statement about the importance of edge classification, posing the question: "given two adjoining retinal areas of different stimulation, under what conditions will the corresponding parts of the behavioral (perceptual) field appear of different whiteness but equal brightness (or 'illumination'), when of different brightness but equal whiteness? A complete answer to this question would probably supply the key to the complete theory of color perception in the broadest sense" (Koffka, 1935, p. 248).

This passage seems to present appurtenance as all-or-none. A luminance ratio in the image is seen as either a reflectance edge or an illuminance edge. The issue here is what Koffka means when he says, "not all gradients are equally effective." At times he seems to mean that those gradients that are not effective for lightness are effective for perceived illumination (all-or-none). But he also seems to suggest that those gradients that are mainly effective for illumination also play a limited (graded) role in lightness.

The empirical data, by the way, support the graded construction. Experiments on the Gelb effect (Cataliotti & Gilchrist, 1995; Gogel & Mershon; McCann & Savoy, 1991, 1969; Stewart, 1959) have consistently shown that the disk appears gray (even light gray), not black, when the white is added.[13] This implies a graded role of appurtenance, with both frameworks influencing the lightness of the disk. And the disk appears lighter as the spatial proximity of the white paper is

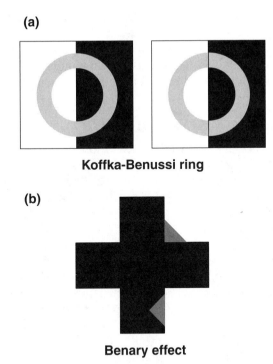

(a)

Koffka-Benussi ring

(b)

Benary effect

Figure 4.2. (a) The Koffka-Benussi ring. The ring appears a homogeneous gray until divided by a thin line. (b) The Benary effect. Although the two identical gray triangles have identical local surrounds, the lower one, which appears to belong to the black cross, appears lighter.

reduced, either laterally (McCann & Savoy, 1991; Stewart, 1959) or in depth (Gogel & Mershon, 1969), consistent with a graded effect of appurtenance. Wishart, Frisby, and Buckley (1997) have reported a graded effect of coplanarity.

The influence of belongingness on lightness had been demonstrated many years earlier by the Gestaltists for several illusions on paper. Both Koffka (1915) and Benussi (1916) had shown that a gray ring laid on two backgrounds, as shown in Figure 4.2a, appears homogenous until a thin vertical line, coinciding with the boundary between the backgrounds, is placed on it. Now a contrast effect shows up in the two halves of the ring. The line segregates the figure into two perceptual groups. A clearer example, shown in Figure 4.2b, was found by Wertheimer, although it bears the name of his student, Benary (1924). The two triangles appear slightly different in lightness, even though they have identical local surrounds. Each borders white on its hypotenuse and black on the other two sides. But one triangle appears to belong to the black cross, while the other appears to belong to the white background. Further variations were reported by Mikesell and Bentley (1930).

The relative weakness of these illusions, by the way, is consistent with a graded effect of belongingness. If belongingness were complete, these illusions would be far stronger.

KARDOS

Despite the importance of Koffka's work on lightness, it was Lajos Kardos who took the Gestalt theory of lightness the farthest. The extraordinary work of this Hungarian Gestaltist has remained unknown since World War II among non-readers of German, in part because his remarkable 1934 monograph *Ding und Schatten* ("Object and Shadow") was not available in English until recently. Kardos, a student of Bühler in Vienna, worked also in London and New York with such people as Koffka, Brunswik, MacLeod, Woodworth, and Heider. He carried out an impressive, highly programmatic set of experiments, including many parametric studies and several crucial experiments.

Kardos took up the problem of lightness right where Katz had left off, with the central challenge posed by multiple fields of illumination within a single image. His theoretical approach was strikingly similar to that of Koffka. Both men emphasized frames of reference, belongingness, and coplanarity. But while Koffka equivocated on whether or not frameworks exert an exclusive control over their members, Kardos established, both logically and empirically, that belongingness and coplanarity apply in a graded, not an all-or-none, manner. Only in limiting cases does a target belong exclusively to a single framework.

The Principle of Co-Determination

Kardos proposed that the lightness of a surface is co-determined by both its relevant field of illumination and the foreign field of illumination, although the main influence is that of the relevant field. The relevant field is the field to which a target surface belongs; the foreign field is the adjacent field of illumination. Perhaps his most important insight was that failures of constancy are the expression of the influence of the foreign field. He studied the competing influences of these fields where they are most equal in strength: in perceptually segmented but weak frameworks.

Kardos produced the most extensive analysis of the grouping factors that segment one framework from another. The most important of these factors is depth. Long before the modern work, Kardos used depth to create dramatic lightness changes while holding the retinal image constant. Had his work not been ignored, we might have been spared decades of confusion on this crucial topic. I myself was un-

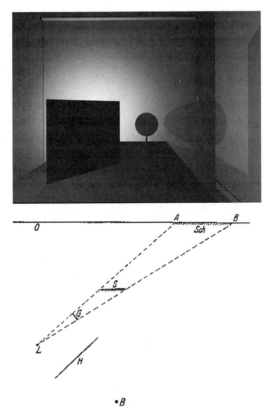

Figure 4.3. Simulation of the Kardos illusion (top) and plan view of the hidden shadow arrangement (bottom). The white target disk (S) appears black to the observer (B) who is shielded from the light source (L) and the shadow caster (G) by a screen (H).

aware of Kardos's work when I demonstrated the same point 45 years later (Gilchrist, 1977, 1980).

The Kardos Experiments

To the extent that Kardos is known at all, he is known for the Kardos illusion, the inverse of the Gelb effect. Just as Gelb showed that a black paper in a hidden spotlight appears white, Kardos showed that a white paper in a hidden shadow appears black. Kardos began his work at the Vienna Psychological Institute using the arrangement diagrammed in Figure 4.3 (reprinted from Kardos, 1934). A light source, a shadow caster, and a white target disk are positioned in space so that the whole space is illuminated except for the disk, which is entirely covered by the cast shadow. The shadow need not be hidden in the usual sense. Although Kardos hid both the light source and the shadow caster behind a screen, they can be in full view without destroying the illusion. But the shadow must be hidden in the sense that (1) only a single surface appears within the shadow, and (2) the boundaries of the shadow must coincide with the occlusion edge bounding the target surface, from the observer's perspective (even though the shadow is larger than the target surface).[14] Kardos refers to this method as *inumbral shadowing*. The term appears to mean that although the disk is physically shadowed, it does not appear to be shadowed.

There are various ways the disk can be made to appear more like its true white color. Kardos first shows that this can be achieved by enlarging the shadow so that the wall forming the retinal background, from the observer's perspective, is also shadowed. The disk now appears lighter and in shadow. Kardos reports that the larger the background shadow, the lighter the disk appears, consistent with Katz's laws of field size and results obtained by Katona (1929), Marzinsky (1921), and MacLeod (1932).

Field Size, Articulation, and Co-Determination

Katz found that constancy increases within a field of special illumination when its size increases and when the degree of articulation within it increases, but he didn't have a theory of this. The Kardos principle of co-determination makes sense out of these rules. When lightness is viewed as the product of a competition between values computed within competing frameworks, it makes sense that the field in which the target lies should get more weight in this competition as it is made larger and more articulated. This implies a modification of the Katz rules. The work by Kardos suggests that the enhanced constancy resulting from larger field size and greater articulation is really a byproduct of the increased weight given to the relevant field. Indeed, under certain conditions, increasing the weight of the relevant field actually produces less constancy, as we will see in Chapter 11.

If enlarging the shadow strengthens target-shadow belongingness, increasing the depth separation between the target and the shadowed background decreases it. Continuing his experiments at Columbia University, Kardos presented the disk at four depth separations from the shadow in its retinal background while holding disk luminance and visual angle approximately constant. Under these conditions, disk lightness varies directly with its location in depth. The closer it is to the wall, the lighter it appears; the farther it is from the wall, the darker it appears. Here we see clear experimental evidence that the belongingness of the disk varies continuously between the two fields of illumination. We also see that lightness depends on depth even when changes in the retinal image are excluded.

Further Evidence against Normal Illumination

When Katz said that enlarging a field of special illumination produces greater constancy, he was also saying that it shifts the lightness of a target toward its "normal" color—that is, toward the color it would have in normal illumination. Thus, if the illumination in the field containing the target is lower than normal, enlarging the field must lighten the target. Kardos disproved this claim by presenting the target within a dim spotlight surrounded by even dimmer prevailing illumination. The illumination level within the spotlight was far lower than normal illumination. Yet when the spotlight was enlarged, the target became darker, not lighter. This result constitutes another sharp blow to the concept of normal illumination. The actual shift in lightness produced by enlarging the spotlight is not toward the lightness the target would have in normal illumination, but rather away from the lightness it would have in the field surrounding the spotlight (the foreign field).

Most of Kardos's experiments included one condition in which the shadow is concealed and another condition in which it is revealed. Several methods were used to conceal the shadow. In his basic illusion, Kardos hides the shadow using his technique of inumbral shadowing in which the borders of the shadow coincide with the occlusion edge at the border of the target. In further experiments the shadow is hidden using Hering's spot-shadow technique in which a heavy black border coincides with the penumbra of the shadow. The shadow is revealed by breaking the coincidence between the penumbra and the black border. When the shadow is revealed in this way, the target appears much lighter, even under conditions that, according to contrast, should produce the opposite result. Kardos also found that as the target becomes larger, less whitening occurs when the shadow is revealed. This result is consistent with the general rules concerning area and lightness that are described in Chapter 9.

Lightness Depends on Depth

Several of Kardos's experiments demonstrate the role of depth perception in lightness. Perhaps the clearest of these is the experiment similar to what is shown in Figure 4.4. A brightly illuminated hole-board was mounted at some distance in front of a shaded background wall. A shaded target disk could be placed either on the background wall or in the plane of the hole-board. The target disk was constant in luminance, visual angle, and retinal position (centered within the hole). Kardos does not give quantitative data for this experiment but

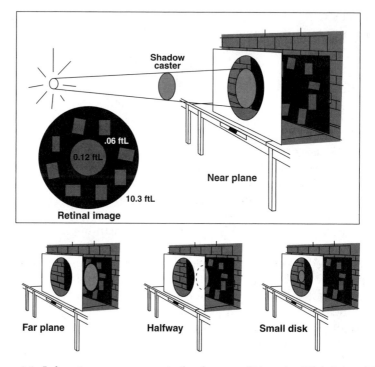

Figure 4.4. Laboratory arrangements for four conditions in Gilchrist and To-dorović's replication of Kardos' experiment on depth and lightness.

reports that the disk appeared substantially lighter in the far plane than in the near plane. Dejan Todorović and I have replicated this experiment (see Chapter 6) using the arrangements shown in Figure 4.4, reporting a difference due to depth alone of 4.4 Munsell steps. In the words of Kardos (1934, p. 48), "The remarkable aspect of this experiment is that *in the whole situation nothing changed except the depth position of a visual object*. The composition and the distribution of light stayed the same; the change only concerned the depth perception. And yet, there was not only a significant phenomenal change of brightness of that depth object, but also a remarkable re-organization of the field. This experiment is paradigmatic for the deep and lawful manner of the dependence of color vision on actual depth relations."

Importance of Kardos

Kardos must be ranked as one of the most important names in lightness history, despite his more recent obscurity. His most valuable contribution was and is the concept of co-determination of lightness by relevant and foreign fields of illumination. The lightness of a given object represents a compromise between its value relative to the relevant field and its value relative to the foreign field. This is an idea toward which many students of lightness had been groping.

Lightness was long suspected to be the product of some kind of compromise. Failures of constancy seem to beg for such a construction. But until Kardos, the components of the compromise had not been successfully identified. Hering had proposed a compromise (or balance if you like) between excitation and inhibition. But the pattern of lightness failures found in empirical work (Jacobsen & Gilchrist, 1988a, 1988b) does not fit the pattern of failures predicted by the opponent process model[15] (see Chapter 5). Woodworth (1938, p. 605) expressed this compromise intuition by noting that perceived values *"usually lie between two extremes, one conforming to the stimulus and the other conforming to the object."* Indeed, Brunswik and Thouless ratios measure just the location of the percept between these poles, and failures of constancy are associated with the pull toward the stimulus pole. But the fact that Brunswik ratios exceed 100% under certain conditions shows that the percept sometimes lies outside these two poles, not between them.[16] Katz evoked a compromise between normal and non-normal illumination, with failures of constancy caused by non-normal illumination. But Kardos showed that for an object placed within a spotlight of below-normal illumination (see page 69), the constancy failure does not go in the direction of the non-normal illumination; it goes in the opposite direction.

According to Kardos, the lightness of an object always lies between its value as determined by the relevant field and its value as determined by the foreign field, with failures of constancy due to the foreign field. He states (Kardos, 1934, p. 29), "The effect of the foreign field is in opposite direction to color constancy. The color of a surface is affected by an illumination that does not illuminate the surface itself. Ideally, the effect of foreign illumination should not exist, but it does. In contrast to relevant factors, this is an irrelevant, 'illegitimate' disturbance factor, which depends highly on temporary conditions and constellations, and induces higher variability of results." I am not aware of any empirical data that contradict these claims.

Kardos shows unequivocally that belongingness is a graded variable. Except in limiting cases, no surface belongs exclusively to a single framework of illumination. This principle could have been deduced on logical grounds alone. Frameworks emerge and recede as we move about the environment, and these periods of transition present the visual system with a serious challenge. Kardos (1934, p. 30) tells how his mentor described such a transition: "Bühler (1922) noted that a well-lit terrace or window looks luminous when observed at night from a 'sufficient distance'. If one comes nearer, the impression of luminosity gradually disappears and a well-lit region (field of special illumination) is segregated: the terrace or the interior of a room with objects and a specific differentiation of colors and depths. During the approach clearly the differentiation develops and the relevant portion of the retina is enlarged."

This vignette shows how the co-determination shifts from foreign to relevant as one approaches the terrace. From a distance, the relevant field is small and unarticulated, hence weak. It appears luminous relative to the dark foreign field. Luminosity is thus the embryonic form of an emerging framework of higher illumination. As one draws nearer, the relevant framework becomes stronger and the luminosity gradually dissipates. But the transition is gradual. There is no logical basis for a sudden shift to local determination.

To be strong, frameworks must be both segregated and articulated. The Kardos illusion lies at one extreme. A white paper in hidden shadow is segregated, but without articulation it cannot form its own framework. When a few more surfaces are added, a weak framework begins to emerge. Kardos focused on such cases because they reveal most clearly the tension between relevant and foreign fields in the determination of target lightness. This tension shows up not merely in the compromised lightness value, but also in the higher variability among matches made by different observers.

Segmenting Fields of Illumination

Kardos gave more attention than anyone else to the question of the factors in the proximal stimulus on which the segregation of visual frameworks is based. In summary, he cited two kinds of factors (Kardos, 1934, p. 57): "Portions of the visual field constitute a field of phenomenally uniform illumination 1. *when they lie within certain contours*, and 2. *when they keep a certain system of relations among themselves.*"

As for contours, Kardos noted two types that segregate frameworks: (1) blurred contours (penumbrae) and (2) depth boundaries (occlusion contours). Penumbrae have long been associated with illuminance boundaries; both spotlights and shadows are typically bounded by them. Occlusion boundaries, except by chance, always divide surfaces that stand in different illumination levels.

As for systems of relations among elements of the retinal image, Kardos also speaks of two kinds: (1) depth relations and (2) luminance relations. Depth relations are highly important for Kardos, as for Koffka. Coplanar regions group together. This principle is not merely a restatement of the principle that occlusion boundaries segregate, as Kardos shows with several interesting examples.

Principle of the Next Deeper Depth Plane

First, a single homogeneous surface that stands alone in its own depth plane constitutes a unique case. Both the Kardos illusion and the Gelb effect are examples. Even though the surface is bounded by an occlusion edge that segregates it, the surface lacks differentiation and thus cannot form its own framework. In this case Kardos invokes the principle of the next deeper depth plane. The isolated surface groups with the depth plane behind it.

Second, in certain situations, two or more surfaces lie in the same depth plane without touching each other. Even though these surfaces are separated from each other by gaps, and each is bounded by its own occlusion contour, they can group together based on coplanarity. Under these conditions, the strength by which they belong to each other depends upon lateral proximity (size of the gap), and the strength by which each belongs to the next deeper depth plane depends on its depth proximity to that plane.

As for luminance relations, Kardos admits that more work is required. But he notes that a given region can appear self-luminous when its luminance lies far above the range of other regions within the same group, even when that region is not segregated by either a penumbra or an occlusion edge. Real achromatic surfaces lie within a certain canonical range, as Koffka also observed (1935, p. 245).

Critique of Kardos

It is not so easy to criticize the work of Kardos. His empirical findings have not been undermined by subsequent work, nor does he contradict himself in any obvious ways. But we can show the limits of his thinking. Kardos showed how illumination-dependent failures of constancy result from co-determination of lightness by multiple frameworks. But he failed to recognize that contrast and other illusions (background-dependent failures) are also products of co-determination. Had Kardos made a crucial modification in his definition of framework, the reach of his theory could have been extended to include that second great class of errors, those that depend not on illumination differences, but on the pattern of neighboring luminances. This shift requires that the frameworks be identified more closely with grouping factors present in the proximal stimulus and less closely with regions of illumination in the distal array. For example, the black and white backgrounds of the simultaneous contrast display do not really appear differently illuminated. But the display does contain grouping factors that segregate, albeit weakly, the two halves of the display. The illusion can be explained by assuming that target square lightness is co-determined by frameworks (or perceptual groups) of different scale. Errors falling within this category are thus associated with too much determination by the "relevant field" rather than too little. This approach is elaborated in Chapter 11.

Ironically, Kardos already had many of the components of this shift. First, he recognized that phenomenal fields do not coincide with actual fields. Frameworks in the phenomenal realm must be explained in terms of proximal factors, not distal: "The objective partition of the whole field into such regions cannot be the immediate cause of the parallel phenomenal organization" (1934, p. 56). Indeed, it is a mismatch between physical fields of illumination and those frameworks that represent such fields in visual processing that provides the basis for Kardos's explanation of constancy failures. Target lightness is partially determined by regions not in the same illumination as the target, representing "an imperfection of the organization into specially illuminated fields" (1934, p. 30). Here the functional framework is larger than its physical counterpart, including too much. Yet something parallel happens in simultaneous contrast. Regions that do not differ in objective illumination (the black and white backgrounds) are nonetheless treated, in part, as though they do. In this case the functional framework is smaller than the physical framework of illumination. Kardos saw the former mismatch, but not the latter.

Kardos did attribute contrast effects to faulty performance: "in all typical contrast situations there exists some unfavorable aspect in the stimulus configuration, so that the above system must go wrong in its performance, which has to lead to 'illusions' concerning object colors." But strangely he did not link this faulty performance in contrast with the faulty performance in constancy. In his discussion of faulty performance in simultaneous contrast (1934, p. 29), he makes the astonishing claim that lightness constancy under a changing level of illumination "certainly does not involve such a faulty performance." Yet much of his book documents precisely the faulty performance in constancy—that is, the "imperfection of the organization into specially illuminated fields." Both contrast illusions and constancy failures can be understood in terms of a mismatch between functional and actual fields of illumination, as we will see in Chapter 11.

Kardos devotes the last chapter of his book to the relationship between constancy and contrast. He states clearly that "Our view has nothing in common with the idea that contrast and color constancy are parallel phenomena." But he fails to see that contrast and *failures* of constancy form the real parallel.

SUMMARY

Important theoretical developments came only once the Gestalt theorists engaged the problem of lightness. During this brief 5-year window, roughly from 1930 to 1935, under the gathering storm clouds of Nazism, the Gestaltists conducted crucial experiments that demolished the theories of Hering and Katz and rendered Helmholtz's cognitive operations unnecessary.

Gelb's paradoxical experiment destroyed Katz's theory of lightness constancy in a single blow, and his countershaded backgrounds experiment demonstrated lightness constancy in the absence of every one of Hering's factors, both physiological and psychological. Koffka proposed an invariant relationship between lightness and perceived illumination and emphasized the role of illumination frames of reference. But the Gestaltist whose lightness work was most advanced was Kardos, despite his current obscurity. Kardos engaged the crucial question of how illumination frameworks are perceptually segmented, identifying two main factors: depth boundaries and penumbrae. In the process he proved that lightness depends crucially on depth perception. Still, his most important contribution was his doctrine of co-determination. Lightness, he showed, is not computed exclusively within the relevant framework. Influences from foreign frameworks also have an impact, and these influences explain the failures of constancy.

The Gestalt theorists demonstrated the crucial role of perceptual organization. Dismissing the Hering/Helmholtz dispute as quibbling, they offered a truly radical departure that broke the grip of the mind/body dilemma. They rejected both the presumption of raw sensations and the importance of high-level cognitive processes. According to the Gestalt theorists, lightness is the product of a single, truly perceptual mechanism, the output of which is experienced as vision. We can only speculate on how lightness work might have developed had this exciting period of time not been cut short by the tragic events surrounding World War II. When the dust settled, lightness research in Germany was essentially destroyed.

5

The Contrast Period

Chronologically the fourth, or contrast, period extended from World War II until the end of the 1960s. Ideologically, however, it began at the end of the 19th century, exhibiting an almost total amnesia for the intervening work of Katz and the Gestaltists. The contrast theorists took up the debate right where it had been left off in 1900, amidst the Hering/Helmholtz controversy—and they sided overwhelmingly with Hering. Two theories came to dominate this period, those of Jameson and Hurvich and of Cornsweet, both derived from Hering. Other important theories of the time, such as Helson's adaptation-level theory and Wallach's ratio theory, were assimilated to Hering's theory of contrast.

This period was driven by a physiological, not a psychological, approach and fueled by the discovery of lateral inhibition. The focus on the physiological response generated by light stimuli had a regressive effect, turning the emphasis away from the objective reference in lightness perception back to the subjective reference. Issues of constancy and veridicality receded to the background.

To understand how this happened, we must look beyond lightness perception to the changes taking place in the field of psychology itself. These changes in turn can be understood only in the context of events in the larger world.

Psychology had emerged as an academic discipline in Germany in the latter half of the 19th century. The first school, known as structuralism, was founded by Wilhelm Wundt with the goal of identifying the elements of the mind through introspection. Wundt had proposed three kinds of elements: ideas, feelings, and sensations, the latter forming the raw materials of perception. This agenda failed to produce consensus.

Two schools of thought sprung up in challenge to structuralism: Gestalt theory in Germany and behaviorism in America. Each held out great hopes for making psychology more materialistic and more scientific. But the two routes chosen to reach these goals were very different.

The Gestalt psychologists sought to do away with the sensation/perception split. They proposed a single process whereby patterns of light projected onto the retina set in motion field forces that culminate in organized patterns of brain activity that are isomorphic to visual experience of the world. Because of its emphasis on phenomenology, Gestalt theory was viewed by the Americans as warmed-over introspectionism. But in fact the Gestaltists took a thoroughly materialistic perspective: their goal was to account for visual experience using the same principles that apply to physics. Köhler, after all, was a student of Max Planck, and he took pains to demonstrate that the same kind of organizing forces he proposed for the brain can be seen in the action of gravity, magnetism, and soap bubbles (Köhler, 1920, excerpted in Ellis, 1938, p. 17).

The behaviorists, by contrast, sought to resolve the mind/body problem merely by denying the mind. They believed that psychology would become a science only when it stopped talking about mental events. The proposal was a bold one: if human behavior can be reduced to stimuli and responses, both of which are concrete and publicly observable, talk of mental events can be simply eliminated.

As to what the outcome of the behaviorist–Gestalt debate would have been had outside forces not intervened, we can only speculate. In actual fact, the near-term fate of the two schools was decided by the events associated with World War II. The three founders of Gestalt theory, two of whom were Jewish, fled to the United States. Gelb was forced by the Nazis to retire in 1933 and died 2 years later. Katz fled to Sweden.

After the war, the center of science shifted from Germany to the United States. The fabric of science in Europe, especially in Germany, was devastated by the war and the Holocaust, but in the United States the prospects for science were better than ever. There had been no fighting on American soil, and indeed the massive spending on the war had pulled the United States out of economic depression. Education and research enjoyed expanding resources. Thus, American science easily came to dominate world science.

This made it more likely that the history would be ignored, as well as contemporary work done elsewhere (Gilchrist, 1996). The tradition of lightness work that had been extinguished by the war was carried on in Japan, Italy, and the Scandinavian countries in the work of Kozaki, Musatti, Kanizsa, Metelli, von Fieandt, and others. But this work was mostly ignored in the field that would now be called "brightness perception."

Inevitably the lightness theories of this period would be dominated by American psychology, which at that time meant behaviorism. Indeed, it was not inevitable that there would be any theories of perception at all. Perception after all is private and need not be accompanied by behavior. However plausibly learning might be reduced to behavioral terms, in perception this approach was fatal. One simply cannot escape phenomenology in the study of visual perception. Visual experience is what has to be explained, and if one does not get that right, one will be trying to explain the wrong thing. Advances in perception were scarce during the behaviorist period.

Most of the history was written off as hopelessly metaphysical. Helmholtz's cognitive theory of lightness represented just the kind of ideas the behaviorists tried so hard to banish. Phenomenology was rejected as warmed-over introspectionism, Gestalt theory as another fuzzy, metaphysical cognitive approach.

BACK TO SUBJECTIVE REFERENCE

In the end, the behaviorists embraced the very subjectivity they were trying to escape. This happened in both avenues that were taken in search of materialism: psychophysics and physiology.

Modern psychophysics barely allows the study of perception without reference to visual experience. Threshold settings and perceptual matches are, after all, behaviors. Behaviorists looked for a simple stimulus–response account of lightness. Some, like S.S. Stevens (1961), reached all the way back to Fechner and Weber. True, he wanted to replace Fechner's logarithmic law with a power law. But fundamental to the thinking of both Stevens and Fechner was the idea of a simple relationship between stimulation and visual sensation. Helmholtz, Hering, and Mach had stressed how poorly visual experience correlates with luminance at the retina. By studying primarily those reduced stimulus conditions under which experience does correlates with luminance, Stevens returned the study of lightness to a preoccupation not with the objective aspect of lightness, but with its subjective side.

Other behaviorists, of course, found in Hering's theory a necessary, if minimal acknowledgement of the role of context. Light stimulation evokes not only excitation but also inhibition. A response that included inhibition was still simple enough to satisfy the behaviorist ideology, yet it was just complex enough to obscure its own inadequacy.[1]

Fechner had stressed the correlation between visual experience and retinal luminance. Helmholtz and Hering had stressed the correlation between visual experience and object reflectance, as did the Gestalt theorists. But for the contrast theorists, visual experience dropped out of the equation. They stressed the correlation between physiological response and light intensity. Thus, the sensation went underground, so to speak, taking the form not of a phenomenon, but of a rate of firing of neural cells. The sensation was replaced by the sensory mechanism.

TERMINOLOGY IN THE CONTRAST PERIOD

The distinction between lightness (as perceived reflectance) and brightness (as perceived luminance) was suppressed during the contrast period. A single term, *brightness*, was typically used to cover both meanings, and the usage was not consistent. Often the term was used for the subjective experience of luminance, but often it was used for the whiteness or blackness of surfaces. This latter usage is revealed by accompanying terms, such as "brightness constancy" and "black." Constancy is a property of lightness, not of brightness; thus, the term "brightness constancy" makes sense only if the term brightness refers to lightness. The term *black* also refers to lightness, because black is a property of a surface, not a property of light.

The term *contrast* itself has been used in a variety of ways (see Chapter 1). I use the term *contrast theories* to refer to theories, such as those of Cornsweet (1970) and Jameson and Hurvich (1964), that rely primarily on the mechanism of lateral inhibition to explain the basic phenomena of lightness. I have tried to consistently use modifiers that indicate whether the term refers to a period of time (contrast period), a mechanism, an illusion (simultaneous contrast), a theory (contrast theory), or merely the physical luminance ratio at a border.

GRADIENT THEORIES

Both Harry Helson and Hans Wallach published important work in the United States during or immediately after World War II (Helson, 1943; Wallach, 1948), but although these two important names open the third, or contrast, period, they do not fit neatly into it. Neither man was a contrast theorist, although there has been confusion on this point, especially in the case of Wallach.

Helson was careful to make reference to all the key figures of the Gestalt period, especially Katz, whose concept of weighted mean luminance was central to adaptation-level theory (though he did not acknowledge Katz's precedence on this concept). Wallach did his graduate work in Berlin with the Gestalt psychologists and fled from Germany to join his mentor, Köhler, at Swarthmore. But in America he sought to distance himself from Köhler's ideas. Wallach was a brilliant experimenter with little interest in theorizing.

Helson's Adaptation-Level Theory

Helson (1943, 1964) presented a theory of lightness perception that would later be expanded into a general theory of perception and, indeed, cognitive functioning. In its simplest form Helson's model states that the lightness of a target depends on the luminance ratio between the target and the average luminance (called the adaptation level [AL]) of the entire visual field. A target with a luminance equal to the AL is perceived as middle gray, luminances higher than the AL are perceived as light grays, and those lower than the AL as dark grays.

The scheme performs reasonably well under a temporal change in illumination, but it fails to account for lightness constancy in spatially separate fields of illumination. It also fails to account for simultaneous lightness contrast. To deal with these problems, Helson weighted the average for proximity to the target surface. For simultaneous contrast, this means that the equal luminances of the two gray squares are divided by slightly different ALs, given that the white and black backgrounds, due to their proximity, get extra weight in the computation of each square's AL. As for lightness constancy, the weighting also makes it more likely that target luminance will be divided by an average taken from the same region of illumination as the target.

Helson's AL concept had obvious appeal. It offered an operationalization of the troubled concept of taking the illumination into account that is not subject to Hering's paradox. It is a relational theory in that the correlate of lightness is a relationship, not an amount—the luminance of the target divided by the AL. Both constancy and simultaneous contrast are dealt with by this same quotient.

AL theory produces veridical lightness values only to the degree to which the collection of surfaces over which the average is taken, called the adaptive window by Adelson (2000, p. 346), is congruent with the physical field of illumination in which the target lies. As Adelson notes, if the adaptive window is too small, it will not contain enough statistics for computing target lightness, but if it is too large it will include surfaces standing in a different level of illumination than the target. Ideally the boundaries of the window should coincide with the boundaries of the field of illumination that includes the target, but the AL model has no capability for recognizing illumination boundaries. Weighting the AL for proximity to the target is a very blunt response to the challenge. In addition, there is a fundamental contradiction between the steepness of the weighting function required to account for simultaneous contrast and that required to account for lightness constancy between spatial fields of illumination. Any weighting gradient calibrated to account for simultaneous lightness contrast would be far too weak to account for lightness constancy of surfaces standing in differing adjacent fields of illumination. Conversely, adjusting the weighting for differing illuminations would predict simultaneous contrast effects far in excess of those actually obtained.

Empirical Work

Helson (1943) reported a study of lightness constancy carried out with Bornemeier, using Katz's light/shadow method. Varying the reflectance of target disks, the reflectance of the backgrounds, and the illumination ratio, they obtained much better constancy using backgrounds of higher reflectance, but poor constancy for disks of lower reflectance. As for illumination ratio, they found, as others had, greater relative constancy for higher illumination ratios. Included in this set of experiments is a countershaded backgrounds experiment in which Helson and Bornemeier claimed to find no constancy. This claim is consistent with Helson's core idea that only the average luminance in the target vicinity is crucial. But the claim is not consistent with their data, which show Thouless ratios ranging from 49% to 66% (depending on target reflectance). These values are commensurate with the 58% Thouless constancy found by Jaensch and Müller (1920).

Helson's work on achromatic surfaces in chromatic illumination (Helson, 1938; Judd, 1940) will not be reviewed, but his proposals on lightness assimilation are discussed later in this chapter.

Wallach's Ratio Theory

In 1948 Hans Wallach published a set of very elegant experiments. Inspired by the Gelb effect, Wallach used two slide projectors to create a display consisting of a disk surrounded by a thick annulus. He was able to independently vary the luminance of either disk or annulus region by interrupting either beam of light with an episcotister of variable opening. He demonstrated that if the luminance of the disk is held constant, it can be made to appear any shade of gray between white and black merely by adjusting the luminance of the annulus. As long as disk luminance is higher than annulus luminance, the disk appears white. As annulus luminance surpasses disk luminance, the lightness of the disk begins to drop, appearing black when the annulus/disk ratio reaches about 30:1.

Wallach conducted an elegant experiment using two such disk/annulus displays (Fig. 5.1). He separated the two displays by about 20° in a dimly lit room, set the luminance values on one disk/ring display to a given ratio, and set the annulus on the second display to a very different luminance level. The observer was then given control over the luminance of the disk in the second display and asked to adjust it until the two disks appeared equal in lightness.

Observers judged the two disks to be equal when the disk/annulus luminance ratio in one display was almost equal to that of the other display. Wallach drew the bold conclusion that lightness is determined

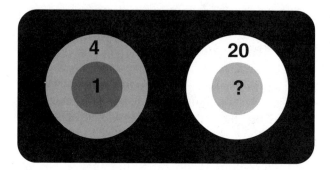

Figure 5.1. Schematic of Wallach's disk/annulus experiment (1948). Observers were asked to set the disks equal by adjusting the right side. The average setting was slightly less than 5. The disks appear equal in lightness when they have equal disk/annulus luminance ratios.

merely by the luminance ratio between a given surface and its surround, without reference to the level of illumination. He added that this explains both constancy and simultaneous contrast, noting that the luminance ratios of adjacent reflectances are just what remain constant when illumination changes, thus explaining constancy, and that the simultaneous contrast illusion is explained by the different target/background ratios of the two gray squares.

Wallach's ratio principle has been considered a pre-eminent example of Gibson's (1966) claim concerning higher-order variables. As for his own theoretical perspective, Wallach never strayed far from his data, but he did suggest (Wallach, 1976) that lightness results from some kind of "interaction" in the brain between the neural representation of the disk luminance and that of the annulus luminance. When conditions, such as a large stimulus area or the presence of penumbra, interfere with this interaction process, then a more primitive process occurs. It is based on absolute luminance rather than relative luminance, and it produces the appearance of luminosity. This luminosity process often yields an impression of illumination, but it is separate from the surface lightness process and plays no causal role in surface lightness.

CRITIQUE OF GRADIENT THEORIES

Helson and Wallach Not Contrast Theorists

During the 1950s and 1960s, the work of Helson and Wallach became widely assimilated into the emerging contrast perspective. Yet, contrary to some writers (Boring, 1942; Freeman, 1967; Kaufman, 1974), neither was a contrast theorist.

Helson took pains to stress the myopia of attributing lightness constancy to a particular mechanism, such as lateral inhibition. Indeed, herein lies what I consider to be a valuable, though neglected, aspect of Helson's thinking. Helson argued that mechanisms such as pupil size, adaptation, and lateral inhibition work together in a coordinated fashion to support the AL principle. He argued that it is the principle being served that is important, not the mechanisms serving that principle, and that those who focus merely on a particular mechanism will be misled. This is an important claim, whatever one thinks about the particular principle advanced by Helson.

Wallach confirmed to me in April 1975 that his was not a contrast theory, and in a subsequent paper (Whipple, Wallach, & Marshall, 1988) he argued that his findings could not be explained by lateral inhibition.

Helson and Wallach are best described as gradient theorists, not contrast theorists. Both sought the correlate of lightness in a gradient, or relationship, in the stimulus array. Contrast theories, as Koffka noted earlier, are based on absolute values.

Easily Assimilated to Contrast Theory

Helson and Wallach did make it easy to assimilate their work to contrast theory. Their work, as that of the whole contrast period, is responsive to the debate between Helmholtz and Hering, suggesting that lightness might be determined without any reference to the illumination level.

Both Helson and Wallach provided grist for the behaviorist expectation that lightness could be explained by relatively simple concepts with little recognition of perceptual structure. Like the contrast theorists, both proposed a simple formula to explain both simultaneous contrast and constancy, and each claimed to have identified the perspective that reveals the parallel between the two. In Helson's words (1964, p. 280), "the data point to a single visual mechanism which is responsible for constancy, contrast and adaptation." Wallach (1976, p. 30) remarks flatly, "there is no essential difference between brightness constancy and brightness contrast." Wallach's ratio findings, especially, were seized upon by the contrast theorists. The apparently easy reduction of those findings to lateral inhibition offered the tantalizing prospect that lightness might be the first important constancy explainable at the physiological level.

Helson and Wallach Not Gestalt Theorists

Still, the theories of Helson and Wallach are not Gestalt theories either. Neither Helson nor Wallach responded to the exciting developments that took place in lightness during the 1930s. Helson largely continued Katz's theory. Despite Wallach's close relationship to the Gestaltists, his work made no real contact with the earlier period in Germany; relative to that work, his ratio idea was simply a non sequitur. He acknowledged that his experiments were inspired by Gelb's illusion, but he never related his findings to Gelb's theory, or to either the findings or the theories of Koffka, Kardos, or Wolff. Unlikely as it might seem, Wallach may not have been very familiar with this other work in lightness. He was known to be economical in his reading of the literature,[2] and it must be remembered that lightness constitutes only a small part of Wallach's work in perception.

Both Helson and Wallach ignored the many countershaded backgrounds experiments reviewed in Chapter 3, each of which revealed substantial degrees of constancy that cannot be explained by AL theory or ratio theory because both targets have backgrounds of equal luminance.

Both Wolff (1933) and Kardos (1934) had shown that a change in the depth separation between a target and its background can substantially change the lightness of the target, even while target and background luminances are held constant. These results pose a serious challenge to the simple models proposed by Helson and Wallach, but neither man referred to them.

Neither Helson nor Wallach has explained why the magnitude of simultaneous contrast is so much less than that of constancy. When measured in the traditional way, as departures from luminance matching, constancy has been shown to be 3.7 times stronger than simultaneous contrast (Gilchrist, 1988), even with highly comparable retinal images.[3]

Wallach (1976, p. 31) has commented on the weakness of the simultaneous contrast illusion relative to the strong results he obtained in his disk/annulus studies. He suggests that in the side-by-side simultaneous contrast pattern, the gray square on the black background also comes to some extent under the influence of the white background, due to its proximity, and this weakens the local ratio effect. But he fails to realize that the same can be said of the Katz light/shadow display used to test lightness constancy. The target in the shadowed region comes under the influence of the brightly illuminated background in the adjacent region. Nevertheless, my empirical data (Gilchrist, 1988) show that departures from ratio predictions are 7.3 times greater[4] in the simultaneous contrast display than in the constancy display, even when this factor of proximity between the high luminance background and its contralateral target is held constant.

Structure-Blindness

Like the contrast theories that followed them, but unlike the Gestalt theories that preceded them, the theories of Helson and Wallach are structure-blind. For example, they are blind to depth relations, to distinctions among reflectance, illuminance, and occlusion edges, and to configurational factors such as T-junctions.

Limitations on the Ratio Principle

The controversial topic of limitations on the ratio principle is discussed later in this chapter.

CONTRAST THEORIES

I will define contrast theories as relatively simple, low-level models based on a simple conception of lateral inhibition.

The contrast period brought a resumption of the Helmholtz/Hering dispute, with the weight of opinion favoring Hering. Several factors allowed the champions of Hering to press for the complete overthrow of Helmholtzian ideas:

1. The behaviorist hegemony in America with its rejection of cognition
2. Wallach's findings suggesting an explanation of lightness constancy without reference to the perception of illumination
3. New physiological findings

Discovery of Lateral Inhibition

By the mid-20th century, technological advances made possible electrical recordings from a single nerve cell such as the large, accessible cells found in the optic tract of the horseshoe crab (Limulus). The Limulus eye is ideal because each nerve fiber receives input from a single facet. Hartline and Graham, recording from a single facet of the Limulus eye, had shown in 1932 that the rate of firing of its nerve fiber is proportional to the intensity of light stimulating that facet. In 1956, Hartline, Wagner, and Ratliff showed that if the light stimulating the facet is held constant, the rate of firing is inversely proportional to the intensity of light shining on adjacent facets, thus providing hard physiological evidence for Hering's theoretical concept of reciprocal interaction. Hartline, Wagner, and Ratliff also found the strength of inhibition to depend strongly on distance. They showed that the inhibiting effect that flows from an excited facet drops off sharply within lateral distances of four or five facets.

The parallel between these physiological discoveries and Wallach's ratio results was obvious. A constant light shines on one photoreceptor, but nevertheless its rate of firing varies inversely with light shining on it neighbors. The lightness of a disk of constant luminance varies inversely with the luminance of its surround.

Empirical Work: The Brightness Induction Literature

The discovery of lateral inhibition inspired a series of brightness induction experiments that were reported during the 1950s and 1960s.

Brightness Induction

The concept of brightness induction is analogous to that of induced motion. Just as a stationary spot appears to move in one direction when it is surrounded by a larger frame of reference moving in the opposite direction, so a disk of constant luminance appears to get darker when the region surrounding it is made brighter. The term "brightness induction" is closely related to the term "contrast" (and both are associated with lateral inhibition), but while contrast tends to imply a perceptual exaggeration of the difference between the disk and its surround, the term "induction" implies merely a transfer of effect from the brighter to the darker.

These experiments shared a common theoretical perspective and a common methodology. The stimuli consisted of luminous patches presented within a dark or dimly lit room. The stimulus display usually consisted of a target square or disk, known as the test field, and an adjacent, nearby, or surrounding region, typically of higher luminance, known as the inducing field.

This stimulus display was considered to be the "simplest experimental arrangement for studying induction effects," in the words of Heinemann (1972, p. 146). Its simplicity allowed rigorous experimental control of the relevant variables. Such a highly reduced display is not at all similar to the complex images normally encountered by humans, but this was not considered a problem from the contrast perspective. These researchers shared the tacit assumption that whatever is found in some local part of the visual field can be generalized to the entire visual field in a rather straightforward manner. The darkness surrounding the stimulus pattern was not considered to be a problem because zero luminance was treated as zero stimulation.

Perceived test field brightness was measured by having the observer adjust the luminance of a separate comparison field so as to match the perceived brightness of the test field. The test and comparison fields were small, often subtending less than one degree, and were presented in different parts of the visual field. Ideally, to avoid retinal interactions between them, they were presented to separate eyes in a technique known as haploscopic presentation.

In most cases the comparison field, controlled by the subject, was presented in isolation against a totally dark background, but in some cases it was presented against a bright white background. Choice of background has been controversial. The use of the dark background has been criticized on two grounds. It has been known since Katz (1935) that such an infield appears in the film or aperture mode, while the test field, as long as it is darker than the surround field, appears as a surface color. It is extremely difficult to make a match across these modes, if it can be done at all. This factor appears to be responsible for the precipitous drop in disk brightness as annulus luminance surpasses disk luminance. Jameson and Hurvich (1961) presented their comparison field against a large white background, arguing that unlike Heinemann's dark background, the bright background allows the expression of both of the opponent processes.

Because the displays were so simple, only several independent variables were available for manipulation, and these were tested repeatedly: (1) the luminance, (2) the size, and (3) the proximity of the fields.

Test and Inducing Field Luminance

The first experiment of this series was reported in 1953 by Diamond. His stimulus consisted of two adjacent square regions of equal size, one the inducing region and one the test region, presented to one eye. A square matching stimulus isolated within a dark surround was presented to the other eye. His results (Fig. 5.2) show clearly that luminance changes in the inducing field have an effect on test field brightness only when inducing field luminance is higher than test field

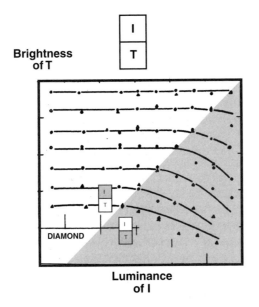

Figure 5.2. Brightness of the test field (T) as a function of the luminance of the inducing field (I) in Diamond's (1953) brightness induction experiment. The induction effect occurred only when the test field was darker than the inducing field. Reprinted with permission.

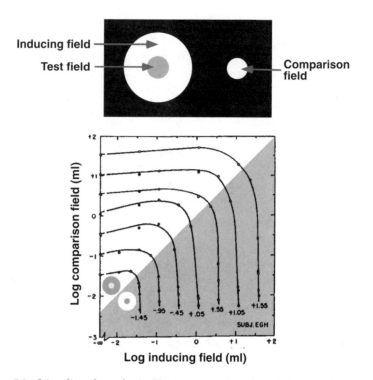

Figure 5.3. Stimuli and results in Heinemann's (1955) brightness induction experiment.

luminance. Diamond reported that when inducing field luminance is lower than test field luminance, little or no darkening effect is exerted on the test field.

Shortly thereafter, Heinemann (1955) reported a similar but more extensive study using a disk/annulus display as the stimulus. His data, which became quite well known, are shown in Figure 5.3.

While Heinemann's results corroborated those of Diamond in showing a pronounced effect only for inducing luminances higher that that of the test field, several differences appeared: (1) The negative part of Heinemann's curve is much steeper than that of Diamond. (2) Heinemann reported that inducing field luminances lower than that of the test field produce a modest enhancement of test field brightness, whereas Diamond found no change. (3) Diamond reported that the inducing field begins to darken the test field exactly when its luminance surpasses that of the test field, but Heinemann found the darkening to begin well before the inducing field luminance reaches that of the test field.

All three of these discrepancies can be traced to the difference in stimuli, the first to the fact that Heinemann's inducing field totally surrounded the test field (see Cataliotti & Gilchrist, 1995) and the other two to differences in relative area of test and inducing fields, discussed at length in Chapter 9.

Results similar to those of Heinemann were reported by Horeman (1965), Saunders (1968), and Fry and Alpern (1953, 1954).

Leibowitz, Myers, and Chinetti (1955) tested constancy over a million-fold illumination range using a gray target on a white, gray, or black background. They found only a modest degree of constancy for the white background and almost no constancy (that is, luminance matching) for the black and gray background. Overall, the poor constancy they obtained can be attributed to their instructions (match luminance) and their matching stimulus (presented against a dark background), both of which favored luminance matching.

Separation between Test and Inducing Fields

Studies of the effect of separation between inducing field and test field on the appearance of a darker test field have been reported by Cole and Diamond (1971), Dunn and Leibowitz (1961), Fry and Alpern (1953), and Leibowitz, Mote, and Thurlow (1953). All found that the perceived brightness of the darker test field increases with increasing separation between the two, when test and inducing luminances are held constant. All of these authors attributed this pattern of results to the reduction in strength of lateral inhibition with increasing distance across the retina. McCann and Savoy (1991) and Newson (1958) obtained analogous results using similar stimuli and measuring lightness, not brightness. But they did not attribute their findings to lateral inhibition.

Test and Inducing Field Size

Experiments testing the role of inducing field size or test field size have been reported by Diamond (1955, 1962a, 1962b), Heinemann (1972), Stevens (1967), Stewart (1959), and Torii and Uemura (1965). In general, the larger the inducing field relative to the test field, the stronger the induction effect, and this general pattern has been attributed to lateral inhibition. But under certain conditions of relative area, no effect of area on strength of induction is found, and no explanation of these findings in terms of lateral inhibition has been given. This issue is discussed in more detail in Chapter 9.

Contrast Explanation of Simultaneous Contrast

In its most basic form, contrast theory (Hering, 1874/1964) says that brightness (not generally distinguished from lightness) is the net result of two opposing forces, excitation and inhibition. For any given location in the visual field, the level of excitation is directly proportional to the luminance at that location. The level of inhibition at the same location is proportional to the average luminance of the immediately surrounding region. As described earlier, in the case of the simultaneous contrast illusion, the neural activity corresponding to the target on the white background is depressed by inhibitory influence of its surround, while the other target does not suffer such inhibition.

Contrast Explanation of Lightness Constancy

The same trade-off between excitation and inhibition has been extended to explain lightness constancy as well. Here is how Wyszecki (1986) has described it: "This simple physiological model is extended to explain the case of lightness constancy, which is observed when the level of illuminance on a given display (e.g., a gray paint chip on a white background) is increased or decreased. Raising the level of illuminance, and thus the luminance of every object in the display, does not result in an increased neural-firing rate because the tendency toward an increased level of excitation of a given neural cell is canceled by a virtually equally increased level of lateral inhibition caused on each such cell by its neighbors. The degree to which the increase in excitation cancels the increase in lateral inhibition determines the degree of approximation to which lightness constancy is observed."

Figure 5.4 shows how this account would be applied to Katz's

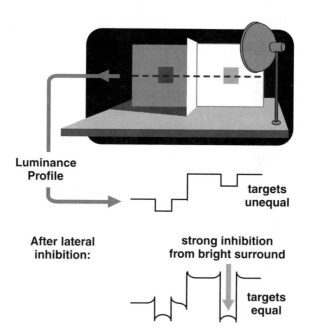

Figure 5.4. Contrast explanation of lightness constancy. Lateral inhibition turns the unequal luminance of the two targets into equal levels of neural activity.

light/shadow arrangement composed of two target disks, one standing in a lighted region and the other standing in an adjacent shadowed region. The observer's task is to match the two disks for luminance (or reflectance) by adjusting one of them. Once the observer achieves perceptual equality, the lighted disk will have a higher luminance than the shadowed disk, as illustrated in the luminance profile at the bottom of Figure 5.4. This profile can be used to illustrate the problem of lightness constancy in its traditional form. How can the two disks appear the same in surface gray when they are so different in luminance level?

According to contrast theory, the two disks produce different levels of excitation at the retina, or at least they would without inhibition. Inhibition lowers the excitation associated with both target disks, because each disk has a surround of higher luminance than itself. But there is greater inhibition acting on the illuminated disk, and this reduces its rate of firing to that of the shadowed disk. In other words, constancy of perceived lightness is explained by constancy of neural rates of firing.

Freeman (1967) reviewed the evidence for a contrast interpretation of lightness constancy. He concluded (p. 186) that when the degree to which constancy fails is taken into account, "the Hering-Jameson-Hurvich theory of opponent induced-response processes accounts well for the results of conditions which produce constancy as well as those in which 'underconstancy' or 'overconstancy' is obtained."

Two Models Based on Hering

Opponent-Process Theory

Hurvich and Jameson (1957; Jameson & Hurvich, 1964) have proposed a formal model of lightness/brightness based on Hering's theory. But while Hering appealed also to peripheral factors other than lateral inhibition and to the cognitive factor of memory color, Jameson and Hurvich focus almost exclusively on lateral inhibition. But they have been especially faithful to Hering in stressing both the degree to which constancy fails and the manner in which it fails. Jameson and Hurvich echo Hering's claim that when illumination changes, the change in excitation equals the change in inhibition (for any given location) only by chance. More typically, either the change in excitation will be greater (producing underconstancy) or the change in inhibition will be greater (producing overconstancy). Jameson and Hurvich support this theoretical claim with an appeal to visual experience: black objects, they assert, appear blacker under brighter illumination.[5] But they also appeal to data.

Claim of Diverging Functions. In 1961 Jameson and Hurvich published a simple experiment that appeared to support their contention that

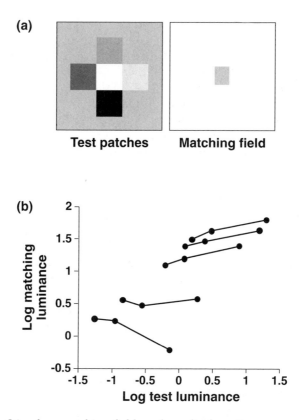

Figure 5.5. Stimulus, matching field, and results from Jameson and Hurvich (1961). Reprinted with permission.

failures of constancy assume the form of both underconstancy and overconstancy. Using a projected pattern of light, they simulated a paper display consisting of a pattern of five gray squares arranged in a cross on a middle-gray background (Fig. 5.5A). Three levels of intensity of the projector, spanning 1.1 log units, were used to simulate three levels of illumination. At each level of illumination, observers made a match for each of the five squares by adjusting the luminance of a comparison square that was presented against a bright white background in a separate viewing chamber that was seen by turning the head 90° to the side.

This matching display, analogous to Wallach's disk/annulus display, is an excellent way to match perceived surface gray. It allows continuous adjustment of a convincing series of grays. Jameson and Hurvich deliberately surrounded their comparison square with a white background rather than a dark background (as Heinemann and others had) because "when the luminance of the inducing field . . . has been increased beyond a certain level, the test area . . . takes on a very black appearance. This blackness cannot be matched by [the comparison field] in its dark surround no matter how much we reduce the intensity of [the comparison field]" (Hurvich & Jameson, 1966, p. 93).

According to the results shown in Figure 5.5B, when illumination increases, light grays become whiter, dark grays become blacker, and only middle grays show real constancy. Since the ratios among squares in the pattern were presumably the same for all "illumination" levels, the ratio principle would predict that all the squares would show constancy. Constancy would appear in the Jameson/Hurvich plot as a set of parallel, horizontal lines rather than the diverging functions they reported. Curves of positive slope, indicating underconstancy, are not unusual in constancy experiments; they reflect the kind of failures of constancy typically found in constancy experiments. But the negative function they reported was atypical. It supported their view that lightness is the net result of opponent excitation and inhibition processes that exactly cancel out only for middle-gray surfaces. Jameson and Hurvich have appealed to analogous findings by Hess & Pretori (1894), Stevens (1961), and Bartleson and Breneman (1967).

Jameson and Hurvich take the pattern of diverging functions to support their claim of intensity-dependence. Lightness, they claim, depends upon both relative and absolute luminance.

Cornsweet's Theory

In 1970, Tom Cornsweet published a book featuring his own model of brightness perception, according to which perceived brightness depends on two successive stages: a first nonlinear stage, followed by a second stage with strong lateral inhibition. Cornsweet's account of lightness constancy differs from that of Jameson and Hurvich in that Cornsweet claims that normally, when the illumination level changes, changes in the excitation and inhibition corresponding to a given retinal locus are equal in strength and thus cancel each other out completely.

Thus, Cornsweet does not agree with Jameson and Hurvich that lightness is intensity-dependent. And he rejects their claim that the ratio principle is limited to relatively small changes in illumination. But he makes a different claim: that the ratio principle is limited to relatively low target/background luminance ratios, breaking down at higher ratios. He has written (Cornsweet, 1970, p. 374), "the brightness of a target is judged to be almost constant when the illumination falling on it and its surroundings is varied over wide limits. . . . Constancy, however, breaks down when the intensities of the retinal images of the target and its surround differ strongly." According to Cornsweet, this occurs because the first, nonlinear, stage in his model is not exactly logarithmic, and he cites Heinemann's data as support for this claim of limitation.

CRITIQUE OF CONTRAST THEORIES

Intensity Dependence and the Claim of Diverging Functions

Grounds for skepticism regarding the Jameson/Hurvich experiment existed from the beginning. The crucial claim of the negative function rests on only a single data point, based on only three subjects, two of whom are the authors. The negative slope appears only in the curve for the black square. Only the third of the three data points drops significantly, without which the curve is effectively horizontal. There was also a logical problem. If lightness diverges this much with only a 12-fold increase in illumination, where do the curves possibly go in the real world, where illumination changes of a million-fold are not unusual? Worse still, by 1974 there were three published failures to replicate the Jameson/Hurvich experiment—Flock and Noguchi (1970), Haimson (1974), and Noguchi and Masuda (1971). Nevertheless, the Jameson/Hurvich finding was reported in virtually all of the perception textbooks at that time.

Believing that only relative luminance is encoded, Alan Jacobsen and I became interested in those few empirical results that seemed to require the encoding of absolute luminance as well as relative luminance. We set up a very careful replication of the Jameson/Hurvich study, making only one change. After finding it impossible to maintain constant ratios (see footnote) using the projection method, even taking every possible step to control stray light, we decided to switch to a front-illuminated paper display.

We soon found what we believed to be an artifactual basis for the diverging curves. Observers in the Jameson/Hurvich experiment had made matches by looking away from the stimulus display to a matching square of variable luminance surrounded by a large white background. This matching technique is a good one, but looking at the bright field in the matching apparatus leaves a large bright afterimage, which then functions as a veiling luminance when one's eyes return to the stimulus display. This has been observed by Noguchi and Masuda (1971, p. 68) as well. A veiling luminance reduces edge ratios (Gilchrist & Jacobsen, 1983), and the effect would be greater for the lower illumination conditions. Such an influence on edge ratios would nicely account for the Jameson/Hurvich curves consistent with the ratio principle.

But, to our surprise, when we tested a group of naïve observers, we got no diverging functions at all; we got excellent constancy. The situation was ironic. We were convinced that if we could replicate the Jameson/Hurvich results, we could tease out the reason for the discrepancy between the Jameson/Hurvich results and those of Wallach. The fact that we could not obtain the diverging functions seemed to prevent us from challenging their claim. What would be the point of adding another failure to replicate to the three already published? Instead, we chose a different tack.

Million-to-One Range

Jameson and Hurvich had suggested that the reason Wallach had not discovered the diverging functions is because he had tested too limited a range of illumination. Wallach's experiments had simulated an illumination range of only eight-to-one, it is true. But Jameson and Hurvich had extended that range to only 12-to-one, a modest extension that would seem unlikely to produce such a dramatically different pattern of results. Nevertheless, the idea of extending the illumination range seemed a good one, and we decided to replicate the study using an illumination range of a million-to-one. Observers made matches using two separate methods. In one condition observers made lightness matches using the Jameson/Hurvich method; they varied the luminance of a target surrounded by a large white background. In a second condition, observers made brightness matches. For this we merely replaced the large white background with darkness, as in the Heinemann (1955) experiments.

Our results (Jacobsen & Gilchrist, 1988) are shown in Figure 5.6. For our lightness matches we got very good constancy with no negative trends at all. For the brightness matches we obtained approximate luminance matches.

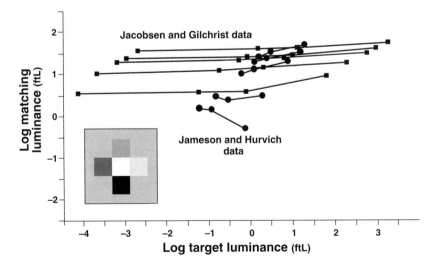

Figure 5.6. Results of Jacobsen and Gilchrist's (1988b) replication (using a large illumination range) superimposed on the original Jameson and Hurvich results. Reprinted with permission from Jameson and Hurvich, 1961, and from Jacobsen and Gilchrist, 1988b.

Supporting Studies

Although no successful replication of their results had been published, Jameson and Hurvich had pointed to two other studies as showing the same finding: the 1894 Hess and Pretori study, and a study published by S.S. Stevens in 1961. We set out to have a closer look at these studies as well.

Hess and Pretori (1894)

Figure 5.7a shows a representative set of curves from the Hess and Pretori study described in Chapter 2. Each curve was obtained in the following way. One center/surround pair, called the test pattern, was adjusted to a given luminance ratio. Then the center of the other center/surround pair, called the comparison pattern, was set to a series

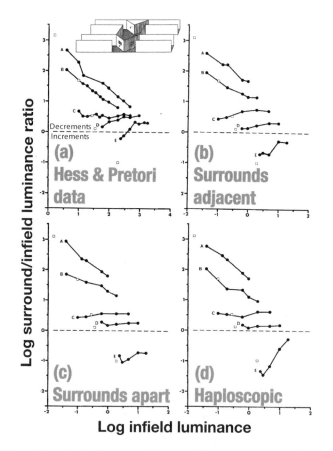

Figure 5.7. (a) Data from Hess and Pretori (1894) compared to (b, c, d) three conditions from Jacobsen and Gilchrist (1988a). Reprinted with permission from Jacobsen and Gilchrist, 1988a.

of values, and at each of these values the observer was required to make the two centers appear equally bright by adjusting the luminance of the surround on the comparison pattern.

The Hess and Pretori results are qualitatively similar to those of Jameson and Hurvich (the curves in Figure 5.7 are converging rather than diverging merely because of a different plotting scheme) but quite different from those of Wallach. Wallach's ratio results would have appeared as a set of parallel horizontal lines in the Hess and Pretori plot. Wallach did not gather data on increments, as did Hess and Pretori, but even for decrements the Hess and Pretori data are very different from the Wallach data.

What could account for the discrepancy in these results? There are three main differences between the studies: (1) Hess and Pretori used square patterns, while Wallach's were circular. (2) Hess and Pretori's standard and comparison patterns were adjacent, while Wallach's were separated by about 20° of darkness. (3) Hess and Pretori's subjects adjusted the comparison surround to make a match, while Wallach's subjects adjusted the comparison center. There is no reason to think that difference (1), pattern shape, would have any effect on the data. Nor should difference (3) matter; if everything is relative it is immaterial whether subjects adjust the center or the surround. Wallach told us that he believed that the adjacency of Hess and Pretori's patterns was responsible for their data, and we began by investigating this difference.

We replicated the Hess/Pretori experiment using three degrees of proximity of the standard and comparison patterns. The patterns were (1) adjacent as in Hess and Pretori, (2) separated by 90° of darkness, or (3) presented haploscopically with 65° of separation. In the adjacent condition (see Fig. 5.7b) we replicated Hess and Pretori's results very closely. But the results in the two non-adjacent conditions (see Fig. 5.7c and 5.7d) were almost exactly the same! Apparently, proximity was not the crucial factor. This left us with quite a puzzle.

Eventually we uncovered two clues, one concerning decrements and one concerning increments.

Decrements. Alan Jacobsen pointed out something that others had missed: a center of constant luminance (as long as it is a decrement) will appear to get darker as the luminance of its surround increases. But there is a limit to this effect. At a certain point the center reaches its maximum darkness, and further increases in the luminance of the surround have no further darkening effect on the center. Evans (1974, p. 85) refers to this as the "black point." Whittle (1994) has called it the "black limit." Heinemann (1955) also refers to it. It occurs at a ratio of approximately 100:1, depending upon other factors. But some of Hess and Pretori's curves (see curve E, Fig. 5.7) showed systematic data well beyond this threshold. All centers beyond this threshold, regardless of the surround/center ratio, should appear identical: completely dark. Any data in this region should be random.

We tested this expectation by setting the standard and comparison surrounds to equal luminance values. The centers were set at values beyond this threshold; specifically, each center was at least 210 times darker than its surround. The two centers were set to very different luminance values, and the observers were required to judge which center was lighter/brighter. We ran this experiment two times. Performance was at chance level both times, even when one center was 8.5 times as bright as the other! This demonstrates that the matches Hess and Pretori obtained in this region cannot possibly represent what they have been presumed to represent, namely center matching.

We are now quite confident that the curves in this region actually represent surround matching, not center matching. But why would subjects match surrounds when they were instructed to match centers? We do not claim the subjects were trying to match surrounds, only that they did. The data in the region beyond the threshold never departed more than 2.5% from exact surround matches. Two factors make surround matching plausible. First, with high contrast decrements, the much brighter surround casts a veiling luminance over the center, due to scattered light in the eye (Fry & Alpern, 1954; Rushton & Gubisch, 1966). In fact, this may be the cause of the "black limit." Subjects may have been trying to match these two veils on the centers, which they could do by adjusting the only value available to them, the luminance of the comparison surround. The veils of course would be equal when the surrounds were equal. But, second, there is an even simpler possibility. Hess and Pretori began each trial by setting the surrounds equal. Since both targets were beyond the darkness threshold and would have appeared totally dark, and thus equal, from the outset of the trial, the subjects may have simply left the surround values untouched.

In either case there is a simple way to avoid the problem: allow subjects to adjust the comparison field itself rather than its surround. It turns out that this method also solves the problem concerning increments.

Increments. The clue concerning increments emerged as we considered a further puzzle. In simple center/surround studies like this one, subjects tend to match the centers for luminance, not luminance ratios, when the center is an increment (Heinemann, 1955). Wallach's ratio results were obtained with decremental centers. Although he made informal comments on the appearance of incremental centers (Wallach, 1976), he never reported data concerning them. We wondered why Hess and Pretori's subjects, and indeed our own subjects, had not matched the luminances of the centers. And then we realized the answer is very simple: the subjects could not match the centers for

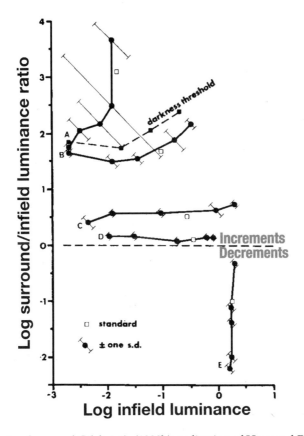

Figure 5.8. Jacobsen and Gilchrist's (1988b) replication of Hess and Pretori, but allowing observers to control infield luminance. The results show luminance matching for decrements, ratio matching (approximately) for increments, and unsystematic results beyond the darkness threshold. Reprinted with permission.

luminance because they were not allowed to! They were given control of only the surround. The obvious solution was to have the subjects adjust the comparison center rather than its surround. Moreover, this was the same solution required by the problem with decrements.

Obviously the entire experiment needed to be run again using center adjustment. This would serve two purposes. For high contrast decrements it would prevent subjects from making a surround match, and for increments, it would give subjects the freedom to match the centers either for luminance or for center/surround luminance ratio. According to the opponent process model that Jameson and Hurvich had derived from Hering, having the subject adjust the center rather than the surround should have no effect on the data. But we had reasons to predict that the data would change dramatically. We predicted qualitatively different results in three domains. (1) In the region of increments we predicted luminance matching (which would appear as a vertical line in the same plot used in Figure 5.7). (2) In the region of high contrast decrements, beyond the "black limit," we predicted completely random data, with high variability. (3) In the region of decrements lying between (1) and (2), corresponding to the black/white surface color range, we predicted ratio matching as Wallach had found. Ratio matching would produce horizontal lines on the graph. A look at Figure 5.8 will reveal that these results are just what we did obtain.

Stevens

What about Stevens' data (1961), presented in Figure 5.9, showing diverging functions as the illumination increases? Jacobsen did not get to this study as part of his doctoral work, but we have since learned that there is really no study to be replicated. The graph that is familiar from Stevens' 1961 paper comes from a Harvard University technical report (1960, No. PPR-246) co-authored by J. Stevens, in which it was presented as a theoretical model. The graph has generally been accepted as representing empirical data (though extremely clean data, with data points falling precisely at the intersections of straight lines).

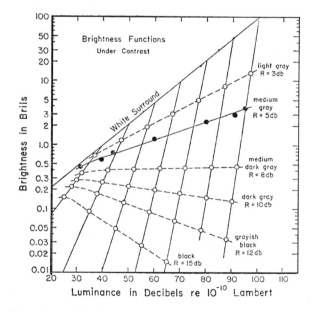

Figure 5.9. Data figure from Stevens (1961). Often regarded as empirical data points, the open circles, showing some negative functions, were not obtained empirically but are merely theoretical. Reprinted with permission.

This misunderstanding can probably be traced to the failure of S. Stevens in his later publication (Stevens, 1961) to make the true nature of these "data points" clear to the reader (p. 86): "These functions were determined in a long series of experiments aimed directly at determining the slopes of the brightness functions for targets seen under contrast."

In a 1974 paper, Flock wrote, "With regard to the negative lines, Stevens indicated (in a personal communication) that supporting data points had only been collected for the lower range in scotopic vision." According to J. Stevens (personal communication, Aug. 3, 1987), the diverging curves published by S. Stevens represent the way S. Stevens would have expected the data to turn out, had a complete study been conducted. Thus, Stevens (1961) did not in fact report empirical data showing diverging functions.

Taking all the evidence into account, the claim of diverging functions must be rejected. Nevertheless, there does seem to be an expansion along some dimension as illumination increases. Things are easier to see. Technically we might say that the number of just noticeable differences between black and white increases under higher illumination. But this doesn't mean that black or dark-gray surfaces actually become blacker in appearance, nor does the pronouncedness of black increase when the illumination becomes brighter. According to Katz (1935, p. 80), the pronouncedness of black surfaces is greater under lower illumination, not higher.

Whatever is the correct phenomenal description of black surfaces under high illumination, there are not sufficient grounds here for rejecting the ratio principle.

Limitations on the Ratio Principle

The weight of the evidence suggests that the ratio principle is not "intensity dependent," nor does it apply only to a limited range of illumination. Within the range of surface grays from white to black and within the range of normal illumination, the ratio principle appears to be the rule. Other contrast theorists have made additional claims concerning limitations on the ratio principle.

Constancy Breakdown at High Contrasts

Cornsweet (1970, p. 283, Fig. 13.4, p. 378; see also Kaufman, 1974, p. 133) claimed the ratio principle breaks down when disk and annulus luminances differ by more than a factor of about five. However, the breakdown referred to in these claims appeared in the data of Heinemann (1955) and are no doubt associated with problems in methodology. Data from virtually all other constancy experiments fail to show this breakdown.

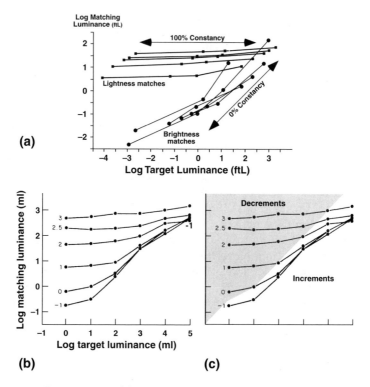

Figure 5.10. Data presented by Heinemann (1989) (b) as evidence against the Gilchrist and Jacobsen (1989) (a) claim that decrements evoke ratio matching (horizontal lines) while increments evoke luminance matching (diagonal lines). But when the decrements and increments are separated (c), Heinemann's own data appear to fall into the same pattern as that found by Jacobsen and Gilchrist (1988b). Reprinted with permission.

Qualitative Boundaries

The ratio principle does indeed have limits, but they are not arbitrary limits. The limits exist either at qualitative boundaries or at the limits of the visual system. For example, the ratio principle applies to decrements, not increments.[6] It ceases to apply at the increment/decrement boundary, which is merely an arbitrary point in terms of absolute luminance but a qualitative watershed in terms of relative luminance.[7]

For example, Figure 5.10a shows the data that Jacobsen and I obtained for lightness and brightness matches in our replication of the Jameson/Hurvich experiment. For lightness matches, the comparison field, seen against a bright white background, was always a decrement. But for brightness matches, the comparison field, seen against darkness, was always an increment. The data show a qualitative difference, with lightness showing matching according to luminance ratio and brightness showing matching according to luminance.

Heinemann (1989, p. 91) has taken issue with this claim, writing that "if they exist at all, these qualitative boundaries are irrelevant to brightness perception." He has argued that we obtained what appear to be two qualitatively different patterns of data merely because we reported only two extreme values of comparison surround luminance (bright white versus darkness). And he offered some of his own previous unpublished data, shown in Figure 5.10b, as a demonstration that when one varies the luminance of the comparison surround in a parametric fashion, a whole fan-like family of curves is produced.

Nevertheless, when the boundary between increments and decrements is located in the Heinemann graph, the qualitative difference is revealed. As seen in Figure 5.10c, on the decrements side of the boundary, one obtains roughly horizontal lines characteristic of ratio matching, while on the increments side, one obtains roughly a slope of +1, characteristic of luminance matching.

Heinemann's claim is ironic because even in the best-known plot of his data, shown in Figure 5.3, the two qualitative patterns of results are clearly seen. Each curve is composed of two basic legs, one leg roughly horizontal and one leg with a steep drop. Except when relative area comes into play (see Chapter 9), the shift from one leg to the other occurs right at the increment/decrement boundary.

Ratio Principle and Complex Stimuli

Additional limitations of the ratio principle emerge when the concept is applied to more complex stimuli. The computational theorists, while accepting Wallach's fundamental insight regarding the relational determination of lightness, noted that the ratio principle (1) cannot account for depth effects on lightness; (2) ignores the role of remote ratios; (3) applies only to reflectance edges, not illuminance edges; and (4) cannot produce lightness values without anchoring rules. All of these claims are examined in detail in subsequent chapters.

Wallach may have overstated his claims for the ratio principle, but he had nevertheless touched on a fundamental topic, the question of absolute versus relative luminance information. This fact has given his work a broad appeal.[8] Others may have talked about relative luminance, but no one had done such a simple yet fundamental experiment.

Constancy Explanation versus Empirical Data

Many attempts have been made to test experimentally whether constancy can be reduced to contrast (i.e., explained by a contrast mechanism). Many of these tests have been rather oblique, but there are several experimental paradigms that get right to the heart of the matter.

The contrast explanation of constancy is best tested by counter-shading the backgrounds to make them equal in luminance, and thus equal in the contrast effects they exert on their enclosed targets. In fact, substantial levels of constancy have repeatedly been obtained under these conditions (see Chapter 3), a result that directly undermines the contrast account. To these earlier studies reporting constancy under countershading we can add four more from the contrast period: Hsia (1943), Evans (1948), Landauer and Rogers (1964), and Oyama (1968). Indeed, we will find even more such results in the computational period (Arend et al., 1971; Gilchrist, 1988; Gilchrist, Delman & Jacobsen, 1983).

Contrast Theory Lacks Rigor

Contrast theories are difficult to evaluate because they tend to equivocate on a series of crucial issues. The contrast approach is rather like a toolbox: various combinations of tools are taken from the box for various purposes. Contrast theory is all things to all people. Consider the following issues on which contrast theories equivocate.

No Consistent Strength

Contrast theories are unable to assign a consistent strength[9] to the inhibiting effect. A target surface of constant luminance will appear to get darker when the luminance of the surrounding region increases, regardless of whether the increase is perceived as due to a change in the reflectance of the background, a change in the illumination, a change in the intensity of a veiling luminance in front of the target, or a change in either the lightness or the transparency of a transparent layer in front of the target. But the amount by which the perceived lightness of the target decreases is very different in each of these cases.

As Kingdom (1997, p. 675) has observed, "In the Hering-based approach, simultaneous contrast is expected to occur irrespective of whether a test region's surround is perceived to be a veiling luminance or a surface differing in reflectance from its neighbours: the phenomenon is due only to the effects of local contrast. Thus no assumption about the nature of the surround is being made."

Gilchrist, Delman, and Jacobsen (1983) showed that the standard 0.75-Munsell-step simultaneous contrast effect jumps to six Munsell steps when the edge dividing the white and black backgrounds is made to appear as an illumination edge by altering the larger context. Piantanida and I (described in Gilchrist, 1994, p. 26) found that retinally stabilizing the black/white border not only makes the two backgrounds appear as one, but also makes the gray targets appear white and black, respectively. It should also be noted that this perceptual change occurs in targets far from the retinal locus of the stabilized edge.

Agostini and Bruno (1996) have shown that the size of the simultaneous contrast illusion approximately doubles when the entire display is presented within a spotlight, like that used for the Gelb effect. There is nothing obvious in the lateral inhibition account that would suggest a doubling of the illusion under these conditions.

There are a number of experiments in the literature in which the luminance of a target and the luminance of its surround are both held constant, yet perceived lightness can vary dramatically. Gilchrist and Jacobsen (1984) showed that a 1:2 target/background luminance ratio produces a light gray appearance (Munsell 6.5) when no veiling luminance is seen, but the same ratio produces a black appearance (Munsell 2.0) when a veiling luminance is perceived to lie across it. In a very different kind of experiment, but using the same constant 1:2 target/background luminance ratio, Gilchrist (1988) found a light-gray appearance when the surround appears white but a black appearance when the surround is made to appear dark gray.

The structure-blind character of lateral inhibition does not allow it to distinguish reflectance from illuminance edges; thus, there is nothing in the model to explain these effects of very different size produced by the same edge ratio.

No Consistent Direction: Disinhibition versus Remote Inhibition

Any model of lightness can be forgiven if it cannot predict lightness in complex images, but contrast theories fail to make clear predictions for some very simple images. For example, if the disk/annulus configuration represents a simple image, then we can take a minimal step toward complexity by adding a second annulus. What should now be the effect on the disk caused by the addition of the second annulus? According to the concept of disinhibition (Hartline & Ratliff, 1957), an increase of luminance of the outer annulus inhibits the activity in the inner annulus, reducing its ability to inhibit the disk. Thus, the net effect on the disk of a luminance increase in the outer annulus is facilitation, not inhibition. But it is sometimes argued that a luminance increase in the outer annulus merely adds to the total inhibition acting on the disk. Jameson and Hurvich (1989) have argued that inhibition can come from remote regions of the visual field. Thus, not even the direction of the effect can be predicted by contrast theory.

Recent years have seen the appearance of a variety of stimuli in which contrast effects work in a direction opposite to that predicted by lateral inhibition (Bressan, 2001a; Gilchrist, 1980). These effects, which create a major headache for contrast models, are described in Chapter 10.

Pointwise Model versus Edge Theory

At times contrast theories appear as pointwise models, while at other times they appear as edge-coded models. Cornsweet (1970, p. 303) states the pointwise version thusly: "the physiological correlate of the brightness of any point is the frequency of firing of the spatially corresponding part of the visual system (after inhibition)." An example of the edge-coded version can be found in this quote from Ratliff (1972, p. 12): "The maximum and minimum in the retinal response may 'set' brightness discriminators in the brain, and provided that there are no intervening maxima and minima (that is, visible contours) the apparent brightness of adjacent areas would not deviate from that set by the maximum or the minimum." Shapley and Enroth-Cugell (1984, p. 268) wrote, "brightness is mainly determined by *the contrast near the border* between an object and its surroundings."

According to the pointwise version, homogeneous surfaces should not appear homogeneous. Bright or dark scallops should appear near the borders, but these are not generally seen by observers. The edge-coded version, typically accompanied by filling-in between borders (Cohen & Grossberg, 1984; Gerrits & Vendrik, 1970; Grossberg & Todorović, 1988), offers a way around this problem. Ironically, as McCourt (1982) has noted, the edge coding/filling-in approach cannot explain illusions such as grating induction, in which such illusory scallops are seen.

But I emphasize that the pointwise and edge-coded versions of contrast theory are very different theories, and there is simply no consensus on which version is implied when lateral inhibition is invoked.

Enhance or Encode?

"Contrast" often means that the perceived difference between the center and its surround is enhanced or exaggerated. For example, Hurvich and Jameson (1966, p. 85) write, "What the contrast mechanism seems to do in all these instances is to magnify the differences in apparent brightness between adjacent areas of different luminances." Cornsweet (1970, p. 300) writes, "This kind of interaction, then, can be said to be a contrast amplifier, in that the contrast between the two outputs is greater with inhibition than it would be without inhibition." Leibowitz (1965, p. 57) notes, "the differences in light intensity which exist in the retinal image are actually exaggerated by the nervous mechanism of the intact eye." Fry (1948, p. 172) writes, "the inhibition mechanism in the retina accentuates the 'contrast' at a brightness contrast border." Leibowitz et al. (1953, p. 456) write, "luminance differences in the fovea are exaggerated by an inhibitory mechanism."

But, as Wyszecki (1986, pp. 9–13) has written, "It is important to note that the term 'contrast' is also used in a different sense, referring to the ratio of the luminances of two adjacent stimuli (achromatic or chromatic), and care must be taken to avoid possible confusion." Whittle and Challands (1969, p. 1106) write, "On this view the role of 'lateral inhibition' is less obvious than usually assumed. It is involved in determining the size of the edge signal, but simultaneous contrast could in principle be just as great in a system without lateral inhibition." In this sense the term *contrast* refers not to any enhancement of the luminance ratio, but only to the ratio itself.

There is simply no consistent use of the term. Does lateral inhibition encode luminance ratios, or does it encode and enhance them?

Enhancement versus Induction (Transfer of Effect): Defining Enhancement

The term *contrast* sometimes means only that when the luminance of the surround is increased, the perceptual effect shows up in the center, as if the change in the surround is transferred to the center. Often the term *induction* is used for this transfer of effect, with *contrast* being reserved for exaggeration of differences. This usage should probably be encouraged, but in fact the two terms are often used interchangeably.

But the critical point is that the "transfer of effect" concept and the "exaggeration of difference" concept are completely separable. This point has been made clearly by Heinemann (1972, p. 146). The increase in luminance of the surround can be perceived as a decrease in intensity of the center with no exaggeration whatsoever. This would mean that the decrease in lightness or brightness of the center is exactly proportionate to the increase in luminance of the surround. Or both effects could happen together. The increase in surround intensity could produce a perceived darkening of the center that is proportionately greater than the increase of the surround.

The "transfer of effect" phenomenon, like induced motion, is a clear, undeniable fact. Yet it is a central fact, and every theory of lightness perception must try to explain it. The concept of "exaggeration" or "enhancement," however, is both more confusing and more controversial. The facts are not so clear here, so neither is it clear what a theory must be able to explain. As Freeman (1967) wrote in a review of the contrast idea, "an experimental analysis of enhanced brightness differences has not, as yet, been performed." Heinemann (1972, p. 147) has described what such a test would entail: "To measure contrast the comparison field must be matched to the test field and to the inducing field when each is presented alone, and again when the two fields are presented simultaneously. If the brightness of either the test or the inducing fields is not affected by the simultaneous presence of the other, or if the brightness of the two fields changes in opposite directions, then it is possible to specify whether the difference in brightness between the two fields increased or decreased as a result of their interaction."

Upward Induction versus Downward Induction

Increasing the luminance difference between a target and its neighbor can produce effects in two opposite directions. In some experiments (Diamond, 1953; Heinemann, 1955) this increasing luminance difference is seen as a darkening of the darker region with little or no change in the brighter region. As Freeman (1967, p. 173) has noted, "inducing-field luminances less than test-field luminances have little effect on brightness judgments" of the test-field. But in other experiments, especially those on luminosity threshold (Bonato & Gilchrist, 1994; Lie, 1977; Wallach, 1976) it is seen as a brightening of the brighter region, with little or no change in the darker region. Contrast theories offer no explanation of why the induction effect goes down in some cases but up in others. Indeed, a fuller picture (see Chapter 9) would show that both upward induction and downward induction occur in all of these experiments. In the brightness induction experiments, however, this was obscured by the fact that no measures were taken of the perceived values of the brighter regions.

Contrast theories have not confronted the question of upward induction, nor can they predict the relative degrees of upward and downward induction.

Physiology No Substitute for Rigor

The fact that contrast theory cannot give clear answers on a range of such basic questions demonstrates that physiological approaches to vision do not guarantee rigor. Just because the neurons are concrete doesn't mean the theory is.

Problem of the Missing Scallops

The strength of lateral inhibition is known to drop off precipitously with distance, becoming negligible within a few degrees of visual angle (Fry & Alpern, 1953; Heinemann, 1972; Leibowitz, Mote & Thurlow, 1953; Stevens & Diamond, 1965). Thus, according to this spatial function (at least in its pointwise version), homogeneous regions should not appear homogeneous. Light or dark scalloped regions (haloes) should appear near the borders. But observers report that homogeneous regions appear homogeneous.

Cornsweet has dealt explicitly with this challenge. Presenting a figure of a light disk within a darker annulus (1970, p. 350), he notes that "the center of the central disk should have almost the same brightness as the middle region of the dark ring. That is clearly not the case." He offers an escape from the dilemma based on an experiment by Davidson (1968) in which scallops are perceived when homogeneous patterns are presented briefly and at low contrast. Hering (1874/1964, p. 148) had similarly noted, "it is important to catch the first impression, because with somewhat longer rigorous fixation the rings very soon become uniformly bright throughout their whole width."

But Cornsweet's workaround has not been generally accepted. Who, for example, would agree that the center of Cornsweet's disk (1970, p. 350, and shown in Figure 10.1) has the same brightness as the middle region of the ring, regardless of the brevity of the exposure? More favored by contrast thinkers have been the following two solutions: (1) averaging within boundaries, and (2) shifting to an edge theory.

Averaging Excitation Levels between Borders

Visible scallops would not be predicted if the regions between borders were filled in with an average of the activation levels of all of the points that lie within those borders, as shown schematically in Figure 5.11. Averaging between borders does predict a contrast effect in the

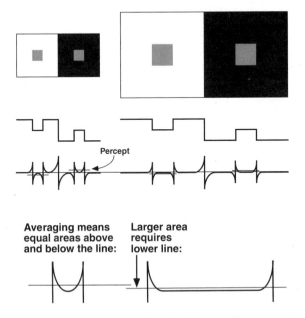

Figure 5.11. Averaging activation within borders predicts a weaker contrast effect for a larger display.

standard textbook display but quickly runs into several other problems.

First, the averaging approach is not consistent with the lack of a viewing distance effect. For an incremental target, averaging should produce a higher level for a retinally smaller target than for a larger target; a smaller decremental target should appear darker than a larger one, as can be seen in Figure 5.11. But Burgh and Grindley (1962) have shown that the strength of simultaneous contrast does not vary with viewing distance, and hence with visual angle.

Second, the averaging approach should produce the same-size illusion with double increments as with double decrements. But in fact there is virtually no illusion with double increments.

Lateral Inhibition as Edge Theory

The problem of the missing luminance scallops is associated with what might be called the pointwise character of lateral inhibition as it is usually understood. The lightness of a given point in the visual field corresponds to the local activity level at that point, even though that activity level depends on inhibition coming from a larger retinal area. When such local activity levels are mapped across the retina, they produce the familiar pattern of scallops shown in Figure 5.4.

But a theoretical leap is required to assume that this early pattern of neural activity should directly map onto the percept. An alternative view is that only the maximum/minimum differences from this pattern are forwarded to higher centers. From this perspective the scallops represent nothing more than a temporary transition in retinal space between a maximum and a minimum and some baseline resting activation level.

Treating lateral inhibition as an edge coding mechanism potentially avoids the problem of the missing scallops as well as the viewing distance problem, and makes the lateral inhibitory mechanism consistent with an edge theory of lightness. But here we face the problem mentioned earlier: are the edges merely encoded, or are they enhanced? Encoding per se explains neither constancy nor simultaneous contrast.

Indeed, merely encoding edge ratios doesn't even produce surface lightness values without additional processes. As more recent models (Adelson & Pentland, 1996; Arend, 1994; Gilchrist, 1979) have made clear, the encoded (but not enhanced) differences must be transformed into levels by adding edge integration and filling-in. These components do yield lightness values (given an anchor), but they do not explain the simultaneous contrast effect: the emerging gray levels for the two targets remain identical, as may be noted in Figure 5.12a.

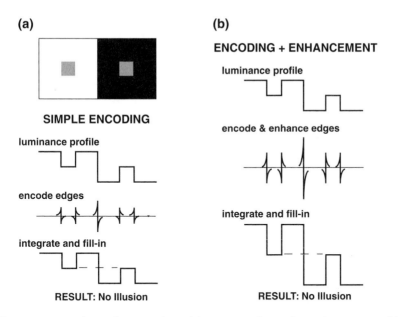

(a)

SIMPLE ENCODING

luminance profile

encode edges

integrate and fill-in

RESULT: No Illusion

(b)

ENCODING + ENHANCEMENT

luminance profile

encode & enhance edges

integrate and fill-in

RESULT: No Illusion

Figure 5.12. Neither edge encoding (a) nor encoding plus enhancement (b) produces the contrast effect.

Lateral Inhibition as Edge Enhancement

For this reason lateral inhibition has been interpreted as an edge-enhancement mechanism. Enhancement has been proposed as a solution to both constancy and simultaneous contrast, but a closer look reveals otherwise.

Edge Enhancement Cannot Explain Constancy

Figure 5.4 shows how edge enhancement is used to explain lightness constancy by reducing the neural activity of the two targets to equal levels, but a fuller account of the observer's visual experience reveals two problems. First, lighted and shadowed disks in such a constancy experiment do not appear identical, or indistinguishable, as in a metameric match. Even when they are adjusted to the same perceived lightness they appear different in brightness, and differently illuminated. As Rock has argued (1983, p. 271), "Given the assumption that lightness is a function of rate of discharge of neurons in the critical region, there would seem to be no basis for explaining the differing phenomenal appearances of two surfaces in differing illuminations that have the same phenomenal lightness. If lateral inhibition leads to the same rate of discharging neurons from the critical region in the two cases, that region should look exactly the same in *every respect*, but it does not." Second, the disks are not the only parts of the display to exhibit lightness constancy. The background walls behind the two disks also appear approximately the same as each other in lightness, even though they too differ in luminance. But there is no way that these regions can be reduced to equal levels through edge enhancement. Indeed, when lateral inhibition is applied to the border between the illuminated and the shadowed portions of the wall, it makes the problem worse by further increasing the difference between them. Remember that lateral inhibition is necessarily blind to whether the luminance edge that triggers it is caused by a change in reflectance or a change in illuminance. Contrast theories seem not to have considered the implications of edge enhancement applied to illuminance edges.

If enhancement of edge differences could serve constancy only when applied to reflectance edges, it is indeed ironic, because if the optic array contained only reflectance edges, there would be no constancy problem. As Wallach (1976, p. 22) has observed, "If our environment were so constructed that illumination were always and everywhere the same, the light reflected by the surface of an object and thus the intensity of the stimulation received in the retinal image of the object would unequivocally represent the reflectance of that surface."

Edge Enhancement and the Loss of Information

The enhancement of edge differences is difficult to reconcile with the requirements of constancy. If lateral inhibition serves merely to encode luminance ratios at the retina, absolute luminance information is lost. This may not pose a serious problem: lightness certainly can be computed without absolute luminance values. But if edges are enhanced by lateral inhibition, information about relative luminance is lost, and this is serious. When local edge information is distorted, the visual system is denied the raw materials it needs to compute things like transparency (Metelli, 1970, 1974) or luminance ratios between non-adjacent targets (through integrating successive edges).

Edge Enhancement Cannot Explain Simultaneous Lightness Contrast

At first glance the enhancement story appears to explain the simultaneous lightness contrast phenomenon. But the enhancement of edge signals does not, by itself, explain simultaneous contrast. Remember that the edge dividing the black and white backgrounds must be enhanced as well as the edges of the targets, unless there is some rule governing selective enhancement. Enhancing the border between the backgrounds cancels out the effects of enhancing the target edges once the enhanced edges are integrated and filling-in is applied. For example, imagine that every edge in the contrast display is doubled in magnitude (followed again by integration and filling in), as shown in Figure 5.12b. The gray targets will still appear identical because the integrated ratio will still be 1:1. So if all edges are enhanced by the same degree, the contrast illusion remains unexplained.

Selective Enhancement

Simultaneous lightness contrast can be explained by edge enhancement only if some edges are enhanced more than others. But what might be the rule that determines the degree of enhancement for each edge? One possibility is that the degree of enhancement might be tied to the size of the luminance step, but there is controversy on this score. According to Hurvich and Jameson (1966, p. 98) Mach stated that "small differences are slurred over by the retina, and large differences stand out with disproportionate clearness." And Helson (1964, p. 292) stated that "relatively small differences in intensity of similar processes in neighboring areas summate, or at least do not inhibit one another, thereby giving rise to assimilation; large differences . . . result in inhibition of less intense excitations giving rise to contrast." Evans (1948, p. 164), on the other hand, subscribes to the more common view of contrast as "a mechanism of vision which increases small differences."

But even were this disagreement to be resolved, it turns out that there is no simple rule that can be consistently applied to the range of simultaneous contrast displays. If we assume that small luminance steps are exaggerated more than large ones, the standard textbook simultaneous contrast display can be explained, that is true. The borders of the two gray squares would be enhanced more than the border between the two backgrounds because the luminance steps at the borders of the gray squares are smaller. However, this scheme fails when applied to other simultaneous contrast displays. In the conventional version of the display, one target square is an increment and the other is a decrement. But, as can be seen in Figure 5.13, when both targets are decrements, this scheme predicts a result that is opposite to that which is actually obtained. Moreover, it predicts a contrast effect when both targets are increments, even though empirically there is virtually no contrast effect in this case.

Contrast effects in these various displays could be explained if the borders of the targets were enhanced more than the borders of the backgrounds, but lateral inhibition is blind to such distinctions. But how would a lateral inhibitory mechanism know which edge was the border of a target and which edge was the border of a background?

It is a fact that a target of fixed luminance appears to darken when

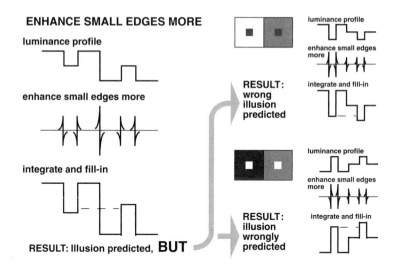

Figure 5.13. Enhancing small edges more than larger edges produces contrast in the standard display but fails to predict the results for double increment and double decrement versions.

the surrounding luminance is increased. Lateral inhibition, in some form, is also a fact. Part of the appeal of contrast theories lies in the seductive conflation of these two facts. But, as Paul Whittle (1994, p. 153) has observed, "To explain brightness contrast in terms of lateral inhibition is like explaining the jerky progression of a learner driver in terms of the explosions in the cylinders of the car's engine. The explosions have a place in the causal chain, but regarding them as causes specifically of the jerks is to be misled by a superficial analogy."

ASSIMILATION (VON BEZOLD SPREADING)

Over a century ago, von Bezold (1874) described and illustrated an effect in which a colored surface appears lighter when overlaid by thin white lines or small white dots and appears darker if the lines or dots are black. This effect, which has sometimes been called the Bezold spreading effect, was given the name *assimilation* by Evans (1948). Over the years this effect has fascinated students of lightness perception because its direction is opposite to that of the more familiar effect known as simultaneous lightness contrast. But despite this opposition in direction, the notion of assimilation has not typically been opposed by contrast theorists. Indeed, it has served as a convenient basket into which a multitude of anti-contrast effects can be placed.

Assimilation and Contrast as Opponent Processes

The apparent symmetry between contrast and assimilation is intriguing because in the case of contrast, the gray target region comes to appear more different from the so-called inducing region, while in the case of assimilation, the gray target comes to appear more similar to the inducing region. This superficial symmetry has led to repeated attempts to treat them as opponent mechanisms, but although a wide consensus has emerged concerning the mechanism underlying simultaneous contrast, no such clear mechanism has been found for assimilation. Just as the term *contrast* has been rather indiscriminately applied to a variety of distinctly different phenomena, so the term *assimilation* has been used in an ad hoc manner. One class of phenomena are said to result from contrast, while those showing opposite results are said to result from assimilation. Escape from this circularity requires at least a description of those stimulus conditions that lead to contrast and those that lead to assimilation. But such attempts have led merely to a situation like the Tower of Babel, as shown in the following list of claims:

1. Helson (1964, p. 292) has claimed that contrast occurs when there are large luminance differences between inducing and test areas and assimilation occurs when there are small differences between inducing and test areas.
2. Helson (1964, 283) also claims that contrast occurs when the inducing region is large relative to the test region, while assimilation occurs when the inducing region is small relative to the test region.
3. Beck (1966) claims that contrast occurs when the lines on a gray background are lighter than the test region, while assimilation occurs when the lines are darker than the test region.
4. Festinger, Coren, and Rivers (1970) claim that contrast occurs when the observer attends to the gray test region, while assimilation occurs when the test region is not attended.
5. Jameson and Hurvich (1989, p. 13) claim that when image elements are small relative to cone diameters, assimilation occurs, but when they are large relative to cone diameters, contrast occurs.
6. Shapley and Reid (1985) have explicitly proposed an antagonistic relationship between contrast and assimilation, arguing that every stimulus engages both mechanisms.
7. Agostini and Galmonte (2000, p. 3) claim "assimilation occurs earlier during the formation of perceptual groups, whereas contrast occurs after the formation of perceptual groups."
8. Bindman and Chubb (2004) claim that "assimilation occurs for a given region R when the contrast difference at R's border is

small in comparison to the contrast difference of edges in the general neighborhood of R." Otherwise, contrast occurs.

In general, none of these claims has been replicated. Indeed, in most cases, the authors have made no reference to the other competing claims.

Many of the observations concerning assimilation suggest a primitive effect of space-averaged luminance, as noted by Whittle (1994, p. 138): "A tempting explanation for von Bezold's effect is simple averaging in a low spatial-frequency channel." This would be similar to the mixtures that result in pointillist paintings and half-tone printing using dot patterns. Burnham (1953) observed that assimilation seems to be facilitated by viewing displays with a lack of sharp focus, in peripheral vision, at greater distances, and with an overall focus.

VOICES OF DISSENT DURING THE CONTRAST PERIOD

In Germany, Gestalt theory had lost on the battlefield what it had won at the negotiating table. In America, it never really took root. But the Gestalt tradition continued, primarily in Italy, Scandinavia, and Japan.

Scandinavian Work

In Norway, Lie (1969a,b) argued for the multidimensional nature of lightness. In Finland, von Fieandt (1966, p. 217) criticized the dualism of traditional theories and suggested that "an interactional pattern of relations among elements could serve as immediate stimuli." Most importantly, the Swedish student of David Katz, Gunnar Johansson (1950, 1964), developed a brilliant theory of motion perception involving the visual analysis of motion stimuli into common and relative components. Not only would this serve as the model for Bergström's elegant theory of lightness (see Chapter 7), but it also heralded the logic of inverse optics brought to center stage during the computational revolution.

Italian Work

Musatti (1953), himself a student of Benussi, suggested that the light composing the retinal image was split into two components: a common component representing the illumination, and a differential component representing surface lightness. Although he called these *assimilation* and *contrast*, they anticipated, if somewhat vaguely, the common and relative components in Bergström's more recent decomposition model.

Metelli (1970) developed the classic theory of perceived transparency. The concept of seeing two colors at one point in the image was simply out of reach for the contrast theorists. More important, Metelli, like Johansson, was one of the first to apply the logic of inverse optics. Perceptual scission into multiple layers was treated as the exact inverse of color fusion (see also Fuchs, 1923). These multiple layers anticipated the intrinsic images of the later computational models.

Kanizsa (1954, 1979) studied the role of belongingness in simultaneous lightness contrast, the role of hard and soft edges on the mode of appearance of a surface, and the brightness effects produced by his now-famous subjective contour figures. He suggested that figural regions show more contrast than ground regions.

Japanese Work

Japanese work on lightness perception took a somewhat different course during the contrast period, not only maintaining continuity with the earlier Gestalt period, but also trying to bring both the questions and the answers of that period into contact with the newly dominant contrast theories. They repeatedly raised uncomfortable questions for the contrast approach. They tested whether constancy could be explained by contrast mechanisms. They measured perceived illumination along with lightness, exploring the possibility of an invariant relationship between the two.

In 1943 Hsia reported a lightness constancy experiment using a Katz-type light/shadow arrangement modified to exclude a contrast explanation. For his lighted and shadowed regions, he used two adjacent boxes. Each box contained a target disk, but the far end of each box was missing so that both target disks were seen against a common distant background of dark cloth. Thus, any contrast effects on the two disks were equal. This experiment is similar in logic to the countershaded backgrounds experiments discussed earlier, providing yet another way to test constancy while excluding differential contrast effects on the two targets. He obtained Thouless ratios in the range of 20% to 40%. Hsia also ruled out contrast effects from the sidewalls of the box by using both black and white sidewalls. Taubman (1945) later obtained higher constancy ratios in a replication of the Hsia experiment. In addition, Hsia reported conditions that confirmed Gelb's paradoxical experiment, and he reported better constancy for dark-gray targets.

Kozaki (1963, 1965) reported a series of experiments featuring haploscopic techniques in which both contrast and constancy were measured. Finding that test field area, inducing field area, and background reflectance influenced contrast in her experiments, but not constancy, she noted that these results are inconsistent with the claim by Leibowitz (1955) that contrast and constancy behave in correlated fashion. Her results also replicated Helson's (1943) earlier finding of higher degrees of constancy with lighter backgrounds, but importantly she noted that the key factor is not background reflectance per se, but

Lightness

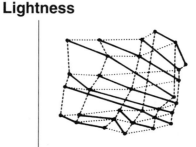

Perceived illumination

Figure 5.14. Data from Kozaki and Noguchi (1976) showing a roughly invariant relationship between lightness and perceived illumination. Reprinted with permission.

whether the targets are lighter or darker than the background. Incremental targets tend to produce luminance matching (low constancy), while decrements tend to produce ratio matching (high constancy). This was confirmed by Jacobsen and Gilchrist (see p. 102).

Oyama (1968) measured both lightness and perceived illumination in an experiment using Hsia's distant background method. He found that matched illumination correlates highly with actual illumination, and he found, as had Beck (1959, 1961), that matched illumination corresponds closely to highest luminance. But he argued that his results are inconsistent with the idea of an invariant relationship between lightness and perceived illumination because while illumination was matched accurately, lightness was not. He also concluded that his results are inconsistent with a contrast interpretation of constancy.

Noguchi and Masuda (1971) reported a failure to replicate the Jameson and Hurvich (1961) claim of diverging functions. They also measured perceived illumination, finding that it depends on highest luminance in the field. Their results also show that perceived illumination depends on largest area, but they did not comment on this. In a subsequent experiment Kozaki (1973) reported that perceived illumination depends on highest luminance and largest area.

Kozaki and Noguchi measured lightness and perceived illumination in two studies (Kozaki & Noguchi, 1976; Noguchi & Kozaki, 1985). In both studies they reported good illumination perception and strong support for the invariance hypothesis concerning lightness and perceived illumination. Figure 5.14 shows this invariance in their data. They found better constancy using white backgrounds (as opposed to black or gray) and better scission of lightness and perceived illumination.

Torii and Uemura (1965) varied test field and inducing field area in a brightness induction experiment similar to that of Heinemann. Their results show that several puzzling features of Heinemann's data can be attributed to the relative area of inducing and test fields. These relationships are discussed in detail in Chapter 9.

Cognitive Perspectives in the United States

One finds almost no Gestalt work on lightness in the United States during the contrast period. Ralph Evans (1948) wrote a book on color during the contrast period that contains excellent passages on the nomenclature and phenomenology of lightness (see also Evans, 1974). Coren (1969) presented a figure of a rabbit containing a gray target area that was reversible for figure and ground. Greater contrast was obtained for this area when it was seen as figure than when it was seen as ground. Coren also showed effects of depth on lightness using the Benary cross figure. Otherwise, dissent from the contrast viewpoint came mainly in the form of Helmholtzian theory and other high-level cognitive perspectives.

Perception of the Illumination

Beck (1972) distinguished cognitive theories from sensory theories on the basis of whether or not explicit reference is made to the perception of illumination. He contributed several experiments on illumination perception. From his results he argued against the idea, found in Koffka and Helmholtz, of an invariant relationship between lightness and perceived illumination. These claims are evaluated in Chapter 8.

Beck did not directly confront the contrast theories. Indeed, in his own theoretical formulation, he struck an ecumenical note, grafting Helmholtzian factors onto a Hering contrast model, with Gestalt grouping factors thrown in for good measure. According to Beck (1972, p. 92), "the perception of lightness involves two components: (a) sensory processes of transduction, enhancement, and abstraction, such as adaptation, contrast, and contour formation, that determine a central neural pattern in accordance with the peripheral luminance distribution; and (b) schemata for the perception of visual surfaces that encode a central neural pattern in terms of lightness differences, differences in surface orientation, or differences in surface illumination." The second of these is further broken down (p. 169): "Two factors influence the assimilation of sensory signals to schemata. First, there are organizational processes; second, there are cues to an altered illumination."

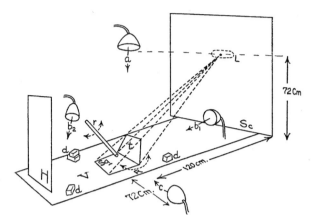

Figure 5.15. Arrangements used by Hochberg and Beck (1954) to test the role of depth in lightness. Reprinted with permission.

Depth and Lightness

The theories of Wallach, Jameson and Hurvich, and Cornsweet all carried the implication that lightness does not depend on depth perception. The luminance ratios of Wallach's ratio principle were ratios of adjacent regions of the retinal image; depth was irrelevant. But Wallach had no strong theoretical stake in this position; it was merely an empirical outcome for him. Curious to know whether his ratio principle depended on depth perception, Wallach had done an unpublished experiment in which the disk was brought toward the observer in stereoscopic space, but without changing the monocular retinal image. He found that this had no effect at all on perceived lightness and concluded that lightness was determined only by the retinal pattern.[10]

But the absence of a depth input into lightness perception was more central to the theories of Cornsweet and of Jameson and Hurvich. Lateral inhibitory interactions at the retina (or at least driven by the retinal pattern) know nothing of the distance that the stimulating light has traveled.

But what about the Mach bent card? There the retinal image is held constant and yet a pronounced lightness change occurs. Hochberg and Beck (1954) tested whether the ratio principle could account for effects of this kind. They mounted a trapezoidal piece of achromatic cardboard vertically in the center of a rectangular table, directly below a light bulb, as shown in Figure 5.15. Several blocks were placed haphazardly near the trapezoidal cardboard. The observer, standing behind a vertical screen at the end of the table, viewed this cardboard target by looking downward at a 45° angle. Various methods, including monocular and binocular viewing, were used to cause the target to appear to be either lying horizontally, coplanar with the tabletop, or vertically, at right angles to the tabletop. Logically the lighting on the target from the overhead bulb should appear much brighter when it appears to lie horizontally than when it appears to stand vertically. If this difference in illumination is taken into account, it should cause the horizontal target to appear darker than the vertical target, despite a constant luminance ratio between the target and its retinal surround.

Hochberg and Beck did not measure the size of the lightness change induced by the depth change, reporting only that their observers were unanimous in perceiving the target to be lighter (although they used the term *brighter*) when it appeared parallel to the direction of the illumination than when it appeared perpendicular to the illumination. They concluded, "The empiricist or 'inferential' position, disconcertingly enough, seems well able to explain the findings." But their forced-choice data indicated only that such an effect exists, leading some to conclude that the effect was quite weak (Cornsweet, 1970, p. 366). Indeed, the depth effect was not found when the blocks were removed.

Epstein (1961) carried out a study similar to the Hochberg and Beck experiment, except that Munsell matches were obtained, and he reported no effect. Beck (1965) later repeated the Hochberg and Beck experiments using Munsell matches. He obtained a significant change of lightness (0.5 of a Munsell step) in only one out of four conditions. In a separate experiment modeled more closely on the Mach bent card he was able to find a perceived lightness difference of 1.25 Munsell steps.[11] Flock and Freedberg (1970), in yet a further replication of Hochberg and Beck, obtained lightness differences ranging from 0.25 to 0.75 Munsell steps.

All of these experiments, inspired by Mach's bent card, manipulated depth by varying the perceived orientation of a target surface. An alternative method involves changing the apparent depth plane of a surface without altering its angle of orientation. Gogel and Mershon (1969; Mershon, 1972; Mershon & Gogel, 1970) were able to produce lightness changes of 0.6 to 1.25 Munsell steps by stereoscopically altering the perceived depth plane of surfaces. Using the familiar simultaneous lightness contrast pattern, Gibbs and Lawson (1974) separated the two gray squares in stereoscopic space from their black and white backgrounds, without altering the retinal image. They found that this produced no change at all in the strength of the contrast effect. Julesz (1971) had earlier demonstrated the same thing using his random-dot stereogram techniques.

Coren (1969) obtained systematic effects of depth on lightness using stereoscopic viewing of the Benary cross figure. The depth relations he simulated and the resulting lightness values are illustrated in Fig-

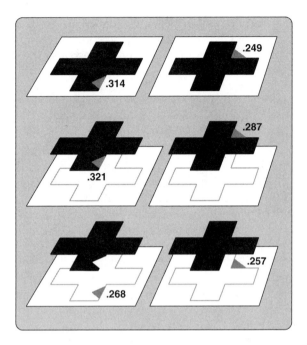

Figure 5.16. Schematic showing various 3D versions of the Benary effect tested by Coren (1969). The numbers represent relative lightness values for each configuration.

ure 5.16. Coren and Komoda (1973) obtained a weak lightness effect using a reversible figure (Fig. 5.17) and argued that the perceived spatial orientation provides cues to the illumination.

Wist and Susen (1973) separated the two halves of the Koffka/Benussi ring (see Fig. 4.2a) in depth while keeping them retinally adjacent. They found that the size of the illusion is inversely related to the degree of depth separation. Wist (1974) presented observers with a four-step luminance staircase that produced pronounced Mach bands when coplanar. But when the four steps were moved into separate depth planes, the Mach bands were greatly attenuated or absent, even though the retinal image remained the same.

In the context of Wallach's elegant ratio theory, with its apparent understandability at the physiological level, all these results were taken by many as damning with faint praise the role of depth perception in lightness perception. Cornsweet, whose model implied no role for depth on lightness, wrote (1970, p. 366), "The literature dealing with perceptual phenomena is preponderantly preoccupied with the effects of 'psychological' factors, while often completely neglecting analyses of physical conditions that account for 99.9% of the magnitude of the phenomena."

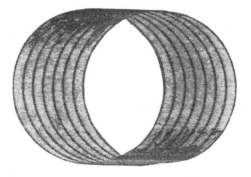

Figure 5.17. Reversible figure used by Coren and Komoda (1973) to produce a weak effect of depth on lightness. Reprinted with permission.

Memory Color

Many studies of memory color were reported during the contrast period (Baker & Mackintosh, 1955; Bolles, Hulicka & Hanley, 1959; Bruner, Postman & Rodrigues, 1951; Delk & Fillenbaum, 1964; Duncker, 1939; Fisher, Hull & Holtz 1955; Hanawalt & Post, 1942; Harper, 1952). These studies, which contain many methodological flaws, generally found weak effects of memory color.

The classic study was reported by Duncker (1939), who presented the profile of either a donkey or a leaf, cut from dull green paper and illuminated by reddish light. A simple disk presented under the same conditions appeared roughly gray. Observers were asked to match both the donkey and the leaf figures using a color wheel. In general the two figures required different matches. But Duncker obtained such a difference for only 6 out of his 11 observers, and he reported that even for those observers, the phenomenal difference was "little more than just distinctly noticeable." And he observed that such past experience effects require somewhat ambiguous conditions, "as long as the configurational factors inherent in the present stimulation are not too strong."

The above authors are agreed that memory colors are found under reduced viewing conditions, including poor illumination and colored illumination. Baker & Mackintosh (1955) covered their stimulus with translucent paper; Delk and Fillenbaum (1964) used waxed paper. Several studies (Bruner et al., 1951; Duncker, 1939) confirmed that memory color effects are not obtained when stimuli are compared side by side. In any case, careful scrutiny tends to eliminate the effects. Bruner et al. (1951) tested and supported the hypothesis that "The smaller the quantity of appropriate information, the greater the probability of an initial hypothesis being confirmed even if environmental events fail to agree with such hypotheses." Bolles et al. (1959) criticized earlier studies for not allowing an exact color match, and they presented evidence that when an exact match is allowed, memory color effects disappear.

The challenge for proponents of memory color is to show that memory color acts upon the percept itself rather than merely on the response made by the observer. This has not been demonstrated. Indeed, many of the features of the above experiments tend to facilitate response effects. These include the passage of time between exposure to test and comparison stimuli, and leading instructions to subjects.

Bolles et al. (1959) concluded fairly "memory colour effects are enhanced by conditions that maximize associative or memory factors and minimize the stimulus support for colour judgment." Overall the evidence for memory color is extremely weak. No evidence exists so far that cannot be attributed simply to response bias.

SUMMARY

With the collapse of science in Europe the spotlight shifted to the United States, where behaviorism was in firm control. Ushering in the contrast period, the behaviorists ignored Katz and the Gestaltists, and rehabilitated Hering. They sought to make lightness theory materialistic by emphasizing physiology, but they used impoverished stimuli that bear little resemblance to complex, real-world images. This period might be called the dark ages in lightness perception, only in part because the experiments were generally conducted in dark rooms.

Led by Heinemann, a group of contrast theorists studied the manner in which the brightness of a luminous region depends on the luminance, size, and proximity of another adjacent or surrounding region. In studying what they called brightness induction, they made no distinction between lightness and brightness. They interpreted their results as products of the mechanism of lateral inhibition, the recent discovery of which had offered the tantalizing prospect that a major constancy could be explained at the physiological level. Theories based on lateral inhibition and derived from Hering were published by Jameson and Hurvich and by Cornsweet. These contrast theories sought to explain not only simultaneous contrast, but also lightness constancy by lateral inhibition.

The elegant work of Helson and Wallach appeared at the outset of the contrast period. Although neither was a contrast theorist, the simplistic nature of their theories allowed their work to be easily assimilated to the contrast mold.

6

The Computational Period

The end of the 1960s marked a new era in lightness perception. The shift from a contrast approach to a computational approach was merely part of a larger change taking place in psychology, a change that ended five decades of behaviorist hegemony. But the cognitive revolution was itself a reflection of changes in the larger world. The Cold War and its need for smarter weapons spawned high levels of funding for artificial intelligence, machine vision, and computational models. Behaviorist objections that internal cognitive functioning, being essentially private, could not be studied scientifically were merely swept aside by the new emphasis on information processing. The encoding, storage, retrieval, and processing of information by computers put the lie to behaviorist claims that talk of cognitive processing is necessarily mystical.

LOOSENING THE GRIP OF PHYSIOLOGY

The shift from contrast thinking to computational thinking had a profound effect on theories of lightness. During the contrast period, theories had been driven by physiology, primarily in the form of lateral inhibition. Consistent with the behaviorist agenda, physiological validity was pursued as a means for making psychology materialistic. But the computer provided an alternative definition of materialism. Computers made of copper and silicon store, process, and retrieve information without a ghost in the machine. And the distinction between software and hardware liberated theorists from the shackles of having to tie each step in visual processing to a known physiological mechanism.

EMPHASIS ON VERIDICALITY

Contrast theorists wanted to claim that lightness perception had been explained at the physiological level, yet these theories seemed very remote from surface color perception in the real world. Machine vision replaced the constraints of physiological validity with a powerful new constraint: that of veridicality. Machine vision has no obligation to neural plausibility, nor does it have any obligation to explain the kinds of error found in human vision. It merely has to work—that is, it has to produce a realistic representation of the physical environment, one, for example, that could allow a robot to operate. Those working on human visual perception were influenced, indeed inspired, by the exciting work taking place in machine vision. Machine vision's emphasis on veridicality resonated with the traditional theme of constancy in psychology, bringing this issue back to the foreground.

Computational models began to speak of inverse optics. In the formation of the retinal image, reflectance and illuminance become entangled with one another according to the laws of projective optics. In principle, they can be disentangled by analytical processes that mirror those of projective optics. In this way reflectance (like other properties of the distal stimulus) is not merely computed, it is recovered (Arend, 1994, p. 169; Horn, 1986, p. 188; Marr, 1982, p. 250).[1]

Objective Reference Paramount

In our historical survey, we have tracked the uneasy tension between the subjective reference in lightness perception and the objective reference. Does the visual experience of lightness and/or brightness reflect the subjective state of the organism, or does it reflect the state of the physical environment? The influence of machine vision turned the spotlight decisively towards the objective reference in lightness, bringing renewed urgency to the question of the match between the perceptual output and the distal stimulus.

This was not the first time that important advances in visual perception resulted from an emphasis on veridicality. Helmholtz and Hering had earlier stirred up interest in vision by emphasizing the remarkable degree to which perceptual experience is faithful to objective reality, not to sensations. Later the Gestalt psychologists defined the constancy of visual perception despite change at the receptor level to be the central problem. The issue of veridicality, which had taken a back seat during the physiologically driven contrast era, was brought to the fore again by machine vision's inescapable concern with veridicality.

Input, Output, and Mediating Processes

Computational models seek to describe a set of operations that transform the input of a system into its output. Thus, we find at the outset of the computational period a reconsideration of both the input and the output of the lightness system. Traditionally, the input to lightness was assumed, with little explicit consideration, to consist of pointwise absolute luminance values.[2] Computational models of lightness redefined the input in terms of relative luminance at edges, consistent with Koffka's earlier approach. The output was also defined in a more sophisticated manner. Whereas contrast theories spoke merely of a unidimensional product called brightness, computational thinking defined the output as multi-dimensional, with at least two perceptual values at each point in the image, one for reflectance and one for illumination level. This richer conception of the output flowed not from phenomenal description, as in Katz's earlier work, but from the realism inherent in machine vision, and from the notion of disentanglement.

To transform the relative luminance values at input into the multiple dimensions of visual experience, various mediating processes were proposed, such as edge integration, edge classification, vector analysis, and selection based on simplicity.

EDGE CODING: RELATIVE LUMINANCE AS THE INPUT

The redefinition of the input as relative luminance rather than absolute luminance was driven in part by the computational distinction between energy and information and in part by empirical evidence, some old and some new. The relatively new findings came from two sources: work on retinal physiology, and work on stabilized retinal images.

Energy versus Information

The term *brightness*, like the broader term *sensation*, reflects confusion between the medium and the message, between energy and information. This distinction is fundamental to computational thinking. Light is treated as a form of energy that carries information about surface lightness in the form of variations in that light energy. Logically, it is the information that is encoded, not the energy. It doesn't matter whether my e-mail message travels over a fiberoptic cable or a more conventional copper cable; the message is the same.

In addition, the emphasis on relative luminance was driven by the realistic perspective of machine vision. To the extent that lightness perception is veridical, it must be based on relative luminance because there is simply no correlation between the absolute luminance of a surface and its reflectance.

Retinal Physiology

Traditionally, retinal photoreceptors had been thought of as photocells, with an output that corresponds to luminance. But by the late 1960s

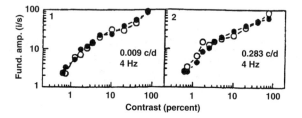

Figure 6.1. Retinal cells encode relative luminance (contrast), not absolute. The curves plot response versus contrast at two patial frequencies for an off-center Y-cell of cat. The open symbols are for a mean photopic retinal illuminance 100 times greater that the filled symbols (from Troy and Enroth-Cugell, 1993). Reprinted with permission.

evidence was accumulating that the output of the retina corresponds to luminance ratios, not luminance. Measurements on ganglion cells had shown that sensitivity at threshold is adjusted so that contrast sensitivity remains roughly constant across a wide range of light levels (Barlow & Levick, 1969; Cleland & Enroth-Cugell, 1970; Derrington & Lennie, 1982; Enroth-Cugell & Robson, 1966). Several writers (Barlow, 1972; Rushton, 1969; Shapley & Enroth-Cugell, 1984; Whittle & Challands, 1969) concluded that this is accomplished by retinal adaptation, and indeed that the purpose of adaptation is "to adjust the luminance *gain* of the retina in such a ways that the magnitude of ganglion cell responses is determined by contrast" (Troy & Enroth-Cugell, 1993, p. 383). Finally, Troy and Enroth-Cugell showed that the response of X- and Y-cells in the cat retina corresponds to luminance ratios (or contrast, as they put it). Data from their study, presented in Figure 6.1, shows that there is a monotonic relationship between the output of the cells and the luminance ratio in the image, and that the output for a given luminance ratio remains roughly constant over a wide range of illuminance.

Stabilized Images

To see a stationary environment, the eyes must be moving. Constant relative displacement between the retinal surface and the optic array appears to be a necessary condition for vision. This condition is normally satisfied by a variety of types of eye movement. In addition to the more familiar types called saccadic and smooth pursuit, there are fairly high-frequency tremors, between 30 and 150 per second (Yarbus, 1967), which continue even when the eye is carefully fixated. If the muscles that move the eye are totally paralyzed, the visual field quickly dissolves to nothing. Paralysis of this kind can be achieved with curare, but there is an unfortunate side effect: the subject also stops breathing. The experiment can be done using a mechanical breathing apparatus but is understandably not popular with human subjects committees.

Of course, displacement of the image across the retina can also be prevented without stopping eye movements if the image can be made to track the eye movements. Ironically, moving the image in this way is called stabilizing the image; the image is made stable relative to the retina. Several techniques exist for this purpose. When this is accomplished, the results are the same as if the eye[3] is paralyzed: vision ceases within a few seconds.

The fact that optimal vision requires some degree of constant movement of the retinal image was noted in an early paper by Adrian (1928). Subsequent research showed that objects stationary relative to the retina are not continuously visible (Ditchburn & Ginsborg, 1952; Riggs et al., 1953). In 1956 Yarbus reported that when objects are completely stabilized on the retina, they become completely invisible within a few seconds.

Pritchard, Heron, and Hebb (1960) described stabilized image experiments using a tiny mirror mounted on a contact lens worn by the observer. An image produced by a miniature projector is reflected off this mirror onto a screen in front of the observer so that each eye movement displaces the image on the screen. Several additional mirrors are inserted into the optic train to equate the angular displacement of the image with that of the eye movement. When the projector light is first switched on, the image is seen. But, Pritchard et al. reported, after a few seconds the image disappears, and shortly afterward Gestalt-like parts of the image reappear. Subsequent work (Barlow, 1963) has shown that this reappearance was due to incomplete stabilization. Given the mass of the lens, a certain amount of slippage occurs when the eye moves, so perfect stabilization is not achieved.

Stabilized images have also been produced using sophisticated eye trackers. Data from the eye tracker can be used either to displace a projected image by rotating mirrors inserted into the optical train or to displace a video image by computerized techniques. But neither of these methods is capable of achieving adequate stabilization.

In 1967 Yarbus published an extraordinary monograph describing an extensive series of stabilized image experiments. Yarbus used a variety of techniques, finding the most complete stabilization using a suction cup attached to the eye itself. He reported that images stabilized in this manner fade away without returning, a result he found even for a dazzling image produced by the filament of an incandescent light bulb mounted on the suction cup. Yarbus (1967, p. 63) concluded, "if a test field (of any size, color, or brightness) becomes and remains strictly constant and stationary relative to the retina, then all contours in the field will disappear after 1–3 seconds and will not reappear."

Stabilized images are most useful for theoretical purposes when only one part of the image is stabilized. Yarbus reported that when a stabilized target falls completely within the boundaries of a non-stabilized homogeneous region, the stabilized target takes on the color of its non-stabilized surround, just as with the blind spot. Krauskopf (1963) published quantitative data showing that when the boundary between a disk and a surrounding ring is stabilized, the observer sees merely a large homogeneous disk with the color of the ring, regardless of the initial colors of disk and ring.

Yarbus takes the radical position that retinal photoreceptors are stimulated only by a change in the light striking them, and he claims that homogeneous regions of ordinary complex images often consti-tute stabilized images:

> Very often, conditions of steady illumination arise on certain parts of the retina in the process of perception. Such conditions arise during the perception of large and uniform surfaces and during small movements of the eyes. If the illumination continues constant for more than three seconds, an empty field appears inside this uniform surface (or sur-faces). The empty field always takes the color of the surroundings and, in ordinary conditions, is never seen by the human subject. In other words, the visual system extrapolates the apparent color of the edges of the surface to its center. In accordance with electro-physiological find-ings, I suggest that in man constancy and immobility of the retinal im-age will banish impulses entering the optic nerve from the eye or will sharply reduce their number. In these circumstances, absence of signals from a certain part of the retina gives the visual system information that this area corresponds to a uniform surface, the color of which does not change and is equal to the color of its edges. (1967, p. 100)

Sensory Systems Encode Change

While Yarbus's conclusions have been challenged, they are consistent with much of what is known about sensory systems in general. Con-sider the sense of touch. On a cold day metal objects feel colder than wooden objects, even though their physical temperature is the same. This is because the temperature sense in the skin is not analogous to a thermometer. It registers the rate that heat leaves the body, which is af-ter all a crucial physiological indicator. Since metal is a much better conductor than wood, it draws heat from the body at a faster rate, and we experience this as coldness. When we leave the cold outdoors and walk into a warm room, the conductivity of the medium (air) is now held constant and the rate of heat loss signals a change in temperature, but the physiological response is not to the temperature per se.

An interesting example of this phenomenon can be seen in the game of baseball. A batter waiting for the ball to be pitched faces the pitcher but holds the bat up behind his or her head, out of sight. Typically the bat is not held still, but is oscillated back and forth before the swing. One might think that holding the bat perfectly still prior to the swing would allow maximum precision. But by oscillating the ball the batter gets a much better feel for the position of the bat, even though that position is changing. A stationary bat makes a partially stabilized tactile image on the surface of the hands.

Or take a familiar example from lovemaking. A vivid experience of one's partner's body requires relative displacement between the two adjacent bodies. Mere contact is not enough. But a fuller treatment of this topic lies beyond the scope of this book.

Further Evidence for Edge Coding

Wallach's Ratio Findings

Wallach's finding that lightness depends on luminance ratios does not prove that ratios are encoded directly, but it is certainly consistent with the idea. Wallach himself assumed that absolute luminance is encoded at the retina, with the ratio computed in the brain. But the work of Yarbus suggests a simpler account of Wallach's finding. Let's take a concrete example: two disks of different luminance (for example, 1 and 5, as shown in Fig. 5.1) but equal disk/annulus ratios (in this case, 1:4 and 5:20) may simply appear equal in gray because photoreceptors stimulated by the 1:4 boundary in one display produce the same neural signal as those stimulated by the 5:20 boundary in the other display.

Edge Code Constant under Changing Illumination

Edge coding, like Wallach's ratio principle, appears to offer a remarkably simple explanation for the traditional problem of lightness constancy: changes in the illumination leave the luminance ratio at the boundary of a target unchanged. Because the edge signal remains constant, so does target lightness. As we will see, encoding edges can explain only part of the constancy problem, but an important part.

Increments and Decrements

Paul Whittle (1994) has called attention to a fact, described more fully later in this chapter, that under reduced conditions, increments and decrements appear qualitatively different. This follows directly from edge coding because increments and decrements have edges of opposite sign.

Weber's Law

The work of Weber and Fechner (1860/1966) implies that the increment threshold for brightness (the weakest visible disk of light) depends not on any absolute luminance but on the luminance ratio at

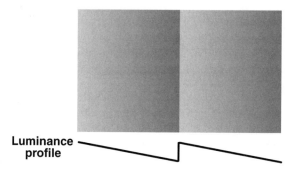

Luminance profile

Figure 6.2. Sawtooth version of the Craik-O'Brien effect. The two rectangles appear different in lightness even though they are identical.

the boundary of the disk, a result that is completely consistent with encoding of relative luminance. We now know that, especially under reduced conditions, this applies to suprathreshold stimuli as well (Fry & Alpern, 1953; Wallach, 1948; Whittle & Challands, 1969).

Craik-O'Brien Contours

The dependence of lightness on contours is also shown by a phenomenon reported by Craik (1966) and O'Brien (1958), and made famous by Cornsweet (1970). Two regions of equal luminance can be made to appear different in lightness when they are separated by an edge having a special cross-section that consists of a combination of one sharp change and one or two gradual changes. Except along the zone near the sharp border between them, the two rectangles have the same luminance level. But the luminance difference at this border seems to be extrapolated across the whole of each rectangle, causing them to appear different. This illusion is often attributed to a greater sensitivity to sharp changes, as compared to gradual. A variation of the Craik-O'Brien illusion using a sawtooth pattern is shown in Figure 6.2.

WHAT ABOUT ABSOLUTE LUMINANCE?

The encoding of relative luminance does not exclude the possibility that absolute luminance is encoded as well.

Is Absolute Luminance Needed?

Most published data on lightness are compatible with the encoding of relative luminance; very few strictly require access to absolute luminance. The claim by Jameson and Hurvich (1961) that lightness is intensity-dependent requires the encoding of absolute luminance, whether or not relative luminance is encoded. But the evidence reviewed in Chapter 5 leaves little empirical support for this claim.

However, several findings concerning human capabilities suggest a role for absolute luminance, namely: (1) failures of lightness constancy (2) perception of illumination, and (3) perception of brightness. All three of these phenomena can be seen in Wallach's experimental setup consisting of two disk/annulus displays, simultaneously visible in a dimly lit room (see Fig. 5.1).

Constancy Failures

First, when the observer sets the lightness of the two disks to perceptual equality, the luminance ratios of the two displays are almost but not quite identical. The error, however small, goes in the direction of a match based on absolute luminance. This error has sometimes been taken to mean that in addition to relative luminance, absolute luminance makes a small contribution to lightness. If so, absolute luminance must be available.[4]

Illumination Perception

Second, the disk/annulus display on the right (see Fig. 5.1) is seen as more brightly illuminated than the display on the left. Wallach attributed this to the higher absolute luminance values in the display on the right, believing that while lightness depends on relative luminance, our sense of the level of illumination depends on absolute luminance.

Brightness Perception

Third, the disk on the right is seen as brighter (more intense) than the disk on the left—that is, it appears to have a higher luminance, a fact that is closely related to but not identical to that of its higher perceived illumination.[5]

It is possible, in principle at least, to explain all three of these facts without absolute luminance. The scheme proposed by Kardos for explaining constancy failures (see p. 71) does not rely on absolute luminance but can be implemented by integrating the luminance ratios at multiple edges. Such an integration of edge ratios can also explain brightness perception and the perception of illumination differences within a scene. Perception of overall illumination level remains problematic in the absence of absolute luminance information. We will consider such possibilities in detail, but only after we first examine the evidence that absolute luminance information is actually available to the visual system.

Is Absolute Luminance Available?

There are two lines of inquiry that could in principle determine whether absolute luminance is available. One involves stabilized images and the other involves ganzfelds. We will review the evidence from each.

Stabilized Image Evidence

If Yarbus is correct that completely stabilized images fade, never to return, it implies that absolute luminance is not available. But this conclusion is difficult to test because perfect stabilization is difficult to achieve.

Among the best-stabilized images are those produced by the blood vessels in front of the retina. The shadows cast by these blood vessels are stabilized because the blood vessels are literally attached to the eye itself and move with it. These shadows are invisible to us and they never become visible under normal conditions.[6] Here we seem to have evidence that a well-stabilized image disappears completely, never to return. Some, however, find this argument unconvincing because such images are of low contrast and low spatial frequency. However, in one experiment, Yarbus (1967, p. 62) stabilized the retinal image of a dazzling incandescent filament, mounted very close to the eye by means of his suction cup. He reports that this image disappeared, never to return for the several-minute time span tested. This is certainly a high-contrast, focused image.

According to some reports (Rozhkova, 1982), binocular stabilized images do not disappear, and monocular stabilized images disappear only due to binocular rivalry: the stabilized image is suppressed by the homogeneous field in the other, covered, eye. This is not entirely logical. It is far from clear why the homogeneity of the darkened eye should win the rivalry, particularly when there is a patterned image in the other eye. The failure of disappearance under binocular conditions could be related to the multiplied difficulty of achieving the proper conditions. One would have to achieve perfect stabilization in both eyes simultaneously for a period of at least 3 seconds, and this is a very difficult requirement to meet.

It must be acknowledged that no one has yet succeeded in making binocular, high-contrast, sharp-edged images disappear completely. Arend and Timberlake (1986) concluded from a very careful set of experiments that the required degree of stabilization had not been achieved and indeed may not be possible. The eye is remarkably sensitive to any changes in stimulation, however tiny. They note, for example, that blood pulsing through the retina is sufficient to destabilize sharp images. Thus, it might not be possible to perform an ultimate test using stabilized images. Arend and Timberlake (1986, p. 241) summarized the situation by writing, "it is not possible with current techniques to reject the hypothesis that all psychophysical detection of visual patterns requires temporal modulation of the retinal image. The simplest model therefore requires only dynamic psychophysical detector mechanisms."

Ganzfeld Experiments

According to the radical view of edge coding, vision should cease if all edges and gradients are eliminated. Removal of all spatial gradients results in what is known as a ganzfeld or homogeneous visual field. We know that lightness perception is absent under ganzfeld conditions. But the question here is whether all sense of light intensity is lost. As Koffka (1935, p. 120) wrote, "Perfect homogeneity would be both temporal and spatial. Would it be too bold to say that if all, not only visual, stimulation were completely homogeneous, there would be no perceptual organization at all?" Barlow and Verillo (1976) tested brightness perception of brief flashes in a ganzfeld, over an eight-log unit range of luminance, using magnitude estimation. They found that the subjective estimates of brightness increased monotonically with luminance and concluded (p. 1294) that "the visual system is capable of performing as a photometer." This experiment does not provide the proper test, however, because temporal stimulation was not homogeneous. It is likely that the responses made by Barlow and Verrillo's subjects were based on the luminance transient at the onset of each trial rather than on the absolute luminance of the ganzfeld itself. This transient information must be eliminated.

Measuring brightness in the absence of both spatial and temporal gradients presents quite a problem. My student Jim Schubert and I (Schubert & Gilchrist, 1992) decided to attack the problem according to the following plan. An observer would be presented with a ganzfeld of medium intensity (9.1 foot-Lambert), which would then, by random selection, either increase or decrease at a very slow rate, well below the threshold for sensing the change itself. After a long period of time (1 hour) and the accumulation of a large change of intensity (3 log units), the observer would be asked for a forced-choice as to whether the ganzfeld was now brighter or darker than at the outset of the trial.

Intuitively there should be no difficulty discriminating merely the direction of a three-log unit change of luminance, but there were both theoretical and empirical reasons to expect that the discrimination might not be possible. Cornsweet (1970, p. 371) has made the claim that for completely homogeneous visual fields (ganzfelds), "all such fields look alike so long as they are above the cone intensity threshold." Anstis (1967) showed that when the luminance of a ganzfeld is ramped in a sawtooth fashion (a gradual increase alternating with a sharp drop), observers report the luminance as constantly stepping down, even though it remains constant on average.

On the other hand, if absolute luminance is not encoded, what is the basis for our sense of the overall illumination level? Illumination variations within a scene (AC illumination) require only luminance relationships, but overall or DC illumination is another matter. Several writers (Evans, 1948, p. 171; Katz, 1935, p. 85; Woodworth, 1938, p. 617) have suggested that overall illumination level is based on the increasing visibility of edges at higher illumination levels. To test this possibility we wanted to test detection of absolute level using a patterned image as well as a ganzfeld.

To eliminate all spatial gradients, we created probably the most homogeneous ganzfeld ever. Previous ganzfeld studies (Bolanowski & Doty, 1987; Gibson & Waddell, 1952; Hochberg, et al., 1951) had used a section of a table tennis ball, fitted to the contour surrounding the eye. We had two concerns about this method. First, the surface of the ball may not be sufficiently homogeneous, and second, it is not an easy matter to achieve homogeneous illumination of all parts of the ball. For one thing, the nose gets in the way. We opted to have a pair of special translucent contact lenses constructed. Binocular viewing was used because Bolanowski and Doty (1987) have shown that binocular ganzfelds do not show "blankout" as do monocular ganzfelds. Not only would the surface of the lens likely be more homogeneous in thickness than the surface of the ball, but since the lens would be located immediately in front of the pupil, greater uniformity would result both from the fact that the operative area (namely the area of the pupil) would be much smaller than the area of the table tennis ball, and because there is much less possibility of focusing on any remaining inhomogeneities.

Of course blinking could not be allowed, and so the eyelids were taped open. To keep the eyeball moist during trials as long as 1 hour, the table tennis ball method was used in addition to the contact lens. This not only trapped moist air inside the ball, but also served to further diffuse the light.

To guarantee the absence of visible temporal gradients, we used a rate of change well below threshold levels that had been previously determined. Yarbus (1967, p. 65) measured the minimum change in the luminance of a stabilized target necessary to make it visible. For a wide range of initial luminance values, he found the threshold rate of change to be 30% per second. Waygood (1969) found approximately a 7% per second threshold rate of change for seeing a luminance change in a ganzfeld. Arend and Timberlake (1987, p. 407) claim that even a luminance change of 0.45% per second can produce substantial changes in contrast threshold. We chose a rate of 0.19% per second.

At this rate, ganzfeld luminance changes by three log units over the course of a 1-hour trial.

Controlling the luminance change presented certain problems as well. We needed a method that would allow a very slow continuous change of luminance, at a known and constant rate, logarithmically, over a large range, potentially six log units. Nor did we want any chromatic changes in the light. Most conventional methods of varying luminance violate one or more of these requirements. Schubert suggested a method that at first seemed outlandish but proved to meet our demanding requirements. We called it the water method. The observer lay on his back with his head just below a rectangular, glass-bottomed aquarium partially filled with dye-containing water. A 1,500-watt quartz halogen source was mounted immediately above the aquarium tank. The luminance of the ganzfeld was changed by slowly increasing or decreasing the level of liquid in the tank. The method is analogous to stacking or unstacking filters. Consequently, it has the fortuitous property that as the level of liquid changes in linear fashion, the illumination of the ganzfeld changes in logarithmic fashion. To a first approximation, the rate of change was determined by the concentration of dye in the water. This rate was then fine-tuned by adjusting a valve controlling the flow of liquid into or out of the tank. The apparatus is illustrated in Figure 6.3.

Besides probing for brightness perception in the absence of all visible gradients, we wanted to test the hypothesis that the presence of edges in the visual field facilitates the detection of the overall luminance of the field. We therefore included a yoked control condition in which the luminance of a patterned image changed in exactly the same way as the luminance of the ganzfeld. The face of the ganzfeld observer served as the patterned stimulus for a control observer, who sat near the prone ganzfeld observer. After 1 hour of change, an experimenter obtained a forced-choice (darker or brighter) from each observer. Hand signals from the control observer and foot signals from the ganzfeld observer ensured that neither observer was aware of the other's judgments.

Our pilot results showed that both observers were correct at the end of each 1-hour trial. These results failed to support the radical hypothesis that absolute luminance information is simply not available.

But how accurate were the brightness percepts? Theoretically, brightness perception could be wildly inaccurate under these conditions and still allow correct forced-choice judgments, since these concerned only direction, not magnitude. Some measure of magnitude was needed for determining how well brightness can be seen without visible gradients and for comparing perception of the patterned field with that of the homogeneous field.

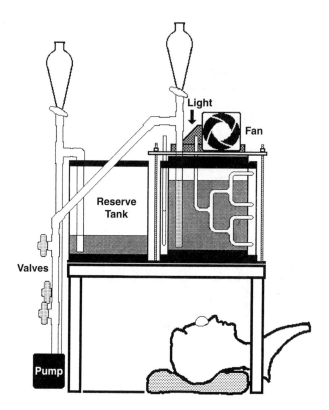

Figure 6.3. Apparatus used by Schubert and Gilchrist (1992) to test brightness perception in the absence of all visible spatial and temporal luminance differences.

Our design did not lend itself to a determination of how much change of luminance was perceived relative to the actual change. To get some measure of this, we took forced-choice judgments from both observers at 1-minute intervals as well as a binary confidence judgment. We defined the threshold as the first trial on which the observer reported confidence that was also correct as to the direction of the change in luminance and followed by 10 successive correct reports of direction of change. The yoked ganzfeld and patterned-image observers served together in each of 10 trials. Direction of change on each trial was random without replacement.

Thresholds for detecting the direction of change were 9.7 minutes for the homogeneous field condition and 11.4 minutes for the patterned field condition. At these times the luminance had changed by a factor of 2.7 in the homogeneous condition and 3.3 in the patterned condition.

Because these data are based on a single subject in each condition (10 trials, five decrements and five increments), they must be viewed with some caution. But they do agree fairly well with ganzfeld results reported by Knau (2000), who also measured the time elapsed and the total luminance change before an observer can report the direction of change. Using three different rates of change, 4%, 0.4%, and 0.04% per second, they found, at all three rates, that observers detected the direction of change after an accumulated luminance change of 0.24 log units. This is about half as much change as was required in our experiment.

As with the hands of a clock, we may speak of two kinds of threshold. We can test how fast a clock hand must be moving for the observer to see the movement itself (as opposed to seeing that movement had occurred). But even when the movement is too slow to see, we can test the threshold for seeing the direction in which the hand has moved. But the appropriate units of measurement are different. The first of these thresholds is measured as a rate of change, but the second is no doubt measured in terms of distance. Likewise, our results, together with those of Knau and Spillman, suggest that while the threshold for seeing a change in luminance is measured as a rate of change, at rates below this threshold, the observer can detect the direction of change when the amount of change reaches a factor of about three. Of course, this ability appears to imply some encoding of absolute luminance information, however crude.

The lack of a difference between the patterned field and the homogeneous field is quite interesting. If valid, it renders moot any schemes of how edges in the field could, through increased visibility or whatever, contribute to a determination of absolute luminance. It also implies that DC luminance and AC luminance are orthogonal— that overall luminance is determined independently of luminance variations within the image.

The apparent independence of absolute and relative luminance brings to mind an analogous distinction from motion. Wallach has described separate subject-relative and object-relative motion systems, the first used to sense the change of angular direction of a single spot of light (in a totally dark environment) and the second used to sense the change of angular distance between two simultaneously visible spots.

Does our approximate 10-minute threshold imply good detection of absolute luminance level? One might regard the glass as half empty or half full. 3:1 is a large jump in luminance; it is almost as great as the difference between middle gray and white. Of course, this change takes place over a time period of 10 minutes. Yet how much change would be required to judge the direction of change in the lightness of an object, even if the change took 10 minutes? We turned to questions of this sort.

Is Relative Luminance Derived from Absolute?

To explore the relationship between absolute and relative luminance information and to test whether relative luminance can be derived from absolute luminance, we carried out a further experiment, using the apparatus shown in Figure 9.6, in which a 4.8° disk was added to the center of our ganzfeld. Either the disk or the ganzfeld background was made to change (either increase or decrease) in luminance at the same rate that had been used in the first experiment.

We measured the amount of time needed for the observer to reliably report whether the luminance difference between the disk and the ganzfeld was increasing or decreasing, using criteria analogous to those we had used for an increase or decrease in the luminance of the simple ganzfeld. We found that observers could detect the direction of change in relative luminance at an average of 1.022 minutes. This is 10 times faster than our observers were able to detect the direction of change of absolute luminance in the simple ganzfeld.

These results imply that relative luminance must be encoded directly. If relative luminance were derived from absolute luminance, relative luminance could not be determined 10 times faster than absolute luminance.

Is Absolute Luminance Derived from Relative?

In our normal habits of thought, we assume that relative luminance is derived from absolute luminance values. Yet logically, absolute luminance (or its functional equivalent) could just as well be derived from relative luminance. Thus, we can identify three possible coding schemes that could provide the combination of absolute and relative luminance information seemingly required to account for overall visual performance.

1. Both absolute and relative luminances are encoded at the retina.
2. Absolute luminance values are encoded and luminance ratios are derived from these.
3. Relative luminance is encoded and "absolute" luminance levels are reconstructed using higher-order luminance relations.

The Whittle Experiments

It is disappointing that neither stabilized image experiments nor ganzfeld experiments have produced a clear decision on whether absolute luminance is encoded. Perhaps the strongest evidence to suggest that absolute luminance is not encoded comes from an unlikely source: a study of center-surround stimuli by Whittle and his associates using a unique haploscopic method. Because the results are rich in implications for several issues, I will describe the work in general terms before returning to its bearing of the encoding of absolute luminance.

Whittle and Challands

Unlike the disk/annulus displays of Wallach, the center/surround stimuli used by Whittle and Challands (1969) were created by super-imposing a square of light on a larger disk of light. Whittle and Challands refer to this large disk as a pedestal (it can also be called a veiling luminance) because the light in the square is added to the light of the large disk where they overlap. Two such displays were created and the observer was required to match the brightness of the square target in one display with that of the other—that is, the observer attempted to equate the targets for absolute luminance. One target/pedestal pair was seen by one eye while the other target/pedestal pair was seen by the other eye, as in other haploscopic presentations. But, in a crucial twist, the two pedestals were binocularly superimposed. Thus, in the binocular view, the two targets appeared side by side on a single large disk (Fig. 6.4a). The observer's task was to adjust the luminance of one target square to match the other in brightness. Using this method, observers found the task very easy. The usual ambiguities of asymmetric matching were absent and variability was remarkably low.

Whittle and Challand's results are shown in Figure 6.4b. The curves are equal-brightness curves. They show, for different levels of background luminance (Log ΔI) in one eye, the luminance increment (Log DI) in that same eye required to maintain brightness equality with the increment in the other eye. The lowest curve is the brightness increment threshold.

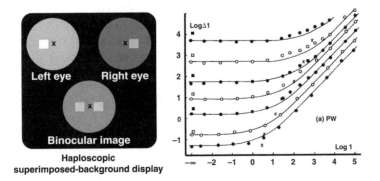

Figure 6.4. Stimulus schematic and equal brightness curves from Whittle and Challands (1969). Each curve shows setting of a target luminance (Log DI) necessary to maintain a constant brightness as the luminance of the background (Log I) is increased. Reprinted with permission.

The data are neatly fitted by threshold-versus-intensity curves (Wyszecki & Styles, 1967). Each curve consists of two branches, a horizontal branch and a branch with slope=1. The unity slope is equivalent to Weber's law and to Wallach's ratio principle. It implies that two targets appear equally bright when the center/surround luminance ratios are equal, or alternatively when the target/background edge ratios are equal. The horizontal branch of the curve represents very low light levels.

We will discuss several conclusions that appear to follow from these data. (1) Suprathreshold targets behave just like the increment threshold. (2) Superimposing a light pedestal on a target darkens the brightness of the target, even though more light is added to the target region. (3) Increments and decrements are highly distinct visually, especially in very simple displays. (4) Remote ratios are obtained by edge integration, not by comparing absolute luminance values. All of these conclusions are consistent with edge coding.

Wallach Meets Weber

Whittle and Challands (1969) had been concerned about the relationship between threshold and suprathreshold targets. Weber's early work on just-noticeable differences had implied that superimposing a pedestal on a just barely visible target of light pushes the target below threshold. This result is consistent with the edge-coding proposal and with results for suprathreshold targets obtained by Wallach (1948) and by Fry and Alpern (1953). But the simple and attractive idea that all inputs, both threshold and suprathreshold, are equally attenuated by a superimposed pedestal had been undermined by the findings of Stevens and Diamond (1965). But in the Whittle and Challands data, the threshold curve (the lowest) is parallel to the other curves representing suprathreshold targets. This suggests in strong terms that both the increment threshold and the brightness of suprathreshold targets are determined by the luminance ratio at the target border.

A New Primitive. It had long been assumed that the absolute luminance at each point in the image constitutes the primitive value for lightness. The work of Whittle and Challands suggests that the primitive values are actually differences or ratios. Thus, if there is any validity to the concept of a brightness sensation, it must be a sensation based on a relationship, not on a level of intensity. This strange concept is called contrast-brightness by Whittle (1994, p. 109): "It can be thought of as a bipolar dimension with zero at zero contrast . . . Positive values correspond to the brightness of increments and negative ones to the darkness or lightness of decrements, separated by a zero of invisibility."

Adding a Pedestal of Light

What happens to the brightness of a spot-in-a-void (Land & McCann's 1971 term for a homogeneous disk of light within a totally dark visual field) when a larger homogeneous disk of light is superimposed on it? If luminance values are encoded, adding the larger disk should increase the brightness of the smaller disk because it adds to its luminance (Schouten & Ornstein, 1939). But the concept of edge coding implies the opposite result. Superimposing the larger disk must actually darken the appearance of the smaller disk because adding the same amount to both sides of the target edge reduces the target/surround ratio. This is what Fry and Alpern (1953) found, and the Whittle and Challands results confirm this counterintuitive prediction.

Increments versus Decrements

The Whittle and Challands results have drawn our attention to an important theme that went unrecognized until surprisingly late: the astonishing separation between increments and decrements. If brightness depends on edge coding, then increments, which have positive contrast, should always be brighter than decrements, which have negative contrast. This is just what Whittle and Challands found: every increment appears brighter than any decrement, regardless of absolute luminance! The simplicity of the Whittle and Challands method suggests that the increment/decrement split occurs at a very early stage, such as encoding.

The total separation of increments and decrements found by Whittle and Challands can be attributed to their haploscopic method, for reasons described in the following point. But even in more conventional experiments, when matching is done between two center/surround patterns presented side by side and simultaneously visible, the separation is remarkably strong. Hess and Pretori's subjects did match increments to decrements, but, as Jacobsen and Gilchrist (1988a) later showed, that is only because the Hess and Pretori method forced them to, as described in Chapter 5. When this flaw is removed, increments are never matched with decrements. Wallach (1948) collected data only for decrements. Heinemann's (1955) data show some matching of increments to decrements, but very few under the conditions most similar to those of Whittle and Challands (background behind both test field and comparison field). In an experiment by Arend and Spehar (1993b) in which test and comparison targets were presented on backgrounds of different reflectance, observers matched increments to decrements when the backgrounds differed strongly in reflectance, but they would tolerate a deviation of up to 0.2 log units from a correct match to avoid matching decrements and increments. When subjects are given the standard textbook version of simultaneous contrast and asked to adjust the luminance of one target so as to match the other, they will match an increment to a decrement but, as Burgh and Grindley (1962) showed, they grumble about the difficulty of the task.

The increment/decrement watershed shows up in another way as well. Displays composed of decrements tend strongly to produce ratio matching, while those composed of increments tend strongly to produce luminance matching. Alan Jacobsen and I obtained this pattern of results both in our replication of Jameson and Hurvich (Jacobsen & Gilchrist, 1988b), graphed in Figure 5.6, and our replication of Hess and Pretori (Jacobsen & Gilchrist, 1988a), graphed in Figure 5.8. We concluded (see Chapter 5) that in simple displays, Wallach's ratio principle applies to all decrements, regardless of the illumination range, but it ceases to apply at the increment/decrement boundary.

Whittle (1994) has suggested that increments suggest light sources while decrements suggest gray papers. This construction fits neatly with the empirical fact that increments elicit luminance matches while decrements elicit ratio matches. But one must be careful about applying this simple rule to complex images. It is probably true, even in complex images, that decrements never appear self-luminous.[7] But increments can look like paper, as does the gray square on the black background in the simultaneous lightness contrast display.

References to the increment/decrement distinction are rare prior to the late 1960s, surely a reflection of the general assumption during that period of absolute luminance encoding. The distinction came hand in hand with the recognition that relative luminance is encoded.

It should be noted that the concepts of increments and decrements do not refer merely to luminance relations. They are higher-order concepts that combine intensity relations with spatial relations. An increment is a higher luminance *surrounded by* a lower luminance. Todorović (1997) calls them "geophotometrical" concepts.

Edge Integration as a Surrogate for Absolute Luminance

Earlier we discussed whether those perceptual qualities such as brightness that appear to depend on absolute luminance are based on the direct encoding of absolute luminance or based on the integration of two or more luminance ratios at borders. The Whittle and Challands findings appear to provide a clear answer to this question.

The key point is that the haploscopic method used by Whittle and Challands prevents the visual system from integrating the edge signals that lie between the two targets. In a side-by-side presentation, such as Wallach's experiment, there are two comparisons relevant to target appearance. Each target luminance can be compared with its surrounding (annulus) luminance, as in Wallach's proposal. But in addition, the luminance of one target can be compared with the luminance of the other target by integrating all the edge ratios that lie between the two.

In the Whittle and Challands experiment, only one of these comparisons can be made. A target can be compared only with its immediate surround. Alternatively, we might say that the targets can be compared with each other through edge-integration in the binocular view, but this would amount to the same thing. The luminance of one target cannot be correctly compared with the luminance of the other target because a critical link in the chain is missing. The ratios at the borders of the backgrounds (pedestals) are not available because they are binocularly superimposed. As a result, two of the three phenomena listed earlier as suggesting a role of absolute luminance are eliminated in the Whittle and Challands experiment: (1) the target of higher luminance no longer appears brighter, and (2) it no longer appears to be more brightly illuminated.

This implies that the brighter appearance of one of the targets in Wallach's experiment, even after the two targets are set to appear equal in lightness, is not based on the direct encoding of absolute luminance. If it were, the same thing should happen in the Whittle and Challands experiment. Even though the two targets appear equal due to their equal edge ratios, the fact that one target has a higher luminance than the other target should be visually experienced in some way, but it is not. The perceptual duality present in Wallach's experiment is absent in the Whittle and Challands experiment. That's why the task is so easy to perform.

This also explains why observers never match increments and decrements in the Whittle and Challands experiments, while they sometimes do in other experiments. Observers match increments to decrements only when integrated ratio information is available. Even when this information is available, however, increments will not be matched to decrements when the two targets are strongly segregated into separate frames of reference.

WHAT EDGE CODING DOES NOT EXPLAIN

The concept of edge coding is not merely a single idea. There are several conceptions of what it means. As I will use the term, it means that the retinal image is initially encoded strictly in terms of relative luminance (not absolute), measured as luminance ratios (not differences), from neural signals arising at borders (not homogeneous regions). At times I will refer to the luminance difference at an edge, and here I mean a difference of log values, which is equivalent to a ratio.

From the computational perspective, edge coding is viewed as roughly equivalent to a scaled-down version of Wallach's ratio principle. During the contrast era, Wallach's ratio principle was treated as an expression of lateral inhibition, which directly determines lightness. Computational theorists have viewed lateral inhibition not as a key process in the achievement of constancy, but merely as a mechanism that implements the initial encoding of luminance ratios. Wallach's finding is treated as psychophysical evidence of this encoding. Although luminance ratios are considered to be the foundation upon which the lightness computation is built, they serve only as the starting point.

Evidence on the crucial role of borders has led many writers to conclude that surface color and lightness are determined simply by the change in color and luminance at the border. Indeed, both Yarbus and Wallach have talked in this way. But this simple formula will not work, for several important reasons.

The Filling-in Problem

If the lightness and perceived color of a surface come from neural signals arising at its border, some additional process, like filling-in, is required to account for the color that appears to cover the entire surface. Some writers, including Ratliff (1972), have suggested that this may be a will-o'-the-wisp problem: once the edge information is encoded, the problem is solved. Others, like Todorović (1987, 1998), have argued from the assumption of isomorphism that there must be a neural representation for the object color, and thus the filling-in problem must be confronted. Arend and Goldstein (1987a) have demonstrated that various gradient illusions seem to require an active filling-in process. Whittle (1994, p. 105) argues that the need for a filling-in solution is unavoidable in the case of a homogeneous target on a non-homogeneous background. Dennett (1991) has argued that the blind spot is not actively filled in, but Ramachandran (1992) has presented convincing evidence to the contrary.

More importantly, what value is used to fill in? Yarbus speaks of the color of an edge, but an edge has no color. Under the edge-coding assumption, as I have defined it above, there is no absolute luminance or color information contained in the edge signal; there is only relative information. Thus, it makes no sense to say that the color of a surface comes from the change at its edge. The edge signal provides information about the luminance difference (in log values). To derive a lightness (or color) value, differences must somehow be transformed into levels. This is an important aspect of the anchoring problem, described in more detail later.

Illuminance Edges

Many of the edges within the retinal image are illuminance edges (not reflectance edges), such as the borders of spotlights or shadows. These edges do not determine the surface lightness of the regions they bound, although they may determine the perceived illumination of those regions.

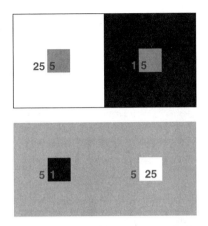

Figure 6.5. Upper and lower targets have equal local ratios, showing that the targets in simultaneous contrast have local ratios as different as black and white, yet the contrast effect is much weaker.

Remote Luminance Ratios

Edge coding by itself, like Wallach's simple principle, puts lightness far too much at the mercy of local ratios. To compute lightness veridically, the visual system also needs information about remote ratios. Consider the problem of lightness computation in complex scenes. Ideally, the visual system would like to compare the luminance of a target surface to that of a white surface in the same illumination. But under a local ratio theory, this could occur only if the target happened by chance to be adjacent to a white. But, as Land and McCann (1971, p. 1) have observed, lightness could be easily determined if the eye could "insert a comparison standard next to the object which it is regarding." The visual system could create the equivalent of such a standard by computing luminance ratios between spatially remote patches. Notice that this problem would not be solved by absolute luminance values, even if they were available. What is required is the relationship between target luminance and the luminance of some standard gray shade, such as white.

The standard textbook example of simultaneous contrast (see Fig. 1.2) also shows the need for remote ratios. A local ratio theory, or edge theory, certainly predicts such an illusion, but it predicts an illusion far in excess of its actual value. Literally, the targets should appear as different as black and white, for the simple reason that the local luminance ratios for the two gray squares are as different from each other as those of a white square and a black square on a common background, as illustrated in Figure 6.5. But the target squares appear almost equal. This suggests that certain remote ratios are playing a part in the computation: either the ratio between each target and the white background, or the ratio between the two targets.

BACKGROUND INDEPENDENCE: A NEW CONSTANCY

As evidence for edge coding accumulated, a new constancy problem began to come into focus. Whenever we move around in the environment or when the object or its background moves, the luminance ratio at the border of the object changes. And the change in the luminance ratio at the border is directly proportional to the change in the luminance of the background itself. And yet such movements produce little or no change in object lightness. Paul Whittle (1994b, p. 128) has described this kind of constancy in a graphic way: "An object moved over different backgrounds does not seem to change much in lightness. To get a good look at a sample of cloth, you may pick it up and take it to a good light, but you don't worry about what background is behind it. It's as though the background doesn't matter. It is not that there is no simultaneous contrast effect, if you look for it; just that it is amazingly small. If brightness were always contrast brightness such objects would flash on and off all the time as they changed from being increments to decrements. They do not."

We have here a new constancy. Ross and Pessoa (2000) use the term *background-independent constancy* to refer to the degree to which object lightness remains constant under these conditions, and to distinguish it from the traditional constancy problem, which they call *illumination-independent constancy*. I have adopted their usage.

Despite the clear evidence of background-independent constancy in our direct phenomenal experience, and given the striking parallel between this form of constancy and the traditional illumination-independent form, its recognition came remarkably late in the study of lightness perception. This can be seen as another symptom of the photometer metaphor. From this perspective, closely tied to the doctrine of local determination, lightness constancy despite a change of illumination was surprising (and thus interesting) because target luminance changes, whereas lightness constancy despite a change of background was not surprising because target luminance remains constant. But from the assumption of edge coding, background-independent lightness jumps out as surprising.

It was precisely those who emphasized the initial encoding of luminance ratios (Arend & Spehar, 1993; Brenner & Cornelissen, 1991; Gilchrist et al., 1983; Walraven, 1976; Whittle & Challands, 1969) for whom the alarm bells began to ring. Earlier Koffka (1931, p. 250), who had emphasized relative luminance, made indirect references to this problem. As Brenner and Cornelissen (1991, p. 72) noted, "If the perceived color of the central surface depends on the ratio between the signals from the two surfaces for each type of receptor, changing the illumination will hardly affect the perceived color. However, moving the central surface in front of a background with different reflectance properties will change the perceived color considerably. This does occur to some extent (chromatic induction), but objects generally do not change color as they are moved around." Land and McCann (1970, p. 3) noted that when a colored paper embedded in a colored Mondrian is moved to a new location "where it is surrounded by new sets of colored rectangles, the color sensation does not change significantly."

The fact that background-independent constancy is not complete also worked against its recognition. Thus, target lightness is always influenced, to some degree, by a change in background, even if these changes are not commensurate. Consider the familiar simultaneous lightness contrast pattern. Even though the two gray targets do not appear black and white, as their local edge ratios should warrant, neither do they appear identical to each other. Contrast theorists cited this difference in appearance as support for their position, neglecting the quantitative shortfall in the difference.

Yet illumination-independent constancy is not complete either. Target lightness is always influenced to some degree by a change of illumination. Perhaps it was assumed that background-independent constancy was much weaker than illumination-independent constancy. But no one had measured the two under comparable conditions.

Illumination Independence and Background Independence: Constancy Strength Compared

The classic paradigm for investigating illumination-independent lightness constancy is that of Katz (see Fig. 3.1). Targets are placed in front of backgrounds that differ in illumination level, and the observer is asked to adjust the luminance of one of the targets to make a lightness match. If background-independent constancy were to be tested in an analogous fashion, one would place the two targets on equally illuminated backgrounds that differed in reflectance. The crucial difference between these two arrangements is whether the backgrounds appear to differ in illumination level or in reflectance level.

Practically speaking, this question can be reduced to that of whether the border between backgrounds appears as an illumination edge or as a reflectance edge. Thus, if a simple way is found to control the appearance of the edge dividing the two backgrounds, illumination independence and background independence can be compared under the same geometric and photometric conditions. This kind of experiment affords another comparison as well, a comparison between the strength of constancy and that of contrast, to use the traditional language. Gelb (1929, p. 666) had objected that the reduction of constancy to contrast was unfair because the two phenomena had been tested under different conditions. The edge-substitution method allows a fair comparison of contrast and constancy effects, in addition to the comparison between the two types of constancy.

An Edge-Substitution Experiment

A sharp-edged shadow was cast across the left half of a large white rectangle (Gilchrist, 1988). The luminance ratio (30.5:1) between the shadowed and the non-shadowed halves of the white paper was equivalent to that between white and black paper. In the center of the left, shadowed side of the white paper, a light gray (reflectance=59%) square of paper was placed. This was the standard target. In the center of the illuminated half of the white paper, a grid of 16 Munsell chips was placed for matching purposes.

In the illumination-edge condition (in that paper called the "constancy condition") the observer saw the entire scene, including the shadow-caster and the location where the shadow fell on the wall and ceiling. It was clear to the observer in this condition that the border between the two backgrounds was an illumination border. Thus, this condition was very similar to many other constancy experiments using the side-by-side technique (Gilchrist, Delman & Jacobsen, 1983; Helson, 1943; Henneman, 1935; Katz, 1935). Observers selected the shade of gray from the grid that appeared most similar in lightness to the target on the shadowed side. In this condition the results were close to ratio-matching—that is, the luminance ratio between the mean matching chip and the background surrounding the grid was almost equal to the luminance ratio between the target square and its background.

In the reflectance-edge condition (called the contrast condition) we made the border between backgrounds appear to be a reflectance border simply by placing a large reduction screen midway between the observer and the display.[8] The screen contained a 5.7° by 9.7° rectangular aperture through which the observer saw the target, the grid, and as much as possible of the left and right backgrounds, without seeing their borders. In this condition the shadowed half of the white paper appeared convincingly as near black in surface color. In this case the average match from the grid nearly matched the target in luminance (rather than luminance ratio), showing the same degree of contrast effect (0.9 Munsell units) found in other studies of this kind (Burgh & Grindley, 1962). The results are shown in Figure 6.6.

To compare these two conditions, it is necessary to identify ideal performance in each. When backgrounds differ in illumination level, targets seen against them should be matched for target/background luminance ratio. But when backgrounds differ in reflectance, targets

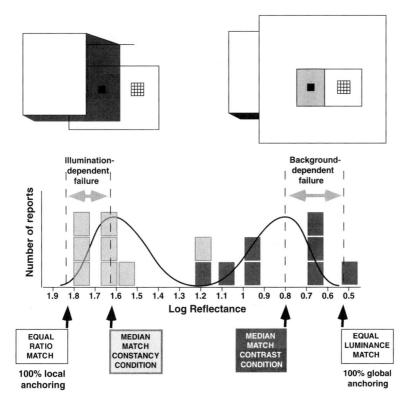

Figure 6.6. Stimulus displays (top) and data obtained in edge-substitution experiment (Gilchrist, 1988). The median matches show that the failure of illumination-independent constancy was equal in magnitude to the failure of background-independent constancy.

seen against them should be matched for luminance. Thus, in the illumination-edge condition an ideal match would be a Munsell 8.5, whereas in the reflectance-edge condition it would have been a match of Munsell 2.1. The obtained matches in these two cases were 7.5 and 3.0, respectively. Thus, in the first case the obtained match fell 1.0 Munsell units short of perfect illumination-independent constancy, and in the second case it fell 0.9 Munsell units short of background-independent constancy.

Bruno (1994) reported a parametric edge-substitution experiment modeled after mine, but using a CRT stimulus. He found substantial background-independent constancy, though less symmetry between the two types of constancy.

Arend and Spehar (1993b) reported a very systematic study of background-independent constancy. The test and comparison stimuli, presented on a CRT screen, each consisted of a square center and surround that was in turn surrounded by a Mondrian border. They found almost perfect constancy for incremental targets. For decrements, constancy was poorer but still substantial.[9]

Better results would be obtained under real-world conditions. Logvinenko, Kane, and Ross (2002) have recently claimed that the simultaneous contrast produced by Adelson's picture of a wall of blocks (Adelson, 1993) completely disappears for a 3D model of the display, even when the two images are close to identical.

Taken as a whole, these studies confirm that background-independent constancy must be considered a major form of constancy, alongside illumination-independent constancy. Rossi, Rittenhouse, and Paradiso (1996) have shown that a significant proportion of cells in primary visual cortex are sensitive to the luminance ratio between a target surface and its surround. This kind of cell could help explain lightness constancy under a change of illumination because local luminance ratios are preserved under such a change. But it would contradict lightness constancy under a change of background: here the local luminance ratio changes even though lightness is constant.

Constancy-versus-Contrast Revisited

These results further undermine the claim that (illumination-independent) lightness constancy can be reduced to contrast. Traditionally, both contrast and constancy effects have been measured as departures from luminance matching.[10] Using this criterion, the constancy effect obtained in my experiment is about six times as large as the contrast effect, in Munsell units. Arend and Spehar (1993a) found a constancy effect 4.5 times as large as the contrast effect, in Munsell units. These results suggest that illumination-independent constancy cannot be realistically reduced to contrast. This reinforces the same conclusion already drawn from the countershading experiments discussed in Chapter 3.[11]

But we can go further. Far from being mutually reducible, contrast and (illumination-independent) constancy become opposites when background-independent constancy and illumination-independent constancy are viewed as parallel phenomena. Contrast is a failure of background-independent constancy.

Challenges to Veridicality

The general interest in veridicality, ushered in by the computational period, led to the recognition of several "environmental challenges to constancy," in Arend's (1994) apt expression. The constancy problem had been drawn in far too narrow a way. Changes in illumination level represent only one of many challenges to veridicality. We have seen how constancy is challenged by a change in the background of an object. The superimposition of a veiling luminance represents another, in this case neglected, challenge to constancy. Indeed, the various challenges are not even confined to the environmental domain. There are also challenges that reside within the organism, such as an inappropriate level of adaptation, as had been noted by Katz (1935, p. 434). But it was the challenge posed by background changes that led the way to a more sophisticated view of the constancy problem.

EDGE INTEGRATION: COMPUTING REMOTE RATIOS

In background-independent constancy, changing the edge ratio of a target produces little or no change in its lightness. We now discuss the converse situation: a change in the lightness of a target with no change in its edge ratio.

Yarbus: Lightness Change with no Change in Local Ratio

Although Yarbus (1967) has said that the color of a surface is equal to the color of its edges, he reports an experiment (p. 96) demonstrating that lightness does not depend merely on the local edge ratio. A disk, divided into a black half and a white half, was presented against a red background, as shown in Figure 6.7. The black and white disk could be stabilized, leaving the appearance of a homogeneous red field. Then two small red disks were added, one on the black hemidisk and one on the white. This produced the normal contrast effect as long as the black and white disk was visible. But when the black

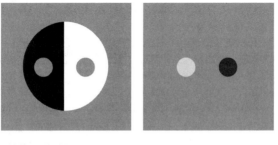

Before stabilization   After stabilization

Figure 6.7. (Left) Stimulus tested by Yarbus (1967). (Right) Approximate appearance of the display after black white hemi-disks were retinally stabilized. (Gray regions shown here were red in the Yarbus study.)

and white disk disappeared through stabilization, the two small red disks, which remained visible and now appeared on a homogeneous red background, appeared very different from each other in lightness. The small red disk placed on the black region appeared "less saturated in color and much lighter" than the red background, while the other disk appeared "darker and more saturated."

Here we find that the lightness of the target changes even though the edge information at its border does not change, and that border remains visible. Krauskopf had shown that stabilizing the border of a target region changes its perceived color even though there is no change in the retinal image. But in the Yarbus experiment, the color (here the lightness) of a target region can be changed by stabilizing an edge that does not border the target region. This implies that the lightness of the red disk depends not only on the luminance ratio between the disk and its immediate background, but also upon the luminance ratio at the edge of the background. Thus, the information at one edge is somehow integrated with the information at the next edge.

Land and McCann's Sequential Ratio Product

In 1971 Land and McCann published a concrete model of edge integration:

> Given a procedure for determining the ratio of reflectances between adjacent areas, the next problem is to obtain the ratio of reflectances between any two widely separated areas in an entire scene. We solve the problem in the following way: Find the ratio of luminances at the edge between a first and a second area, and multiply this by the ratio of luminances of the edge between the second and a third area. This product of sequential ratios approaches the ratio of reflectances between the first and third areas, regardless of the distribution of illumination. Similarly, we can obtain the ratio of reflectances of any two areas in an image, however remote they are from each other, by multiplying the ratios at all the boundaries between the starting area and the remote area.

Land and McCann illustrated this using a display (Fig. 6.8) in which an achromatic Mondrian was illuminated by a fluorescent tube placed along its bottom edge, casting an illumination gradient across the Mondrian. The position of the tube was adjusted so that a near-black patch (r=12%) at the bottom border of the Mondrian had the same luminance at its center as a near-white patch (r=75%) at the top. The veridical appearance of these patches provides a good example of lightness constancy. In addition to computing remote ratios, Land and McCann argued that their algorithm also separates reflectance edges from illuminance edges, a claim evaluated later.

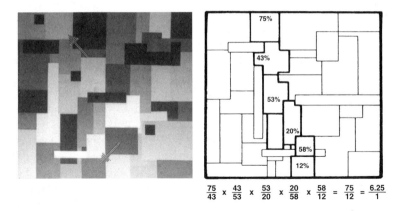

$$\frac{75}{43} \times \frac{43}{53} \times \frac{53}{20} \times \frac{20}{58} \times \frac{58}{12} = \frac{75}{12} = \frac{6.25}{1}$$

Figure 6.8. (Left) Photograph of Land and McCann's (1971) Mondrian pattern illuminated by a fluorescent bulb placed along the bottom edge. Targets indicated by arrows have identical luminance. (Right) Schematic shows that an integration of the chain of edge ratios falling between the two targets can be used to calculate the reflectance ratio between the targets.

Arend, Buehler, and Lockhead

At about the same time, Arend, Buehler, and Lockhead (1971) offered clear empirical data that demonstrated qualitatively an effect of edge integration. In a simple but critical experiment, two adjacent background regions of equal luminance were made to appear different in lightness by dividing them with a Craik-O'Brien contour (discussed on p. 132). Equal increments were then placed in the centers of each of these backgrounds, creating the luminance profile shown in Figure 6.9. The question is how the incremental targets would appear. There were three possibilities:

1. The targets could appear equal. They have equal luminances and they stand on backgrounds of equal luminance, and their local edge ratios are equal.

Figure 6.9. Luminance profile of stimulus tested by Arend, Buehler, and Lockhead (1971). The incremental target on the left appears lighter than the target on the right.

2. The target on the background that appeared brighter could appear darker than the target on the darker-appearing background. This would be the outcome if contrast were a function of the phenomenal brightness of the background as well as its physical brightness.
3. The target on the background that appeared brighter could appear brighter. This is what happened in fact. It has been replicated by Knill and Kersten (1991), and it makes good sense. Given that the luminance ratio ratios of the two targets are detected to be equal, it means that one target is perceived to be lighter than its background by the same degree as the other target is perceived to be lighter than its background. Any difference in the backgrounds must in turn show up in the targets. This is edge integration.

Arend and his colleagues performed this experiment as a test between two distinct interpretations of the edge determination concept (1971, p. 367):

> According to the first hypothesis, which we call the absolute information hypothesis, the perceived colors are directly determined from the spectral compositions and intensities of the light, modified only by local contrast and adaptation effects. The resulting colors are extrapolated from the contours to the enclosed areas where there is no temporal change in the stimulus, and therefore no change information.
>
> According to the second hypothesis, which we call the difference hypothesis, the contour responses provide change information only. When a point on the retina is traversed by a contour, the temporal change on that point is simply the difference between the spectral compositions and illuminances of the light on the two sides of the contour. The difference information allows only the specification of the relative colors on the two sides of the contour. The resulting perception is then extrapolated to the enclosed unchanging areas. Only the relation between the various parts of the visual field, the relative color distributions, is specified by this hypothesis. How this distribution is located in a color space is not specified.

These results imply that edge information is strictly relative and must be combined with other edge information. Arend (1973) later published a more formal account of the complementary processes of the retinal differentiation that produces edges and their subsequent integration. Yet we must assume that all edges in such a chain contain only relative information, and this underscores the importance of the anchoring problem that will be addressed in some detail later.

Koffka

The experiment by Arend et al closely parallels the countershaded backgrounds experiment of Koffka and Harrower (1932) that was described in Chapter 3. In both experiments, targets of equal luminance were placed on adjacent backgrounds that, while equal to each other in luminance, appeared very different in lightness. Although Koffka and Harrower used countershaded backgrounds to satisfy the background conditions, they obtained the same qualitative results as Arend et al.

Using the terms S_1 and S_2 for the backgrounds (surrounds) and I_1 and I_2 for the targets (infields), Koffka (1935, p. 248) frames the question much as I have done above, asking:

> Will I_1 look equal to I_2, or if it does not, in which direction will they differ from each other? One way of arguing would be this: Since S_1 looks whiter than S_2, I_1 should, by contrast, look blacker than I_2. This prediction neglects the fact that the gradient S_1-I_1, expressed by the ratio S_1/I_1, is exactly the same as the gradient S_2-I_2, S_2/I_2, since physically $S_1=S_2$ and $I_1=I_2$. If then the appearance of the inlying fields depends upon the gradient which connects them with the surrounding field, I_1 should look whiter than I_2. That this must be so will appear when we consider the case where the two inlying fields are physically almost of the same intensity as the two outlying fields so that they look almost equal to them. Then I_1, looking almost equal to S_1, must look white and I_2 correspondingly black.

Notice that this analysis lays out the basic elements of edge integration, which is not entirely surprising since his concept of edge determination was always that which Arend et al. refer to as the "difference information hypothesis." On the following page Koffka writes, "we explain the appearance of one object by the gradient of stimulation which connects it with another and by the appearance of the latter," which in turn depends "on conditions beyond" these two. This is another instance in which Koffka was ahead of his time.

Assimilation versus Edge Integration

Inspired by certain parallels between edge integration and the older concept of assimilation, several writers (Shapley & Reid, 1985; Shevell, Holliday & Whittle, 1992; Whittle, 1994) have made a renewed attempt to present contrast and assimilation as opponent processes. In doing so, they alter the concept of assimilation in two important ways. First, assimilation and edge integration are collapsed together. Second, while contrast depends on the luminance of the surrounding or inducing region, assimilation is held to depend on the brightness of that region, not its luminance.

Shapley and Reid (1985) use Figure 6.10 to illustrate the convergence of edge integration and assimilation. According to their analysis, the two annuli, which are physically equal, appear different by contrast with the black and white backgrounds. The central targets, on the other hand, have equal local contrast ratios and thus, by con-

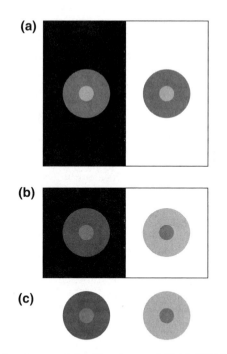

Figure 6.10. (a) Stimulus used by Shapley and Reid (1985). Reprinted with permission. (b) Integration of concentric edges makes the target on the right appear darker. But local contrast also makes the right target appear darker, as seen when outer backgrounds are removed, as in (c). Left and right targets are always equal in luminance.

trast alone, should appear identical. Shapley and Reid argue that they appear different because each assimilates to the lightness of its surrounding annulus. They suggest that this is equivalent to the linkage of each target to its remote surround by integrating the target boundary with the outer annulus boundary. Shapley and Reid use this stimulus arrangement to separately manipulate contrast and assimilation, concluding that assimilation antagonizes only about 50% of the effects of contrast.

Edge Integration Is Not Assimilation

To me, the identification of edge integration with assimilation does not seem correct. Assimilation is, by definition, opposite to contrast, but edge integration is not, in general. Whittle speaks of edge integration as "counteracting contrast-coding," but this is not the same as "opposing" contrast. Edge integration does not have a consistent direction of effect on a surface, as assimilation does; it is highly dependent on context.

Figure 6.10b shows an example in which both contrast and edge integration work in the same direction. The small disks are equal in luminance. Integration, as Shapley talks about it (that is, integrating the two concentric edges), makes the right-hand disk appear darker than the left-hand disk, just as in the figure above it. But contrast also makes the right-hand disk appear darker, as can be seen when the black and white backgrounds are removed, shown below in Figure 6.10c.

Rather than opposing contrast, edge integration should be thought of as "contrast at a distance." What is important about integration is not that it opposes contrast (which it does do sometimes) but that it puts the target surface into relationship with a larger context (not merely the local surround). Assimilation, on the other hand, is more local.

It is not even clear what edge integration predicts in Figure 6.10a. Shapley and Reid claim it predicts that the target on the right will appear darker than the target on the left. But an integration of all the edges that occur between the two targets predicts that they should appear identical. The result depends on how many edges are integrated.

DEPTH PERCEPTION AND LIGHTNESS

An important component in the shift from contrast to computational thinking was the issue of how lightness is related to depth perception. In view of the abundant evidence that has accumulated on the role of depth in lightness, it seems strange to realize that for about 30 years following World War II, the consensus was that depth does not play an important role.

Rock's Question

I offer the following behind-the-scenes account in the hope that it will prove useful to younger investigators. I was a student in graduate school at that time and my mentor, Irvin Rock, gave me a problem that became the basis of my doctoral thesis. Recalling the Mach demonstration, Rock pointed to a corner that protruded into his office. Although one side of the corner received much brighter illumination than the other side, both sides appeared as roughly the same surface color. But when the two sides were made to appear coplanar, by viewing the corner through a hole, the shadowed side now appeared as a much darker shade of surface gray. He asked if that example didn't seem to imply the taking into account of illumination. The demonstration is very compelling and the implication seemed inescapable: because nothing changes except the perceived spatial arrangement, the change of surface lightness must be caused by the change in apparent depth.

Rock himself had been a student of Wallach, and though he liked Wallach's work on the ratio principle very much, his theoretical perspective had been slowly shifting in a Helmholtzian direction.[12] I myself

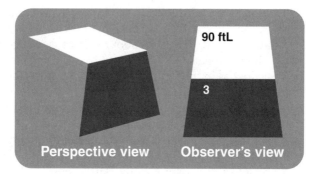

Figure 6.11. Stimulus tested in the first part of Gilchrist's (1980) experiments on depth and lightness. The target surfaces formed a dihedral angle (left) but appeared coplanar when viewed monocularly (right). The perceived depth arrangement (coplanar versus dihedral) had no effect on lightness.

had been quite taken by Wallach's elegant ratio theory. To me the Helmholtzian account seemed vague. Yet, as Rock pointed out, his corner example, and the closely related Mach bent-card illusion, seemed to contradict Wallach's ratio theory and to support the inferential theory. Though Rock and I did not interpret my subsequent findings in the same way, I have always been indebted to him for launching my work on lightness perception by giving me such a great problem.

I immediately set about to replicate this example under laboratory conditions. Wanting the observers to perceive the two depth organizations as unambiguously as possible, I borrowed the Hochberg and Beck (1954) technique involving monocular and binocular viewing of a trapezoidal target. I created the display illustrated in Figure 6.11. The stimulus consisted of a dihedral angle joining the trapezoidal surface to a square surface of equal reflectance. Viewed monocularly the two surfaces appeared coplanar; binocularly they appeared at right angles. I mounted a light bulb above the display, out of sight of the observer, so that the upper square surface was directly illuminated and the lower trapezoidal surface was shadowed. This produced an illumination ratio of 30-to-1, chosen to equal that of a white surface next to a black surface under the same illumination. Separate groups of observers viewed the display either monocularly or binocularly and indicated perceived lightness by making matches from a separately illuminated Munsell chart.

The results showed absolutely no effect of perceived spatial arrangement. In both conditions the upper square appeared white and the lower appeared black, regardless of whether the actual surfaces were both white, both black, or both gray. On the face of it this was consistent with the relative lack of effect found in so many previous studies (see Chapter 5). But because of the compelling nature of the Mach

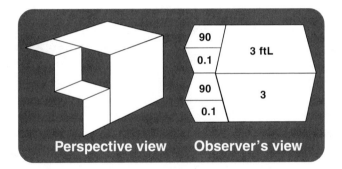

Figure 6.12. Pilot stimulus used by Gilchrist to produce depth effects on lightness. Large upper patch (3 ftL) appeared almost black and large lower patch appeared almost white, even though their retinal neighbors were identical.

bent-card illusion I was unwilling to accept that verdict. I speculated that perhaps observers were more ready to report differences than similarities, as if the common surface color of the upper and lower targets was too obvious to mention. To test this possibility I used a black paper for the upper target and a white for the lower. Now the two targets were exactly equal in luminance. I expected that now surely the observers would report the dramatic difference in surface color between the two targets. But to my surprise, observers now reported the two targets to be equal in surface lightness: both middle gray.

This implied, of course, that the two targets were not perceived to be differently illuminated, and so I began to introduce cues to the illumination. I allowed the light bulb to be seen by the observer and I placed a number of objects near the stimulus in order to reveal the direction of the lighting. Nothing worked. The two targets continued to be seen as equal in lightness.

Here was a strange situation: a black surface and a white surface were seen as the same shade of gray even though their location in different planes was obvious. I recognized that this configuration contained both the Gelb effect and the Kardos illusion. And thus I knew that the true colors (or similar colors) would be revealed if a real white paper was placed adjacent (and coplanar) to the upper, black target and a real black paper were placed adjacent to the lower, white target. But this would make a different context for the two targets, even in the retinal image. Could the crucial information be added to the display such that it would affect the retinal context of the two targets equally? The answer was to add two white papers, both with a horizontal orientation. Each would be retinally adjacent to one of the two targets, but only one would appear to lie in the same plane. Two black papers would be added in an analogous fashion. This technique resulted in the display shown in Figure 6.12.

Now observers perceived the upper target as near black and the lower target as near white, even though the targets had equal luminance and equal retinal surrounds! Also, the lightness of the lower target changed dramatically when its spatial orientation was changed through monocular viewing.

Coplanar Ratio Principle

This display suggested that luminance ratios between retinally adjacent but non-coplanar papers play little or no role in lightness. Coplanar ratios, however, are very effective. I articulated a coplanar ratio principle: lightness depends on luminance ratios between adjacent retinal regions that appear to be coplanar. I then set out to test this hypothesis in a series of experiments using separate planes that were either perpendicular to each other or parallel to each other.

Parallel Depth Planes

The coplanar ratio principle is demonstrated most simply by the experiment illustrated in Figure 6.13. The observer looked through a pinhole and saw a dimly illuminated near plane containing a doorway through which was seen a brightly illuminated far plane. Three paper squares were seen within the doorway. One was a black square mounted on the near wall but protruding slightly into the doorway. Another was a white square clearly located[13] on the far, brightly illuminated wall. The target square was actually a white square located in the dim illumination of the near plane, but it could be made to appear in either the near plane or the far plane by manipulating the interposition cues (Ittleson & Kilpatrick, 1951). The two resulting stimulus configurations are shown in Figure 6.13. In the near condition, eight subjects saw the target as almost white (average Munsell match 9.0), while in the far condition eight other subjects saw the target as almost black (average Munsell match 3.5).

Because there was no important difference between the retinal images produced in these two conditions, the substantial difference in perceived lightness could only be due to depth. One could say that the difference in target lightness is due to the difference in perceived illumination of the two planes. But there is a simpler formula. Lightness can be said to depend only on ratios between perceptually coplanar regions.

A Critical Test

In the experiments illustrated in Figure 6.13 the coplanar ratio hypothesis predicted a change in lightness when models based on the retinal image (Cornsweet, 1970; Jameson & Hurvich, 1964; Wallach,

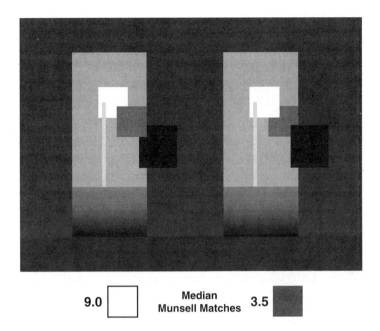

9.0 ☐   Median
Munsell Matches **3.5** ■

Figure 6.13. Stimulus tested in the second part of Gilchrist's (1980) experiments on depth and lightness. When the target appeared to lie in the near plane (left) it appeared almost white, but when it appeared to lie in the far plane (right) it appeared almost black, despite no significant change in the retinal image. Note that the 2167:1 luminance range cannot be conveyed by ink on paper.

1948) would predict none. But it is possible to create a test in which the coplanar ratio hypothesis predicts a difference in one direction while the retinal ratio models predict a difference in the opposite direction. Such a test is shown in Figure 6.14.

A large horizontal white square was attached along one edge to a vertical black square to form a dihedral angle. A smaller trapezoidal black surface coplanar with the white square was attached to the corner so that it extended into midair like a diving board. A similar but white trapezoidal surface was attached to the black square so that it extended vertically above the black square. The two trapezoidal surfaces served as the targets. As in the earlier experiments, the primary light source was mounted directly above the white square (though unseen by the observer) so that the white square and the black target were directly illuminated. The black square and the white target in the vertical plane were indirectly illuminated only by light reflected off a black screen in front of the display. The amount of reflected light was adjusted by varying the size of a piece of white paper attached

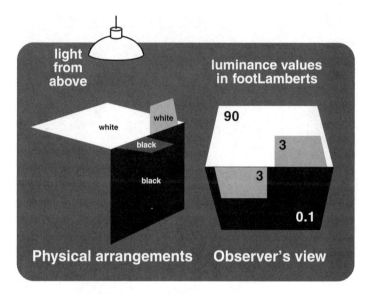

Figure 6.14. Stimulus display tested in the second part of Gilchrist's (1980) experiments on depth and lightness. Monocular observers, who perceived targets as coplanar with their backgrounds, saw lower target as almost white (Munsell 7.75) and upper target as almost black (Munsell 3.75). Binocular observers, who perceived targets as protruding (as at left), saw the opposite lightness values (lower target 3.0, upper target 8.0). Note that the 900:1 luminance range cannot be conveyed by ink on paper.

to this screen until the luminance of the vertical white target was exactly equal to the luminance of the horizontal black target. Thus, the illumination ratio between the horizontal plane and the vertical plane was equal to the reflectance ratio between white and black, namely 30-to-1. This also meant that the luminance of the white background square was 900 times greater than that of the black background square.

The observer was separated from the display by the vertical black screen and viewed the display from a 45° angle by looking through either one or two small apertures in the screen. When the display was viewed monocularly, the targets appeared coplanar with their retinal backgrounds, as shown in Figure 6.14b. When viewed binocularly, the targets appeared in their true spatial positions. Separate groups of observers served in the binocular and the monocular conditions. They indicated perceived lightness by selecting matches from a Munsell chart located above the viewing apertures.

Consider first the theoretical predictions for the binocular condition. One may not be able to derive specific Munsell values from the retinal ratio models, but they would certainly have to predict that the upper target will be seen as darker than the lower target, because although the targets are equal in luminance, the upper target is surrounded on three sides by a very bright region, the lower target by a very dark region. The coplanar ratio principle, on the other hand, would predict not only that the upper target will be seen as lighter than the lower target, but perhaps that it will be seen as white and the lower target as black.

In fact, the upper target was seen as near white and the lower target as near black. Under monocular viewing, which created a reversal of the perceived coplanar neighbors, the results were reversed as well. Not only did these results favor the coplanar ratio principle over the retinal ratio models decisively, but also they seemed to leave no room for a retinal ratio component. For example, imagine there is a lightening or darkening effect that is dependent solely upon retinal adjacency and independent of coplanar ratios. In the binocular condition this retinal effect would work against the coplanar ratio effect, whereas in the binocular condition the retinal effect and the coplanar ratio effect would work in the same direction. Thus, the difference between the two targets should be greater in the monocular condition than in the binocular condition. This did not occur.

Implications

I made the following conclusions based on my results.

Lightness Depends Strongly on Depth

I believe my results established that lightness clearly depends on depth perception. The results obtained from earlier tests had been mixed, and those results showing an effect had not shown a large effect. In my experiments, depth alone moved values almost from one end of the lightness scale to the other, with no serious change in the retinal image.

Lightness Is Computed in the Brain, Not the Eye

My results challenged the prevailing assumption that computed lightness values are already encoded in the neural signals leaving the retina. If lightness depends on depth, and depth is computed in the brain (not in the eye), then so is lightness.

Consequences for Theory

These results are most troubling for lightness theories based on lateral inhibition, which, unlike Wallach's ratio theory, are tied to the retinal pattern in a fundamental way. If a change in perceived spatial arrangement can change the apparent lightness of a surface from black to white, without any change in the retinal image, it simply cannot be argued that lateral interactions that occur prior to depth processing are decisive. Wallach's response to my work was quite favorable, and perhaps this is not surprising. His retinal definition of ratios had been driven by an empirical result he obtained; it had never been central to his thinking.

As for the Helmholtzian perspective, it could be argued, as it is in relation to the Gelb effect, that the role of the neighboring coplanar surface is to reveal the conditions of illumination. But in the absence of coplanar luminance ratios, all other cues to the illumination failed. I found no effect of orientation of the target with respect to the light source. And traditional illumination cues like visibility of the light source and the presence of both cast and attached shadows were ineffective.

Irvin Rock himself (1977) has offered an interpretation of those results within a Helmholtzian framework, arguing that the visual system assumes that coplanar (and adjacent) surfaces receive the same amount of illumination. It cannot make that assumption for noncoplanar surfaces. The novel feature of this account is that the visual system does not have to take into account the *actual amount* of illumination; it only has to take into account that two or more surfaces have the *same level* of illumination. This important difference adds a great deal of plausibility to the concept of taking-into-account.

Percept/Percept Coupling

In my first report (Gilchrist, 1977), I argued that my results showed that depth precedes lightness in visual processing. Noting that in my parallel planes experiments, depth was determined by interposition, while in my dihedral angle experiments, depth was determined by stereopsis, I argued that it is perceived depth itself that causes the lightness percept, an instance of percept/percept coupling (Epstein, 1982). I retracted that claim in a subsequent report (Gilchrist, 1980, p. 534) in favor of the idea that lightness and depth are part of a single parsing that cannot be separated into stages.

Conditions for Producing Depth Effects

Little or no effect of depth on lightness had been reported in a series of previous papers (see Chapter 5). In a paper entitled, "When does perceived lightness depend on perceived spatial arrangement?" (Gilchrist, 1980, p. 533), I noted, "The conditions that produced these large spatial position effects differed in two important ways from conditions that have failed to produce such effects. The first ... concerns the need for separate ratios in the two conditions." In other words, the target needs a different coplanar neighbor in each plane. "A second difference ... concerns the range of luminances within the display. In each of the displays that produced a spatial position effect, the visual system is presented with at least a 900:1 range of luminances. In previous experiments . . . the luminance range did not exceed 30:1, a value such that, in all cases, it could have been created with pigments alone, using a single level of illumination."

Lightness, Brightness, and Perceived Illumination

The dependence of perceived lightness on perceived depth is not the full story. As I wrote about the tabs experiment (Gilchrist, 1980, p. 532):

> First, the observers reported that the two tabs appeared to have similar intensities even though one appeared black and one appeared white. For example, one observer commented that the tabs would have the same intensity in a photograph of the display. Second, observers reported that the horizontal surfaces appeared more brightly illuminated than the vertical surfaces. For a complete description of the targets, one would have to say that one target appeared as a dimly illuminated white, while the other appeared as a brightly illuminated black.

When a surface in one of my experiments appeared to move from one plane into another, the change in its surface lightness was always accompanied by an opposite (and probably equal) change in its perceived level of illumination, as in Koffka's invariance theorem. Although brightness doesn't change, the way that brightness is parsed into illumination and surface reflectance components does.

Subsequent Work

Schirillo, Reeves, and Arend (1990) measured both lightness and brightness in a replication and extension of my parallel planes experiment (Gilchrist, 1977, 1980), introducing three important changes from the method I had used. First, their stimuli were presented on a high luminance range[14] CRT screen. Second, their depth appearance was created by stereo cues, using a mirror stereoscope. Third, and perhaps most substantive, their observers made brightness matches in addition to lightness matches. Those results confirm that brightness, unlike lightness, does *not* depend on perceived depth arrangement.

Regarding lightness matches, Schirillo, Reeves, and Arend obtained the same qualitative pattern of results that I had obtained. However, the difference they obtained between the lightness of the target in the far plane and the lightness of the target in the near plane was approximately half as great as the difference I had obtained. Schirillo et al. used the same observers for both the near condition and the far condition, whereas I used separate groups. In my lab we have repeatedly found that the use of the same observers in the two conditions cuts the lightness difference between conditions approximately

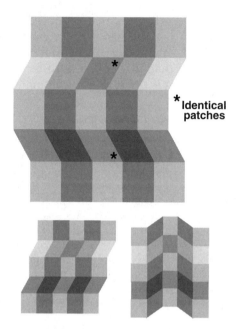

Figure 6.15. Adelson's (1993, 2000) corrugated Mondrian (top). (Lower left) Illusion remains with staircase variation. (Lower right) No illusion when targets lie in same plane. Reprinted with permission.

in half. I have referred to this effect as a "hysteresis effect." There appears to be a strong tendency for a target surface to continue to appear as the same shade of gray as it appeared in a prior display, as long as the retinal image is largely unchanged, even if the second display suggests (whether because of depth information or additional contextual information; see Gilchrist et al., 1983) a very different gray shade.

Adelson (1993, 2000) has created a number of images that illustrate the role of depth in lightness. Perhaps the best known of these is called the corrugated plaid (Fig. 6.15). The two target squares, with stars, are equal in luminance but appear different in lightness, presumably because they appear in different depth planes that are differently oriented with respect to the light source. Adelson's theoretical ideas are discussed in Chapter 12.

Knill and Kersten (1991) have shown that when different occlusion boundaries are used to create different 3D shapes in the Craik-O'Brien illusion, different lightness values result (Fig. 6.16, and see the discussion of their work on p. 182).

Logvinenko and Menshikova (1994) placed a white cone on a table so that it cast a triangular shadow across the surface of the table

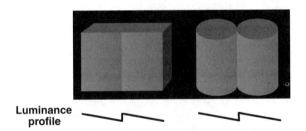

Luminance profile

Figure 6.16. Stimuli from the Knill and Kersten (1991) experiment. Rectangles at left appear different in lightness, while cylinders at right appear to have the same lightness. Reprinted with permission.

(Fig. 6.17). When they then had observers view the scene from above using a pseudoscope that reversed left- and right-eye images, the cone appeared as a conical recess into the surface. The shadow was then perceived as a gray triangle. The lightness of the triangular region thus varied as a result of the altered depth appearance.

Both Spehar et al. (1995) and Taya et al. (1995) found effects on lightness using 3D versions of White's illusion. Pessoa, Mingolla, and Arend (1996) have also shown an effect of depth on lightness, and Bloj, Kersten, and Hurlbert (1999) have reported an effect of depth on perceived color via an effect of mutual illumination.

Research groups at the labs of both Maloney (Boyaci et al., 2003)

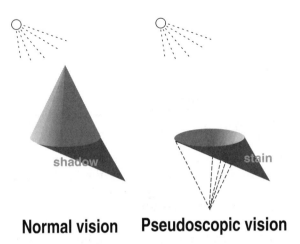

Normal vision   Pseudoscopic vision

Figure 6.17. Percepts resulting from two viewing conditions in the Logvinenko and Menshikova (1994) experiment. The depth reversal caused the cast shadow to appear as a change in surface lightness. Reprinted with permission.

and Brainard (Bloj et al., 2004; Ripamonti et al., 2004) have recently reported experiments testing lightness constancy for a target surface at various degrees of slant in relation to the light source. Boyaci et al. produced a stereo simulation of a scene containing a number of objects, including a large cube with both a lighted and a shadowed side visible to the observer. A target surface was shown at seven different slants covering 100°. Its left edge was always attached to the middle of the shadowed face. Ripamonti et al. presented a gray test card within an illuminated booth containing several objects, including a rectangular block and a large palette containing 36 gray samples. Both cast and attached shadows were visible.

Both groups reported modest degrees of constancy, and both groups attributed that constancy to an estimate by the observer of the properties of the illumination (Bloj et al., 2004; Boyaci et al., 2003).

These results are inconsistent with the coplanar ratio principle in the strictest sense. Nevertheless, the Helmholtzian interpretation is not required; there is a Gestalt alternative. Although the target did not have an adjacent, coplanar neighbor in these experiments, approximations did exist. In the Boyaci et al. experiment, for example, the target in one position was parallel to, nearly coplanar with, and nearly adjacent to the front illuminated face of the cube. In the other extreme position, it was adjacent to and nearly coplanar with the shadowed face of the cube. The results could be a weighted average of these two luminance ratios. In other words, the more coplanar the two surfaces and the closer to adjacent, the stronger the influence of the ratio between them. This modified version of the coplanar ratio principle is consistent with the anchoring theory outlined in Chapter 11. Data supporting this account can be found in Kardos (1934), Wishart et al. (1997), Stewart (1959), and Gogel and Mershon (1969).

Conflicting Claims

Shortly after my reports appeared, several writers (Frisby, 1979; Marr, 1982, p. 258) claimed that my results could not be replicated. The work to which Marr alluded was never published, so there is no way to examine it. Frisby included a 3D version (using colored glasses) of my tabs experiment in his book. However, the limited dynamic range of print on paper would not have allowed the kind of depth effects I had found. Frisby himself (Buckley, Frisby & Freeman, 1994; Wishart, Frisby & Buckley, 1997) later co-authored several papers showing effects of depth on lightness.

More recently several experiments have been published showing little or no effect of depth on lightness, accompanied by denials of the coplanar ratio principle. Dalby, Saillant, and Wooten (1995) used ster-

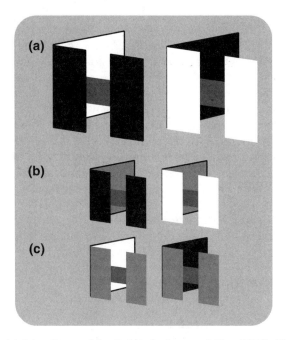

Figure 6.18. (a) Stimuli tested by Zaidi, Spehar, and Shy (1997). The target on the right appears lighter, showing that grouping by T-junctions outweighs grouping by planarity. (b) The effect of T-junctions has been neutralized, revealing the latent coplanar grouping. (c) The effect of coplanarity has been neutralized.

eopsis to determine whether a target annulus appears coplanar with a near-plane disk or with a second, far-plane surrounding annulus. They made the following sweeping conclusion (p. 331): "We conclude that before the relative depth location of an object is determined, its lightness value is known through sensory-level processes."

Zaidi, Spehar, and Shy (1997) have published experiments that they claim "refute the coplanar ratio principle." But it appears that both Dalby et al. and Zaidi et al. have ignored one of the two conditions I had given for obtaining such depth effects, namely an extended luminance range. Dalby et al. used a range of less than 2:1. Zaidi et al. used a range of 82:1, which is not substantially larger than what can be obtained with pigment on paper. My colleagues and I (Gilchrist, Bonato, Annan & Economou, 1998) replicated the Zaidi experiments, obtaining the same results when we used their stimulus, shown in Figure 6.18. But when we increased the luminance range in the display to 900:1, we obtained an effect in the opposite direction that was about nine times larger than the effect they had obtained.

Earlier Work by Kardos

Unpublished work by Dejan Todorović and me replicating and extending one of the earlier experiments of Kardos was mentioned earlier and shown in Figure 4.4. A circular target of fixed luminance was perceived to lie in either a brightly illuminated near plane or a dimly illuminated far plane. The average Munsell matches were 2.75 in the near plane and 7.15 in the far plane, even though the retinal image was essentially identical in the two displays.[15] This finding goes beyond those of my earlier depth/lightness experiments in that, in the near plane, the target was not retinally adjacent at any point to its coplanar surround. I had concluded from my earlier work that retinal adjacency was a necessary if not sufficient condition for coplanar determination. It may be that retinal adjacency is not necessary when the target is completely surrounded by the inducing field.

In the halfway position the target was matched to a 5.2. When a smaller disk was used, the target was matched to a 3.2, suggesting a role for proximity.

EFFECTIVE AND INEFFECTIVE EDGES

My depth experiments had shown that some edges are effective in determining lightness and some are not. But what about the "ineffective edges"—are they merely thrown away? Koffka had spoken about effective and ineffective edges much earlier, as noted in Chapter 4. Like Wallach, Koffka had emphasized the role of luminance ratios, referring to them as "gradients." But, unlike Wallach, Koffka (1935, p. 248) recognized that only certain ratios are critical for lightness, as in the passage I quoted earlier: "not all gradients are equally effective as regards the appearance of a particular field part; rather will the effectiveness of a gradient vary with the degree of appurtenance obtaining between the two terms of this gradient." *Appurtenance* was Koffka's term for belongingness. Appurtenance between two regions forming an edge means that they belong to the same framework of illumination, as do the coplanar regions in my experiments. Thus, effective gradients are those that lie within a framework of illumination, while ineffective gradients are those that divide two frameworks.

By implication, the edges that are ineffective for lightness are just those that lead to the perception of the illumination. Thus, the question of how these two kinds of edges are distinguished becomes crucial. Recall that Koffka (1935, p. 248) gave great importance to this question. Gibson (1966, p. 215) reflected his mentor's influence when he asked, "Why is a change in color not regularly confused with a change in illumination?"

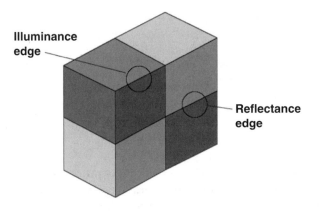

Figure 6.19. The two circled edges are identical locally, but they are perceived as different (Adelson, 2000). Reprinted with permission.

EDGE CLASSIFICATION

By the nature of ecological optics, both reflectance and illumination (or more precisely, changes in them) are represented by a common currency, namely edges, in the retinal projection. Edges that represent changes in the illumination can be locally identical to edges that represent changes in surface reflectance. But they derive from two basic transitions in the distal stimulus. A reflectance edge is a change in the reflectance of a surface, a change in its molecular structure. An illuminance edge is a change in the intensity of illumination on a surface. These edge types can be locally identical, as illustrated by Adelson and Pentland (1996) in Figure 6.19.

As the role of edges came to be increasingly emphasized, my students and I made the point in several papers (Gilchrist, 1979; Gilchrist, Delman, & Jacobsen, 1983; Gilchrist & Jacobsen, 1984) that these two fundamental classes of edges in complex images must be distinguished. Throughout the contrast period (Cornsweet, 1970; Wallach, 1948) and even into the computational period (Arend, 1973; Horn, 1986; Land & McCann, 1970), models dealing with edge ratios implied that all edges are reflectance edges.

My concept of edge classification was consistent with the problem as posed by Koffka, who sought the conditions under which a retinal gradient is perceived as either a change in reflectance or a change in illuminance—that is, my concept of classification implied an all-or-none distinction. On the other hand, when Koffka talked about gradient effectiveness, he presented the problem as a graded, more-or-less, matter.

Illuminance edges in turn come in two general varieties, cast and attached. Cast illuminance edges, such as the boundaries of a spotlight or a shadow, are projected onto a surface. They are often caused by an object, either opaque or transparent, that comes between the light source and the surface. Attached illuminance edges are changes in the incident illumination due to the 3D shape of the surface. They might be sharp, as at a corner, or gradual, as in a smoothly curved surface.

There are other kinds of edges as well in complex images, such as the borders of light sources, of glossy highlights, of transparent surfaces, and of veiling luminances. Every edge or gradient in the retinal image is produced by a change in some property of the physical world, and for the most part these gradients are correctly recognized perceptually. Occlusion contours are unique because they usually combine a difference of reflectance with one of illumination. But the major distinction is between reflectance edges and illumination edges.

There is clearly no direct route from retinal edges to lightness values. We have identified at least two processes that must intervene. The edges must be classified and they must be integrated. Evidence for both of these processes emerged from the study described next.

Another Edge-Substitution Experiment

Earlier in this chapter, I described an edge-substitution experiment (Gilchrist, 1988) demonstrating that whether an edge is perceived as an illumination edge or as a reflectance edge can have far-reaching consequences for the appearance of the rest of the visual field. In these cases the target surfaces changed lightness when a remote edge, not bounding the target surface, was induced to change its edge classification. Earlier my students and I (Gilchrist, Delman & Jacobsen, 1983) had published another edge-substitution experiment that, while similar, had a different focus.

We began by constructing a stimulus that produced a retinal image identical to the conventional simultaneous contrast display composed of two equal gray targets standing on adjacent black and white backgrounds. But in our display, the backgrounds actually differed in illumination, not reflectance. The laboratory arrangements are shown in Figure 6.20. A rectangular middle gray panel was suspended in midair in a laboratory room illuminated solely by two 300-watt incandescent light bulbs. A rectangular piece of black paper, suspended near the bulb, cast a shadow that covered the entire gray rectangle, causing it to appear black, as in the Kardos illusion. Now the left half of this panel was illuminated with a square beam of light that extended beyond the panel on three sides, while its fourth, sharply focused, edge divided the panel exactly in half. Thus, by means of a Gelb effect (on the left) and a Kardos illusion (on the right), the appearance was created of two adjacent panels, one white and one

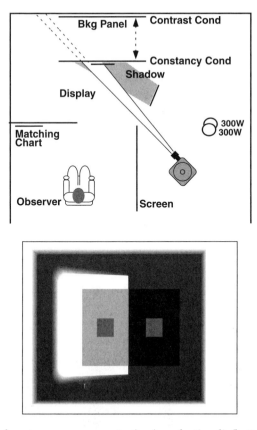

Figure 6.20. Laboratory arrangements (top) and stimuli (bottom) from Gilchrist, Delman, and Jacobsen's (1983) edge-substitution experiment. When the illumination edge was revealed by the outer context, the targets appeared as almost black and almost white. Without the context, the targets appeared almost equal, as in a typical simultaneous contrast display.

black, with no special illumination. To complete the simulated contrast display, a pair of equi-luminant targets was added, one centered on the left half and one on the right. To compensate for the different illumination levels, the left square was black and the right square was white.

One group of observers viewed this display and made matches from a chart that allowed for matching of both reflectance and illumination levels. They saw what appeared to be a standard simultaneous contrast pattern. The two targets appeared roughly middle gray, differing by the usual half a Munsell step. Illumination matches to the two halves of the display were equal, and the two backgrounds were matched as black and white respectively.

A second group of observers viewed the same display, but under conditions that revealed the true lighting arrangements. This was achieved by mounting a large white panel immediately behind, and coplanar with, the display, so as to intercept those regions of the projector beam and the cast shadow that extended beyond the display itself. These observers gave very different matches for the illumination levels on the two halves of the display. They also gave very different lightness matches for the two targets, matching the left-hand target to a charcoal gray and the right-hand target to a white. The left and right backgrounds no longer appeared as black and white; they now appeared to differ by only a few Munsell steps.

The different results cannot be explained by contrast mechanisms.[16] The display itself, subtending 5.1° vertically and 6.8° horizontally, was constant across the two conditions. The fact that a change in perceived classification of the central edge produced changes in target lightness is consistent with the claim that lightness depends not merely on information at its edge, but on the integration of successive edges. And it shows that the perceptual classification of edges exerts a profound effect on lightness.

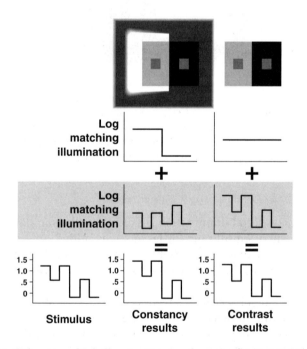

Figure 6.21. When matched illumination levels and matched lightness levels are combined, the results for the constancy condition (middle column) and the contrast condition (right column) are similar to the profile of the retinal image (left column) (Gilchrist, Delman & Jacobsen, 1983).

Both perceived illumination levels and perceived reflectance levels showed departures from constancy, but the departures were complementary—that is, when a profile of the perceived illumination array is combined with a profile of the perceived reflectance array, as seen in Figure 6.21, the resulting profile closely matches the luminance profile of the display. This outcome is consistent with both a layered conception of the retinal image and with Koffka's invariance theorem concerning the interrelationship of lightness and perceived illumination.

All-Black Rooms and All-White Rooms

Imagine you stepped into a world in which every surface has the same color. Would you perceive that color correctly, without other colors for comparison? Now imagine two rooms filled with objects. One room, including all the contents, is painted completely white. The other room is painted completely black. Each room is illuminated by a light source not in your visual field. Could you tell which room is white and which room is black?

The intuitive answer is yes. But what might be the basis for the discrimination? The white room would have a higher overall intensity, of course. Now let's say we neutralize this intensity difference by increasing the illumination in the black room and/or decreasing it in the white room. Could the rooms now be discriminated?

Consider the images of the two rooms. Painting each room a single shade of gray would not produce a homogeneous image. There would still be illumination edges, both cast and attached. This leads to another question: Would the illumination edges be correctly perceived as such? Or would they be perceived as variations in surface gray level? Without an edge classification component, most theories of lightness perception predict that the various surfaces will be perceived as different shades of gray.

Here are the answers. The two rooms can be discriminated. The black room and the white room do not make identical images, even if their average luminance is equated by adjusting the illumination levels. The difference in the two images is due to the role of indirect, or mutual, illumination. Each surface reflects some light, and this reflected light serves as a light source for nearby surfaces. This mutual illumination tends to homogenize the image, reducing contrasts. And there is proportionately more indirect illumination in the white room than in the black room. In the black room, 97% of the light is absorbed in every reflection. There is thus very little indirect light, and the resulting image shows high contrast. But the image of the white room is far more homogeneous, owing to the copious amounts of indirect light.

Alan Jacobsen and I created two small cubical (2 feet on each side)

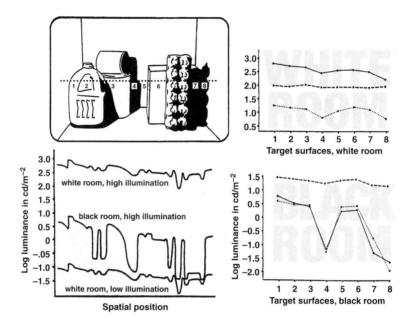

Figure 6.22. (Upper left) Image of the black room showing path of luminance profile and eight tested points. (Lower left) Luminance profiles in various conditions. The right column shows luminance values (solid lines), lightness matches (dashed lines), and illumination matches (dotted lines) for eight test points. Reprinted with permission from Gilchrist and Jacobsen, 1984.

rooms (Gilchrist & Jacobsen, 1984). They were furnished with identical arrangements of objects, including cylinders, cubes, plastic milk jugs, and egg cartons (Fig. 6.22). One room, including its furnishings, was painted entirely matte black. The other room was painted matte white. Observers viewed these rooms by looking through a horizontal aperture in the near wall. The black room was illuminated by a 200-watt, clear incandescent light bulb, placed in the near upper left-hand corner, and baffled so that it could not be directly seen by the observer. The white room was tested with two illumination levels, one using a 200-watt bulb, as in the black room, and one using a much dimmer bulb, such that the luminance at every point in the white room was lower than the corresponding point in the black room.

For each room, nine naive observers were asked (1) to report whether or not the room appeared homogeneous in surface lightness, (2) to make a lightness match for the room as a whole, and (3) to match each of eight test points (indicated in Fig. 6.22) both for lightness and for perceived illumination level, using the matching apparatus shown in Figure 6.23. This apparatus allowed the illumination on a Munsell chart to be varied by sliding an occluding panel that

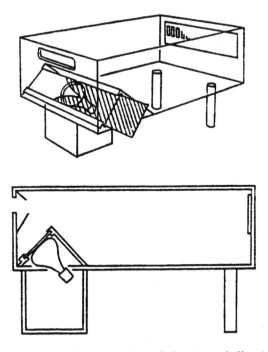

Figure 6.23. Apparatus used for matching lightness and illumination in Gilchrist and Jacobsen's (1984) experiment. Sliding the aluminum panel (shown as hatched) alters the level of illumination on the Munsell chart on the far right end. Reprinted with permission.

controlled the size of the aperture through which light entered the chamber. The observer first indicated the perceived lightness of a test spot by selecting a matching chip from the Munsell chart under a preset medium level of illumination. Then the observer was asked to set the illumination level on that Munsell chip to match the perceived illumination level on the test spot.

All 27 observers reported the rooms to be homogeneous in lightness. The brightly illuminated white room was seen as white (median Munsell match 9.0), the brightly illuminated black room was seen as middle gray (Munsell 5.5), and the dimly illuminated white room was seen as light gray (Munsell 7.5). Matches for the eight points are shown in Figure 6.23. In these graphs the profiles of the lightness matches and the illumination matches can be compared with the profile of the physical luminance values for the eight test spots. Notice that the profile for perceived illumination closely parallels the physical luminance profile, while the profile for perceived reflectance is relatively flat. We have no explanation for the error in overall illumination level for the white room, although the pattern of relative illumination levels is quite accurate. In the black room, both overall and relative (DC and AC) illumination levels were accurately matched.

These results indicate quite clearly that the variations in luminance in the two images are indeed perceived as variations in illumination, not as variations in surface reflectance, indicating that illuminance edges are perceived as such. Many concurrent models of lightness perception, if fed images such as these, would have made predictions sharply at variance with those obtained. A detailed analysis of these predictions can be found in our 1984 paper. Contrast models probably miss the mark most widely. Not only would the excitation levels aroused by the various luminances show pronounced variations, but also the inhibitory process would only further exaggerate these differences.

As with the edge-substitution experiment described above, these results are consistent with a layered conception of the retinal image. The sum of the perceived illumination profile and the perceived reflectance profile closely matches the physical luminance profile.

Chromatic Rooms: Separating the Color of the Light from the Color of the Objects

The logic of black rooms and white rooms can be extended to colored rooms and colored illumination. For example, a red room in white light looks different than a white room in red light (Gilchrist & Ramachandran, 1992; Langer & Gilchrist, 2000). The difference lies in a negative correlation between the luminance gradients and the chromaticity gradients. In the room with red surfaces, the lower the luminance, the more saturated the red light. This happens because the light that illuminates the shadowed areas is light reflected from other red surfaces. In the white room with red illumination, there is no gradient correlation. Whether the luminance is high or low, the saturation is constant.

When there is more than one source of colored light, a positive gradient correlation is produced. For example, when a colored floodlight illuminates the outside of a building, and there is other ambient light in the environment, the color is immediately attributed to the lighting rather than to the surface itself. Here the higher the luminance, the more saturated the color. Color theory has hardly begun to deal with such basic problems.

Factors in Edge Classification

Edge Sharpness

The first factor that naturally comes to mind is edge sharpness. Illumination edges tend to be gradual, due to their penumbrae, and reflectance edges tend to be sharp. Under relatively simple conditions, this factor can be decisive, as demonstrated many years ago by Hering (1874/1964, p. 8) in his famous shadow/spot experiment, described in Chapter 2.

Edge sharpness has been explicitly presented as a factor in edge classification by both Land and McCann (1971) and by Bergström (1977), but in different ways. Land and McCann argue that edge classification is a low-level process. Illumination gradients, being typically shallow, simply drop out automatically due to the relative insensitivity of the visual system to gradual luminance changes. Bergström argues that illumination gradients are seen, but based on their shallow profile, they are classified separately from reflectance edges.

Land and McCann's (1971, p. 9) sequential ratio product, mentioned earlier, is implemented by inputs from a chain of closely spaced detector pairs. They write, "Such a chain cannot miss an edge and will not react to substantial but gradual changes of illumination across the field. Such a chain will also be completely indifferent to change of illumination as a function of time." This model, which has been described by Hurlbert (1986) and endorsed by Marr (1982) and Horn (1974), removes illumination gradients from the integration, but only when the illumination gradients are shallow, as in Land and McCann's Mondrian illuminated from below (see Fig. 6.8).

Bergström's account requires no insensitivity to shallow gradients, but merely classification by edge sharpness. Consider his interpretation of the Craik-O'Brien illusion. Consistent with his perceptual vector analysis model of surface lightness (described on p. 198), Bergström suggests that the display is seen as two adjacent rectangles of different lightness, illuminated from the side. The illusion we see merely reflects the lightness component of the display, while illumination is represented separately as an overall luminance ramp.

Are We Insensitive to Shallow Gradients? There seem to be at least three versions of the insensitivity hypothesis: (1) shallow gradients below a certain threshold are simply invisible (Land & McCann, 1971), (2) amplitude is underestimated for all shallow gradients, including visible ones, and (3) sensitivity is poor for low spatial frequencies (Cornsweet, 1970). What does the evidence show?

1. To be invisible, a gradient must be extremely shallow and probably too shallow to provide much help to lightness constancy. In addition, there is a serious logical problem, expressed by Marr (1982, p. 258): "The problem is that if the threshold is too low, it will not remove the illumination gradient; but if it is too high, it will remove valuable shading information." In fact, McCann (2001, p. 110) has given up the threshold gradient idea, writing, "we could not find psychophysical support for the 'rate of change on the retina threshold' mechanism."

2. Evans (1959, p. 143) presented the display shown in Figure 6.24

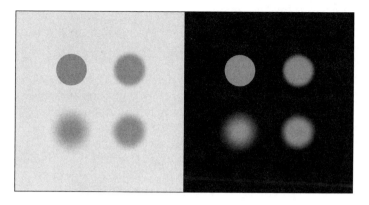

Figure 6.24. The sharpness of the boundary determines how different each disk appears from its background.

to illustrate the insensitivity. The sharp disks clearly appear to differ more in luminance from the background than the fuzzy disks. MacLeod (1940, 1947) varied the breadth of a luminance ramp surrounding a dark disk on a lighter background. He found that the disk region appeared more similar to the background when the boundary was gradual, as opposed to sharp. And the more gradual the boundary, the lighter the disk appeared. Others have reported analogous findings (Shapley & Tolhurst, 1973; Thomas, 1966; Thomas & Kovar, 1965).

The Craik-O'Brien contour makes a similar point, but Knill and Kersten (1991) have presented opposing evidence. They showed that when the top and bottom edges of the Craik-O'Brien display are replaced with scalloped bounding contours, creating the appearance of two abutting cylinders (see Fig. 6.16), the illusion disappears—that is, the two cylinders appear to have the same lightness. Knill and Kersten measured this effect by placing a darker square target patch in the center of each region divided by the sharp change. Naive observers adjusted the luminance of one of these two targets until it appeared as the same lightness as the other. When the display appeared flat, the target on the background that appeared darker had to be increased in luminance by 5.8% to appear equal to the other target. But when the display appeared 3D, only a 0.3% increase was required. Having the observers match targets embedded within the background regions rather than the background regions themselves is good because it makes the task more indirect. It allows an inference about the perception of the Craik-O'Brien contour without testing a surface that is bounded by that contour. This directly contradicts the sensitivity explanation because if the information contained in the shallow gradients had been lost early on due to lack of sensitivity, this information could not be retrieved simply because the perceived 3D arrangement had changed.

3. The modulation transfer function, made familiar by Cornsweet (1970), illustrates the drop in sensitivity to both high and low spatial frequencies. However, McCann et al. (1974) and Hoekstra et al. (1974) have shown that the lowered sensitivity for low spatial frequency goes away when the number of cycles presented to the observer is held constant.

Does Edge Sharpness Explain Edge Classification? The Knill and Kersten (1991) version of the illusion supports Bergström's account of the Craik-O'Brien illusion. The two cylinders appear the same lightness because now both the sharp and the gradual luminance changes are processed together as illuminance changes, as each is associated with a change in surface planarity.

But an illuminance edge need not be gradual to be correctly classified. Arend and Goldstein (1987, 1990) have clearly shown that Land and McCann's results are obtained even with a sharp gradient of illumination. They obtained lightness matches for targets on a Mondrian that were separated by three kinds of illumination gradient: an abrupt step, a linear gradient, and a simulation of side illumination. They obtained close to perfect lightness constancy in all cases. My students and I (Gilchrist et al., 1983) had earlier shown good constancy using an abrupt illumination gradient on a simple Mondrian. Both we and Arend and Goldstein argued that the visual system could achieve this result by correctly identifying the illumination edge as such and excluding it from the edge integration (sequential product) between the two targets.

In one variant of the sensitivity story, illuminance varies more gradually over space than reflectance, but Arend (1994, p. 179) makes an impressive case that this is not valid.

Several additional points suggest that luminance ramps do not reliably signal illuminance boundaries:

1. Reflectance edges are sometimes gradual, but they are nevertheless normally perceived as reflectance edges. In MacLeod's 1947 experiment, described above, the luminance ramp influenced lightness even though it did not appear as an illuminance boundary.

2. Illumination edges are frequently sharp. Attached illumination edges are as sharp as the 3D form change. Corners, for example, often produce very sharp illumination gradients. Even cast illumination edges will be sharp if the illumination is from a point source or if the object casting the shadow is relatively close to the surface on which it is projected.

3. Whatever is the sharpness of the physical gradient in the environment, the important question (at least for sensory thresh-

olds) is the sharpness of the retinal gradient, and this varies with viewing distance. Even very gradual changes of illumination become sharp in the retinal projection with large viewing distance.

We can conclude that edge sharpness is indeed a factor in the classification of edges, especially under simple conditions, but it is only part of the story.

Coplanarity

Depth perception is vital to edge classification. An edge that divides two regions that lie in the same plane is usually seen as a reflectance edge, unless the edge is gradual. An edge, such as a corner or an occlusion edge, that divides two non-coplanar regions is seen, either completely or partially, as an illuminance edge.

X-Junctions

Systematic luminance relationships at X-junctions carry information that specifies edge type. For example, when a reflectance edge intersects an illuminance edge, the junction has the property of ratio invariance. On the other hand, when one illuminance edge intersects another, the junction is difference invariant, not ratio invariant. Thus, in principle, a difference-invariant X-junction allows the classification of both intersecting edges as illuminance edges. A ratio-invariant X-junction, however, does not completely specify the intersecting edges. It specifies that the two intersecting edges are of different types, but not which is which.

These relationships underlie several delightful demonstrations. Although Figure 6.25 is merely a schematic with limited luminance range, the reader, with a bit of imagination, might capture some of the visual experience. A large matte black paper is mounted on a wall and a disk of white paper is placed somewhere on the black paper. Near the white disk, a round spotlight with a sharp edge is projected onto the black paper by a slide projector. It takes some fiddling with the projector and the room illumination, but it is possible to equate both the luminance and the color temperature of the white disk and the spotlight. When this is done, the two become indistinguishable, and both appear as white paper disks.

The spotlight is then moved so as to partially intersect the paper disk. Now the percept changes dramatically. One of the two disks appears to be composed of illumination, while the other can continue to appear as white paper. But either disk can appear as the spotlight. And the display is reversible: when the perception of one disk shifts from spotlight to paper, the other disk makes the opposite shift. One method that guarantees that an observer will experience the reversal

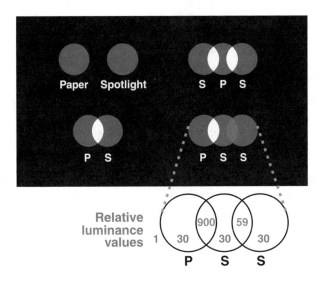

Figure 6.25. Ratio invariance at intersections of paper disk and spotlight, and difference invariance at intersections of two spotlights.

is to add a second, identical spotlight that overlaps the paper disk on the other side of the paper disk (see Fig. 6.25, upper right). Although the actual order of the disks is spotlight/paper/spotlight, observers who have not witnessed the preparations almost always report a single spotlight in the center and two flanking paper disks. This appears to be another instance of Bergström's principle of minimum number of light sources (Bergström, 1994). The true state of affairs can be easily revealed by various methods, such as waving a hand directly in front of the display, and this typically produces visual surprise in the observer.

If the three disks are now arranged in the order paper/spotlight/spotlight, the difference between ratio invariance and difference invariance can be easily seen. The intersection of the paper disk and the spotlight is far brighter than the intersection of the two spotlights. That is because the luminance increments of the two spotlights merely add together, while those of the spotlight and the paper multiply.

Motion

Motion can disambiguate reflectance and illuminance edges. Katz (1935, p. 49), quoting Bühler: "If you attempt to brush a small shadow which looks like a spot of dirt from the arm of your coat, a slight arm movement is quite sufficient to restore your peace of mind by changing it into its proper mode of appearance." Von Fieandt and Moustgaard (1977, p. 371) observe that movement reveals that a gray spot of dust on a jacket is actually a spot of sunlight. Hurvich and Jameson (1966, p. 86) report the same thing.

Other Approaches

Various solutions to the edge-classification problem have been offered, primarily in the context of machine vision. Boulter (1980) proposed a two-stage lateral inhibition mechanism that is based on the assumption that the spectral composition of light changes across a reflectance edge, but not across an illuminance edge. Witkin (1982) has argued that the degree of correlation of image intensities on both sides of an edge allows classification. His scheme is primarily useful for detecting occluding contours, given that, at such contours, regions widely separated in 3D space are projected to adjacent locations in the image. Rubin and Richards (1984) have suggested several tests for an illuminance edge, one based on the assumption that the various spectral components will all have the same sign of change at the boundary, and another based on the assumption that whichever spectral component has the maximum intensity on one side of the boundary will also have the maximum on the other side. Gershon et al. (1986) noted that the Rubin and Richards algorithms assume that the ambient lighting has the same spectral distribution as the direct lighting, an unreliable assumption. They propose an alternative method that takes into account the color of the ambient illumination. However, they note (1986, p. 1706) that because their method is not completely reliable, "an additional computation must be carried out by higher-level spatiochromatic mechanisms."

None of these methods is very reliable. The assumption that the chromaticity does not change at an illuminance border does not apply to occlusion boundaries or corners. The change in light at a corner, for instance, is likely to include a chromatic component because the two sides of the corner face in different directions, thus receiving light of different colors. None of these algorithms could account for the edge-classification results in either the edge substitution experiment just described or the experiments with white rooms and black rooms. What they all have in common is an attempt to account for edge classification without exploiting the context of the edge. The human system is known to rely heavily on context. Although the human visual system might exploit some of these local regularities in the image, this has not yet been demonstrated.

Before leaving edge classification, it should be noted that if the visual system were able to parse the retinal image into common and relative components, as proposed by Bergström (1977, 1994), much of the work of edge classification would be done. Bergström contends that the common component represents illumination, while the relative represents reflectance. This is described in more detail in Chapter 7.

LIGHTNESS AND BRIGHTNESS

The terms *lightness* and *brightness* have perennially produced confusion. In short, lightness is perceived reflectance, while brightness is perceived luminance. Lightness is the perception of a permanent property of a surface; brightness is the perception of the sheer intensity of light at a given location in the visual field, regardless of what combination of reflectance and incident illumination causes that intensity. Lightness is the normal mode of seeing. Brightness is a special mode, often used by painters, in which we attempt to attend to the energy stimulating our retina, rather than to the shade of gray of a surface. Nor does brightness represent perceived illumination, although we sometimes speak of the "brightness" of the illumination. Adjacent light-gray and dark-gray papers in the same illumination differ in brightness.

Arend and his colleagues (Arend & Goldstein, 1987, 1990; Arend & Spehar, 1993a, 1992b) measured both lightness and brightness in CRT displays that simulated multi-illuminant scenes. Alan Jacobsen and I (Jacobsen & Gilchrist, 1988b) measured lightness and brightness using illuminated paper displays in our replication of Jameson and Hurvich (1961), described in Chapter 5. We both obtained the same pattern of results. While lightness tracked reflectance (simulated or physical), brightness roughly tracked luminance. And the lightness matches tracked reflectance more closely than the brightness matches tracked luminance.

SUMMARY

For lightness, the renaissance came at the end of the 1960s, with the advent of the computer and machine vision. While the contrast theorists had treated light itself as the stimulus, the computational theorists recognized that it is the information carried by light (in the form of edges and gradients) that is important. Inspired by the work of Yarbus and Wallach, researchers like Whittle, Arend, and me embraced the radical assumption that what is encoded at the retina is not the absolute intensity of light at each point, but only the relative intensity at borders. But this also implied a subsequent process of edge integration. I advanced the distinction between reflectance and illuminance edges, suggesting that constancy could be achieved only if edges were classified before being integrated (Gilchrist, 1979; Gilchrist et al., 1983).

From the computational perspective, lateral inhibition was viewed more modestly as the mechanism responsible for encoding the edge ratio. And the contrast theory of lateral inhibition was dealt a more serious blow when I reported dramatic effects of depth perception on lightness, even while holding the retinal image constant.

Beyond the traditional form of constancy with respect to changing illumination level, the new emphasis on edge encoding led to the recognition of a second, equally important form of constancy: constancy with respect to changing background reflectance. This resolved the long-debated problem of the relationship between contrast and constancy. Contrast and constancy are not parallel phenomena. Rather, contrast is a failure of the second type of constancy: background-independent constancy.

7

Computational Models

The computer revolution produced two quite different streams of work. These streams are represented by decomposition models and brightness models, respectively. Perhaps the sharpest difference between these streams concerns the treatment of physiology. If the brightness models were driven by physiology, the decomposition models were driven by veridicality. While the decomposition modelers saw in the computer revolution a chance to deduce, just like those working in machine vision, the logical steps necessary to derive veridical lightness percepts from proximal input without concern for physiological data, the brightness modelers saw it as a chance to create computer models of neural functions.

Decomposition models and brightness models can be roughly aligned with Marr's second and third levels of understanding computational devices. The decomposition modelers have been primarily concerned with algorithm; they choose to defer the question of implementation. Brightness modelers, on the other hand, have been more concerned with implementation. Marr's first level, concerning the goal of the computation, has been explicitly addressed by the decomposition modelers but largely ignored by the brightness modelers.

DECOMPOSITION MODELS

Central to the decomposition models is the idea of inverse optics. Because separate properties of the visual scene, such as illuminance and reflectance, become entangled by the optics of image formation, they can be disentangled by inverting the process. Some of these models, called intrinsic image models, speak literally of parsing the image into overlapping layers, while others talk more generally about extracting separate components from the image.

The roots of this logic lie in Gestalt theory. One of the earliest to build an inverse optics model was Johansson (1950, 1975, 1977), whose analysis of retinal motions into common and relative components was simply the mirror image of the synthesis of retinal motions caused by the combination of observer and object movements.[1] The same can be said of Metelli (1970), who simply inverted the laws of color fusion to obtain perceptual scission. Moreover, Metelli's model was explicitly an intrinsic image model.

Inverse optics implies a complementary relationship between the synthesis by which the image is formed and the analysis applied to the retinal image by the visual system, as just noted. But if the retinal image is parsed into separate layers, this further implies a complementary relationship between lightness and perceived illumination, just as proposed by Koffka in his invariance theorem (see Chapter 4). This complementarity can be seen in graphs (see Figs. 6.21, 6.22, and 5.13) from several experiments in which measures of both lightness and perceived illumination were taken (Gilchrist et al., 1983; Gilchrist & Jacobsen, 1984; Kozaki & Noguchi, 1976).

More than any earlier theories, these models give a prominent place to the analysis of the information available in the retinal image. This emphasis is consistent with the current interest in ideal observer analysis (Kersten & Yuille, 2003), as well as Gibson's (1966, 1979) earlier analysis of affordances in the optic array. However, the decomposition theorists stop short of Gibson's claim regarding the degree to which distal properties are specified in the image, believing that image information must be supplemented with constraining assumptions.

Veridicality is a central concern of decomposition models, reflecting the profound influence of machine vision. Failures of constancy are not a central concern. This focus on veridicality, missing during the contrast period, had been seen earlier. It had captured the interest of Helmholtz and Hering and had been considered the central problem in lightness by the Gestalt theorists.

Physiological validity is not a pressing matter for decomposition models, nor is there any interest in the question of sensations. There is a highly rational quality to these models. Don MacLeod has suggested that they have a tidy quality: a place for everything and everything in its place.

Barrow and Tenenbaum: Intrinsic Images

The converging agendas of human lightness and machine vision in the early years of the computational period can be seen in the striking parallel between two independently conceived models of lightness, one from human work (Gilchrist, 1979) and one from machine work

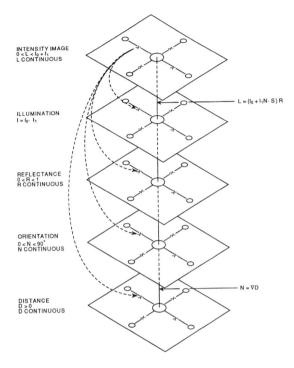

Figure 7.1. Barrow and Tenenbaum's (1978) intrinsic image model. Reprinted with permission.

(Barrow & Tenenbaum, 1978). Both models incorporated the same core idea, that the retinal image can be fruitfully treated as a multiple image composed of separate layers. And both models proposed methods for parsing the image into its component layers, although the methods differed somewhat.

Barrow and Tenenbaum's model was presented in a remarkable paper that acknowledged, from the outset, their common cause with human vision (Barrow & Tenenbaum, 1978, p. 3): "those in computer vision might do well to look harder at the phenomenology of human vision for clues that might indicate fundamental inadequacies of current approaches; those concerned with human vision might gain insights by thinking more about what information is sought, and how it might be obtained, from a computational point of view."

Barrow and Tenenbaum referred to the component layers of the input light-intensity image as "intrinsic images," as shown in Figure 7.1. The intrinsic images of primary interest are those that represent surface reflectance and incident illumination. But as Adelson and Pentland (1996, p. 2) have noted, "In addition one may derive images representing surface depth and orientation, which Marr called the

2 1/2 D sketch (Marr 1982)." Barrow and Tenenbaum argued that such intrinsic images could be recovered only by making assumptions about the world and exploiting the constraints implied by those assumptions. The different layers are not independent of each other, but rather they mutually constrain one another. So, for example, if a gradient of luminance is used for shape-from-shading in the orientation map, it is not available to be seen as a reflectance gradient, and reflectance is seen as homogeneous at that location.

Gilchrist: Classified Edge Integration

In a 1979 paper (Gilchrist, 1979; see also Gilchrist et al., 1983) I proposed that the retinal image be viewed as a pattern of illumination projected onto a pattern of surface reflectances. I suggested that reflectance and illumination can be disentangled by parsing the image into these two intrinsic layers. The approach, which might be called classified edge integration, contains three essential ingredients: (1) edge extraction, (2) edge classification, and (3) edge integration. The input is assumed to consist of luminance ratios at edges and gradients. Once these edges and gradients are classified, they are separately integrated within each class, producing two mappings of the retinal image: a reflectance map and an illuminance map.

Such a scheme has several nice features. First, the problem of illumination-independent constancy is solved automatically. Patches of the same reflectance located in separate regions of illumination emerge in the reflectance map with the same value. Second, perception of the illumination is explained, as is the general phenomenon of two perceptual values at each locus in the image. The devil is in the details of edge classification, of course. No wonder Koffka said that a solution to edge classification "would probably supply the key to the complete theory of color perception in the broadest sense" (Koffka, 1935, p. 248).

The model does not account for errors in lightness perception; neither simultaneous lightness contrast nor illumination-dependent failures of lightness constancy are explained. The model was driven by an attempt to account for the impressive veridicality achieved by the visual system, and the question of errors was intentionally deferred.

Several lines of research produced data consistent with this layered model. In reports of both the early edge-substitution experiments (Gilchrist et al., 1983) and the experiments on black rooms and white rooms (Gilchrist & Jacobsen, 1984) we showed that if the profile of lightness matches made by observers is added to the profile of illumination matches (see Figs. 6.21 and 6.22), the resulting profile closely matches the luminance profile of the retinal image itself.

Other evidence showed that causing a reflectance edge to appear as an illumination edge is functionally equivalent to making the edge disappear through retinal stabilization. The Yarbus experiment de-

scribed earlier used a stimulus essentially like the standard simultaneous lightness contrast display. He reported that when the boundary
between the white and black backgrounds was visually removed by
stabilizing it, the targets came to appear very different in lightness.
Likewise, Tom Piantanida and I found that we were able to make the
gray targets of a simultaneous contrast display appear black and white
by stabilizing the boundary between the white and black backgrounds
(described more fully in Gilchrist, 1994). In the 1983 edge-substitution
experiments, we obtained essentially the same results, not by stabilizing the boundary between the black and white backgrounds, but
rather by making that boundary appear as an illumination edge.

Differentiation and Integration

The idea that edges derived from differentiation at the retina are subsequently integrated, a key part of my intrinsic image model, was laid
out earlier by Land and McCann (1971) and Arend (1973, 1994), and
later by Marr (1982) and Blake (1985a). These models are similar to
mine except that they do not include an edge classification component.
Land and McCann assumed that this problem was solved by the relative insensitivity of the visual system to gradual luminance ramps,
which are often associated with illumination borders. Arend (1994)
acknowledged that although edge classification presents a serious
challenge to models, it is a necessary component of any complete
model. Likewise Marr (1982, p. 260) wrote, "to make a success of a
scheme based only on relative measurements, we have to make a basic
distinction between changes in the image due to changes in reflectance
. . . and those due to changes in illumination."

Layers

Edge Coding Implies Layers

It was not an accident that theorists who began by assuming edge
coding would arrive at a layered concept. Edges and layers are intimately related, especially when those edges are classified. While the
layers are obvious phenomenally, they are not represented explicitly
in the image. However each layer contains boundaries, and these
boundaries are represented explicitly in the image as edges. This close
connection is graphically illustrated in work by Walraven (1976) and
Whittle (Whittle, 1994a, 1994b).

Walraven's Missing Link

Walraven superimposed (additively) a small disk of red light on a
small disk of green light while these were both superimposed on a
larger red disk. The observer was asked to make the resulting disk appear optimally yellow by adjusting the intensity of the green disk.

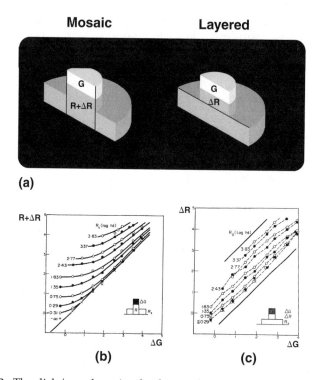

Figure 7.2. The disk/annulus stimulus has traditionally been treated as a disk surrounded by a ring, but the visual system appears to treat it as an increment added to (or a decrement subtracted from) a larger disk. Straight lines emerge only when a layered analysis is used (Walraven, 1976). Reprinted with permission.

Because the small red disk was superimposed on the large red disk, the amount of red light physically present at the locus of the small disk was the sum of the red light in the large disk (R) plus the red component in the small disk (ΔR). When Walraven plotted this variable ($R + \Delta R$) against the amount of green (ΔG) in the small disk, he obtained the curves shown in Figure 7.2, left. However, Walraven found that if only the incremental red (ΔR) is plotted against ΔG, the result is the straight line shown on the right. This implies that the only red light that contributes to the yellow appearance of the small disk is the red light in the small disk, or as Walraven puts its, the difference between the red light inside the border of the small disk ($R + \Delta R$) and the red light outside that border (R). The top part of Figure 7.2 illustrates Walraven's observation that what had traditionally been regarded as a *disk surrounded by an annulus* is treated by the visual system as an *increment added to a pedestal* (or a decrement subtracted from one). The results obtained by Whittle and Challands (1969), described earlier, show the same thing for achromatic stimuli: the brightness of the disk is determined by the change in light at its border.

Thus, we see in the work of Walraven and Whittle that a simple pattern like the disk/annulus pattern is treated by the visual system as a layered structure. This seems ideally suited to our phenomenal experience of complex scenes as composed of a pattern of illumination projected onto a pattern of surface reflectances.

Transparency

Whatever the usefulness of a layered conception for theories of lightness itself, there is one topic in which the concept of layers simply cannot be avoided: the perception of transparency. Here we experience the separate layers explicitly. The classic work on transparency is that of Metelli (1970, 1974). He derived his theory of transparency by working backward from the physics of looking through an episcotister, which is a spinning disk containing both opaque and open sectors. Gerbino (1994) has applied coding theory (Leeuwenberg & Buffart, 1983) to this topic, showing that perception of transparency satisfies the simplicity principle (Hatfield & Epstein, 1985).

The effect of transparency on lightness can be seen dramatically in the illusion by Anderson and Winawer (2005) shown in Figure 7.3. Here, although the left-hand and right-hand disks are physically identical, the right-hand disks appear as white pieces partly occluded by black clouds, whereas the left-hand disks appear as black pieces partly occluded by white clouds. Anderson and Winawer have manipulated the information contained at the intersections of the disk and cloud boundaries to produce a different segmentation into layers.

The kind of transparent surfaces typically studied contain both a

Figure 7.3. Illusion produced by Anderson and Winawer (2005). The disks on the left and on the right are identical, but they appear very different because the perceptual layers are different.

filter component and a veil component—that is, the transparent material filters out some of the light coming through the material, but in addition, light reflected off the front surface of the material is added to the pattern of light coming through the material. The filter component is equivalent to a shadow in multiplicative effect on the image (Metelli, 1975). But the veil component, which is an additive component, has a very different effect on the image, mathematically. The fact that humans exhibit lightness constancy in the presence of both multiplicative and additive layers provides a serious challenge to lightness theory.

Veiling Luminance

Arend (1994) speaks of environmental challenges to constancy, only one of which is that posed by changing illumination. We have already made a distinction between illumination-independent constancy and background-independent constancy. But constancy is also achieved in the face of a very different challenge, one that has been largely ignored, although it is very important: constancy despite a veiling luminance. One example of veiling luminance is fog. In the case of a homogeneous veil, a constant amount of light is added to each point in the retinal image. This has the effect of reducing the contrast of edges seen through the veil. Notice that although adding a veiling luminance and increasing the illumination level both produce an increase in luminance at each point in the image, the effects on luminance ratios at edges are very different. While increasing the illumination brightens the image, luminance ratios at edges are preserved. But when a veiling luminance is added, edge contrast ratios are reduced. As a result, visibility is reduced in the presence of a veiling luminance. Consider a familiar example. It is often difficult to see a person's face when looking into the windshield of an automobile because the sky is reflected in the slanted glass.

Alan Jacobsen and I (Gilchrist & Jacobsen, 1983) showed that despite this contrast reduction, lightness constancy survives the veiling luminance remarkably well. We created a veiling luminance by reflecting a homogeneous sheet of light off the front surface of a clear piece of glass inserted diagonally into a viewing tunnel. One of three scenes was viewed through the tunnel: an outdoor campus scene, an indoor still-life display, and a two-dimensional Mondrian pattern. Each scene contained a luminance range of about 30:1. The luminance of the veil was adjusted to equal the highest luminance within the scene. Thus, the addition of the veil reduced the luminance range to approximately 2:1. Each scene was viewed by one group of observers through the veil and by a separate group without the veil.

For the simple Mondrian pattern, the results were not surprising. Without the veil, the Mondrian appeared, veridically, to contain the entire range of grays from white to black. Observers viewing the scene through the veil did not perceive the veil, but perceived the Mondrian as composed solely of light-gray patches. The highest luminance appeared white and the lowest luminance appeared as a Munsell 6.6, consistent with its 1:1.9 luminance ratio with the highest luminance. This result agrees with those reported in prior studies (Fry & Alpern, 1954; Rushton & Gubisch, 1966; Walraven, 1973; Whittle & Challands, 1969) involving veiling luminance in very simple (disk/annulus) displays.

However, in the case of the two 3D displays, perceived lightness values were only slightly affected by the addition of the veil. When viewed through the veil, the darkest surface in the scene was perceived as Munsell 2.9 in the outdoor scene and Munsell 2.1 in the still-life display. Had these lightness values been based simply on the ratio between the target and the highest luminance, as with the Mondrian display, they would have both been 7.2. It should also be noted that constancy through a veiling luminance always goes hand in hand with perception of the veil itself.

This represents something close to 100% constancy, more than is often obtained in traditional constancy experiments in which illumination level is varied. Herein lies a major challenge to lightness theories, none of which can account for this result. Lightness constancy appears to survive both an increase in illumination level and the addition of a veil, two very different mathematical transformations of the image, and strong testimony to the adaptability of the visual system.

Perhaps it should be added that constancy through a veiling luminance is not a minor phenomenon. Besides examples like fog (Henry et al., 2000) and reflections off glass and water, the same challenge exists when contrast is reduced in a TV or CRT picture. A final example will show that the visual system may confront this problem literally at all times. Reduced visibility caused by glare is a veiling luminance problem. When there is a glare source in the visual field, visibility of other edges in the scene is reduced because the retina is unable to absorb all the light from the glare source and the excess light is scattered across the retina. Glare is a relative matter, and as long as some parts of the retina receive stronger light than others (scarcely an unusual situation) some degree of light will be scattered.

Todd, Norman, and Mingolla (2004) presented observers with a simulated image of an egg-shaped object covered by a Mondrian-like pattern with a glossy finish. Their observers were quite successful at discounting the glossy highlight in order to judge the underlying reflectance of the matte component.

What tells the visual system that a veil is present in the scene? How does the visual system determine the intensity of the veil? This information would seem to be necessary if the true luminance ratios at borders are to be correctly recalibrated. These and other questions have not yet been answered, and this problem is wide open for further research.

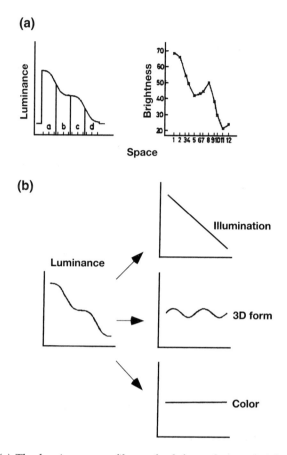

Figure 7.4. (a) The luminance profile on the left produces a brightness profile as shown on the right, suggesting a kind of normalization. (b) The luminance profile can be mathematically decomposed into three simpler components (Bergström, 1977). Reprinted with permission.

Bergström's Common and Relative Components

Bergström (Bergström, 1977a, 1982; Bergström, Gustafsson & Putaan-suu, 1984) has proposed a way of recovering reflectance and illuminance from the image by analyzing light in the retinal image into common and relative components, analogous to Gunnar Johansson's elegant theory of motion perception. Johansson was Bergström's mentor; indeed, Johansson's mentor was none other than David Katz.

The gradient stimulus shown in Figure 7.4a played a key role in the development of Bergström's conception and can be used to illustrate it. Bergström noted that this stimulus produces a brightness paradox (Bergström, 1970, 1977). The brightness at locus c appears greater

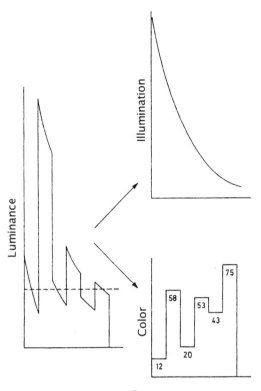

Figure 7.5. The luminance profile on the left represents Land and McCann's (1971) Mondrian illuminated from below (see Fig. 6.8). It can be decomposed into a common component (top right) associated with the illumination and a relative component (lower right) associated with surface lightness (Bergström, 1977). Reprinted with permission.

than that of locus b, even though the physical intensity is higher at b. If one describes the stimulus as a whole, it appears like a corrugated roofing tile, illuminated from the left. This phenomenal description led Bergström to propose that the stimulus is visually analyzed into the three components shown in Figure 7.4b. A gradient of illumination (high on the left, low on the right) accounts for the general downward slant of the function in Figure 7.4b. The remaining sinusoidal variation is attributed to the 3D shape of the surface. When these two components are extracted, what remains is merely a homogeneous reflectance (Bergström, 1977).

Bergström (1977) shows that this approach also provides a nice account of Land and McCann's Mondrian illuminated from below (Fig. 7.5). The luminance profile running from the top light-gray patch to the bottom dark-gray patch is shown in Figure 7.5a. Extracting the illumination gradient or common component from this profile (see Fig. 7.5b) reveals a relative component consistent with Land and McCann's report.

Common and Relative Information at Edges

Just as Johansson's motion analysis is revealed under the minimal conditions of two spots of light, so Bergström's analysis can be elegantly illustrated using the simple disk/annulus stimulus. Consider Walraven's chromatic example. Walraven shows that the color of the disk is determined by the change in light at the border of the disk. This is just another way of talking about the relative component. But Walraven talks about the common component as well, suggesting that the light that is common to the disk and the annulus does not contribute[2] to the color of the disk. According to Bergström, this common component, signaled by the outer boundary of the annulus, is not discarded, but specifies the color of the illumination.

Thus, it is not surprising that when the relative component is eliminated through retinal stabilization, only the common component remains. As Krauskopf (1963, see Chapter 6) has shown, when the boundary of the disk is stabilized, the observer sees merely a large, homogeneous disk, not a large disk with a hole in it.

Minimum Principle

Bergström's (1977) analysis into common and relative components provides a minimal encoding of the stimulus. In addition, Bergström has formulated an explicit minimum principle: *the preferred perceptual organization will always be that which minimizes the number of light sources.* One example of this has already been given in my report (see Fig. 6.25) that a white paper disk partly intersected by two round spotlights is perceived as a single spotlight intersecting two paper disks. Other examples come from various experiments in which Bergström has simulated attached shadows using projected patterns of light.

Bergström Effects

Bergström has produced a series of dramatic 3D effects by projecting patterns of light onto simple paper displays. For example, when a square-wave pattern composed of high- and low-intensity horizontal strips is projected onto a paper Mondrian pattern, as illustrated in Figure 7.6, the Mondrian appears pleated, much like a set of Venetian blinds. This 3D construal reduces the number of light sources from two (representing the two phases of the square wave) to one. Various

Stimulus

3D Percept

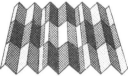

Figure 7.6. The top pattern readily produces the 3D percept shown below it. Reprinted with permission from Bergström et al., 1984.

experiments by Bergström and his colleagues using this basic method have established the following findings:

1. Stimulus complexity is important for these effects. Much stronger 3D effects are produced when the pattern is projected onto a Mondrian display than when it is projected onto a homogenous surface. According to Bergström, the multiple reflectance values in the Mondrian more successfully reveal the common component, noting that "it takes variation to reveal invariance" (Bergström et al., 1993, p. 656). This is all the more remarkable given that horizontal edges in the Mondrian remain strictly horizontal, providing depth cues that the Mondrian is flat. Nevertheless, the greater the number of such edges, the stronger the impression of pleating.
2. Ratio-preserving X-junctions play an important role. The strength of the 3D effect varies directly with the number of such junctions.
3. When the projected grating is oriented horizontally, perceptual reports reveal a preference for seeing overhead lighting, whereas no left–right preference is found when the grating is oriented vertically. In addition, Bergström (Howard, Bergström & Ohmi, 1990) was among the first to establish that the visual system prefers lighting from overhead rather than from

above—that is, 3D effects reverse when observed with the head inverted.

Temporal Modulation of Illumination

In addition to these static effects, Bergström has shown that perceived motion in depth can be produced by temporal modulation of projected illumination. In one experiment, two halves of a Mondrian pattern are separately illuminated by adjacent slide projectors, the intensities of which are sinusoidally modulated over time in counterphase. Observers report various depth illusions, depending on factors like the degree of blur in the boundary of the projected fields. In some cases observers report seeing a corner oscillating from convex to concave, while in other cases a pair of swinging doors is seen.

Careful observation will reveal many illusory 3D effects in everyday scenes, produced by cast illumination gradients. In recognition of Bergström's pioneering work, I suggest that such effects be called Bergström effects.

AMBEGUJAS

The most recent and most astonishing of Bergström's (Jakobsson et al., 1997) illusions has been dubbed AMBEGUJAS, a contraction of the authors' names, reminiscent of Land and McCann's contraction of retina and cortex into Retinex. Two fields of illumination are projected onto a panel containing three adjacent vertical rectangles that differ in gray shade (Fig. 7.7). Adjacent, sharp-edged fields of colored illumination are projected onto the upper and lower halves of the panel, respectively. As Bergström has repeatedly shown, the display will tend strongly to appear 3D. But in this case there are two potential organizations. The display appears to fold, either along the horizontal boundary dividing the two projections or along the vertical boundaries dividing the gray rectangles.

When the folds appear vertical, the observer sees a folded wall, something like a vertically pleated dividing screen. The upper and lower halves of this wall or screen appear to be painted with two well-saturated colors. But when the panel appears to be folded horizontally, all color tends to drain away from the display. The observer sees the three gray shades folding around the horizontal corner. The two planes divided by the fold appear to be illuminated by light of different color temperature, but very unsaturated. At times the color difference seems to disappear altogether.

This illusion must be seen to be believed. It is remarkable that the same stimulus can lead to such different percepts. But there is another, somewhat unsettling, implication concerning the status of the common component. Bergström notes that the relative component is always more salient in our visual experience than is the common com-

Stimulus

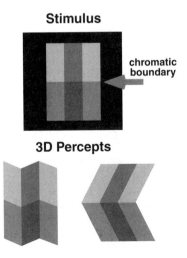

3D Percepts

Figure 7.7. AMBEGUJAS: the stimulus at top readily produces either of the 3D percepts shown below it. When the upper/lower chromatic difference is seen as a property of the surface (lower left), the color is rich and solid. But when it is seen as a property of the illumination (lower right), the color is fainter and sometimes disappears completely. Reprinted with permission from Jakobsson et al., 1997.

ponent. Johansson has made the same observation concerning the common component in motion. And many authors have noted that the color and intensity of the illumination is typically not perceived as clearly as that of the surface reflectance.

This lack of salience is also consistent with general principles of adaptation, and it is not surprising that a color that fills more of the field of view is less salient. But in the AMBEGUJAS phenomenon, the colored regions take up exactly the same part of the visual field, regardless of the perceived 3D structure. In the other Bergström experiments we have discussed, as in the work of Johansson, the common component is not a matter of choice; it is dictated by the stimulus pattern. Whether or not we are fully able to specify an algorithm for extracting the common component, the existence of such an algorithm is assumed. But in the AMBEGUJAS phenomenon, the display can be voluntarily organized in two ways. The strength of the colors seen seems to depend on a choice made by the observer concerning the common component.

Adelson and Pentland: The Workshop Metaphor

Adelson and Pentland (1996) have created a very useful metaphor for the lightness problem faced by the visual system. A team of specialists

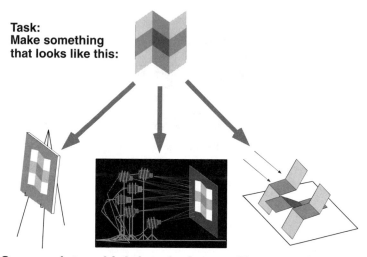

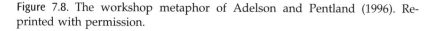

Figure 7.8. The workshop metaphor of Adelson and Pentland (1996). Reprinted with permission.

who build theatrical sets is asked to create the physical arrangements that will produce the top image in Figure 7.8. One member of the team is a painter, one is a lighting designer, and a third member bends metal. Each of the three members is able to create the desired image using his or her own skills. The painter can paint the image on a planar surface. The lighting designer can arrange a set of nine lights of varying intensity, each of which projects one of the parallelograms in the desired image. Finally, the metalworker can cut, bend, and arrange pieces of metal to create the image.

The fact that the image can be reproduced using each of the three specialties alone illustrates the ambiguity of the retinal image. How is the visual system supposed to determine what physical arrangements give rise to any given image? Adelson and Pentland note that this many-to-one mapping problem illustrates a fundamental problem inherent in the inverse optics approach. They propose to solve this problem by exploiting assumptions about regularities in the physical world. These assumptions are built into the workshop metaphor by assigning a specific cost to each step taken by one of the specialists. Thus, simple and common operations are cheap, while more complex and unusual operations are more expensive. A supervisor coordinates the work of the specialists so as to produce the desired image for the lowest overall cost.

Adelson and Pentland (1996, p. 417) describe a sequence of processes to produce the optimal outcome as follows: "The shape process goes to work first and generates its best guess about the shape, seeking the 3-D configuration that explains the 2-D shapes with minimal cost. Then the lighting specialist seeks to explain as many grey-level edges as possible by adjusting the light source direction. Finally the reflectance specialist is allowed to explain whatever is left over. This particular hierarchy gives good solutions to many simple polyhedral images." The shape process is further detailed, at least for polygonal shapes, in terms of a very effective algorithm proposed by Sinha and Adelson (1993) that maximizes the number of right angles and prefers planar surfaces and compactness.

The Adelson/Pentland model shares many features with the earlier Bergström model, including a fundamental minimum principle, represented by Adelson and Pentland as minimum cost.

BRIGHTNESS MODELS

Brightness models are the modern descendents of contrast theories. Their roots can be traced back to Mach and Hering, through Campbell and Robson, Cornsweet, and Marr. It may seem strange to model brightness, or perceived luminance, given that luminance is a proximal quality. But these theorists generally subscribe to the sensation/perception distinction, and they regard brightness as the raw sensation out of which lightness, with the help of cognitive operations, is built.

Although brightness models could arguably be ignored in a book on surface lightness, there are several reasons to include them. First, under homogeneous illumination, lightness and brightness can be treated as equivalent. Second, these models contend that brightness is the first stage of the lightness computation. And these models claim to account for a number of lightness phenomena.

Their ambitious project has been nothing less than to bring together the known facts of physiology and psychophysics in a concrete computer model, a lofty goal if it could be achieved.

These models are elaborate contrast models rooted in the fundamental concept of lateral inhibition. There are several basic components that are common to all of these models. First, each begins by convolving the retinal image by a set of spatial filters based on receptive fields. Some of these models are 2D; others are 1D, usually with a promised expansion to two dimensions. Most are multi-scale; some have only a single scale.

Marr

Marr's program was broader than that of either the brightness models or the decomposition models. In the end he sought to produce lightness values, not merely brightness values. And while the decomposition models accepted edge encoding as a given, Marr sought to explain how edges could be detected in a noisy image using what is known about the wetware. It was this part of his work that inspired so much of the subsequent brightness literature.

Watt and Morgan

Acknowledging the success of Marr's scheme for locating edges (Marr, 1982; Marr & Hildreth, 1980), Watt and Morgan noted other problems with the approach. To determine the degree of blur in an edge, for example, Marr relied on the correlation among spatial filters of different scale. While for a sharp edge, the amplitude of the filter response will be equal for filters at all scales, for a blurred edge the correlation will be reduced, with smaller filters showing a weaker response. But they noted that a second edge nearby will similarly reduce this correlation.

To deal with this and other problems, Watt and Morgan (1985) published a model of spatial primitives in human vision called MIRAGE. First the convolution responses of filters across all spatial scales are combined to produce a single composite convolution-response pattern. Then this response pattern is interpreted, using a set of interpretation rules, to indicate the location, contrast, and blur of features such as bars and edges present in the image. The representation that is interpreted is symbolic in the sense that its features, while not similar to those of the image itself, code for those features. MIRAGE has been generally regarded as successful at predicting the Chevreul illusion, vernier acuity data, Mach bands, and edge blur data, but MIRAGE seems to have trouble with luminance ramps. Fiorentini et al. (1990) argue that either it can predict ramps or it can predict the Mach bands at the ends of a ramp, but not both. The model also produces spurious zero-crossing where no feature exists, and it has difficulties when there are two nearby or superimposed features (Kingdom & Moulden, 1992; Morrone & Burr, 1988). Pessoa et al. (1995, p. 2214) argue that "by providing scene descriptions that employ a vocabulary that only includes 'edges,' 'bars,' and 'plateaus,' MIRAGE does not properly describe brightness phenomena."

Grossberg et al.

Over the years, Grossberg and his associates (Cohen & Grossberg, 1984; Grossberg, 1983; Grossberg & Mingolla, 1987; Grossberg & Todorović, 1988; Pessoa, Mingolla & Neumann, 1995) have presented a series of neural/computational models of human vision, including lightness and brightness. These models originally evolved from conventional contrast models based on lateral inhibition.

Although these models have varied from one publication to another, certain themes have persisted. First, each model can be divided into a series of stages as well as two separate streams. One stream, called the boundary contour system (BCS), involves the encoding of location and luminance change of borders in the image. The other stream, called the feature contour system (FCS), is concerned with the brightness levels filled in within borders. As Pessoa et al. (1995, p. 2202) describe the BCS/FCS framework, "boundaries are used to generate filling-in compartments where featural quality ('brightness' in our case) is diffused, or spread. The final diffused activities correspond to the predicted brightness, whereby boundaries control the process of filling-in by forming gates of variable resistance to diffusion."

The brightness model presented by Grossberg and Todorović (1988) is quite representative. At the first stage, photocell-like units corresponding to the rods and cones encode luminance. The second stage codes luminance ratios using on-center and off-center cells corresponding to retinal ganglion cells and lateral geniculate cells. The third stage encodes the direction of luminance using the difference of two Gaussians with shifted centers. This stage is roughly modeled on cortical simple cells.

At stage 4, the orientation of boundaries is encoded while the polarity of the contrast is lost. For example, a level 4 cell representing a given orientation is activated by any level 3 cell of the same orientation at that location, regardless of its contrast polarity. This stage was added primarily because such cells are known to occur in monkey cortex. At stage 5, all the orientations are pooled and this information is input to the feature contour system.

Stage 6, the final stage, is composed of a syncytium of cells arranged so that activity at any location readily diffuses away from that location by successive cell-to-cell activation. The initial activity level is determined by inputs from the on- and off-cells of stage 2. The activation spreads until it encounters a boundary signaled by stage 5 of the boundary contour system.

The Grossberg/Todorović model successfully modeled simultaneous lightness contrast. But it failed to model Mach bands and gradient induction, and it has difficulties with transitivity effects such as staircase luminance patterns that have been modeled by others using edge integration. As Pessoa et al. (1995, p. 2202) have noted, "The 'steps' of the staircase presumably block diffusion, and it is not evident how a filling-in model can predict that different steps appear with different brightnesses (since 'border contrast' is the same everywhere)." The model also fails for White's illusion and the Benary illusion.

Recently Hong and Grossberg (2004) have published a model of lightness (not brightness) that claims to model a series of findings reported in Gilchrist et al. (1999) concerning lightness compression effects found when various Mondrian patterns are presented within a spotlight. But without an explicit recognition of the distinction between reflectance and illuminance boundaries, the model is unable to account for the very different behavior of patches inside the spotlight versus outside. The most interesting new idea in this model, called the blurred highest luminance rule, involves an attempt to accommodate the role of both relative luminance and relative area within a single concept.

Morrone and Burr

Morrone and Burr (1988) have offered a local energy model based on the recognition that lines and edges occur in the image where Fourier components come into phase, creating a local energy maximum. Their 1D model incorporates two classes of filter: even-symmetric and odd-symmetric. The outputs of these filters are combined nonlinearly and the result is used to label image discontinuities as either "bars" or "edges" in a feature map. The feature map is extracted at each spatial scale and these maps are then combined across scales. The local energy model successfully detects and identifies lines and edges. It predicts Mach bands, but not at luminance steps, where they do not appear. A major problem for the model, however, is that it predicts a homogeneous output for a sine wave grating (McArthur & Moulden, 1999; Pessoa et al., 1995; Ross et al., 1989). Several authors (Kingdom & Moulden, 1992; Pessoa et al., 1995) have noted that because the notion of phase relations doesn't capture amplitude, the local energy model cannot account for the missing fundamental waveform presented at both high and low contrast.

Kingdom and Moulden: MIDAAS

Kingdom and Moulden (1992) reexamined the question of how information at different spatial scales should be combined. The result was a variation of MIRAGE that they called MIDAAS. The main point of departure was that MIDAAS applies the interpretation rules at each scale and then combines interpretations across scale, whereas MIRAGE applies a single interpretation to the multi-scale combination. The model is multi-scale but one-dimensional, like MIRAGE, and uses only on-center filters. This model provides a good account of both the high- and low-contrast versions of the missing fundamental waveform. It can also account for both luminance ramps and their attendant Mach bands. In addition, MIDAAS can handle simultaneous contrast and the Chevreul illusion. However, it fails to predict White's illusion, gradient induction, the Benussi ring, and certain Craik-O'Brien figures. Pessoa et al. (1995) argue not only that there are additional implicit rules in the model, but that the rules, which constitute the core of the model, must be revised to accommodate 2D effects.

Pessoa, Mingolla, and Neumann (1995)

These authors offered a "neural network model of brightness in the tradition of filling-in theories." Their model is one-dimensional and multi-scale and uses both on-center and off-center filters. It is isomorphistic rather than symbolic—that is, the output of the model is held to mimic the perceived brightness distribution in a pointwise fashion. Although the model was developed within the BCS/FCS framework, it incorporates an extensive series of modifications relative to Grossberg and Todorović (1988). These include on and off channels with separate filling-in domains, multiple spatial scales, a new circuit for simple cells, a recurrent competitive circuit, and a new FCS sporting both contrast-driven and luminance-driven channels. The authors sought to demonstrate that an isomorphistic neural network model could achieve the same success as the MIDAAS model and could correctly predict brightness gradients within a BCS/FCS framework.

The model successfully predicts Mach bands where they occur, high- and low-contrast missing fundamental waveforms, and luminance staircases. McArthur and Moulden (1999) have questioned the validity of the luminance channel in Pessoa et al. They also suggest that the Pessoa et al. model is not consistent with known physiology, arguing that work by Lennie et al. (1990) implies that filling-in occurs before on/off channel combination, not after, as in the Pessoa et al. model. The model has not yet been applied to grating induction.

Heinemann and Chase (1995)

These authors have presented a brightness model intended to provide an early vision stage for a pattern recognition model and to simulate the results of Heinemann's (1955) classic brightness induction experiments. The model has three stages. In the first stage the retinal image is convolved with the conventional difference of Gaussians. The dynamic range produced by the first stage is then compressed in logarithmic fashion and a floor is created by replacing values that fall below a threshold value with that threshold value. From the output of stage two at each point is subtracted a value equal to the average of all points in the image, much as in Helson's (1938) adaptation-level formulation.

The model successfully simulates the original Heinemann (1955) data, including the surprising brightness enhancement effect.[3] The model is able to simulate the Craik-O'Brien effect, due to an auxiliary assumption that "brightness judgments are based on the average brightness of the nodes that lie within the area being judged." The model does not predict White's illusion or the Benary effect.

McArthur and Moulden (1999)

These authors have published what is essentially a 2D version of MIDAAS. It operates at multiple scales and includes both on and off channels. The model successfully simulates Mach bands where they appear. The model seems to account for grating induction, Craik-

O'Brien contours (except at high contrast), and the Chevreul illusion. It is partially successful on the Hermann grid. The model fails to predict White's illusion, the Benary effect, and the Shapley and Reid "assimilation" effect (see Fig. 6.10). It also fails to predict staircase contrast, predicting contrast effects for increments but not decrements (compare Fig. 11.17 with Fig. 11 in McArthur & Moulden). But McArthur and Moulden must be commended for their candor in laying out the failures of their model.

Blakeslee and McCourt: ODOG

Blakeslee and McCourt (1997, 1999, 2001; Blakeslee et al., 2005) have presented a simple spatial filtering model that appears to account for a wide variety of illusions. The model is 2D, multi-scale, and multi-orientation. It uses the standard difference of Gaussian filter, with several novel wrinkles. The filters are oriented, consisting of a central excitatory region flanked by a pair of inhibitory regions. And the model includes filters of lower spatial frequency than seen before in such models. For each point in the stimulus, the output of every filter, including all scales and all orientations, is summed, with one important qualification: the outputs of each orientation are normalized to the same maximum value. The normalization stage is the key to understanding how this model predicts assimilation phenomena such as White's effect: here the normalization process shifts the relative contribution to brightness of the different spatial scales in the stimulus from fine to coarse, allowing the coarse scales, which blur the test and grating bars, to predominate.

At least qualitatively, the model has proven successful in simulating simultaneous contrast, Mach bands, grating induction, Shapley and Reid's (1985) "assimilation" figure, Hermann grid, White's illusion, the Torodović illusion, Adelson's corrugated Mondrian, and the Benary effect. This is even more impressive given that no free parameters of the model have been changed.

Of all the brightness models, the ODOG model is probably the most widely endorsed currently.[4] Thus it will be examined most closely.

The model in its present form fails to predict the Craik-O'Brien illusion and the effect of the black line in the Benussi ring.

Although the model accounts for simultaneous contrast in a gross way, a closer look reveals several failures. First, gray targets are predicted to differ in lightness almost as much as the black and white backgrounds, a result that is not realistic. The model predicts that the illusion is largest for targets near the mean luminance, although several reports (Economou, Annan & Gilchrist, 1989; Güçlü & Farrel, 2005; Logvinenko & Ross, 2005) showed that in fact darker targets show the strongest illusion while lighter targets show the weakest illusion (when measured in log reflectance). The model fails to predict the absence of the illusion with double increment targets, as reported in many studies. I don't believe the model predicts the enhancement of the illusion with articulated backgrounds (Adelson, 2000; Bressan & Actis-Grosso, 2004; Gilchrist et al., 1999). And the model predicts a simultaneous contrast effect more than three times bigger than White's illusion (see Fig. 4 in Blakeslee et al., 2005), although most published data show White's illusion to be stronger (compare the two displays in Figs. 10.2a and 10.5). The model fails to predict a greater error for the target on the black background than for the target on white.

The model even stumbles on its flagship illusion, grating induction. It predicts the same magnitude of induced effect for square-wave and sine-wave gratings, even though McCourt (1982) showed that the sine-wave version is stronger.

In addition to these specific failures, the ODOG model shares important failures of brightness models in general. Outlined in Chapter 12, these include the failure to account for (1) lightness constancy with spatially varying illumination, (2) edge classification, and (3) the role of depth in lightness.

SUMMARY

Computational thinking, reflecting the influence of machine vision, brought a renewed emphasis to veridicality and the problem of constancy. These highly rational models have been guided by the logic of inverse optics. Objective properties, like reflectance and illumination, become entangled in the formation of the retinal image, but they can be recovered by decomposition processes that mirror those by which the image is composed. Physiological validity has not been a pressing matter for the decomposition models, nor have they shown much interest in the question of sensations, failures of constancy, or illusions.

Barrow and Tenenbaum, in their model of machine vision, coined the term *intrinsic image* to describe a set of component images inherent in the retinal projection. Gilchrist (1979) proposed that the retinal image can be parsed into a pair of overlapping maps representing reflectance and illumination by encoding edges, classifying them, and integrating within each class. Intrinsic image models explicitly employ the concept of layers, much as was found in the earlier decomposition model proposed by Metelli for perceived transparency.

Bergström, inspired by the decomposition model of his mentor, Johansson, suggested that retinal illumination is parsed into common and relative components, associated with illumination and reflectance respectively. Adelson and Pentland offered a similar model couched in their elegant metaphor of a theatrical workshop.

Such decomposition models easily displaced the simplistic contrast explanations of constancy. But because the computational model bypassed the problem of errors in lightness, they offered no explanation for simultaneous contrast. Thus, lacking a credible rival theory, explanations of simultaneous contrast based on lateral inhibition have survived until today.

The computational era spawned a very different class of models as well, called brightness models, that view brightness, or perceived luminance, as the first stage in lightness. These modern contrast models attempt to explain a range of brightness effects, like simultaneous contrast and Mach bands, using simple spatial filters based on received physiological mechanisms. Brightness models are structure-blind in that they have no provision for either acknowledging the crucial dependence of lightness on depth perception or distinguishing illuminance and reflectance edges.

8

Illumination Perception

NEGLECT OF ILLUMINATION PERCEPTION

What MacLeod (1932) has called "the troublesome problem of illumination perception" has witnessed a strange history. Unlikely as it may sound to a nonspecialist, a variety of lightness theorists have denied that we perceive the illumination. At best the issue has been ignored. Consider the following survey of views.

Helmholtz (1866/1924, v. 2, p. 287) spoke of "eliminating" the illumination, as if discounting means discarding: "In visual observation we constantly aim to reach a judgment on the object colors and to eliminate differences of illumination." It was a contaminating factor, to use Wallach's term, which had to be gotten rid of. Perhaps Helmholtz meant only that the illumination was eliminated from our judgment of object color. But according to Katz (1935, p. 234) Helmholtz "came to consider the perception of illumination in general as something out of the ordinary." At any rate Helmholtz gave little indication that the perception of illumination was a problem to be studied or discussed in its own right.

Hering and his followers took such pains to discredit Helmholtz' use of perceived illumination as the basis of surface lightness that they have seemed to want to deny that illumination is perceived at all. At the least they have ignored the question. As Katz (1935, p. 38) pointed out, "one searches Hering's writings in vain for a statement that the experience of illumination is an independent factor in ordinary colour-perception." This is not to say Hering didn't talk about illumination in the physical sense. He discussed its role in creating the constancy problem but saw it essentially as an intrusion (Hering, 1874/1964,

p. 14): "the eye must inform us, not about the momentary intensity or quality of the light reflected from external objects, but about these objects themselves. It can do this, of course, only when the objects are sufficiently illuminated. Continual change in this illumination, however, is not only not needed for this information, but it would, on the contrary, make it difficult or entirely impossible for the eye to fulfill its essential task if it were not offset to some extent by compensating mechanisms." But on the issue of whether or not illumination is perceived, Hering says little, and what he does say allows only minimal illumination perception: "Most people notice even large differences in two illuminations only when they are presented side by side or in rapid succession."

Jaensch (1919) said of constancy that the illumination is "abstracted." His student, Kroh (1921), gave this expression precision: "In order that we may avoid misunderstandings, may I point out that in our use of the verb 'abstract' we are merely expressing the fact that a particular illumination is not seen." Wallach (1976, p. 32) comments, "the perception of illumination is not relevant to the issue of constancy. However, illumination, too, is sometimes perceived and this fact must now be explained." Cornsweet (1970, p. 380) has written, "our perceptions are correlated with a property of objects themselves (i.e., their reflectances) rather than with the incident illumination." Friden (1973) wrote a paper based on the claim that the more conditions favor lightness constancy, the more they produce insensitivity to the illumination. Hurvich and Jameson (1966, p. 88) regard perception of the illumination (as well as of surface lightness) as a matter of interpretation, not of seeing per se.

According to an influential model introduced by Land (Land & McCann, 1971) but endorsed by such prominent investigators as Marr (1982) and Horn (1974), illumination is filtered out of perception by virtue of the fact that the visual system is relatively insensitive to the shallow gradients of illumination borders.

MacLeod commented on the strange neglect of illumination. He would no doubt be surprised to discover that his remarks, written in 1932 (p. 9), are just as applicable today: "Phenomenally 'illumination' is as valid a datum of experience as 'visual object.' The comparative recency with which it has been recognized as such may be attributed to the slow development of the phenomenological point of view. Until recently illumination has been a factor to be controlled, not to be studied." Apparently MacLeod spoke too soon.

A Symptom of the Photometer Metaphor

In short, the perception of illumination has rather consistently been denied, ignored, or minimized, despite our daily experience of both the overall illumination level and illuminance variations within the scene. As noted earlier, the neglect of illumination perception is a symptom of the photometer metaphor. Cornsweet (1970) seems to get painted into a corner in this way. Central to his account of lightness constancy is his analysis of how the rate of firing of cells exposed to a patterned array could remain invariant after an overall change of illumination on the array. But as Irvin Rock once pointed out to me, this model explains too much! It is a model of lightness identity, not lightness constancy. We are not talking about a metameric match. A gray surface in bright illumination and a gray surface in shadow do not appear identical in all respects, only with respect to surface reflectance. One gray still appears brighter than the other. One appears more brightly illuminated than the other. Reducing the neural activity associated with the two gray papers to identity implies that the illumination is not seen.

Affirmation of Illumination Perception

Perhaps the earliest writer on record as affirming the perception of illumination level was Alhazen (1083/1989, p. 142), who wrote, "Sight . . . recognizes the light of the sun and differentiates between it and the light of the moon or of fire."

Katz approached color perception from a thoroughly phenomenological perspective, from which recognition of the experience of illumination was unavoidable: "It is a fact which we simply cannot deny that we perceive changes themselves in the brightness or hue of the illumination, as long as they transcend a certain limit, and that at any time we are in a position to give a fairly good report of the existing illumination" (Katz, 1935, p. 434).

The Gestaltists placed a premium on good phenomenology, and they paid much respect to Katz on this score. As noted earlier, analyzing the retinal images in terms of edges and gradients, as Koffka did, encourages the recognition of illumination perception just as a pointwise approach discourages it. Koffka pointed out that retinal edges and gradients fall into two broad classes, both in terms of their physical cause and in terms of how they are perceived: reflectance edges and illuminance edges.

Woodworth (1938, p. 599), in the tradition of Helmholtz, referred to "registering" the illumination "so as not to imply in all cases an explicit perception of the illumination." Nevertheless Woodworth gave full recognition to the usual visual experience of illumination. He described what should be too obvious to require statement: "We notice the change when the light is turned on or off, when the sun goes behind a cloud, when we pass from a dark to a light room. Looking out of the window in the morning for a weather observation, we know instantly from the light on the ground, trees or buildings whether the sun is shining and about how brightly it is shining."

Woodworth continued, "it is not enough to register the general illumination, since different parts of the visible environment are differently lighted. Can we perceive regions of different illuminations? Nothing is more certain. High lights and deep shadows are seen as definitely as are object colors. The flecks of sunlight under the trees, the shadow of a house or of a person—examples could be multiplied indefinitely. A shadow is often seen as filling space; a dark corner seems filled with shadow, even when there is no object there to reveal the darkness by its dim reflection." "Our objective tendency extends to illumination conditions as well as to object colors. We are on the watch for both and are not easily deceived."

The perception of illumination has received its most adequate treatment from (1) those who have placed a strong emphasis on phenomenal experience, and (2) those who have been most critical of the photometer metaphor, especially the Gestalt psychologists.

Neither MacLeod nor Helson was a Gestaltist or a phenomenologist strictly speaking, but each was strongly influenced by both Katz and the Gestaltists. MacLeod translated Katz's 1935 book. Perhaps this helped MacLeod to be so clear about the phenomenal status of illumination. "Every visually perceived object is an object in such and such an illumination," he wrote (MacLeod, 1932, p. 8).

Helson (1964, p. 280) offered the adaptation level as "a single visual mechanism which is responsible for constancy, contrast and adaptation" that "renders unnecessary such explanatory molar concepts as noticing or discounting the illumination." But was he denying the perception of illumination or merely denying it a causal role? In the context of discussing lightness constancy in lower forms of animals, Helson (1943, p. 248) asked whether this means "that changes in general illumination pass unnoticed as Jaensch asserted or is there some means by which object color is distinguished from the illumination in which it appears?" His answer is decisive: "Perception of illumination is, as Katz has insisted, as immediate as awareness of object color."

According to Evans (1974, p. 195), "The fact remains, however, that a person can judge the absolute level of illumination, at least for order of magnitude, for all levels."

The intrinsic image models accommodate the perception of illumination very nicely. Patterns of illumination and patterns of surface color can be treated as overlapping layers, much as in a Venn diagram. Duality is no problem here because a given point within the image can have a value of surface lightness that is associated with the reflectance edge that encloses it, but at the same time it can have a value of perceived illumination that is associated with the illuminance edge (or gradient) that encloses it.

EMPIRICAL EVIDENCE

What are the facts of illumination perception? First of all, we know from everyday experience that we do perceive illumination levels. Variations of illumination within scenes are very well perceived. We see shadows and we perceive the difference between mild shadows and deep shadows. As for the overall level of illumination in the environment, this may not be perceived as well, perhaps merely due to its low spatial frequency. Bergström maintains that just as in Johansson's motion analysis, the common component (that is, illumination) is less salient than the relative. Still, though, we easily tell the difference between sunny and cloudy days, between noontime and dusk. We generally know without using a light meter whether there is enough illumination for reading.

But we are less motivated to notice illumination levels. Illumination level is a transitory quality, extrinsic to the object, which is regularly brushed aside as the visual system homes in on permanent object qualities such as reflectance. Kardos (1934, p. 5) brought naïve observers into his laboratory and asked them to describe everything they saw. Except for some artists, the observers never mentioned shadows. When cast shadows were brought to their attention, the typical response was, "Oh, you also wanted that." Kardos concluded that "Shadows are generally not attended to, but can be, since they are optically given." But even when prompted, observers did not report attached shadows: "Self-shadows or relief-shadows, it turns out, strictly speaking do not exist phenomenally at all." Kardos (1928) also made quantitative measurements of perceived illumination.

RELATIONSHIP BETWEEN LIGHTNESS AND PERCEIVED ILLUMINATION

An important theoretical question, closely related to the question of how well illumination is perceived, concerns the relationship between perceived illumination and perceived surface lightness. Four major positions can be distinguished.

Position 1: Lightness Is Derived from Perceived Illumination

This position is most clearly associated with Helmholtz, who maintained that lightness is determined by evaluating the luminance of a surface relative to the perceived level of illumination. Katz (1935, p. 50) agreed, writing, "there is a non-derived, non-inferred, primary impression of the illumination of the visual field which is experientially prior to the experience of the specific colours of the objects which fill the visual field." This dependence of lightness on perceived illumination has come to be known as the "albedo hypothesis," and it implies a tight coupling of the two factors. This means that if the luminance of a target is held constant, an increase in its perceived lightness should be accompanied by a decrease in its perceived illumination, and vice versa.

In a 1977 paper entitled "In defense of unconscious inference," Irvin Rock, while not claiming that the level of illumination is taken into account, suggested merely that the visual system infers that coplanar surfaces receive equal amounts of illumination.

Position 2: Lightness and Perceived Illumination Are Mutually Dependent, but Neither Is Prior

Koffka (1935, p. 244) explicitly proposed an invariant relationship between lightness and perceived illumination without the causal ordering implicit in the albedo hypothesis (see Chapter 4). Likewise, Gelb's (1929, excerpted from Ellis, 1938, p. 276) view of perceived lightness and perceived illumination as parallel phenomena is obvious in his statement that "Severance of illumination and that which is illuminated and perception of a resistant and definitely coloured surface are two different expressions of one and the same fundamental process." The Gelb effect for which he is known was introduced to illustrate the intimate relationship between perceived lightness and perceived illumination, not to attribute causality.

Kozaki and Noguchi (1976; Noguchi & Kozaki, 1985) use the term "lightness-illumination invariance hypothesis," which I will simply call the invariance hypothesis, to distinguish the simple coupling idea from Helmholtz's albedo hypothesis. They write (1976, p. 11), "the tendency to lightness constancy will be larger under the condition in which a change in illuminance can be accurately registered." Musatti (1953) would agree that perception of the illumination goes hand in hand with good lightness constancy: "According to Kardos, the possibility of splitting the chromatic sensations into object color and environmental illumination assures, within some constraints, the constancy of the chromatic appearance in spite of large variations in the illumination." Logvinenko and Menshikova (1994) have produced evidence against the invariance hypothesis, but consistent with a modified form of the hypothesis.

According to Bergström (1977), luminance variations in the retinal image are analyzed into variations in surface lightness, illumination level, and 3D form. Thus, the combination of perceived reflectance and perceived illumination level would be constant for a given luminance, as Koffka proposed. The same invariance is implicit in the decomposition aspect of Adelson and Pentland's (1996) workshop metaphor, as well as my intrinsic image model (Gilchrist, 1979; Gilchrist et al., 1983), and that of Barrow and Tenenbaum (1978).

Empirical evidence supporting Koffka's invariance theorem can be seen in Figures 6.21, 6.22, and 5.13.

Decomposition models are equivalent to the scission models in perceived transparency. The scission concept is evident when Gelb speaks of the "Severance of illumination and that which is illuminated." The analogy seems almost inescapable in cases where a shadow with sharp edges takes on an appearance like a neutral density filter. Indeed, Metelli (1975) published a paper on this topic with the title "Shadows without penumbras."

Metelli's idea is that color scission is the inverse of color fusion. When one surface is perceived to lie behind another, transparent, surface, the local retinal stimulation is thought to be split into two complementary components, one for the transparent layer and one for the surface seen through the transparent layer. As long as the local stimulus value is constant, any change in the perceived value of one layer must be accompanied by an equal and opposite change in the other layer. Intrinsic image models apply the same layered concept to illumination and surface reflectance.

Phenomenally we seem to experience a pattern of illumination superimposed on a pattern of surface colors, and it is plausible to imagine that these perceived layers are produced by a parsing of the retinal image itself. In such models, the question of which comes first, perception of illumination or perception of surface lightness, becomes meaningless—like asking, when a cookie is broken into two pieces, which piece is broken off first.

Rutherford and Brainard (2002) reported an experiment testing both the albedo hypothesis and the invariance hypothesis. The observer viewed two rooms containing objects of various shapes. Each room contained a variety of shades of gray and the two rooms were identical except that each surface in one of the rooms (the light-gray room) was lighter gray than the corresponding surface in the other room (the dark-gray room). Observers first adjusted the illumination level in one room to match that of the other room. The rooms appeared equal in illumination level only when the level in the dark-gray room was physically higher than that of the light-gray room. Then a target rectangle was placed on the wall of each room and observers were asked to adjust the luminance of one of these targets so as to match the other target in lightness. The targets appeared equal only when the target in the dark-gray room was darker in reflectance. Thus, targets of equal luminance did not appear equal in lightness even though illumination levels in the two rooms did appear equal, and the authors note that this contradicts hypotheses that link lightness to perceived illumination. On the other hand, the mismatch found in the data appears relatively modest.

Position 3: Lightness and Perceived Illumination Are Simply Independent

From this perspective, both the priority of perceived illumination and the coupling of lightness and perceived illumination are rejected. Hering, Helson, and Wallach all constructed models of lightness perception that did not include perceived illumination as a component. If illumination is perceived, they considered this to be a separate matter.

According to Helson, the lightness of a surface depends on the relationship between the luminance of the surface and the average luminance within the visual field. This average luminance might be considered as a surrogate for perceived illumination, but it could in principle be computed by a low-level mechanism, and it need not be represented consciously.

When Wallach wrote, "the perception of illumination is not relevant to the issue of constancy" (1976, p. 32), he meant two things: first, that lightness does not depend on a prior registration of illumination, but second, that the degree of lightness constancy and the degree of illumination perception are orthogonal. The albedo hypothesis is rejected.

Beck (1959, 1961, 1972) has argued most explicitly that perceived lightness and perceived illumination have separate stimulus correlates and that therefore the albedo hypothesis is not valid. In one experiment (Beck, 1959) he presented pairs of textured, spotted, and striped patterns haploscopically to observers who were asked to adjust the illumination on one pattern (using a variable transformer) so as to equal the illumination on the other pattern. Each pattern contained only two gray levels. He found first that observers were able to match illumination levels quite accurately. Second, his results showed that illumination levels appear equal when the highest luminance in one pattern equals that of the other pattern. Other bases for the matching, such as matching for average luminance, were not supported.

Although Beck argued that lightness and perceived illumination have separate stimulus correlates, it is interesting to note that he found that perceived illumination depends on the highest luminance in a pattern, just as does the perceived lightness of a surface (see Chapter 9).

In a subsequent paper Beck (1961) reported seven additional experiments of a similar nature, using different surface textures and the presence or absence of a white background. Beck concludes that his results do not support the albedo hypothesis, but in fact five out of his seven experiments produced results consistent with the albedo hypothesis. Beck himself concedes this for four of the experiments: "In Exp. II, III, VI, and VII, lightness constancy was accompanied by a relatively accurate judgment of surface illuminance" (p. 374). He notes that in experiment IV both lightness and perceived illumination were matched inaccurately, but he fails to point out that these two errors were correlated exactly as would be expected by the albedo hypothesis. In that experiment, the stimuli consisted of one piece of medium-gray and one piece of dark-gray flannel cloth. These stimuli are not really composed of two separate gray levels, as are most of the other stimuli, and they are presented under reduction conditions, much as in the Gelb effect. So it is not at all surprising that the lightnesses of these flannel pieces are seen, incorrectly, as equal to each other, and both as light gray. But, like in the Gelb effect, the error in perceived lightness is accompanied by an equal and opposite error in perceived illumination. And of course stronger support for the albedo hypothesis is provided by coordinated errors in lightness and perceived illumination than by coordinated constancies, because the coordination is less likely to be coincidental.

In general the Beck experiments are difficult to interpret and cannot be regarded as constituting a serious challenge to the albedo hypothesis.

Position 4: Veridicality of Lightness and Perceived Illumination Are Negatively Correlated

At this point there is a strange twist in the story. A number of writers appear to subscribe to a veridicality tradeoff between lightness and perceived illumination. According to this line of thinking, lightness constancy is associated with an insensitivity to the illumination, rather than with a sensitivity to it. This position was taken most explicitly by Friden (1973) in a paper called "Whiteness constancy: Inference or insensitivity?" He argued from an experiment on category judgments of illumination and reflectance that the more conditions favor lightness constancy, the more they produce insensitivity to illumination: "illumination does not serve as noise perturbing the object property of surface albedo but rather that in a well-articulated field, Os show an insensitivity to illumination changes. This implies that Os do not have the ability to separate perceptually albedo and illuminance." This argument has been stated by a series of other writers as well.

Helson (1943, p. 249) argues that if an illuminated gray paper and a shadowed gray paper appeared "alike in every respect, it would mean that we cannot distinguish between bright and dim illuminations. The failure in this case to achieve complete constancy serves as a cue to the fact that the illuminations are different." Likewise Jameson and Hurvich (1989, p. 5) have written that if lightness constancy were "a perfectly compensatory mechanism, then there would certainly be no need for experience with, or judgments of, different levels of illumination, because their effects, at least for uniform illuminations and diffuse object surfaces, would never be registered at all beyond the most peripheral level of the visual system." Hering (1874/1964, p. 17) wrote, "Without this approximate constancy . . . If the colors of objects were to be continuously changed in this way along with the illumination changes, then . . . the momentary color in which a given object appears to us could serve as a criterion for the intensity or quality of its illumination." Flock (1974, p. 194), commenting on Helson's work, wrote, "Yet there was a problem. If everything remained constant, then there was no stimulus for specifying the change in the ambient level of illumination." Discussing the task of a lightness perception algorithm, McCann (1988, p. 211) has written, "If the algorithm succeeds in calculating reflectance, then all traces of the illumination will be removed from the computed image." In this view, lightness and perceived illumination are governed by a zero-sum game. By logical extension, if lightness perception were perfect there would be absolutely no sense of the illumination level, and (it can be presumed) if lightness constancy failed completely, perception of the illumination would be complete.

This veridicality tradeoff idea, however, is wrong, both logically and empirically. First, failures of lightness constancy cannot serve as a cue to the illumination. We are not normally aware when lightness constancy has failed. We simply see what we see. Unless we walk around with a Munsell chart constantly checking our lightness percepts, we remain blissfully ignorant of any failures of constancy.

Second, veridicality tradeoff is simply not consistent with the facts. Both Katz and Gelb noted that the minimal conditions for the perception of surface color and the perception of illumination level are the same. In a totally homogeneous visual field, or ganzfeld, no surface color is seen and no specific level of illumination is experienced. As soon as a single border is introduced into the field, both specific surface shades and a specific level of illumination are immediately seen. In the Gelb effect, when a single piece of black paper is presented in a spotlight, there is a failure of both lightness constancy (the black paper appears white) and illumination perception (the spotlight is not perceived). When a white background is placed behind the black paper, then both lightness and illumination are perceived correctly.

SUMMARY

Achieving lightness constancy requires that the impact of illumination on the retinal image be separated from that of surface reflectance. But is the illumination itself perceived? Perception of the illumination has often been neglected or minimized when it has not been simply denied. This follows from a traditional conception in which the retinal image is assumed to contain a single value at every point. That value, however modified by contextual processes, is assigned to lightness and thus unavailable to perceived illumination.

To the extent that illumination is perceived, how is that percept related to lightness? According to Helmholtz, lightness is derived from perceived illumination and thus the two factors are related in an in-

variant and complementary way. Koffka and the decomposition theorists accepted this invariance but denied that either factor depends
on the other. Hering, Wallach, and Beck argued that the two factors
are simply independent. Still other writers (Friden, 1973; Helson, 1943)
have argued that we cannot be sensitive to both illumination and reflectance. To the extent that we achieve lightness constancy, we must
be unaware of the illumination.

9

The Anchoring Problem

MISSING LINK IN THE DECOMPOSITION MODELS

The final component required for a complete theory of veridical perception is an anchoring rule or set of rules. Although it has not been widely recognized, most theories of lightness perception, including decomposition theories, can, at most, assign only relative lightness values to the surfaces in a scene. They may predict, for example, that a particular surface is five times lighter, or three times darker than a neighboring surface.

But our perceptual experience of a surface has an absolute quality that must also be accounted for. Surfaces do not merely appear as lighter or darker than one another, by some factor. Rather, each surface appears to have a specific shade of gray. When I see a surface as white, I am not saying that it appears three times lighter than its neighbor. After all, a middle gray might also be three times lighter than its neighbor. I am saying that it appears to have a specific value of lightness—that is, white.[1]

Generally, models of lightness perception have yielded only relative lightness values, at best, that is, target lightness only relative to the lightness of other surfaces within the same scene. To produce absolute lightness values requires an anchoring rule. This is a rule that identifies a specific value of lightness (like white or middle gray) with some property of the retinal image (like highest luminance, average luminance, or largest area).

Anchoring and Scaling

Anchoring is part of the larger problem of mapping luminance values onto lightness values. The other part is what I will call scaling. Scaling concerns how intervals (specifically ratios) on the luminance scale are translated into intervals on the lightness scale. For example, Wallach's ratio principle amounts to a 1:1 scaling rule. Edge enhancement, often found in contrast theories, implies an expansive scaling rule: the interval on the lightness scale is larger than the interval on the luminance scale to which it corresponds. Brown and MacLeod's (1997) gamut expansion is a further example. While scaling deals with intervals on the luminance and lightness dimensions, anchoring deals with locations on these dimensions. An anchoring rule identifies a given location on the scale of perceived lightness values (such as middle gray or white) with some variable taken from the proximal stimulus (such as highest luminance or average luminance).

Anchoring is similar to normalization, but it is a normalization on the lightness dimension, not the luminance dimension. Absolute luminance may be lost at encoding, but recovering it is not the problem. The visual system doesn't need absolute luminance information, but it needs to produce absolute lightness values.

The ambiguity of absolute luminance values in the proximal stimulus is widely known and understood. If I tell you that the luminance of a given surface is 120 foot-Lamberts, this tells you nothing about the lightness of that surface. What has not been recognized is that relative luminance values are scarcely less ambiguous. For instance, if I tell you that the luminance of a target surface is five times higher than the luminance of its adjacent retinal neighbor, although I give you some additional information, you still do not have enough information to assign a specific lightness value to the target. The adjacent neighbor might be black, in which case the target must be middle gray. But if the adjacent neighbor is middle gray, then the target is white. In fact it is possible that the adjacent neighbor is white, in which case the target must be self-luminous. So the solution is not even restricted to the range of opaque grays.

HIGHEST LUMINANCE VERSUS AVERAGE LUMINANCE

Although a clear statement of the anchoring problem has been lacking in the literature, several anchoring rules have been invoked. Wallach emphasized his ratio principle, which is a scaling rule, not an anchoring rule. But he mentioned, almost in passing, that the highest luminance in his disk/annulus display is perceived as white and serves as a standard. Evans (1974, p. 204) wrote, "The perception of a true white object in a scene therefore tends to be independent of illumination color or intensity; it is seen as the anchor-point, so to speak, of the object frame of reference in its vicinity, quite independent of its psychophysical variables as a stimulus."

The highest luminance rule has also been invoked by Land and McCann (1971), Horn (1986), Marr (1982), and others in the machine vision tradition. Newson (1958, p. 95) wrote, "Other things being equal, the brightest area in the neighborhood of the test surface is of fundamental importance in controlling the appearance of the test surface."

A different anchoring rule can be found at the heart of Helson's (1943, 1964; Judd, 1940) adaptation-level theory.[2] In the simplest description of this approach, any surface with a luminance value equal to the average luminance in the entire scene is perceived as middle gray. Luminance values higher than this are seen as light gray or white, lower luminances as dark gray or black. I will call this the average luminance rule. This rule is implicit in several more modern approaches, especially in the chromatic domain, where it is known as the gray world assumption (Buchsbaum, 1980; Hurlbert, 1986; Hurlbert & Poggio, 1988). Furthermore, this rule is implicit in the concept of equivalent surround (Bruno, Bernardis & Schirillo, 1997; Schirillo & Shevell, 1996; Valberg & Lange-Malecki, 1990) and in various experiments that include a control for space-averaged luminance of a target's surround. Helmholtz, Hering, Mach, and Katz had all proposed the average luminance as the basis for perceived illumination, a concept closely related to the anchor. Helmholtz promoted both the average luminance and the highest luminance in different passages.

An important hint was given in 1965 by Kozaki (p. 146): "Why constancy is promoted by the co-existence of higher reflectance stimuli should be explored. For this problem, proportional law (Wallach, 1948) and adaptation-level theory (Helson, 1943) have not offered sufficient explanation."

Several writers have also hinted at a bipolar anchoring rule, with the highest luminance seen as white and the lowest seen as black (Kirschmann, 1892, p. 546; Rock, 1982, p. 210).

Empirical Data Support Highest Luminance Rule

Experiments testing between these two alternative rules have appeared in the literature only very recently. In general the results favor the highest luminance rule and not the average luminance rule. We will review the evidence for this conclusion.

Xiaojun Li and I (Li & Gilchrist, 1999) tested these rules under the simplest conditions possible for lightness perception,[3] namely two regions that fill the entire visual field and whose luminance ratio is less than the range between black and white (30:1). To exclude any other luminance values, including darkness, from the visual field, we painted two shades of gray side by side on the interior of a large opaque hemisphere that filled the observer's entire visual field. One half of the hemisphere was painted black (Munsell 2.5) and the other half middle gray (Munsell 5.5), creating a 5.3:1 luminance range. We found that when an observer's head is positioned inside the hemisphere and the lights are turned on, the middle gray half appears

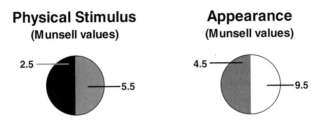

Physical Stimulus
(Munsell values)

Appearance
(Munsell values)

Figure 9.1. The black and gray interior surfaces of the dome shown at the left are perceived as gray and white, as shown on the right (Li & Gilchrist, 1999). Reprinted with permission.

completely white and the black half appears middle gray. This result, shown in Figure 9.1, decisively favors the highest luminance rule. If the average luminance rule were correct, the two halves of the display would appear to have lightness values equidistant from middle gray; the lighter half would appear light gray and the darker half dark gray. No white (or black) would be seen.

Cataliotti and I presented observers with a 15-patch Mondrian containing a restricted (10:1) range of gray shades, extending from black to middle gray. The Mondrian was presented in a spotlight within an otherwise dimly illuminated lab room. The highest luminance in the Mondrian, physically a middle gray, was seen as white. The perceived lightness values of all the surfaces in the Mondrian were not distributed symmetrically about middle gray. For instance, no surface at all was seen as black. In a separate experiment we placed observer's heads inside a Mondrian world, a trapezoidal-shaped chamber, all the interior surfaces of which were painted with a restricted range (4:1) Mondrian pattern containing dark-gray shades no lighter than Munsell 4.0. Again, the highest luminance appeared white and no black surfaces were seen. The average luminance rule has been tested indirectly in several experiments on equivalent backgrounds conducted by Bruno (1992), Schirillo and Shevell (1996), and Bruno, Bernardis, and Schirillo (1997). In general they obtained evidence more consistent with the highest luminance rule than with the average. Bruno, Bernardis, and Schirillo (1997, p. 651) concluded that their results were "not statistically distinguishable from the highest luminance expectations." But Valberg and Lange-Malecki (1990) have reported that a target surrounded by a highly articulated (colored) Mondrian has the same lightness as a target of equal reflectance, surrounded by a gray background set to the space average of the Mondrian. Brown (1994) has produced evidence in the chromatic domain that contradicts the gray world assumption. The highest luminance rule is also supported by the basic finding in various brightness induction experiments: changes in inducing field luminance affect test field brightness only when the inducing field has the highest luminance.

PROBLEMS WITH THE HIGHEST LUMINANCE RULE

Although the existing literature supports the highest luminance rule, certainly as compared with the average luminance rule, several facts suggest that the highest luminance rule is only part of the story.

The Luminosity Problem

The biggest problem for the highest luminance rule (one might call it a glaring problem) concerns the perception of self-luminous surfaces. Some surfaces in the world around us appear brighter than white. They appear to emit more light than they receive, as if they have their own internal light source. The very appearance of self-luminosity directly contradicts the highest luminance rule, according to which white is a ceiling above which no surface can appear.

Consider a common example, as illustrated in Figure 9.2. Many modern office buildings have suspended ceilings that are composed of large, square white panels, but some of the square panels are actually light sources, containing fluorescent light fixtures. According to the highest luminance rule these self-luminous panels should appear opaque white, relative to which the rest of the white ceiling should appear gray or black. But instead the ceiling appears white (or light gray) and the fluorescent panels appear self-luminous.

How can we account for this result? It contradicts the highest lu-

Figure 9.2. Here the ceiling appears white (or close to white; some constancy is lost in the photograph) even though it is not the highest luminance.

minance rule. Nor can the average luminance rule solve the problem.[4] Somehow the solution seems to require that geometric factors be taken into account. Discussing his experiments with disk/annulus stimuli, Wallach (1976) observed that when the disk is brighter than the annulus, it appears self-luminous: "If the spot (disk) is more intense (than the annulus), it will show no color other than white. An increase in the intensity difference will cause a different kind of quality, that is, luminosity, to appear in addition to the white and a further increase will merely cause luminosity to become stronger" (Wallach, 1976, p. 8, parenthetical comments added).

The Direction-of-Induction Problem

So far we have treated the anchoring problem as one of how absolute lightness values can be derived from relative luminance values. But there is a different and equally useful way to state the problem: When the luminance difference between two adjacent regions is increased, will the darker region appear to darken further, or will the lighter region appear to become lighter?[5] If both change, will they change by equal amounts? This question is presented in schematic form in Figure 9.3. Bergström (1977) and Schouten and Blommaert (1995b) have framed the anchoring problem in this way (Fig. 9.4). Stated in this way, the problem of anchoring lightness is very similar to that of anchoring motion. When relative motion occurs between two objects, which object will appear stationary and which will appear to move? Induced motion, for example, is primarily a fact about anchoring in the motion domain.

Notice that *the highest luminance rule is consistent only with downward induction.* But in fact, both downward induction and upward induction have been obtained empirically.[6]

Imagine there is a square piece of middle-gray paper on the wall in the room in which you are sitting. If we have some way to grad-

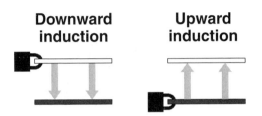

Figure 9.3. Downward versus upward induction. An increase in the luminance difference between two regions can produce a darkening of the darker region, a brightening of the brighter region, or a combination of these. This is the anchoring problem in another form.

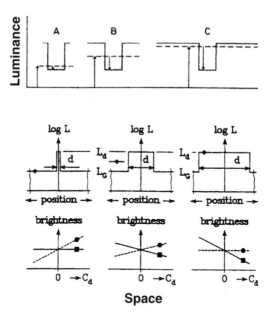

Figure 9.4. The direction of induction depends on the relative areas of target and surround. In the upper figure, the dashed line indicates shift of the common component (analogous to the anchor) as relative area shifts from target to surround (Bergström, 1977; reprinted with permission). In the lower figure, as relative area shifts from target to surround, upward induction of target shifts to downward induction of surround (Schouten & Blommaert, 1995; reprinted with permission).

ually increase the luminance of the piece of gray paper, it will begin to appear lighter and lighter gray. At some point it will appear completely white. As we continue to increase its luminance it will begin to appear as a kind of super-white, and finally it will come to appear self-luminous. This should not happen according to the highest luminance rule. The paper should appear white when its luminance is the highest in the room, but further increases in its luminance should not affect the appearance of the paper itself, but rather should cause all other surfaces in the room to darken in surface lightness.

To Bonato and me, the twin problems of luminosity perception and upward induction implied that the highest luminance rule either cannot be the correct rule, or at least, cannot be the only rule of anchoring. We noted a regularity in Wallach's results that could potentially resolve the dilemma. The data Wallach published as support for his ratio principle were obtained exclusively using decremental displays—that is, displays in which the disk had a lower luminance than the surrounding annulus. And for these kinds of displays the highest luminance rule works just fine. The annulus always appears white, regardless of its luminance, as long as it is the highest luminance, and the perceived lightness of the disk depends merely on the luminance ratio between the disk and the annulus. But in incremental displays, when the disk has the highest luminance, the highest luminance rule no longer seems to apply. The highest luminance, in this case the disk, appears brighter than white, and further increases in the luminance of the disk do not necessarily have a darkening effect on the perceived lightness of the annulus. We might say that the highest luminance rule applies to decremental disks, not to incremental disks, but this is an awkward formulation that does not fully explain the results.

Testing the Surround Rule

Fred Bonato and I noted a factor that can be applied to both incremental and decremental displays in the Wallach experiments: the annulus always appeared white. The annulus is the highest luminance only for decrements. When the disk is an increment, the annulus is not the highest luminance. However, in both cases the annulus surrounds the disk, forming its immediate background. This suggested a new hypothesis: a surround rule, according to which, for simple displays at least, the surround tends to appear white. Decremental disks appear as some shade of opaque gray and incremental disks appear self-luminous.

To test this hypothesis it was necessary to revisit the Wallach experiments, making three changes. First, we collected data for incremental displays as well as for decremental displays. Second, we tested the perception of the annulus in addition to the perception of the disk. And third, we measured observers' lightness percepts using a Munsell scale. Wallach, for his purposes, had required observers to adjust the luminance of the disk in a disk/annulus pair to match their percept of the disk in a second disk/annulus pair that had different absolute luminance values. Using this technique the experimenter can determine that two disks appear equal in lightness, but not the specific lightness appearance of either disk. Because anchoring concerns precisely the absolute lightness value, rather than merely the relative, we used a Munsell scale.

For each different disk/annulus luminance ratio, observers matched both the disk and the annulus using a separate apparatus in which a comparison square embedded within a Mondrian could be adjusted in luminance to appear as any shade of gray, or self-luminous with any degree of brightness.

The results we obtained (Gilchrist & Bonato, 1995) are shown in Figure 9.5. The two small diagrams in the figure illustrate the ideal results under the highest luminance rule (top) and the surround rule (bottom). Qualitatively the obtained results are most similar to the pattern predicted by the surround rule, but a small influence of the

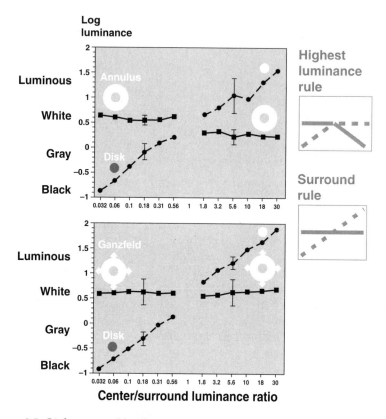

Figure 9.5. Lightness and brightness matches for a disk/annulus display (top) and a disk/ganzfeld display (bottom) (Gilchrist & Bonato, 1995). Ideal patterns of results under two anchoring rules are shown at the right. Adapted by permission.

highest luminance rule can be seen in the data as well. First, notice that the line representing the annulus in the decremental displays and the line representing the annulus in the incremental displays are not collinear. There is an offset, with the annulus appearing darker gray in all incremental displays than it appears in any of the decremental displays. Second, it can be noted that the lines representing both the disk and the annulus in incremental displays appear to be rotated slightly in a clockwise direction relative to their ideal form under the surround rule. A subsequent experiment using a great luminance range revealed that the line representing the annulus in incremental displays is not completely horizontal but has a small, statistically significant negative slope (see Gilchrist & Bonato, 1995, Fig. 6, p. 1434).

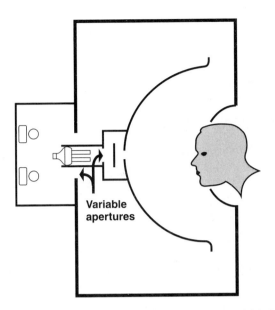

Figure 9.6. Apparatus for presenting a disk within a ganzfeld. Separate vari-able apertures control the luminance of the disk and the ganzfeld indepen-dently (Gilchrist & Bonato, 1995). Adapted with permission.

Disk/Ganzfeld Stimulus. We reasoned that this compromise between the pattern expected by the highest luminance rule and the pattern expected by the surround rule occurred because the disk/annulus stimulus is not the optimal stimulus for this kind of a test. The disk/annulus stimulus allows a third region within the visual field: the dark background against which the disk/annulus display is seen. This cre-ates other relationships within the visual field besides the disk/an-nulus relationship, which is of central interest. We suspected that this region of darkness within the visual field (or perhaps the presence of the outer border of the annulus) somehow allows the data to take the more complex form we had obtained. Our solution was to repeat the experiments using a disk within a ganzfeld. The apparatus is shown in Figure 9.6.

The results are shown in the bottom of Figure 9.5. With the disk/ganzfeld stimulus the data take a very simple form that is completely consistent with the surround rule. No traces of the highest luminance rule can be seen in the data. In addition to the clear pattern of data we had obtained, the surround rule seemed sensible. Figure/ground considerations had been shown to be important for a variety of per-ceptual qualities, which would now include perceived lightness. Fur-thermore, the surround rule, unlike the highest luminance rule, ap-peared to be consistent with the facts of self-luminosity.

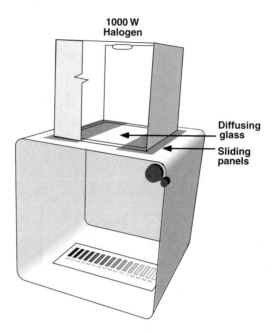

Figure 9.7. Apparatus for matching illumination levels.

Bonato and I also took measurements of perceived illumination. Observers adjusted the illumination level in the apparatus shown in Figure 9.7 to equal the apparent illumination in the ganzfeld. Figure 9.8 shows both illumination matches and disk lightness matches for decremental disks. Although variability was relatively high, the means show good illumination matching. And overall the results are consistent with Koffka's invariance theorem.

EXPERIMENTS ON AREA: SURROUND RULE FAILS

But apparently we were wrong on the surround rule. In our disk/ganzfeld experiments, relative area is confounded with surroundedness. The ganzfeld surround has a much larger area than the disk. Xiaojun Li and I set out to tease apart area and surroundedness using simple patterns painted on hemisphere interiors, as shown in Figure 9.9. To our surprise we found that the results that Bonato and I had obtained could be attributed, perhaps entirely, to relative area, not to surroundedness.

To test the role of relative area in the absence of figure/ground considerations, we compared the dome described earlier (equal areas of black and gray) with a second dome in which the border between the two gray shades was shifted to the right so that now the black

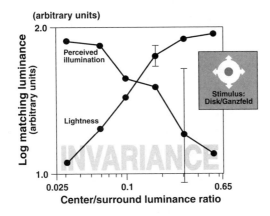

Figure 9.8. As ganzfeld luminance decreases, the increase in the lightness of a disk of constant luminance is roughly mirrored by its decreasing level of perceived illumination, consistent with Koffka's invariance theorem (Gilchrist & Bonato, 1995). Adapted by permission.

region came to occupy a much larger proportion of the observer's visual field than the gray region. The results of this comparison are shown in Figure 9.9b. While the middle-gray region appeared white in both regions (the 8.9 is not significantly different from the 9.5), the black region appeared substantially lighter when its area was increased.

We then pitted relative area against surroundedness in several center/surround configurations. We compared a small disk in a ganzfeld with a large oval in a ganzfeld. The large oval was drawn so that its boundaries were as far out in the periphery as possible while at the same time guaranteeing that its entire boundary would be within the visual field of any observer fixating its center. Both incremental and decremental displays were tested, and the same two shades of black and middle-gray paint, with a luminance ratio of 5.3:1, were used. The results for decrements are shown in Figure 9.9c and 9.9d (Li & Gilchrist, 1999). Notice that the surrounding ganzfeld appeared white, regardless of the area of the center, but the large oval was seen as substantially lighter than the small disk. This result, together with the results from the split ganzfeld, suggests that as surfaces become larger, they also appear lighter gray.

The results for incremental displays using the small disk and the large oval are shown in Figure 9.9e and 9.9f. In both cases the incremental center appeared white. The ganzfeld surround produced a lower mean Munsell value in the large oval condition than in the small disk condition. Although this particular difference fell just short of statistical difference, there is good reason to believe that the difference

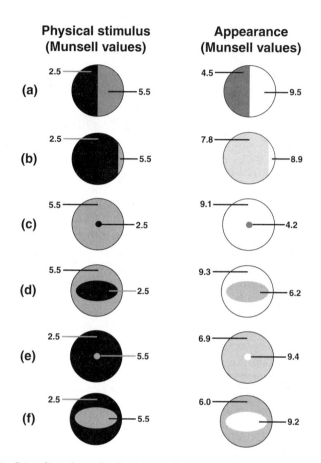

Figure 9.9. Stimuli and results from Li and Gilchrist's (1999) experiments with domes. Reprinted with permission.

is real and probably larger than what we obtained. In several other experiments we have conducted using a small incremental disk in a ganzfeld surround, we obtained lightness judgments for the ganzfeld surround between 8 and 9 on the Munsell scale (Gilchrist & Bonato, 1995). We are inclined to take these values as more representative and assume that the 6.9 value we obtained for the ganzfeld surrounding the small disk is misleadingly low, due either to chance variability or to some uncontrolled factor. Under this logic, the ganzfeld surround is substantially lighter in the small disk condition than in the large oval condition, and these results are consistent with the effect of area found in our split dome conditions and in our decremental center/surround conditions.

The 6.0 value we obtained for the ganzfeld surround in the large oval condition is especially damaging to the surround rule. According to the surround rule, the surround in such a simple display must always appear white, whereas here it appeared only slightly lighter than middle gray.[7]

These results suggest a clear role of area on perceived lightness. Furthermore, they leave little or no room for an effect of surroundedness over and above the effect of area. In general we can say that we have uncovered a tendency for the largest area, in such a simple display, to appear white, consistent with Helson's (1964, p. 292) remark that "within certain limits area acts like luminance, that is, increase in area has the same effect as increase in luminance." Notice that "the larger, the lighter" effect seems to apply only when the area of the darker of the two regions is larger than the area of the lighter of the two. For example, the small disk (in the decremental case) was rated as a Munsell 4.2, not significantly different from the appearance of the gray region when it filled half of the visual field, as in the split dome condition. In other words, enlarging the area of the small disk to the point where it fills half of the visual field had no effect at all on its perceived lightness. The main effect of area on perceived lightness seems to kick in only once the area of the darker region begins to exceed the area of the lighter region.

When the area of the darker region is less than the area of the lighter region, anchoring appears to be based exclusively on the highest luminance rule. The surround rule, proposed earlier by Gilchrist and Bonato (1995), was offered as a substitute for the highest luminance rule. However, the effect of area on perceived lightness that we have uncovered, which could be dubbed the largest area rule, is not a substitute for the highest luminance rule but seems to coexist with it. The critical question now becomes, precisely how does the highest luminance rule combine with the largest area rule in the anchoring of surface lightness?

Highest Luminance or Largest Area?

We have two tendencies. The highest luminance wants to be white and the largest area wants to white. Notice that in many such simple displays the largest area and the highest luminance belong to the same region. This is true for most simple displays that have been reported in the literature. Indeed, the very popularity in this field of the disk/annulus display, in which the disk is darker than the annulus, may reflect an intuitive yet unarticulated appreciation of the role of area. As long as the region with the largest area also has the highest luminance, there is no conflict between the two rules: that region is anchored firmly at white, and the lightness of the darker region is simply a function of the luminance ratio between the two. But when the darker region comes to have the larger area, there is a conflict between these two tendencies.[8] This conflict seems to produce a variety of strange effects.

Effects Produced by Luminance/Area Conflict

Among these effects are (1) gamut compression: the perceived range of lightness values is less than the physical luminance range in the display, (2) Heinemann's (1955) enhancement effect, (3) the fluorence phenomenon of Evans (1974, p. 100), (4) Schouten and Blommaert's (1995b) brightness indention effect, and (5) the phenomenon of self-luminosity.

THE AREA RULE

Collating all the empirical evidence we have gathered so far, we can state the effect of area on lightness in the following way: In a simple two-part display, when the darker of the two regions has the larger area, increases in the area of the darker region produce an increase in its lightness value, and finally, when the darker region becomes much larger than the lighter region, the lighter region comes to appear self-luminous. These relationships are shown graphically in Figure 9.10.

According to the area rule as I have stated it, gamut compression[9] should clearly occur in two of the displays: the split dome with the eccentric border (Fig. 9.9b) and the incremental small disk (Fig. 9.9e). In the first of these, we obtained a perceived range (ratio between matched reflectance of lighter and darker region) of 1.4:1. This was only 26% as big as the actual range (5.3:1). In the second case we obtained a perceived range of 2.1:1, only 40% of the actual range.

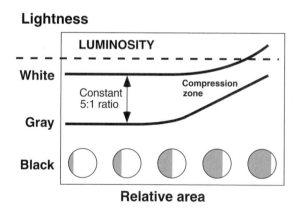

Figure 9.10. Predicted lightness in a two-part dome as relative area shifts. Luminance values are constant (Gilchrist et al., 1999). Adapted with permission.

Gamut compression should occur also in either the incremental case or the decremental case of the large oval condition. The reason for uncertainty here is that there are several complications in determining the relative area in these two conditions. Our goal had been to make the area of the center oval larger than that of the ganzfeld background. However, to guarantee that the boundaries of the large oval fell within the visual system for all observers, it was necessary to be somewhat conservative in constructing the size of the large oval. Second, the effective area of the ganzfeld surround is difficult to determine. For one thing, that region does not appear to stop at the boundaries of the visual field. This is a well-known fact. Second, to the extent that the large oval is seen as figure and the ganzfeld is seen as ground, the ground is perceived to extend, at least to some extent, behind the figure (Rubin, 1921). Later I present evidence that it is perceived area that is critical, not retinal area. At any rate, both of the large oval conditions, the incremental and the decremental, produced a modest level of compression.

According to the area rule, no compression should occur in the two remaining conditions, the split dome condition and the small disk decremental condition. In fact, a modest gamut expansion (7.5% for the split dome and 15% for the small disk) was produced in these conditions. This kind of gamut expansion, which I call scale normalization, is discussed further on pages 263–264.

Li and I proposed that the gamut compression we obtained in some of our domes experiments is produced by a competition between the tendency for the highest luminance to appear white and the tendency for the largest area to appear white. Note that in Figure 9.10, after the area of the darker region becomes more than 50% of the total area, and we continue to increase its area at the expense of the area of the lighter region, the conflict between highest luminance and largest area intensifies. At this point the lighter region takes on a pre-luminosity super-white appearance. This phenomenon has been labeled fluorence by Ralph Evans, although he has applied it mainly in the chromatic domain. In the achromatic domain it seems to apply to the appearance of a surface that is brighter than white but not bright enough to appear self-luminous.

The same conditions that produce fluorence or super-white are the conditions under which Heinemann's enhancement effect occurs in a disk/annulus display, suggesting that Heinemann's enhancement effect is the manifestation of fluorence under disk/annulus conditions. Gamut compression may represent an attempt by the visual system to accommodate the conflicting demands of the highest luminance rule and the largest area rule, but it is an uneasy resolution, involving a discrepancy between the range of physical luminances in the display and the range of perceived lightness values. Presumably the visual system can tolerate such discrepancy only as long as it does not become too great. When the discrepancy becomes large, other perceptual qualities must be invoked to keep the total visual experience roughly commensurate with the proximal stimulus. Fluorence and the enhancement effect do just this. By perceiving the highest luminance as a super-white, perhaps a very highly reflective white, the visual system at least partially acknowledges the strength of the luminance difference between the two regions.

Schouten and Blommaert (1995b) reported a brightness indention phenomenon that we believe functions in the same way. They conducted experiments using a display consisting of two disks seen within a ganzfeld. Taking brightness measurements for the ganzfeld as well as the two disks, they ran into a problem. When both disks are increments, the ganzfeld background does not appear homogeneous but rather appears to have a dark halo around each disk. They report that this indention phenomenon occurs only when the two disks are brighter than the ganzfeld background. In other words, it occurs only under the conditions to which the area rule applies. I suggest that the indention phenomenon is another product of the conflict between the highest luminance rule and the largest area rule. An incremental disk seen within a ganzfeld wants to appear white because it is the highest luminance, but the ganzfeld background also has a claim on white by virtue of its very large area. But seeing both the disk and the ganzfeld background as white, even if they are seen as somewhat different shades of white, would contradict the substantial luminance difference between those regions. By creating an illusory brightness gradient in the ganzfeld background, the visual system reduces the conflict. Where the ganzfeld background comes near to the incremental disk it appears darker, consistent with the luminance difference between disk and ganzfeld. Farther away from the disk, the ganzfeld background brightens, consistent with the tendency for a large region to appear white. Newson (1958, p. 87) described the same phenomenon in his experiments on the Gelb effect. Bonato and I have also observed brightness indention in our disk/ganzfeld experiments.

Of course, devices like fluorence and brightness indention are effective only up to a point. If the area advantage of the darker region over the lighter region becomes great enough, or if the luminance advantage of the lighter region over the darker region becomes great enough, the contradictions can be resolved only by perceiving the lighter region as self-luminous. This seems to be exactly what happens, although there is also evidence of a certain degree of resistance by the visual system to perceiving self-luminosity, possibly an example of Bergström's claim that the visual system tries to minimize the number of perceived light sources.

Luminosity and the Area Rule

The area rule, like the surround rule, accommodates the existence of self-luminosity in a way that the highest luminance rule could not. But in addition the area rule is far more consistent with the empirical data than is the surround rule. Perhaps more importantly, the area rule goes far toward describing the intimate coupling between surface lightness perception and the perception of self-luminosity, at least in these relatively simple displays. Any change in relative luminance or relative area will affect both our lightness percepts of the regions and the probability of perceiving self-luminosity in the lighter region. The area rule also solves the puzzle of upward and downward induction. In general, the greater the relative area of the darker region, the more the upward induction. The greater the relative area of the brighter region, the more the downward induction. We have already seen schematics by Bergström and by Schouten and Blommaert showing these relationships in Figure 9.4. We will return to a more detailed discussion of the perception of self-luminosity after we survey the relevant literature on area effects in lightness and brightness.

Area Rule: The Empirical Evidence

Although the area rule that emerged from our experiments with domes had not been found in the literature, it is very consistent with the results of perhaps a dozen published reports on the effect of area on lightness/brightness.

In most of Wallach's experiments, the disk was both darker than the annulus and smaller in area (about one-fourth as large as annulus area). Thus, the area rule would not apply. However, Wallach did report on several probe experiments that he made on the effect of area using decremental disks. In one probe he reduced the area of the annulus so as to be the same as the area of the disk. He found this had no effect on perceived lightness values, and this is consistent with our rule. In a further probe, he reduced the size of the annulus to an area only one-fourth that of the disk. This produced a pronounced effect of area upon perceived lightness, causing the decremental disk to appear substantially lighter than would otherwise be the case. This is completely consistent with our findings. Wallach (1948, p. 323) implied a key feature of our area rule when he observed, "It seems that, once the ring has an area equal to that of the disk, any further increase in its width does not affect the resulting color of the disk."

Burgh and Grindley (1962) tested the strength of simultaneous lightness contrast as a function of the overall retinal size of the contrast display. They found no effect at all, which is consistent with our area rule because they did not vary the relative area of the lighter and darker regions.

Stewart (1959) varied relative area in the Gelb effect. A large black disk was made to appear white by presenting it alone in a hidden beam of light. Its lightness value was substantially lowered by the introduction of a smaller white disk into the beam, adjacent to the black disk. Stewart varied the size of the smaller white disk and tested the resulting perception of the large disk. Because the white disk was always brighter than the black disk and because it always had a smaller area than the black disk, all of Stewart's conditions fall within the area zone. Consistent with this, Stewart obtained a pronounced effect of area on perceived lightness, with the black disk appearing lighter as the white inducing disk became smaller.

Diamond (1955) and Stevens (1967) have both reported studies in which perceived brightness was measured as a function of relative area. Diamond worked with adjacent rectangular patches, while Stevens worked with a disk/annulus pattern. Both obtained pronounced variation in perceived brightness primarily within the zone of the area rule (see Fig. 32 in Gilchrist et al., 1999).

Newson (1958) presented a display consisting of a darker square center and a lighter square surround, illuminated by a spotlight, as in the Gelb effect. Holding both center and surround luminance constant, he tested perception of the center while surround area varied from zero to an area roughly equal to that of the center. This range is just equivalent to the area zone, and he obtained a strong effect on center lightness. In fact, his curve, shown in Figure 9.11, reached an asymptote just where the area of the surround comes to equal that of the center, indicating that further increases in surround area would not affect center lightness.

Kozaki (1963) tested brightness haploscopically using a square center/surround stimulus in a dark field. The area of the surround was always greater than the area of the test field. When her test field was an increment, she obtained an effect consistent with the area rule. But she also obtained a weak area effect when the test field was a decrement.

Yund and Armington (1975), using disk/annulus stimuli that all fell within our area zone, obtained an effect of surround-to-center area ratio on contrast strength. Although their results are consistent with the area rule, they claimed that a metric based on the distance between center and surround edges fit their data better. However, Burgh and Grindley (1962) obtained no effect at all by varying the distance between center and surround edges.

Using a reversible rabbit figure, Coren (1969) found greater contrast for a gray area when seen as figure than when seen as ground. As with our domes experiments, Coren's results can be explained by the area rule, given the larger perceived area of the background, as it appears to extend behind the figure.

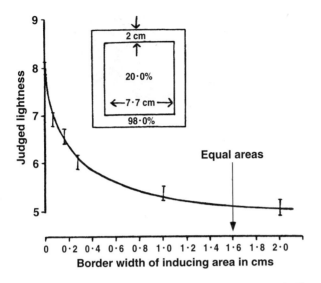

Figure 9.11. Data from Newson (1958). Notice that he obtained effects of area on lightness only when the darker region (center) was larger than the brighter region, consistent with the area rule. Reprinted with permission.

Heinemann (1955)

Our area rule appears to shed a good deal of light on Heinemann's findings. Heinemann studied the perceived brightness of a disk surrounded by an annulus as the luminance of the annulus was increased from zero to a level higher than the disk luminance. Some of the results he obtained are shown in Figure 9.12. Included in the same figure is a schematic showing the results that would be expected to occur in his experiment from an anchoring perspective, but using only the highest luminance rule and ignoring area effects. The first part of the curve is horizontal, indicating that as long as the disk is the highest luminance, it will appear a constant white. The second part of the curve is a straight line with slope of −1, indicating that when the annulus is the highest luminance, disk lightness/brightness goes down exactly in proportion to increases in annulus luminance, according to the ratio principle. The breakpoint between the two parts of the curve occurs at the increment/decrement threshold.

To a first approximation, Heinemann's obtained results fit the ideal results based on the highest luminance rule. However, there are three discrepancies. First, the downward slope is much steeper than a straight line of slope −1. Second, the horizontal part of the curve shows a modest upward bulge that Heinemann has referred to as the

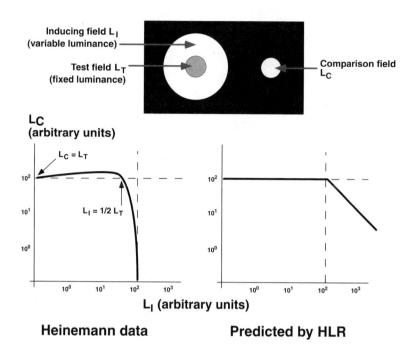

Figure 9.12. Stimulus display and results from Heinemann (1955), plus ideal results under the highest luminance rule.

enhancement effect—that is, increases in the luminance of the annulus produce a slight increase in the perceived brightness of the disk even when annulus luminance is lower than disk luminance. Third, the knee or breakpoint in the curve (the point at which the curve crosses its initial value on the y-axis) does not occur right at the increment/decrement threshold, as it should according to the highest luminance rule. It occurs a bit before this point is reached. In other words, the perceived brightness of the disk begins to decrease even before the annulus luminance becomes greater than the disk luminance. I will call this the "breakpoint offset." This strange feature of Heinemann's data has received almost no attention.

The first discrepancy is a simple matter that has already been resolved. The precipitous slope Heinemann obtained can be directly attributed to the kind of matching stimulus he used, namely a single disk surrounded by darkness. It has been pointed out by Katz (1935), Wallach (1976, p. 5), and others that this kind of stimulus always appears self-luminous, regardless of its luminance level. It cannot be used to match the surface gray appearance of a decremental test disk (Katz, 1935, p. 53). The steep drop in Heinemann's curve merely reflects the frantic, indeed futile, attempt by the observer to get rid of the self-luminous quality in the matching disk by reducing its luminance. In an additional experiment Heinemann (1955, Exp. 2) added an annulus to his matching disk, and this did produce a −1 slope for decrements.

As for the enhancement effect and the breakpoint offset, there are three important clues in the literature:

1. These features are not always present in Heinemann's data.
2. The presence and size of both the enhancement effect and the breakpoint offset vary together. Either both occur or neither occurs.
3. Both features vary with relative size.

These puzzling results can be understood in terms of our area rule. Consider what happens to the perception of both the disk and the annulus as we increase annulus luminance starting from zero—that is, moving from left to right in the Heinemann graph (see Fig. 9.12). Keep in mind that because the area of the annulus is always larger than the area of the disk, the zone to which our area rule applies is the zone of increments, which means the left half of the graph. Within this zone the annulus benefits from an area effect, causing its lightness/brightness to increase somewhat above the level it would have merely by taking the disk luminance as white and deriving the annulus lightness by the disk/annulus luminance ratio (as per Wallach, 1948).

The enhanced lightness of the annulus in turn puts an upward pressure on the appearance of the disk, causing it to appear fluorent, or super-white, which I believe is the enhancement effect. Now, what about the breakpoint offset? This is the point at which disk brightness/lightness starts to drop. From an anchoring perspective this should occur as soon as the annulus becomes the anchor, meaning as soon as the annulus comes to appear white. Remember that because of the additional lightness boost the annulus gets by virtue of its relatively large area, the annulus comes to appear white *before* it has the highest luminance.

According to this analysis, then, both the enhancement effect and the breakpoint offset should occur only under conditions to which the area rule applies: when the area of the annulus is greater than the area of the disk. In fact, this is exactly what the brightness induction results have already revealed. Perhaps this is best shown in Figure 9.13, which is taken from a study of annulus area reported by Heinemann (1972, Fig. 7). The two lines are tracings from the two extreme values of annulus area tested by Heinemann. Line A in the graph was produced by a stimulus with an annulus-to-disk area ratio of 3.6:1; for line B the ratio was 0.15:1. Thus, the area rule applies to line A but not to line B.[10] One can readily see that both the enhancement effect and the breakpoint offset appear only in line A, but not in line B. Torii

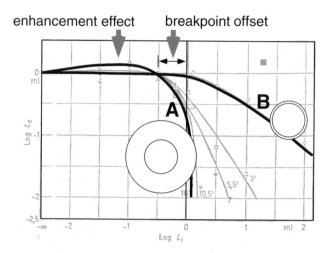

Figure 9.13. Data from Heinemann (1972) with variable annulus area. Notice that the enhancement effect and the breakpoint offset appear most pronounced when the annulus/disk area ratio is greatest. Reprinted with permission.

and Uemura (1965) have also shown that both the enhancement effect and the breakpoint offset disappear when the area of the annulus is reduced to equality with the area of the disk.

Heinemann and Chase (1995) have recently offered a mathematical account of the enhancement effect, but the account offers no explanation of the breakpoint offset, or why the breakpoint offset varies with the enhancement effect, or why the enhancement effect and the breakpoint offset vary with relative area.

THE PERCEPTION OF SELF-LUMINOSITY

The perception of self-luminosity refers to the fact that some surfaces in our visual environment appear to be brighter than white. They appear to emit light, as if the source of the light lies within or behind the surface rather than in front, as with an opaque surface. The paradox is that while self-luminous surfaces stand out sharply in our visual experience and appear qualitatively different from opaque surfaces, it is difficult to find simple qualitative factors in the optic array that distinguish self-luminous from opaque surfaces. For example, it is often the case that a luminous surface is the highest luminance in the field. Yet it would be incorrect to say that the highest luminance in the field always appears self-luminous. Some scenes simply do not contain a luminous surface. Moreover, the highest luminance in the field appears to play a crucial role in defining a white surface. Certainly the highest luminance in the field cannot be used as a marker for self-luminosity and simultaneously as a marker for white.

The perception of self-luminosity is inextricably bound up together with the issue of the perception of opaque surface lightness. The point of contact is the anchoring problem. The question of how the visual system identifies the luminance value that lies at the boundary, which we will call the luminosity threshold, dividing opaque lightness values from self-luminous regions is none other than an alternative way to state the anchoring problem.

Measuring the Luminosity Threshold

Fred Bonato and I conducted a series of experiments in which we measured the luminosity threshold under a variety of conditions (Bonato & Gilchrist, 1994, 1999). Some of our stimuli were very simple; others were quite complex. We tested the luminosity threshold on backgrounds of different reflectance and within regions of different levels of illumination.

Our first experiment was designed to measure the luminosity threshold on backgrounds of different reflectance but in a complex visual scene. By looking through a tiny aperture in the middle of a large screen our observers saw a large portion of the laboratory (Fig. 9.14), including lab benches, a sink, a clock on the wall, and other objects. The only illumination came from a 250-watt halogen light bulb mounted behind the screen but very close to the viewing aperture. A large rectangular piece of paper was mounted on the far wall of the laboratory just opposite the viewing aperture. In the center of this large rectangular paper a smaller square region appeared, the luminance of which could be increased in steps. Although this square region appeared to lie on the surface of the rectangular background, in fact it was physically located much closer to the observer, on a large sheet of clear glass, invisible to the observer, through which the laboratory scene was viewed, as shown in Figure 9.14. The distance of this glass from the light source was adjusted so that a physically black piece of paper attached to the glass would have exactly the same luminance (and indeed virtually disappear) as its white rectangular background. According to the inverse-square law of illumination, and given that the reflectance of the white paper was approximately 25 times that of the black paper, the white paper had to be about five times as far away from the light source as the glass.

By replacing the black target square on the glass with identical squares of higher reflectance, the luminance of the target square could be increased in steps. A series of target luminance values was presented to the observer in random order, and on each trial the observer was required to choose whether or not the target appeared self-

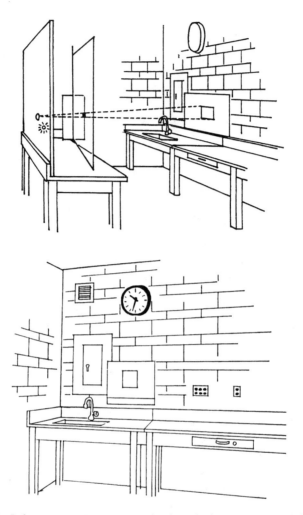

Figure 9.14. Laboratory arrangements (top) and observer's visual field (bottom) in Bonato and Gilchrist's (1994) luminosity threshold experiments. Reprinted with permission.

luminous. Three different large rectangular backgrounds were used, one white, one middle gray, and one black.

The results are shown in the top graph of Figure 9.15, in which the percentage of luminosity reports is plotted against the target-to-background luminance ratio. Using this measure we obtain three separate sigmoid functions and three separate measures of the luminosity threshold, one for each background. These results make it clear that self-luminosity perception is not a simple function of the contrast between the target and its background.

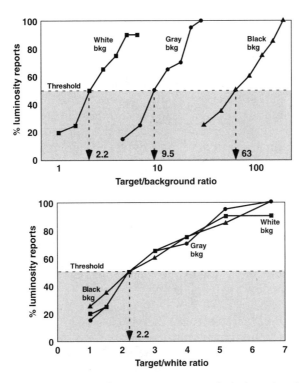

Figure 9.15. (Top) Percentage luminosity reports plotted against local luminance ratio of target. (Bottom) Luminosity reports plotted against the ratio of
target luminance and the luminance of a white surface (Bonato & Gilchrist,
1994). Reprinted with permission.

But there is a deeper consistency in these data that is revealed in
the bottom graph of Figure 9.15. Here the percentage of luminosity
reports is plotted against the ratio between the luminance of the target
square and the luminance of a white surface in the same plane,
whether or not the background of the target happens to be white.
Plotting the data in this way reveals that the three functions come
together in a single function, with a target/background threshold ratio
of 2.2.

It should not come as any surprise to find that the visual system
does not define the luminosity threshold by a measure as local as the
target-to-background luminance ratio. Yet it is not at all clear how the
visual system could recover the luminance of white in the same plane,
which is a necessary component of the x-axis in the bottom graph of
Figure 9.15.

The coincidence of the three curves in this bottom graph in Figure
9.15 demonstrates that the luminosity threshold exhibits background-

independent constancy (that is, constancy despite changes in the background), just as opaque surface gray colors do. If instead of putting a bright target on each of the three backgrounds as we did in the luminosity threshold experiment, we were to place a middle-gray surface on each of the same three backgrounds, we would find that the perceived lightness values would be very similar, despite the very different target-to-surround luminance ratios in the three cases. Of course, the middle-gray target paper on the black background would look about three quarters of a Munsell step lighter than the middle-gray paper on the white background, but this simultaneous contrast effect, or failure of background-independent constancy, is small relative to the change in local target-to-surround luminance ratio. But for the luminosity threshold, we did not obtain even this small degree of failure of background-independent constancy. This is consistent, however, with other results (Arend & Spehar, 1993; Gilchrist, 1988) showing that background-dependent failures are absent or tiny when both targets are increments relative to their immediate surrounds, as is the case in our luminosity experiment.

The existence of constancy with respect to a change in the background implies that somehow the visual system is able to take into account the lightness value of the background. However, we cannot assume that background lightness is calculated without error. Thus, it becomes important to consider the luminosity threshold in relationship to the perceived lightness of the background.

This can be understood by invoking the concepts of upward and downward induction discussed earlier. In our initial luminosity threshold experiment, the increasing luminance difference between the target and its surround as we increase target luminance is mainly expressed perceptually in terms of upward induction resulting in self-luminosity. But a small portion of the change is expressed as downward induction in the surround. In that experiment we did not take measures of the perceived lightness value of the surround. However, in a subsequent, virtually identical experiment (Bonato & Gilchrist, 1999), we did, at least for the white surround. The data we obtained show that for a target with a luminance value right at threshold (that is, 26.99 cd/m^2) the perceived lightness of the white surround is in fact Munsell 8.5 (65% reflectance). This means that while the luminosity threshold for a target on the white background occurred when the target was 2.2 times the luminance of the background, it was only 1.6 times the luminance that, by extrapolation, would be perceived as white. This conversion was performed simply by dividing our obtained value of 2.2 by the ratio of the physical reflectance of the white background (90%) to its perceived reflectance (65%).

Luminosity Threshold in Simpler Displays

In simpler displays, such as the disk/annulus, the trade-off between upward and downward induction is even more pronounced.

Lie (1977) conducted what he called a "colour/shadow discrimination." Presenting a square version of Wallach's disk/annulus stimulus, Lie increased the luminance level of the central target until the observer "felt sure the two fields were differently illuminated."

Although Bonato and I did not think of our experiments specifically in the context of edge classification, we consider Lie's construction to be reasonable, at least for such simple displays. Indeed, in our first experiment testing the luminosity threshold on homogeneous white, gray, and black backgrounds, we classified the response as reporting luminosity whether the target appeared to have its own internal light source or whether the target appeared to represent a special patch of bright illumination projected onto the homogeneous surface. The only practical difference between Lie's task and our task appears to be that Lie required a higher degree of confidence in the perception of luminosity, or special lighting. Bonato and I defined the luminosity threshold as that luminance which elicits luminosity reports 50% of the time, or the luminance at which the target appeared equally likely to be luminous or opaque, whereas Lie defined the threshold as the luminance at which the observer felt sure that the target was differently illuminated from its surround (i.e., not opaque). If our definition represented the 50% level in terms of luminosity reports, Lie's definition probably reflects a level closer to 70% or 80%.

Lie obtained a threshold at a center/surround luminance ratio of 4 to 1. This result appears to be consistent with our findings when the different criteria are taken into account. Looking at our data (bottom graph of Fig. 9.15), it is quite obvious that if we had used a 70% to 80% definition rather than our 50% definition, we also would have obtained our threshold at a luminance ratio of 4 to 1. Wallach's informal observations using the disk/annulus stimulus appear consistent with these figures as well. Wallach reported that, for his stimulus, the disk appears luminous when its luminance is between two and four times higher than that of the surrounding annulus.

Zavagno and Caputo (2001) have recently reported experiments on the perception of luminosity using a stimulus composed of luminance ramps. At first glance, their results appear inconsistent with our findings, but I would argue that they used a different criterion for luminosity than ours, one that may be understood in the context of picture perception.

Illumination Level and the Luminosity Threshold

In another experiment we measured the luminosity threshold for a target in each of two differently illuminated Mondrians. The stimulus

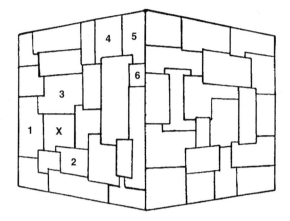

Figure 9.16. Dihedral Mondrian stimulus used to measure luminosity threshold in highly illuminated and dimly illuminated planes. Lightness matches were taken for numbered patches (Bonato & Gilchrist, 1994). Reprinted with permission.

display is shown in Figure 9.16. It consisted of two Mondrians placed at right angles to each other, each containing 20 patches. One Mondrian was brightly illuminated and one was dimly illuminated. The illumination ratio between the two Mondrians was 30:1, a ratio equal to that between white and black. Each Mondrian contained one target square whose luminance was adjustable over a large range. In fact, each of these targets was an aperture, although it appeared to be a surface coplanar with the surrounding Mondrian. Separately illuminated panels of different shades of gray could be mounted behind the target aperture to change the luminance of the target. This dihedral Mondrian stimulus was presented against a homogeneous background of 192 cd/m² within a vision tunnel (Fig. 5 in Bonato & Gilchrist, 1994). In all other respects this experiment was equivalent to the experiment previously described.

The results are shown in the top graph of Figure 9.17, which shows two very different threshold values, when the threshold is defined in terms of the absolute luminance of the target. This result shows clearly that the luminosity threshold is not determined by any absolute luminance value. We can also see in these results that the luminosity threshold exhibits illumination-independent constancy, or constancy with respect to changes in illumination level. Just as the illumination on the brightly illuminated Mondrian was 30 times higher than that of the dimly illuminated Mondrian, so the luminosity threshold on the brightly illuminated Mondrian occurred at a luminance value 25 times higher than for the dimly illuminated Mondrian.

These results also show that a region does not have to be the high-

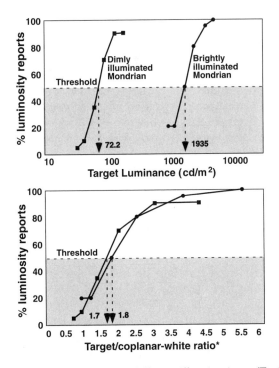

Figure 9.17. Luminosity threshold in different illuminations. (Top) Percentage luminosity reports plotted against target luminance. (Bottom) Luminosity reports plotted against the ratio of target luminance and the luminance of a coplanar white surface (Bonato & Gilchrist, 1994). Reprinted with permission.

est luminance in the scene to appear self-luminous. The target on the dimly illuminated Mondrian began to appear luminous at a luminance value far lower than the luminances of many of the nonluminous patches on the brightly illuminated Mondrian. However, it is probably necessary that the target have the highest luminance in its own framework to appear luminous.

In the bottom graph of Figure 9.17, the percentage of luminosity reports is plotted against the ratio between target luminance and the luminance perceived as white within each Mondrian separately. The calculation of the luminance of a white in each Mondrian was performed as described for the previous experiment, extrapolating from Munsell matches made to patches in each surrounding Mondrian. This graph reveals that in the dimly illuminated Mondrian, the luminosity threshold is reached at a value 1.7 times that of a perceived white in the same plane. The corresponding value for the highly illuminated Mondrian is 1.8. These values are quite similar to the 1.6 value obtained in our initial luminosity threshold experiment.

Ullman's Proposal

There has been very little prior empirical work on the perception of self-luminosity. Ullman (1976) has given a very well-reasoned analysis of the problem of visual detection of light sources, particularly with regard to the inadequacy of a number of intuitive algorithms. He gives a list of six potential metrics that are obvious candidates for the basis of luminosity detection, and he argues, mainly on logical grounds, that none of these six factors can work. The factors are:

1. Highest intensity in the visual field
2. High absolute intensity value
3. Local contrast
4. Global contrast
5. Intensity compared with the average intensity of the scene
6. Lightness computation

Each of these six factors is ruled out empirically by one of the two experiments that have just been described. Highest intensity in the visual field, high absolute intensity, global contrast, and intensity compared with the average intensity of the scene are all inconsistent with the results of the luminosity threshold experiment using the dihedral Mondrian. Local contrast, as a predictor of luminosity, is inconsistent with the results of our experiment measuring the luminosity threshold on white, gray, and black backgrounds. And finally, the lightness computation, which is attributed to Land and McCann (1971), is unable to account for the luminosity results of either of these experiments.

Ullman (1976, p. 209) offers an algorithm for detecting a light source: "Given two adjacent areas, compute both their intensity ratio and their gradient ratio and compare the two. If the ratios are not equal, one of the two areas is a light source." Ullman's algorithm is based on the observation that self-luminous regions, unlike opaque surfaces, typically contain shallow gradients that are inconsistent with shallow gradients in the surrounding context. For example, consider a gray wall illuminated by a lamp near the left end of the wall. This entire gray wall will contain a shallow illumination gradient going from relatively bright on the left to relatively dim on the right. If a piece of white paper is attached to this wall it will also contain the same left-to-right shallow gradient. On the other hand, if a self-luminous region is somehow embedded in this wall, it will not, except by chance, contain a shallow gradient consistent with that of its surround. The gradient within the luminous region will depend on how it is constructed. The luminous region might be completely homogeneous, but it would more typically have a hot spot in the center.

Ullman's proposed algorithm is thus based on a solid ecological observation. However, it cannot be a sufficient condition, because a surface that is darker than its surrounding region will never appear

luminous, even if its shallow gradients are inconsistent with the surrounding region. Nor can his algorithm be considered a necessary
condition. This is shown by the fact that we obtained the perception
of luminosity in the experiments just described in the absence of Ullman's inconsistent gradients. Nevertheless, Yamauchi and Uchikawa
(2004) have shown a lower threshold for perceived self-luminosity in
the presence of Ullman's gradient inconsistency.

Lightness and Luminosity: One Dimension or Two?

Our results indicate quite clearly that the luminosity threshold behaves as if it were a value of surface lightness. It exhibits the two
main forms of lightness constancy, illumination-independent constancy despite changes in the level of illumination, and background-
dependent constancy despite changes in the background. This makes
sense because, in a very real way, the threshold is part of the lightness
scale. It is the upper boundary of the lightness scale, not the lower
boundary of luminosity. Thus, it is part of the lightness scale in the
same sense that the shore is part of the continent, not part of the ocean.
Of course, by definition it is the boundary dividing the zone of opaque
surface lightness values from the zone of luminous-appearing surfaces. But just as Nakayama (Nakayama & Shimojo, 1990; Nakayama
et al., 1995) has discussed Rubin's ideas of figure and ground in terms
of border ownership, so the luminosity threshold can be thought of
as a border that is owned by the lightness scale, not by the luminosity
scale.

Perception of the brightness of a luminous surface is based on absolute luminances, while the perception of surface lightness is based
on relative luminance. More concretely, if an observer is given control
of the luminance of a luminous surface and asked to adjust it so as to
appear the same as another luminous surface, the observer will make
the two luminous regions equal in terms of their absolute luminance
value, regardless of any differences in background or level of illumination. But if an observer is given control of the luminance of an
opaque surface and asked to make it equal in lightness to another
opaque surface, the observer will adjust the luminance of the target
until the two surfaces being matched stand in an equal relationship
to their own surrounds.

Luminosity Threshold versus Brightness Matching

From this analysis we can infer that the luminosity threshold does not
behave like a luminous surface, but rather like an opaque surface. The
distinction between the behavior of the luminosity threshold and the
behavior of a luminous surface is more clearly illustrated in a subsequent unpublished experiment that Bonato and I conducted, also using the dihedral Mondrians, in which we obtained both luminosity

thresholds and brightness matching of two luminous regions. We reasoned that if the luminosity threshold depends on relative luminance while brightness matching depends on absolute luminance, a strange paradox should occur under certain conditions.

Imagine that the luminance of the target in the shadowed Mondrian is set to the value at which 50% of the observers report luminosity—that is, at the threshold. Now imagine that we increase the luminance of the target by a factor of perhaps two or three, such that 95% of observers perceive it to be self-luminous. The luminance of the target will now be roughly equal to the luminance of a middle-gray surface in the brightly illuminated Mondrian. We predicted that if the observer is now asked to adjust the luminance of the luminous target on the illuminated Mondrian so that it appears equal in brightness to the luminous target on the shadowed Mondrian, the observer will not be able to perform the task. This is because when the observer increases the luminance of the target on the illuminated Mondrian until it begins to appear luminous, it will already appear much brighter than the target on the shadowed Mondrian. But when the observer attempts to compensate for this difference by reducing the luminance of the target on the illuminated Mondrian, this will quickly make that target appear opaque, and not luminous at all.

On the other hand, if the target on the brightly illuminated Mondrian is first set to a luminous appearance and then the observer is asked to match its brightness by adjusting the luminance of the target on the shadowed Mondrian, we predicted that this task should be relatively easy and the match should be based on absolute luminance, not relative luminance.

In fact, these are exactly the results we obtained. We set the target on the shadowed background to a luminance value of 79 cd/m^2, a value 3.5 times higher than that of a perceived white in that framework, at which 90% of the observers in our previous experiment reported the target to be luminous. But this value was equal to that of a surface that would appear as Munsell 3.7 on the brightly illuminated Mondrian. Eleven observers were asked to adjust the target on the lighted Mondrian so as to make the two targets equally bright; all 11 observers reported that they were unable to perform the task. In a second condition we set the target on the lighted Mondrian to a value of 2,401 cd/m^2 (also equal to 3.5 times the luminance of a perceived white in that framework) and asked observers to make a luminosity match by adjusting the target on the shadowed Mondrian. None of the observers reported any difficulty on this task. The mean setting was 410 ftL. A setting of 700 ftL would represent a perfect luminance match, while a setting of 28 ftL would represent a perfect ratio match (that is, the ratio of the target luminance to the highest luminance in the Mondrian). The same observers were asked to set each of the two targets right at the luminosity threshold. They had no difficulty with this task either, and it is reassuring to note that the thresholds we obtained this way, using the method of adjustment, are essentially the same as those we obtained in our previous experiment using the method of constant stimuli.

Lightness and Luminosity: Two Dimensions in One

These results can help to resolve a puzzle concerning the relationship between surface lightness and luminosity: Do they represent two separate dimensions, or do they represent two regions along a single dimension divided into two parts by the luminosity threshold? In other words, is it valid to consider perceived lightness values and perceived brightness values of luminous surfaces as parts of a single continuous dimension? Treating lightness and luminosity as part of a single dimension is supported by the observation that for a given target imbedded in a Mondrian, we can make that target appear to have any surface lightness value and many different brightness values merely by adjusting a single dimension of the stimulus, namely the luminance of the target. If we start with a low luminance value, the target will appear black. If we increase its luminance it will come to appear middle gray, then white. Then it will move through a kind of super-white zone that Evans calls fluorence. As we continue to increase its luminance it will cross the luminosity threshold, coming to appear as a light source. As we increase its luminance further it will appear as a brighter and brighter light source.

On the other hand, the idea that lightness and luminosity (brightness?) represent separate dimensions is supported by the observation that lightness matches are based on relative luminance, while brightness or luminosity matches are based on absolute luminance. Figure 9.18 is consistent with the results we obtained in these experiments, and we believe it illustrates the correct way to think about the relationship between lightness and brightness or luminosity. The lightness scale is taken to be a scale of finite length, about 30:1, which is overlaid on, and slides along, an underlying luminance dimension that extends infinitely away from an origin of complete darkness. This figure illustrates that the luminosity threshold does indeed belong to the lightness dimension. It represents the upper limit of the lightness dimension. It does not represent the lower limits of the luminance dimension. But the figure also illustrates the sense in which lightness and luminosity, for any given level of illumination, can be thought of as collinear dimensions. Sliding the lightness scale up and down along the underlying luminance scale is equivalent to raising or lower the illumination on a Mondrian. Thus, depending on the illumination level on a Mondrian, when the luminance of the target crosses the luminosity threshold and begins to appear self-luminous, it may become luminous at different levels of absolute intensity.

Figure 9.18. The finite lightness scale can be thought to slide along the infinite luminance scale. Consequently, the luminosity threshold, the upper boundary of lightness, can occur at any luminance value.

Self-Luminosity and the Area Rule

Because the luminosity threshold is part of the lightness dimension, it should also be subject to the area rule—that is, for a target of increasing luminance, the proportion of upward induction (movement toward luminosity) and downward induction (darkening of background) should depend on the relative area of the target and its background.

Consistent with this analysis, and according to the area function, increasing the size of a target should raise its luminosity threshold by increasing the efficiency of downward induction at the expense of upward induction. Bonato and I (Bonato & Gilchrist, 1999) tested this prediction, using our open lab paradigm. We replaced the target used previously with a target 17 times larger in area. Some minor modifications of the apparatus were necessary to accommodate the larger target, and we used only the white background. The details can be found in our research report (Bonato & Gilchrist, 1999). Otherwise the method is identical to that of our prior experiments.

The results are shown in the top graph of Figure 9.19. The main result is that larger targets require a higher luminance for a luminous appearance. The threshold value we obtained for the large target was

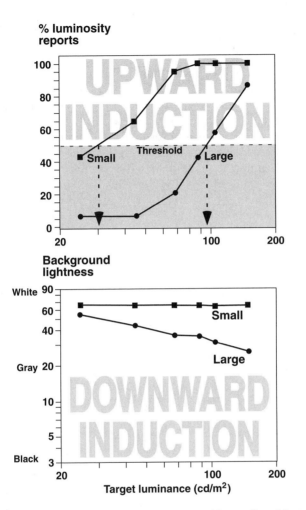

Figure 9.19. (Top) Percentage luminosity reports with small and large targets. (Bottom) Change in background lightness as target becomes brighter (Bonato & Gilchrist, 1999). Reprinted with permission.

101 cd/m², three times higher than the threshold (34.6 cd/m²) we obtained previously using the small target. The higher threshold required for the large target means that increases in the luminance of the large target induced less luminosity than did the same increase in the small target. This implies in turn that increases in the luminance of the large target should induce more grayness into the surround than would an equal luminance increase in the small target. The bottom graph of Figure 9.19 shows that this is indeed the case. Here the perceived lightness value of the surround is plotted as a function of the target luminance. For the small target, there was little or no dark-

ening of surrounding lightness as the target was made brighter. But for the large target, there was a substantial amount of darkening. As the luminance of the large target was increased from 23.2 cd/m² to 138 cd/m², the perceived lightness of the background dropped from Munsell 7.7 to Munsell 5.6.

Because of the relatively strong downward induction produced by the large target, at the luminosity threshold the lightness of the background was perceived to be Munsell 6.2. Extrapolating from this value to the luminance of a perceived white, we find that the large target crossed the luminosity threshold when its luminance was 2.2 times the luminance of a perceived white. This can be compared to the 1.6 value we obtained for the small target and the values of 1.7 and 1.8 we obtained for the lighted and shadowed Mondrians in the dihedral Mondrians experiment.

Retinal Area or Perceived Area?

Whenever size is found to be an independent variable, it is necessary to ask, as Rock's work has established so well, whether it is perceived size or retinal size that is effective. Fred Bonato and I (Bonato & Gilchrist, 1999) examined this question. We used the disk/annulus stimulus for convenience. First we mapped out the luminosity threshold for a baseline display size and viewing distance. Then we conducted two additional conditions: a retinally larger condition (with perceived size held constant) and a phenomenally larger condition (with retinal size held constant). In the retinally larger condition the same-size stimulus display was used, but the observer was moved to one-third the viewing distance, yielding a retinal image three times larger. Perceived size was held constant to the degree that size constancy held. In the phenomenally larger condition, a display three times larger was used, but the observer was moved to three times the baseline distance.

The results are shown in Figure 9.20. In short, the phenomenally larger target produced a higher luminosity threshold but the retinally larger target did not. This implies that the luminosity threshold depends on the perceived size of the target, not on its retinal size. Although the retinally larger target did not produce a significantly higher threshold compared to baseline, a glance at Figure 9.20 reveals that curve for the retinally larger condition is shifted to the right, relative to that of the nearer but retinally smaller target, by a small but consistent amount. It is reasonable to suppose that this small difference might reflect a small failure of size constancy. When the observer is moved to a position three times closer to the display, a small failure in size constancy would cause the display to look a bit larger than under baseline conditions, and this small increase in perceived

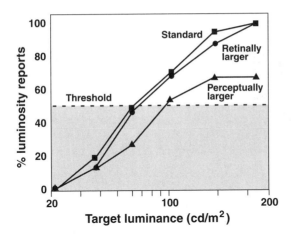

Figure 9.20. The luminosity threshold increases with increase in perceived target size but not retinal target size (Bonato & Gilchrist, 1999). Reprinted with permission.

size may be responsible for what appears to be a slightly higher threshold curve for the retinally larger condition.

The ratio between the luminosity threshold and the luminance of a perceived white was 2.0 for our small target and 2.8 for our perceptually larger target.

The finding that the luminosity threshold depends on perceived size of the target, not retinal size, was tested by Bonato and Cataliotti in an interesting way. They used a stimulus created by dividing a rectangular space into two regions of equal area using the profile of a face (Fig. 9.21). Although the physical area of the two regions is equal, the perceived area of the two is not. The background region on the right side is perceived to have a larger area than the face region on the left side, consistent with Rubin's (1921) observation that ground regions are perceived to extend behind figural regions. Bonato and Cataliotti (2000) found a higher luminance threshold for the background region (67 cd/m²) than for the face region (29 cd/m²). This is consistent with Coren's (1969) finding that a gray region surrounded by black appears lighter when it appears as figure than when the same gray region appears as background. Shimojo and Nakayama (1990) used an ambiguous apparent motion quartet to determine the functional amount of amodal extension of partially occluded rectangles.

In a closely related experiment, Bonato and Cataliotti tested the luminosity threshold for a square target and a trapezoidal target. Although the physical area of the two targets is equal, the perceived area of the trapezoidal region is larger because it is perceived as a rectangle lying in a horizontal position. They measured a luminosity threshold

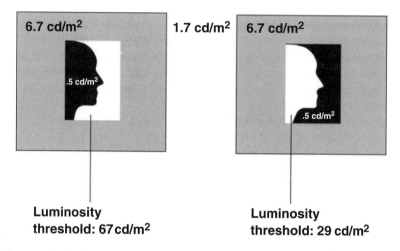

Figure 9.21. Higher luminosity threshold for background region with larger perceived area than figural region, despite equal retinal areas (Bonato & Cataliotti, 2000). Reprinted with permission.

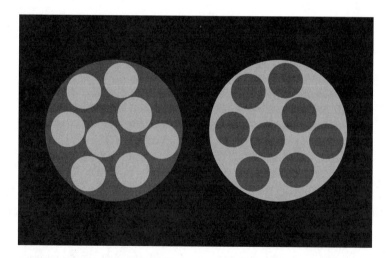

Figure 9.22. The Wolff illusion (1934). The small dark disks on the right appear darker than the equi-luminant large background disk on the left. Though both regions have the same physical area, the perceived area of the background region is larger because it appears to extend behind the small disks. Wolff suggested that figural regions show greater contrast than background regions, but the effect is consistent with the role of perceived area in anchoring. Reprinted with permission from Gilchrist et al., 1999.

for the trapezoidal target that was significantly higher than for the square target.

Defining area in perceptual terms seems to explain another illusion as well: the Wolff illusion (Wolff, 1934), shown in Figure 9.22. The light disks on the right appear lighter than the light background on the left and the dark disks on the left appear darker than the dark background on the right. In retinal terms the combined area of the disks is equal to the visible area of the background. But because the background appears to extend behind the disks, it has a greater perceived area. Thus, the area rule is consistent with the Wolff illusion.

SCALE NORMALIZATION

Besides the highest luminance rule and the area rule, there is some evidence for a third, weaker rule that concerns lightness range rather than lightness level. The perceived range of grays within a framework tends toward the canonical range between black and white. When the range of luminances within a framework is less than 30:1, some expansion occurs. The coefficient of expansion varies inversely with the range. When the range is greater than 30:1, some compression occurs. I will refer to this as the "scale normalization rule."

This rule has not been established empirically as well as the highest luminance and area rules, but the rule is consistent with several reports. All of our domes experiments (Li & Gilchrist, 1999) produced expansion, except those to which the area rule applies. Brown and MacLeod's (1997) gamut expansion is an example of scale normalization. And the contrast-contrast effect presented by Chubb et al. (1989) and shown in Figure 9.23 can also be considered a scale normalization effect. In this view, the central region on the right appears

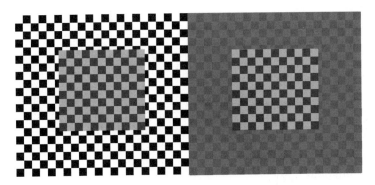

Figure 9.23. Contrast-contrast illusion (Chubb et al., 1989). The two interior sets of squares have identical contrast, although the right-hand set appears to have higher contrast.

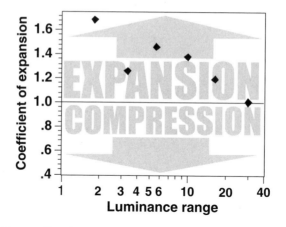

Figure 9.24. The smaller the luminance range in the disk/ganzfeld, the greater the coefficient by which perceived lightness range exceeds luminance range in the stimulus.

to have greater contrast because the right-hand framework that it is part of has a smaller luminance range than the framework on the left. Data from Gilchrist and Bonato (1995) showing scale normalization in the disk/ganzfeld are shown in Figure 9.24.

Logically, the highest luminance rule and the scale normalization rule could be replaced by a single bipolar anchoring rule. According to this idea, which has been suggested by at least Kirschmann (1892, p. 546), Koffka (1935), and Rock (1983, p. 210), lightness is anchored simultaneously by both the highest and the lowest luminance. But overall, bipolar anchoring does not appear to be consistent with the data.

SUMMARY

There is wide agreement that lightness depends on relative luminance. But relative luminance can only produce relative lightness. To produce the specific gray levels found in visual experience, anchoring rules must also be invoked. The basic anchoring rule is that the highest luminance appears white. Darker regions are seen relative to this standard, according to Wallach's ratio principle. Anchoring in simple images (two surfaces that fill the entire visual field) can be completely described by adding two additional rules: an area rule, whereby surfaces appear lighter as they become larger, and a scale normalization rule, whereby the perceived range of gray shows a tendency to normalize on the range between white and black.

When the luminance of a target surface is made about 1.7 times that of a surface perceived as white, it begins to appear self-luminous.

Increasing its luminance further makes it appear brighter. Self-luminosity is qualitatively different from surface lightness. Perceived brightness of a self-luminous region depends on its absolute luminance; it does not follow the ratio principle. The luminosity threshold, however, is logically part of the lightness scale—its upper limit. Empirically, the threshold behaves as a lightness value—that is, it shows both illumination-dependent and background-dependent constancy.

Increasing the luminance difference between two adjacent surfaces in a simple display can cause the darker region to appear darker still (as in the brightness induction literature), the lighter region to appear lighter still (as in luminosity threshold experiments), or both. Which of these occurs depends on the relative area of the two regions, according to the area rule of anchoring.

10

Errors in Lightness

In 1992 Mario Zanforlin once opened a talk by remarking that if you take a hand calculator, enter 2 times 2, and get 4, you have the correct answer, but it tells you nothing about how the calculator works. But if you get 3.9999999 there is a small error in the answer, and that error constrains the possible explanation of how the calculator works.

The motivation for a systematic study of lightness errors is compelling:

1. Lightness errors are everywhere.
2. The errors are systematic, not random.
3. The pattern of errors must be the signature of the visual system.

I emphasize that the pattern of errors has enormous potential for revealing the nature of the visual software by which lightness is computed (Gilchrist, 2003). Indeed, the pattern of errors would appear to constrain models more than veridicality. One could more easily imagine two models that equally predict veridicality than two models that predicted the same pattern of errors. I am not suggesting that this is a totally new idea, but I believe it has not been applied in a systematic manner. Theories have attempted to explain lightness illusions largely in a piecemeal manner (but see Gregory, 1997). The overall pattern of lightness errors has never been surveyed in a single publication.

It is a curious fact that lightness illusions (such as simultaneous contrast) and failures of lightness constancy have always been treated as separate phenomena. This is further evidence that the pattern of lightness errors has not been approached in a coherent manner. In this chapter I will treat illusions and failures of constancy as merely part of a single pattern of errors.

Is the Lightness System Basically Faulty?

Before plunging into the issue of errors in lightness perception, let us briefly review some of the arguments given earlier for building a model of veridical perception:

1. The degree of veridicality in lightness perception is truly impressive, especially in view of the various challenges to constancy posed by such factors as different illumination levels, different backgrounds behind a target surface, and various layers in front of the target, layers with both veil (additive) and filter (multiplicative) components.
2. Performance of the lightness system is underestimated by laboratory experiments using reduced displays. Veridicality is better with more complex images typical of everyday conditions.
3. Survival requires a high degree of veridicality. Reality monitoring must be central to visual functioning; veridical perception cannot be an accident of the system.
4. An understanding of how veridicality is achieved is likely to provide a framework within which the errors can be understood.

A fruitful study of lightness errors need not challenge any of these points. The size of the errors is not crucial, only that the errors be systematic. Fingerprints at a crime scene may be very faint; it is necessary only that the pattern be detectable.

DEFINITION OF ERRORS

Conceptually, an error is a discrepancy between the distal stimulus and the percept, whether called an illusion or a failure of constancy. I will define errors in a simple-minded way, inspired by the kind of practical problems we find in daily life, as when, for example, we bring back the wrong color of paint from the paint store. I will define a lightness error as *the difference between the actual reflectance of a target surface and the reflectance of the matching chip selected from a Munsell chart.* This definition applies to real scenes with real papers and objects. For photographic prints, slide projections, and CRT images, one can merely substitute the reflectance of the target surface that was photographed or simulated.

Although the Munsell chart incorporates those conditions known to favor good constancy (white background, high articulation), my definition does not strictly require that the chart itself be perceived with no error at all. It does, however, require that errors in perception of the chart be small relative to the errors one is trying to measure. Galileo timed the period of the chandelier at Pisa using the human pulse. Thus he discovered the law of the pendulum, which was then used to build clocks, which in turn were used to time the human pulse with greater accuracy. The pulse, despite its errors, was good enough to discover the constant period of the chandelier.

I will approach the topic of errors in lightness perception in two ways. First, I will examine the nature of errors predicted—either explicitly or implicitly—by the major theories of lightness perception. This should serve to emphasize the point that every model of visual functioning has an associated pattern of predicted errors (and vice versa). I hope to show that an analysis of the errors predicted by competing models is a powerful method for evaluating those models, although it has never been systematically done in the literature.

Second, I will attempt to survey the facts with respect to errors in lightness perception, excluding theoretical bias as much as possible. But that description will be used to constrain a model of lightness perception. Two conclusions will emerge: (1) current models of lightness perception predict substantial errors that do not in fact occur, and (2) many important errors that do occur are not accounted for by current models.

ERRORS PREDICTED BY THEORIES OF LIGHTNESS

Our analysis of predicted errors will be hampered by a lack of concreteness in many theories of lightness, but we will concentrate on those errors that most clearly and inescapably follow from each theory.

Helmholtz

Vagueness is a major problem in Helmholtz's theory. But in the broadest sense, of course, Helmholtz views lightness perception as intelligent behavior, and the product of learning. MacLeod (1932, p. 21) wonders whether the Helmholtzian model should predict any errors in lightness perception at all: "One is tempted to ask in this connection why, if learning is capable of effecting such an astounding transformation in experience, the constancy of colour is only approximate and never complete." In any case, Helmholtz's theory appears to predict more errors in children and animals. But this prediction is not borne out. Locke (1935) found smaller constancy failures in monkeys than in humans; Burzlaff (1931) and Brunswik (1929) found equal degrees of constancy in children and adults.

Woodworth (1938, p. 605), who took a generally Helmholtzian perspective, wrote that judgments in constancy experiments "usually lie between two extremes, one conforming to the stimulus and the other conforming to the object." Both the Brunswik ratio and the Thouless ratio were created to measure just where the perceptual judgment lies between these two poles. Judgments lying outside these poles have generally not been taken seriously. This is inherent in Thouless' concept of "phenomenal regression to the real object." The regression is away from the proximal stimulation.

Empirical evidence shows that the percept does not in fact always lie between the stimulus and the object. Under certain conditions over-constancy occurs. For example, when one piece of gray paper is placed in bright illumination on a background brighter than itself, and another piece of identical gray paper is placed in a shadowed region on a background darker than itself, the gray paper in shadow will appear lighter gray than the paper in bright illumination, even though its luminance is much less than that of the paper in the bright illumination (Helson, 1943, p. 255).

Rock (1984, p. 44) has argued that errors in general are caused by an intrusion into perception of what he calls the proximal mode. Thus, when an object is seen at a very great distance, one may be struck by the unusually small visual angle subtended, and this may cause the object to appear a bit smaller than it would at a nearer distance. But errors caused this way can produce only under-constancy, not over-constancy.

Hering

Hering emphasized the role of four factors, three relatively peripheral and one cognitive. His cognitive factor was memory color. An obvious outcome implied by this factor is that the accuracy of lightness perception should be substantially reduced for unfamiliar objects. For the record, there is virtually no evidence that this is true (see Chapter 5).

But according to Hering, most of the heavy lifting in lightness perception is done by three sensory mechanisms: pupil size, adaptation, and lateral inhibition. Each of these implies specific conditions that should produce errors. When the pupil size is inappropriate to the prevailing conditions of illumination, systematic errors should occur. Specifically, if pupil size is artificially reduced by looking through a pinhole, all visible surfaces should appear somewhat darker in surface color. Likewise, if the pupil is artificially enlarged, by use of atropine for example, all surfaces should appear lighter than they are. Although there is no published study of lightness under these conditions, it is easy to confirm that lightness values are not changed by looking through a pinhole.

Analogous arguments can be made concerning adaptation. Immediately following exposure to a bright adapting field, surfaces should appear darker in lightness than they are. Immediately after dark adaptation they should appear lighter. We have all had the experience of stepping out of a dark cellar into bright sunlight. This leaves us temporarily with inappropriate degrees of pupil size and adaptation, which we experience as a kind of blinding. But I do not think it is correct to say that objects in the bright sunlight really appear lighter in surface color. Logically there are four possibilities: (1) All surface lightness values might be temporarily raised. (2) The illumination might appear temporarily brighter than it really is, with no effect on surface color. (3) Brightness levels might be affected, with no effect on objective properties like lightness or illumination. (4) None of these might be affected.

Likewise, when one moves from bright sunlight into a dark cellar, everything at first appears very dark, in some sense. We can say that the dynamic range is dramatically but temporarily compressed. It is certainly difficult to distinguish the various objects; edges are harder to detect. And we can even say that the number of jnd's between perceived white and perceived black is greatly reduced. But none of this necessarily implies that the perceived surface lightness values are systematically distorted. Experiments of this kind are needed.

Hering's third physiological factor, lateral inhibition, plays a central role in all of the contrast theories that fall within the Hering tradition and is widely believed to explain simultaneous contrast. But we will find that many variations of simultaneous contrast cannot be explained by lateral inhibition.

According to the spatial function of lateral inhibition, homogeneous surfaces should not appear homogeneous. In general, the simple fact is that homogeneous surfaces appear homogeneous. There are special conditions under which we perceive modest bright or dark scallops near edges. But the spatial function makes a more concrete prediction. Cornsweet (1970, p. 350) presents a figure (reproduced in Fig. 10.1) consisting of a near-white disk surrounded by a dark gray-annulus, noting that his inhibition-based model predicts that the center of the disk ought to appear almost the same brightness as the middle region of the annulus. He acknowledges, "This is clearly not the case."

Lateral inhibition is inherently tied to the 2D retinal pattern. This implies that any two displays that produce the same retinal pattern must be seen as having the same lightness values, even if they are composed of different reflectances in different spatial orientations. The various experiments on depth and lightness (Gilchrist, 1977, 1980; Knill & Kersten, 1991; Schirillo, Reeves & Arend, 1990;) show that the visual system does not exhibit such simple-minded errors.

Lateral inhibition is blind to important structural aspects of the field, such as the distinction between reflectance and illuminance edges. As long as there is no difference in edge sharpness, a condition easily satisfied, lateral inhibition must make the same response to an

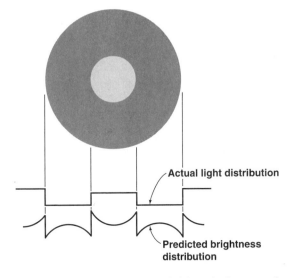

Figure 10.1. According to Cornsweet's model (1970), the central region of the disk should appear equal to the central region of the annulus. Reprinted by permission.

illuminance edge that it makes to a reflectance edge. This factor predicts a wide range of serious lightness errors that did not occur.

These predictive failures apply not only to Hering, but also to the theories of Cornsweet, and Jameson and Hurvich, whose theories make their own peculiar predictions as well.

Jameson and Hurvich

For all its apparent rigor, the Jameson and Hurvich opponent process model does not produce specific predicted lightness values. Partly this is due to a series of ambiguities in the lateral inhibition concept, including the lack of an anchoring rule and a failure to specify the strength of contrast. But partly it is because in the end, Jameson and Hurvich do not claim to have a theory of lightness. They claim to have a theory of brightness and darkness, a kind of raw sensation of light intensity. How these levels of brightness and darkness are mapped onto the lightness dimension, and whether differences are seen as reflectance differences or illumination differences, is considered by Jameson and Hurvich to be a matter of interpretation. And no rules are given as to how this interpretation process works.

Yet certain lightness predictions follow from the Jameson/Hurvich model. As illumination increases, light grays are held to become lighter while dark grays are held to become darker (see diverging functions, p. 91). The empirical evidence shows, however, that when constancy fails due to increased illumination, dark grays become lighter, not darker.

Cornsweet

Cornsweet (1970, p. 374) claims that "the brightness of a target is judged to be almost constant when the illumination falling on it and its surroundings is varied over wide limits. . . . Constancy, however, breaks down when the intensities of the retinal images of the target and its surround differ strongly." Cornsweet based this claim on Heinemann's data (p. 283, see also Fig. 13.4, p. 378): "So long as the intensities of the test spot and its surround did not differ by more than about five-fold, the subjects showed good very good constancy." But many experiments have shown good constancy well beyond this ratio (Arend & Spehar, 1993a, 1993b; Jacobsen & Gilchrist, 1988a, 1988b). Indeed, several studies have shown better constancy with greater target/background ratios (Flock & Noguchi, 1970; Hsia, 1943; Kozaki, 1963; Noguchi & Masuda, 1971, p. 65; Oyama, 1968).

But Cornsweet's model itself (at least for temporal illumination changes) seems to predict perfect constancy. According to Cornsweet, when the general level of illumination changes on a pattern of surface colors, the change in inhibition levels exactly cancels out the change in excitation levels, leaving the rate of firing associated with a given surface unchanged. But real empirical data show that lightness is only rarely so constant. Normally there is some degree of under-constancy. Here we have an example of a theory that fails to predict errors that are known to occur.

Helson

Adaptation-Level Theory

In its simplest form, Helson's adaptation-level theory of lightness perception (Helson, 1964, 1943) holds that the lightness of a given surface is a function of the luminance of that surface divided by the average luminance of the entire field of view. Clearly this simple scheme would predict gross errors when the visual contains spatially adjacent fields of different illumination level. This is one of the reasons Helson postulated a weighted average, with the contribution of each part of the scene to the average weighted according to proximity to the target.

Even with the weighting, however, the Helson formula predicts the wrong pattern of errors. Because Helson offers no way to make sure that the average luminance is taken only within a given field of illumination, it is inevitable that the average will include surfaces from an adjacent field of illumination. This will produce under-constancy, but that under-constancy will apply to all shades of gray equally. As we will find in the staircase Gelb effect (p. 310), illumination-dependent failures of constancy show a gradient of error. In the higher illumination, dark grays are lightened more than light grays, while in lower illumination light grays are darkened more than dark grays.

Helson's model also predicts errors that do not occur when the zone within which the average is taken contains a skewed distribution of reflectance values. For example, when the field contains a truncated range of gray shades, Helson's model predicts that the perceived lightness values will center on middle gray, with no whites or blacks visible. But when Cataliotti and I (Cataliotti & Gilchrist, 1995) presented observers with a truncated range of grays covering the walls of a small room that filled the entire visual field, only white and light-gray surfaces were perceived.

Wallach

Both Helson and Wallach predict a simultaneous contrast illusion far stronger than what actually occurs. Wallach attributes this discrepancy to the fact that in addition to the local ratio of each target and its background, the ratio between each target and the contralateral background also plays a (weaker) role. But this account fails to recognize that exactly the same argument must be made in the case of a lightness constancy display with side-by-side lighted and shadowed fields. Yet in this case, the obtained data approximate the ratio predictions.

Other problems stem from the fact that Wallach's ratios are local ratios, with no provision for edge integration. As illustrated in Figure 6.5, a white square and a black square resting on a common gray background have exactly the same local ratios as the two middle-gray targets in the simultaneous contrast display. Yet the perceived lightness values differ wildly in the two situations.

Wallach's theory must predict zero lightness constancy when the two backgrounds are made equal in luminance by the technique of countershading (see Chapter 3). Yet, as many experiments have shown, substantial constancy occurs here. Wallach's ratio model also predicts serious lightness errors whenever a target is bounded by either a depth edge (corner or occluding edge) or a sharp illumination boundary, because in those cases the two terms of the ratio will lie in regions of very different illumination level.

Land and McCann

Within the Land and McCann (1971) model of lightness perception, the only means of distinguishing reflectance and illuminance edges is through edge sharpness. But of course illuminance edges are often quite sharp. These must be treated as reflectance edges by the model, just as in models that have no mechanism for edge classification at all. This predicts failures of lightness constancy much larger than those obtained empirically. On the other hand, shallow reflectance gradients should not be sensed at all, another prediction not consistent with the facts. And the model fails to predict the simultaneous contrast illusion.

The foregoing is far from an exhaustive survey of predicted errors, even for the models considered. But perhaps these examples help to point out (1) the general lack of specificity in models of lightness perception, (2) the need for greater specificity, and (3) the power of an errors analysis in testing models, especially as models become better specified.

OBTAINED ERRORS

Now we approach the question of errors from the opposite direction. Instead of starting with lightness theories and then deriving predicted errors, we start with empirical results, describing the actual pattern of lightness errors as reported in the literature, and then use this pattern to drive a theory of lightness.

Legitimate and Illegitimate Errors

Before continuing we must make an important distinction between what I will call *legitimate errors* and *illegitimate errors*. Legitimate errors typically involve a lack of information. A good example is the simple Gelb effect. A disk of black paper is suspended in midair and illuminated by a spotlight, making it appear white. This is certainly an error, and the largest possible error. It must be noted, however, that the black disk in the spotlight makes exactly the same retinal image as a white disk in room light. Apart from extrasensory perception, there is no way to avoid such an error. The information is simply not in the stimulus. An ideal observer (Kersten & Yuille, 2003) would necessarily make the same error.[1]

Illegitimate errors, on the other hand, are not the result of missing information. An ideal observer would make only legitimate errors, not illegitimate errors. Simultaneous lightness contrast is an illegitimate error. An even better example is the staircase Gelb effect that will be described in the next chapter. In these cases, there is sufficient information available to the visual system so that, if it were programmed as described by the intrinsic image models, it would get the correct lightness values. Instead the system makes sometimes huge and seemingly unnecessary lightness errors. Such errors have much to teach about how the visual system works.

We now review these illegitimate errors, putting theoretical perspectives aside as much as possible. We will group them into two classes, as failures of the two basic types of constancy: failures caused by different illumination levels and failures caused by neighboring reflectances.

Failures of Illumination-Independent Constancy

Most of what the empirical literature shows about illumination-dependent failures of constancy can be summarized by six components.

The Fundamental Error: Lightening in High Illumination, Darkening in Low

Although the visual system copes admirably with the challenge of different levels of illumination, it can also be said that every change in illumination, especially every spatial change, causes at least some error. Surfaces on the brighter side of the illuminance border appear lighter than they are, or surfaces on the darker side appear darker than they are, or both.[2] This means that illumination-dependent failures of constancy take the form of under-constancy, not over-constancy.[3] This is the fundamental illumination-dependent failure. Surfaces tend to be lightened in high illumination and darkened in low illumination (Gilchrist, 1988; Gilchrist et al., 1983).

The failure of constancy here is a genuinely perceptual error; it is not an artifact of the observer's misunderstanding of the task. Expert observers (i.e., the experimenters) show this error as well. There are errors that result from observer task-confusion, but these are not included in our definition of errors in surface lightness.

Illumination Difference: Larger Errors with Larger Difference

The size of the error associated with an illuminance border generally depends on the size of the illuminance change: the greater the illuminance difference, the greater the constancy failures. (If, however, the error is measured using a Brunswik ratio or a Thouless ratio, then error size declines with greater illuminance change because they measure the size of the error relative to the size of the illumination change.)

Standard Gradient of Error: Error Size Depends on Target Reflectance

When constancy fails in high illumination, surfaces appear to lighten. But do all shades of gray lighten by equal amounts? The answer is no. In high illumination, especially if the high illumination fills only part of the visual field, dark-gray surfaces lighten more than light-gray surfaces. In low illumination, light grays darken more than dark grays. I will refer to this pattern as the *standard gradient of error*.

The same pattern was there in my early work on depth and lightness (Gilchrist, 1980; see Chapter 6). I reported Munsell matches only for the target patches, which were typically either whites in shadow or blacks in bright illumination. These showed fundamental errors of about 1.5 Munsell steps. But the whites in bright illumination and the blacks in shadow were always seen without error.

It should be noted that testing for the standard gradient of error requires the use of a Munsell chart; the gradient will not be revealed by the method of adjustment used in the classic form of lightness constancy experiment introduced by Katz (1935, p. 121). There a target in a field of high illumination is adjusted so as to match another target in an adjacent field of low illumination. Under such conditions, constancy can fail simultaneously in both the high illumination and the low illumination, but in opposing, self-canceling, directions. Thus, it should not be surprising that in the classic literature on lightness constancy conducted using this method, contradictory findings have been reported concerning the degree that constancy depends on the reflectance of the targets. Katz (1935, p. 121) and Evans (1948, p. 164) reported better constancy for light grays, while others (Flock & Noguchi, 1970; Hsia, 1943; Kozaki, 1963; Noguchi & Masuda, 1971; Oyama, 1968) have reported better constancy for dark grays.

Background Reflectance: Larger Errors with Darker Backgrounds

In his original constancy experiments, Katz (1935) obtained poor levels of constancy, due at least in part to his use of gray backgrounds behind each of the targets, as opposed to a white background, even though Hering (1874) had already noted that greater constancy is obtained with lighter backgrounds. The same finding has since been reported by Kardos (1934), Helson (1943), Leibowitz, Myers, and Chinetti (1955), Hano (1955), and Kozaki (1963, 1965).

Framework Size: Larger Errors with Smaller Frameworks

According to Katz's laws of field size, the degree of constancy within a field of illumination depends on the size of the field (see Chapter 3). Empirical evidence in support of this has been reported by Henneman (1935), Kardos (1934), MacLeod (1932), Cataliotti and Gilchrist (1995), and Agostini & Bruno (1996), among others. Errors are greatest with small fields of illumination and become progressively smaller as field size grows.

Framework Articulation: Less Error with Greater Articulation

Katz was the first to report that the strength of lightness constancy varies with the degree to which the lighted or shadowed fields are articulated. Supporting empirical evidence is ubiquitous (Adelson & Pentland, 1996; Arend & Goldstein, 1987; Burzlaff, 1931; Henneman, 1935; Kardos, 1934; Katona, 1929; Kozaki, 1963; Schirillo & Arend, 1995; Wishart et al., 1997).

Failures of Background-Independent Constancy

The visual system maintains an impressive degree of constancy in the lightness of a target despite changes in its background, or neighboring gray levels. Yet because this challenge is never fully met, changes in background inevitably produce lightness errors. Although often small, these errors are very systematic. We will review the various factors that influence error size in the basic simultaneous contrast pattern first, and then describe the many delightful variations that have appeared.

The Fundamental Error

Targets on dark backgrounds appear lighter and targets on light backgrounds appear darker. This is the basic error. The magnitude of this error is typically between 0.5 and 1 Munsell step in the standard textbook version shown in Figure 10.2.[4]

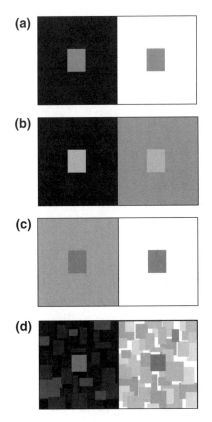

Figure 10.2. The contrast illusion found in the standard simultaneous contrast display (a) is absent or greatly reduced with double increments (b), unlike with double decrements (c). Articulating the backgrounds strengthens the illusion (d).

Error Varies with Background Luminance Difference

Not surprisingly, the size of the error increases as the luminance difference between the two backgrounds increases, at least up to some limit.

Little or No Error with Double Increments

In the standard textbook display, one target is an increment and one target is a decrement. When both targets are increments, as illustrated in Figure 10.2b, the contrast illusion either disappears (Agostini & Bruno, 1996; Arend & Spehar, 1993b; Diamond, 1953; Gilchrist, 1988; Heinemann, 1955; Jacobsen & Gilchrist, 1988b; Kozaki, 1963, 1965) or is dramatically reduced (Bressan & Actis-Grosso, 2001; Schirillo & Shevell, 1997; Zemach & Rudd, in 2005). This fact, ignored by contrast theories, presents us with an important clue as to the source of simultaneous contrast. This clue does not mean that the illusion requires both a decrement and an increment. The illusion remains when both targets are decrements, as seen in Figure 10.2c.

Additional Factors in Simultaneous Contrast

Articulating the black and white backgrounds strengthens the illusion, as shown in Figure 10.2d, even when this reduces the difference in average luminance between backgrounds (Adelson, 2000; Bressan & Actis-Grosso, 2004; Gilchrist et al., 1999). Varying the distance from which the simultaneous contrast display is viewed has no effect on the size of the illusion, even though this changes the retinal distance from the center of each target to its background (Burgh & Grindley, 1962). Introducing a luminance ramp between the black and white backgrounds strengthens the illusion (Fig. 10.3; also see Shapley, 1986). Agostini and Galmonte (1997) have produced a strong example of this, shown in Figure 10.3, by superimposing gray targets on a pattern of luminance ramps used by Zavagno (1999) to create a glare effect.

Wolff (1933) claimed that the simultaneous contrast illusion is either eliminated or greatly reduced when the gray targets are perceived to lie in a very different depth plane from the light and dark backgrounds, But Gibbs and Lawson (1974) and Julesz (1971) reported no such effect. These latter studies used stereoscopic depth, while Wolff used an actual depth difference. The additional cues present in Wolff's study, like accretion and deletion at target edges due to observer motion, might account for the different results.

Agostini and Bruno (1996) have shown that the size of the simultaneous contrast illusion approximately doubles when the entire display is presented within a spotlight, like that used for the Gelb effect. The effect is not the result of high illumination, per se. As the scope of the spotlight is gradually enlarged, the size of the contrast effect is correspondingly reduced to its standard textbook strength.

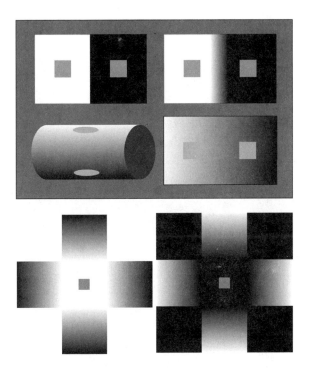

Figure 10.3. Simultaneous contrast displays with luminance ramps in the backgrounds. Bottom display due to Agostini and Galmonte (1997) and Zavagno (1999).

Apparently a CRT screen functions somewhat like a spotlight. Agostini and Bruno found the same doubling of the contrast effect when presented on a CRT screen. This potentially important finding suggests that the more recent CRT-based lightness literature cannot be automatically integrated with the older paper-based research.

Laurinen, Olzak, and Peromaa (1997) superimposed shallow luminance modulations on each of the four parts of the simultaneous contrast display, as shown in Figure 10.4. They found that the contrast effect is substantially weakened if the modulation frequency on each target is different from that of its background. When the frequency of each target is the same as that of its background and when the backgrounds differ in frequency, the contrast effect is enhanced.

Grouping Principles Play a Role

The Koffka (1915) ring, shown in Figure 4.2a, shows that little or no contrast effect is obtained if the two gray targets merge into a single region. However, a thin black line drawn in the appropriate location is sufficient to restore the contrast effect.

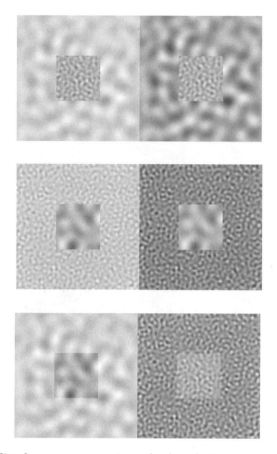

Figure 10.4. Simultaneous contrast is weak when the targets are grouped with each other by similarity but each is dissimilar from its background (top and middle, after Laurinen, Olzak & Peromaa, 1997). Contrast is strong when each target is similar to its background but the two targets are dissimilar (bottom). Reprinted with permission.

The Benary effect (see Fig. 4.2b), created by Wertheimer and studied systematically by Benary (1924), shows that two gray targets with identical local contexts can nevertheless show a contrast effect if they are grouped, by perceptual structure, with black and white regions respectively. Notice that both triangles border white along the hypotenuse and black along the other two sides. But perceptually one triangle clearly appears to belong to the cross, while the other triangle appears to belong to the white background. According to my measurements (Gilchrist, 1988), the Benary effect has 71% of the strength of the conventional contrast effect.

The role of perceptual organization in channeling the contrast effect is even more dramatically illustrated in an effect that has come to be

Figure 10.5. White's illusion (White, 1986). The gray bars are all identical. The bars on the right appear lighter gray even though most have more white on the border than black.

called White's illusion (White, 1981). Here the perceived contrast effect contradicts the expectation based on local context. Notice that in Figure 10.5, the gray bars that appear lighter actually share a longer border with white neighbors than with black neighbors. Moreover, unlike the Benary effect, which is a bit weaker than the standard contrast effect, White's illusion is stronger, typically about 1.5 Munsell steps. White himself attributed the illusion to assimilation. But Anderson (2001) has produced three versions of White's illusion (Fig. 10.6) that appear to argue strongly against this interpretation. In these cases even the direction of the difference between target bars on the left and right displays is opposite to that predicted if target lightness assimilates to the lightness of the flanking stripes. Spehar et al. (2002) have shown that the direction of White's illusion is reversed when the two target bars are both lighter or both darker than the contextual stripes, an effect opposing assimilation. Kingdom and Moulden (1991), reporting a series of experiments designed to maximize the possibility of finding assimilation effects in White's illusion, conclude that it plays no important role in the illusion.

The Todorović illusion (Todorović, 1997), shown in Figure 10.7, shows that the direction of the perceived contrast effect can oppose the effect expected by local context even when the aspect ratio of white and black adjacency is pushed to remarkable lengths.

Checkerboard contrast, as presented by DeValois and DeValois (1988) and illustrated in Figure 10.8, goes even farther. On a black-and-white checkerboard pattern a gray square is substituted for one of the black squares, while another gray square is substituted for one of the white squares. The gray substituted for the black appears lighter than the other gray despite the fact that it is totally surrounded by white. This illusion is relatively weak and unstable (Gilchrist et al., 1999, p. 817). The deWeert illusion (deWeert, 1991), shown in Figure 10.9, is topologically similar to checkerboard contrast and may have the same explanation.

Assimilation predictions

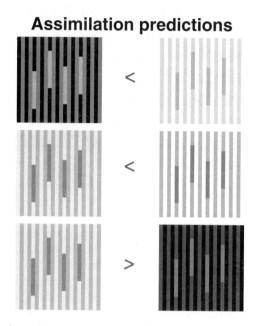

Figure 10.6. In these examples, relative lightness values are opposite to those predicted by an assimilation theory of White's illusion (Anderson, 2001). Reprinted with permission.

Figure 10.7. The Todorović illusion (Todorović, 1997) is topologically equivalent to White's illusion but an even more extreme version.

Figure 10.8. Checkerboard contrast (after DeValois & DeValois, 1988). The gray square with all black adjacent neighbors appears paradoxically darker than the square with white neighbors, suggesting grouping by diagonals.

Figure 10.9. The DeWeert illusion (DeWeert, 1991). The three interior gray regions are identical. Reprinted with permission.

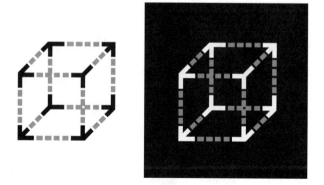

Figure 10.10. The left gray dashes, which are surrounded by the higher luminance background, appear lighter than the right dashes surrounded by the darker background (Agostini & Galmonte, 2002). Adapted with permission.

Complete Reversal of Contrast

Recently several new illusions have appeared that completely reverse the direction of contrast, as predicted by contrast theories. The first of these, shown in Figure 10.10, was presented by Agostini and Galmonte (2002). The dashed parts of the Necker cube appear lighter in the left figure, even though these dashes are completely surrounded by the lighter background.[5] Apparently this happens because each set of dashes is anchored by the cube to which it strongly belongs. Elias Economou constructed a display we call *reverse contrast*, shown in Figure 10.11. We found (Economou et al., 1998) that the strength of the illusion is systematically related to the strength of the grouping factors present in the set of flanking bars. Our findings are presented on page

Figure 10.11. Reverse contrast illusion (Economou, Annan & Gilchrist, 1998). The left gray bar, though completely surrounded by black, appears darker than the right gray bar, completely surrounded by white.

Figure 10.12. The dungeon illusion (Bressan, 2001). The perceived difference between the two gray squares contradicts a local contrast explanation. Reprinted with permission.

323. Paola Bressan (2001) has produced a strong anti-contrast illusion that she calls the dungeon illusion (Fig. 10.12).

Adelson Illusions

Some of the most remarkable lightness/brightness illusions have been produced in recent years by Ted Adelson. Four of these are shown in Figure 10.13.

Adelson's illusions often are not easily categorized as illumination-dependent or background-dependent constancy failures. They are background-dependent failures in the sense that they can be created by arranging bits of gray paper in a mosaic, and Adelson typically measures the background-dependent errors in his displays.[6] Yet the mosaic typically results in a pictorial representation of a illumination-independent constancy situation. The illusions shown in Figure 10.13 are mosaics that create the impression that some targets lie behind a strip of neutral-density filter. In other Adelson mosaics the impression of different levels of illumination is created. We saw this clearly in Adelson's checkered shadow (Fig. 1.1), surely the most effective demonstration of the problem of lightness constancy ever produced. The two floor tiles indicated have equal luminances but appear very different in gray shade. Adelson's corrugated plaid, shown in Figure 6.15, creates the impression of different depth planes, each with a corresponding level of illumination.

Crispening

The crispening effect, named by Takasaki (1966), is a sort of exaggeration of luminance differences for luminances near the background level. A given luminance difference (log difference, that is) near the background luminance appears larger than that same difference much further from background luminance. An excellent quantitative analysis of this effect can be found in Whittle (1994a).

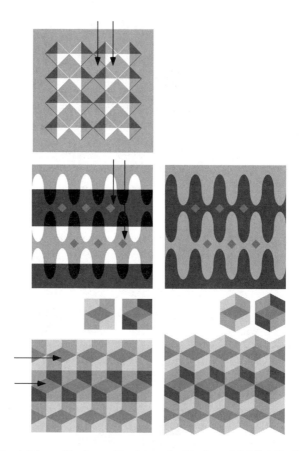

Figure 10.13. Adelson illusions. (Top) Argyle illusion. (Middle) Snake illusion. (Bottom) Wall of blocks. Reprinted with permission from Adelson, 1993, 2000.

Gradient Illusions

Many delightful errors in lightness involve luminance ramps. In addition to those that heighten the simultaneous contrast illusion, we have seen the fuzzy spots of Evans (Fig. 6.24), the Craik-O'Brien illusion (Fig. 6.2), and Bergström's gradient paradox (Fig. 7.4).

Several more gradient illusions are shown in Figure 10.14. Blakeslee and McCourt (1999, 2003) have constructed a multiple scale filter model to explain McCourt's (1982) gradient induction effect, and other illusions. Arend and Goldstein's (1987a) induced gradient is analogous but simpler. Pawan Sinha has added his own creative twist: he used an induced gradient to make a bar containing a real gradient appear homogeneous. When equi-luminant targets are then placed on this bar, they appear inexplicably different.

Figure 10.14. Several gradient illusions. (Top) Induced gradient (Arend & Goldstein, 1987). (Middle) Grating induction (McCourt, 1982). The bottom illusion is by Sinha. See text for explanation.

Figure 10.15 (top) shows an exceptionally strong version of Adelson's wall of blocks, created by Logvinenko (1999) by adding luminance ramps to the vertical diamond segments. Figure 10.15 (bottom) shows the diamond illusion (Watanabe, Cavanagh & Anstis, 1995), a delightful version of the Craik-O'Brien illusion.

BUILDING A THEORY OF LIGHTNESS ERRORS

How does one begin the task of building a theory to account for the almost dizzying range of errors, including those we have reviewed? Can some of these errors be viewed as more important than others? And is it possible to group the errors into classes?

Though both the traditional categories of illusions and failures of constancy should be equally regarded as errors, they represent two main classes of error. In current terminology, these are failures of the two classes of constancy (with changes of illumination or changes of

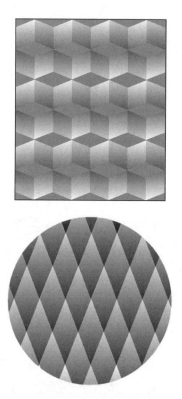

Figure 10.15. (Top) Covering the vertical diamonds in Adelson's wall of blocks illusion (see Figure 10.13, bottom) with luminance ramps produces a strong illusion. The horizontal diamonds are equal in luminance (after Logvinenko, Kane & Ross, 2002; reprinted with permission). (Bottom) The diamond illusion (Watanabe et al., 1995). The diamonds are all identical.

background). For each type of constancy failure we will begin with the fundamental error. If a candidate model cannot easily explain the fundamental failure, there is little use in pursuing it farther.

The Big Challenge

A central challenge for a theory of lightness errors will be to bridge these two broad classes of errors with a single model.

As we saw in Chapter 3, historically many theories have tried to account for illumination-independent lightness constancy and simultaneous contrast (which is a background-dependent failure) with a single model. A related but different attempt has been to account for illumination-independent constancy and background-independent constancy with a single model. Here the intrinsic image models have proven their strength. But the challenge for a theory of errors is different still: to account for illumination-dependent failures and background-dependent failures with a single model.

Decomposition Models: Clues to the Errors?

The arguments for basing a theory of lightness perception on veridical perception have already been given (see p. 267). Yet there was another consideration as well. Even if a decomposition model could not, by itself, account for lightness errors, the hope was that it would provide a framework within which the errors could be understood. Can the errors be chalked up to a failure of one or more of the components of the model?

The first component in my intrinsic image model (Gilchrist, 1979) is edge encoding. It has already been shown that anything that interferes with edge encoding can produce errors. Retinal stabilization of edges provides the best evidence of this (Krauskopf, 1963; Yarbus, 1967). But this produces legitimate errors, and we really want to understand the illegitimate errors. Certain illusions involving luminance gradients have been attributed to a failure to encode the full amplitude of change in shallow gradients. But this argument, which has itself been challenged (see p. 181), applies to only a limited domain of illusions.

In 1988 I proposed a common model for both illumination-dependent and background-dependent errors. It was inspired by the striking parallels between the two types of constancy, as illustrated in Figure 10.16. The following statements apply equally to the two displays:

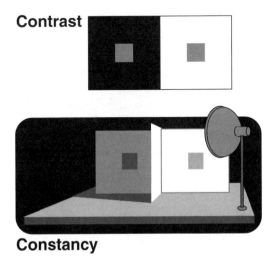

Figure 10.16. The simultaneous contrast illusion and the constancy setup are very similar in structure.

1. The display can be said to entail a large framework that is composed of two smaller frameworks.
2. If the two targets have exactly the same luminance, the target on the left (that is, the target on the darker background) will appear lighter than the target on the right. The lateral inhibition account was driven primarily by this observation, but additional facts need to be considered.
3. If the two targets stand in the same luminance ratio to their respective backgrounds, the target on the right (that is, the target on the brighter background) will appear lighter.
4. Points 2 and 3 above imply that a lightness match lies somewhere between a luminance match and a luminance ratio match.

But several important differences between the two displays should also be noted:

1. The border between the backgrounds is perceived to be an illuminance border in illumination-independent constancy but a reflectance border in background-independent constancy.
2. When measured in the traditional way, as deviations from a luminance match, the illumination-independent constancy effect is an order of magnitude larger than the contrast effect (background-dependent failure). This neglected fact is very damaging to the lateral inhibition story.
3. A veridical lightness match would be represented by a luminance ratio match for illumination-independent constancy but a luminance match for background-independent constancy.
4. Empirical results lie closest to a luminance ratio match for illumination-independent constancy but closest to a luminance match for background-independent constancy.

Earlier I described an edge-substitution experiment designed to compare the two types of constancy under equivalent photometric conditions. The lightness matches obtained in that experiment revealed yet another parallel: the deviation of the lightness match from a veridical match was the same for both types of constancy—that is, in the illumination-independent situation, the obtained match deviated from a luminance ratio match just as much as the obtained match deviated from a luminance match in the background-independent situation.

A Competition Model of Constancy Failures

The symmetrical pattern in the matching data can be observed in Figure 6.6. This pattern is very reminiscent of comments that Ralph Evans makes in his first book (1948) regarding the Hess and Pretori display. Hess and Pretori (1894/1970) had done one of the earliest lightness/

brightness matching experiments using a pair of side-by-side center/ surround displays. Their apparatus, though ingenious, did not make it visually clear whether the backgrounds differ in reflectance or illumination. Evans set up a model of the Hess and Pretori display. He reports (p. 166) that:

> As soon as the brightness difference became very large some sort of attitude had to be taken toward the figure in order to obtain consistent data. At large differences the appearance of the central squares took on an indeterminate, fluctuating sort of quality, and the observer was equally dissatisfied with the match over a relatively large range of intensities. Binocular vision was used in a room which was not wholly dark. Under these conditions it was quite apparent that there were four surfaces visible, and it became possible to ask the observer to consider their appearance in either of two quite different ways. The whole figure could be seen as cube viewed from one edge with gray squares on each of the two sides, or it could be seen as two apertures through which what appeared to be a single separately illuminated surface was seen. The results obtained by asking the observer to take either one of these two attitudes were quite satisfying. The indeterminateness ceased at once. When the perception was that of a cube with gray squares the matches moved far in the direction of the ratios required by complete brightness constancy. When the perception was that of a uniformly illuminated rear surface seen through two apertures, the results moved equally far toward having identical intensities (luminances) on the two sides.[7]

Evans' two attitudes correspond to the two appearances of my contrast/constancy display (Gilchrist, 1988). Seeing the display as two faces of a cube is equivalent to seeing the difference between the backgrounds as a difference of illumination, whereas in the case of seeing two apertures, the backgrounds appear as coplanar and would appear to differ in reflectance. The qualitative report of his results bears a striking resemblance to my quantitative results. When the backgrounds appeared to differ in illumination "the matches moved far in the direction of the ratios," and when they appeared to differ in reflectance, "the results moved equally far toward having identical intensities (luminances)."

This symmetry suggested a new way to understand lightness contrast and failures of lightness constancy in general. My proposal assumed that the visual system is somehow capable of integrating edge ratios (see Chapter 7) and of classifying them into either reflectance or illumination edges. To perform veridically, the visual system should match luminance ratios when the backgrounds differ in illumination, and match luminances when the backgrounds differ in reflectance. Operationally these correspond to either fully including the border between backgrounds or fully excluding it from the integration. The obtained results indicate that the system does not succeed either in fully excluding the background/background border in one case, or in fully including it in the other case. It is as if the urge to exclude it and the urge to include it compete with each other, and neither can be entirely eliminated. The hypothesis is that both kinds of operations are invoked in every constancy situation, regardless of appearance.

But this model has not held up as a general model of errors. Bruno (1994) has shown that the symmetry I obtained in the size of illumination-dependent and background-dependent failures may have been peculiar to the specific conditions in my experiment: it does not appear to hold up under parametric changes in background luminances. Worse, the model fails to account for the majority of the errors listed under our survey of errors given earlier. Nor can the model account for the dramatic errors in the staircase Gelb effect yet to be described.

The only remaining component in the veridicality model is the late-coming anchoring component. Can anchoring provide the key to errors? As we will see, the answer appears to be yes. But it does so, as we will see, in a way that deeply undermines the intrinsic image models.

SUMMARY

Errors in perception, while of little interest in machine vision, offer a powerful access to the secrets of human vision. These errors are systematic, not random, and they can only come from visual processing. Thus the pattern of errors must be the signature of the human software used to compute lightness. Lightness errors have been used sporadically but not systematically to reveal the human lightness algorithm. Many errors predicted by lightness theories simply do not occur, and there are many lightness errors lacking a theoretical account. Failures of constancy (illumination-independent constancy) and illusions have traditionally been treated as separate phenomena, but this separation is unwarranted and these errors are here grouped together.

This chapter represents an attempt to survey and organize the many lightness errors reported in the literature. These errors can be broadly grouped into two categories: illumination-dependent and background-dependent errors. These represent failures in the two basic types of constancy. The fundamental illumination-dependent error is this: surfaces in high illumination tend to appear lighter than they are, while those in low illumination tend to appear darker. Other errors of this type depend on size of the illumination difference, gray level of the target, gray level of the background, and size and articulation of the region of illumination.

The fundamental background-dependent error is shown by the simultaneous contrast illusion: targets on bright backgrounds appear too dark, while targets on dark backgrounds appear too light. Other errors of this type depend on background luminance, presence of luminance ramps, grouping factors, articulation of the framework, and whether the target is an increment or a decrement.

11

An Anchoring Model of Errors

The lightness model described in Gilchrist et al. (1999) is presented here in more detail. Its principal strength is the wide range of lightness errors it can accommodate. Central to the model is its construction of the relationship between simple and complex images. But first we will consider lightness in simple images.

ANCHORING IN SIMPLE IMAGES

Let us begin with a definition of simple images. I will define the simplest image as one that contains only two shades of gray, and these fill the entire visual field. There has not been complete agreement on what constitutes the simplest image. Evans (1974, p. 84) has argued that a spot seen against darkness constitutes the simplest image. Heinemann (1972, p. 146) has nominated the disk/annulus display. Koffka (1935, p. 111) has argued that a completely homogeneous visual field (ganzfeld) is simpler than a point of light in a dark field, but he did not claim that such an image produces lightness. For that, at least one edge is necessary. As Wallach noted (1963, p. 112), "Opaque colors which deserve to be called white or gray, in other words 'surface colors,' will make their appearance only when two regions of different light intensity are in contact with each other."

In practice, this can be achieved by placing the observer's head inside a large dome, as described in Chapter 9. Under these simple conditions, the computation of lightness can be exhaustively described by three rules.

1. Highest luminance rule. The highest luminance is defined as white (reflectance 90%), and the darker region is seen relative

to this standard, using the Wallach ratio principle. The formula, which applies to both regions, is:

$$\text{Lightness} = (L_t/L_h * 90\%)$$

where L_t is the luminance of the target, L_h is the highest luminance, and lightness is defined as perceived reflectance.

2. Area rule. Area is held to influence lightness only when the darker region has the larger area. For a two-region dome, the combined formula for highest luminance and area is:

$$\text{Lightness} = (100-A_d)/50 * (L_t/L_h * 90\%) + (A_d-50)/50 * (90\%)$$

where A_d is the area of the darker region, as a percentage of the total area in the field. Note that as A_d increases, lightness also increases. When A_d is 50 or less, this formula reduces to formula 1 above.

3. Scale Normalization Rule. The range of perceived grays in the dome is expanded in proportion to the degree to which the physical luminance range is truncated relative to the canonical range of 30:1. If the physical range exceeds 30:1, the perceived range is proportionately compressed. The formula is:

$$\text{Perceived Range} = (1+(.56 * (\log 30 - \log R))) * R$$

where R is the actual range. The value .56 represents the slope of the regression line obtained by plotting perceived range against actual range in a disk/ganzfeld experiment reported by Gilchrist and Bonato (1995) and shown in Figure 9.24. Expansion always projects away from the anchor, just as compression always collapses toward the anchor. Perceived reflectance of a specific patch is predicted by combining this formula with formula 1 above, as follows:

$$\text{Lightness} = ((1+(.56 * (\log 30 - \log R))) L_t/L_h * 90\%)$$

Domes that contain more than two regions will still be considered simple as long as they contain no segmentation factors, which are described later.

SIMPLE VERSUS COMPLEX IMAGES

The fact that we could achieve such a command of the rules of anchoring in simple images is gratifying. But the significance of this is very limited unless these findings can be applied to complex images. The question of how simple images are related to complex images has been addressed sporadically, but it has never gotten the attention it deserves. The induction experiments of the contrast period were based on the tacit assumption that the behavior of isolated points of light can be directly extrapolated to all the points that compose a complex image. Why else would one care so much about the brightness of spots of light in a dark room? But with the computational period came experiment after experiment contradicting this assumption of direct extrapolation.

Arend (Arend & Goldstein, 1987; Arend & Spehar, 1993a) has criticized disk/annulus experiments as fatally flawed, suggesting that such stimulus conditions are too ambiguous to teach us anything about lightness in complex scenes. Clearly the results obtained under simple conditions cannot be mindlessly applied to complex images. And yet, it would be surprising if there were no systematic relationship between lightness in simple images and lightness in complex images.

THE APPLICABILITY ASSUMPTION

At the heart of the anchoring model lies a critical assumption about the relationship between simple and complex images: the rules of anchoring found in simple images are applicable to frames of reference embedded within complex images. The same anchoring rules are held to apply to both. The values so computed in local frameworks do not represent the final perceived values, however, until they are combined with values computed globally. This is the Kardos principle of co-determination. But the anchoring model holds that the formulae describing the lightness computation within a given framework are the same whether a simple image inside a dome, a local framework such as a shadow, or (presumably) the entire visual field. These rules are three: the highest luminance rule, the area rule, and the scale normalization rule.

Area and the Applicability Assumption

Ana Radonjić and I recently completed an extensive experiment that tested the role of area in simple images but in a larger sense was really a test of the applicability assumption. Nine domes were created. Each one had the same two shades of gray, but in different proportions, using radial sectors, as seen in Figure 11.1. We had several reasons to revisit the question of area. The predicted area rule graphed in Figure 9.10 was based on only a few data points. And the radial sector method removed the confound between relative area and retinal eccentricity; the proportion of light and dark was always the same in the fovea and in the periphery, as long as the subject fixated the central vertex.

The results presented in Figure 11.1 show that lightness was significantly influenced by relative area only when the darker region was greater than 180°. This confirms the shape of the curves predicted in Figure 9.10. More importantly, however, it implies that the area rule

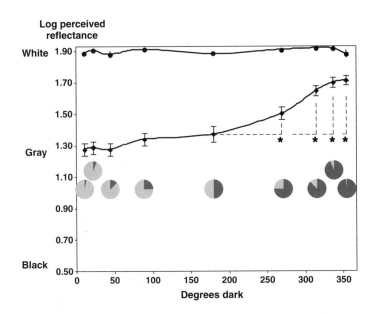

Figure 11.1. Perceived lightness of light and dark regions within a simple image that filled the observer's entire visual field, as relative area was varied, with luminance values constant.

obeys the applicability assumption, given that the area rule has already been demonstrated several times (Diamond, 1955; Newson, 1958; Stevens, 1967; Stewart, 1959) in complex images.

It should be noted, however, that these results did not show the gamut expansion predicted by the scale normalization rule—that is, in those domes to which the area rule does not apply, the range of perceived reflectances was slightly less than the actual range (approximately 5:1), casting some doubt on the status of the scale normalization rule.

Frameworks in Complex Images

A complex image will be defined as an image that contains at least one segmentation factor or more than one framework. A framework will be defined by a group of patches in the retinal image that are segregated, or a group of patches that belong together or are grouped together.

Frameworks of illumination can be seen clearly in some of the wonderful photographs by Cartier-Bresson, one of which is shown in Figure 11.2. In Figure 11.2 I have added a set of probe disks. Though the disks are equal in luminance, they appear as different shades of gray within the different frameworks. Adding probe disks to Adelson's

Figure 11.2. Probe disks of identical luminance appear different within different frames of reference. (Henri Cartier-Bresson, *Trastevere, Rome, Italy, 1959.* Photograph courtesy of Magnum Photos.)

checkered shadow image (Fig. 11.3) shows that it is not the local contrast ratio that determines the lightness of these disks, but rather the framework within which each falls. The disks on squares A and B have identical local contrast (their backgrounds are also identical), and yet they appear different in lightness. The disks flanking the letter A have very different local contrast and yet they appear roughly equal in lightness, and the same holds for the disks flanking the letter B. The weak simultaneous contrast effect seen there is small relative to the difference between disks inside the shadow and disks outside.

Consistent with these effects, Rock et al. (1992) showed that achromatic targets are phenomenally grouped based on their equal perceived lightness, not on equal luminance values or on equal local luminance ratios.

Figure 11.3. All of the probe disks added to this Ted Adelson display are identical, but those inside the shadow appear light gray while those outside the shadow appear dark gray. Within each of these regions it matters little whether the disk is on a light square or a dark square (http://web.mit.edu/persci/people/adelson/checkershadow_illusion.html). Reprinted with permission.

Segmenting Frameworks

Clearly an important question is how such frameworks are identified within the retinal image. The anchoring model postulates two strong factors and series of weaker ones. The strong segmentation factors are the factors identified by Kardos: penumbra and depth boundaries (i.e., corners and occlusion edges). The Gestalt grouping factors create weaker frameworks as well. The black background in a simultaneous contrast display, for example, would be a weak framework. To these grouping factors we can add T-junctions and X-junctions. Grouping factors, of course, are just the flip side of segmentation factors. When frameworks interpenetrate one another, like the set of black squares in checkerboard contrast, it is more appropriate to speak of grouping factors than segmentation factors.

Co-determination

Because frameworks in complex images are not completely isolated from each other functionally, the rules of anchoring must be applied to them using the Kardos principle of co-determination. In other words, each target surface in a complex image is a member, virtually by definition, of more than one framework, each of which exerts an influence on its lightness. In the model, a separate lightness value is computed for a given target within each of the frameworks to which

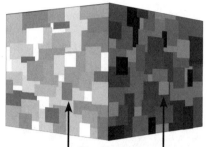

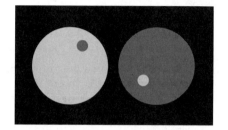

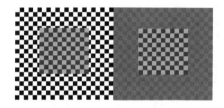

Figure 11.4. Applicability assumption: The three rules of anchoring that govern simple frameworks (domes) can be seen at work in frameworks that are part of complex images. (Top) Highest luminance rule. (Middle) Area rule. (Bottom) Scale normalization rule.

it belongs, including the global framework (the whole image) and at least one local framework. Then a weighted average is taken to determine perceived lightness.

Co-determination in complex images can be seen in the three displays shown in Figure 11.1. Each display is composed of two side-by-side frameworks. I will treat each pair of frameworks as a global framework, ignoring the larger context.

Figure 11.4, top, illustrates the highest luminance rule. Consider the two targets marked as equal in luminance. The target on the shadowed right side appears approximately white, because it is the highest luminance in its framework. It would be seen as pure white if the image on the right were painted onto the inside of a dome so that it filled the whole visual field. However, in the context of the adjacent lighted Mondrian, that target appears light gray rather than white. This illustrates the co-determination. Both parts of the compromise are phenomenally available here. If there were local anchoring but no global anchoring, the right-hand target would appear white. If there were no local anchoring, it would appear the same as the left-hand target. Clearly the percept lies between these values.

Figure 11.4, middle, shows the area rule at work. The small dark disk on the left appears darker than the larger disk on the right (even though they are physically equal), and the small light disk on the right looks lighter than the large disk on the left (also physically equal). If anchoring were totally global, these perceived differences wouldn't exist. But if anchoring were totally local, the differences would be much greater. If each of the two patterns were painted onto the inside of a dome, for example, the small disk on the left would appear slightly darker than it does here and the large disk on the right would appear much lighter, almost white, due to the area rule. Again, the differences that we see in these iso-luminant disks show the co-determination because they lie between zero difference and the extreme difference of the two-dome case.

The Wolff illusion (Fig. 9.22) shows the same thing for perceived area.

Contrast-contrast (Chubb et al., 1989), seen at the bottom, can be viewed as an application of the scale normalization effect to complex images. The left half of the display contains a full luminance range but the right half does not. Thus, in the right half the perceived range is expanded, and this is seen as greater contrast. Again, the illusion seen here is much weaker than if each half were presented separately within a dome, due to the role of global anchoring that is induced by placing them side by side.

Weighting the Co-Determination

The lightness of any given target is a weighted average of the values computed for that target in both the global framework and any local frameworks. The weighting depends primarily on the strength of each local framework. For a target belonging to the global framework and one local framework, the formula is:

$$\text{Lightness} = W_1(L_{tl}/L_{hl} * 90\%) + (1-W_1)(L_{tg}/L_{hg} * 90\%)$$

where W_1 is the weight of the local framework and $1-W_1$ is the weight of the global framework. L_{tl} and L_{hl} represent target luminance and highest luminance in the local framework; L_{tg} and L_{hg} represent these values in the global framework.

The strength of a local framework depends mainly on its size, its degree of articulation, and the strength of its segregation. Greater articulation and larger size give the framework greater weight. Quantifying the strength of the weights will require more work, but a rough idea can be gotten from existing data. For example, in the textbook example of simultaneous contrast, if the gray targets appear to differ by about one Munsell step, a typical result, this implies a local framework weight of about 12%. Cataliotti and Gilchrist (1995) found that when a group of five squares is placed on a group of five squares (the staircase Gelb effect display, to be described soon), the black square appears as a Munsell 5.5. This implies a local framework weight of about 40%. The five squares have greater articulation than a local framework in the simultaneous contrast display (5 versus 2), and they are more strongly segregated (by a depth boundary).

Coplanarity as a Graded Variable

In my experiments that led to the coplanar ratio principle (Gilchrist, 1980) I treated belongingness due to coplanarity as an all-or-none affair, even though Kardos (and Koffka with less clarity) had presented it as a graded factor, as required by the principle of co-determination. Other work (Gogel & Mershon, 1969; Wishart et al., 1997) suggests that the Gestaltists were correct.

LIGHTNESS COMPUTATION IN COMPLEX IMAGES: A SUMMARY

1. Complex images are segmented into frameworks.
2. Within a given framework each target is assigned a value according to three rules of anchoring for simple images: highest luminance, area, and scale normalization.
3. Local values are weighted according to the area and articulation of the local framework, and these values are combined with the global values.

Modification of Katz's Rules

Katz's law of field size and his principle of articulation have been incorporated into the model, but with some modification. First, the model reflects the empirical findings that the law of field size works for perceived size but not for retinal size. More important, Katz claimed that greater field size and articulation produce greater constancy within a field. In the model, however, these factors produce stronger anchoring within the framework (or field). In many cases this would lead to greater constancy, but not in all cases. When the backgrounds in simultaneous lightness constancy are articulated, as shown in Figure 10.2d, the result is less constancy—that is, a greater illusion.

ROOTS OF THE MODEL

This anchoring model emerged somewhat by accident in an experiment designed to pit the anchoring notion against a contrast notion.

Anchoring versus Contrast

In our work on the anchoring problem, we had repeatedly found that results that had been reported earlier from the perspective of contrast or induction could be understood as well or better from the perspective of anchoring. For example, the highest luminance rule accounts for the empirical finding that contrast effects primarily involve influences from the brighter region to the darker. In addition, the role of relative area in anchoring seems to account for those situations in which upward induction is obtained. These findings led to the obvious but radical possibility that everything that had previously been attributed to contrast (or induction) is really a manifestation of anchoring. Thus, Joe Cataliotti and I (Cataliotti & Gilchrist, 1995) conducted a series of experiments designed to tease apart contrast and anchoring interpretations of phenomena typically attributed to contrast.

It is well known that, in general, a target surface will appear darker when a brighter region is placed next to it. We chose a dramatic example of this phenomenon, one frequently invoked to illustrate contrast: the Gelb effect. We used the spatial function of lateral inhibition to distinguish between anchoring and contrast accounts of this effect. It is generally agreed that contrast effects due to lateral inhibition decrease rapidly with lateral distance between the inducing region and the target. Shapley and Reid (1985) had also proposed that edge integration weakens with distance in a similar way. But anchoring involves no such fall-off. As long as the target and inducer lie within the same framework (or field of illumination), the distance between them should not matter. We were able to create several experiments that exploited this difference.

Staircase Gelb Effect

Our basic experiment involved a stepwise version of the Gelb effect.[1] First we suspended a black square (reflectance 3%) in midair and illuminated it with a bright projector spotlight so that it appeared completely white. The illumination intensity at the target location was 30 times that of the ambient room illumination, adjusted to give a black surface in the spotlight the same luminance as white in ambient illumination. Then we added a dark-gray square (reflectance 12%) next to the black square. Then, in like fashion, a middle-gray square (30%) was placed in the next position, then a light-gray square (60%), and finally a white square (90%). This left a horizontal row of five squares, arranged in ascending steps, roughly equal on the Munsell scale,[2] from black at

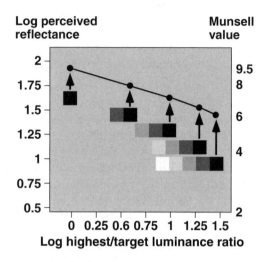

Figure 11.5. Perceived lightness of black square in a spotlight as lighter squares are added. The amount of darkening depends only on the amount by which each new square raises the highest luminance in the group, but not on its proximity to the black square.

one end to white at the other. The projector beam formed a horizontal rectangle to accommodate all five squares. Observers matched each target using a 16-step Munsell chart under separate illumination.

Our test would be the amount of darkening produced in the black target square when each brighter square was added to the group. According to the spatial function of lateral inhibition (and to Shapley and Reid's claim), the darkening of the target should decrease as new, brighter squares are added in positions successively more distant from the target. But according to anchoring, the darkening should depend merely on the degree to which each new square increases the maximum luminance in the group.

Our results are shown in Figure 11.5. If the darkening effect of the highest luminance were weakened by distance, we would have obtained a negative but positively accelerated curve. But we obtained a straight line, which strongly supports the anchoring prediction. We found no evidence for a spatial function, despite the fact that the brightest square, the white square, was separated from the target square by 4.5° of visual angle.

In another condition we switched the position of the dark-gray square and the white square so that the white square was now adjacent to the black target square. Ten additional observers matched the target square under these conditions, producing a mean Munsell of 6.0, exactly the same mean shown in Figure 11.5 when the white square was far from the target.

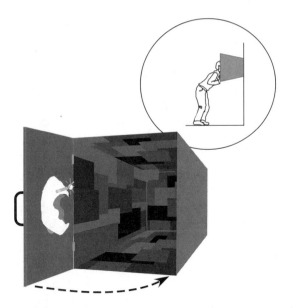

Figure 11.6. The Mondrian world (Annan & Gilchrist, 2004). The lightest squares, physically dark gray, appear white. Adapted with permission from Gilchrist et al., 1999.

In a further experiment we explored the spatial function by testing 10 additional observers at one-third the viewing distance. This multiplied all the visual angles within the display by a factor of three, producing a separation of 13.5° of visual angle between the target square and the white square. The spatial function of lateral inhibition clearly refers to retinal distance, not perceived distance. Despite the greater retinal separation, not one of the squares appeared significantly darker in the far condition compared to the near.[3]

We conducted a modified version of our basic five-squares experiment using a 4.6° square Mondrian composed of 15 squares ranging in reflectance from black to middle gray (Munsell 6.0). This Mondrian was presented in a special beam of light just as with the five squares. Ten naive observers matched the perceived lightness of all 15 squares in the Mondrian. Then a white square was added to the Mondrian and a separate group of 10 observers again matched all 15 squares. All 15 squares appeared darker when the white square was present. However, we found that the darkening of squares adjacent to the white square was not significantly greater than the darkening of remote squares.[4]

And finally, to eliminate the possibility of uncontrolled influences from the larger surround, we replicated the Mondrian experiment in what we called a Mondrian world (Fig. 11.6). Observers' heads were placed within a trapezoidal chamber, all of the interior surfaces of which were covered with a Mondrian pattern composed of dark-gray shades ranging from black to dark gray (Munsell 4.0). One group of observers matched a subset of these squares and a separate group of observers matched the same squares after a real white square had been introduced into the display. Again we found no difference between the darkening effect on adjacent squares and that on remote squares.

Uniform Influence of Anchor within a Framework

We concluded that when the highest luminance is increased within a group of surfaces that belong together so as to constitute a frame of reference, the standard of whiteness used to compute gray shades of lower values is changed for all elements within the framework, regardless of distance from the highest luminance. This implies that concepts like contrast and induction are better understood in terms of anchoring.

It should be noted that the lack of spatial function applies only to members of a single framework. When two isolated surfaces are presented in midair at some distance from each other, and one of the two is the highest luminance in the field, the lightness of the darker square depends in a systematic way on the separation between them. This is a solidly established empirical result (Cole & Diamond, 1971; Dunn & Leibowitz, 1961; Fry & Alpern, 1953; Leibowitz, Mote & Thurlow, 1953; Newson, 1958; Stewart, 1959) that also makes sense from an anchoring perspective. The greater the proximity between the two targets, the more they form a group and the more the lightness of the darker target is anchored by its relationship to the brighter target.

New Finding: Strong Compression of Gray Scale

The straight line shown in Figure 11.5 shows that the anchoring power of the highest luminance is roughly homogeneous across the members of the coplanar group. But the shallow slope of this line reveals a new finding, a strong compression on the lightness scale (the y-axis) that caught us completely by surprise. The darkening effect of each higher luminance was much less than one would expect based on Wallach's ratio principle supported by edge integration. Although the five squares physically spanned the entire gray scale from black to white, they were perceptually compressed into the upper half of the gray scale, and the darkest square appeared no darker than Munsell 6.0.

This is a substantial and surprising failure of lightness constancy, and the failure has a very specific pattern. It is not the case that each of the five squares shows the same degree of erroneous increase in its perceived lightness. There is a gradient of constancy failure, with black showing a whopping failure of about half of the entire gray scale, white showing no failure at all, and the other three squares showing failures proportionately spaced between these. This amounts to a compression of the gamut of perceived gray shades, and we will refer to this as *gamut compression* after Brown and MacLeod's (1997) term *gamut expansion*.

Why Is the Gamut Compression Surprising?

We expected that once the true white had been added to the group of squares, the black square, with a luminance 30 times less than white, would finally appear black. Certainly a disk surrounded by an annulus 30 times brighter appears black. Nor can the compression be explained by the separation between the white and black squares, because the compression remains when the two squares are adjacent. This compression is a prime example of an illegitimate error, described in Chapter 10.

The Gelb effect is one of the most celebrated phenomena in lightness. In virtually all descriptions of the illusion, even by authorities like Katz (1935), Koffka (1935), Woodworth (1938), Wallach (1963), Evans (1948), and Helson (1964), the black target is said to appear black when a white paper is placed next to it. However, the empirical results tell a different story, one that is consistent with the compression we obtained. Even when a white target and a black target are presented side by side within the spotlight, the black target does not appear black; it appears lighter than middle gray. Stewart (1959) who conducted the most systematic study of the Gelb effect, reported Munsell values of 6.9 to 8.5, depending on conditions. Newson (1958) reported values of 5.5, 4.9, and 5.3. Gogel and Mershon (1969) reported a value of about 4.75.[5]

The Gelb target appears black in the spotlight only when it is completely surrounded by white (Horeman, 1963; McCann & Savoy, 1991).

Source of the Compression

What can account for such a dramatic compression in lightness values? Three possible hypotheses can be suggested: (1) adaptation, (2) a lightness ceiling effect, and (3) co-determination.

1. *Adaptation.* The five squares constitute an island of bright light surrounded by a sea of dimmer light. Perhaps in its adaptation to the ambient illumination, the visual system cannot accommodate the entire range within the spotlight. But this hypothesis seems to be knocked out by a simple variation: if a narrow rectangular white border is placed around the perimeter of the five squares, but still within the spotlight, the compression is almost completely eliminated! Somehow the white border seems to insulate the five squares from influence by the global (or foreign) framework. I refer to this as the *insulation effect* but cannot explain it further. A black border has no such effect,

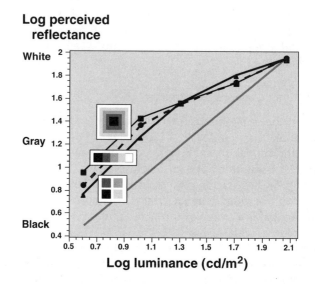

Figure 11.7. Lightness matches for the five gray shades under three configurations. Compression is reduced when the black square is surrounded by a white border, regardless of whether the border makes contact with the black square. Adapted with permission from Gilchrist et al., 1999.

and a middle-gray border seems to provide half as much insulation as a white border (see Gilchrist et al., 1999, Fig. 12). Apparently such insulation cannot be reduced to a contrast effect. It is necessary merely that the five squares be surrounded by the white border; they need not make any contact with it, as can be seen in Figure 11.7 (from Gilchrist et al., 1999).

2. *Ceiling effect.* When all five squares are presented simultaneously in the spotlight, the brightest one or two squares appear self-luminous. It might be argued that the compression we observe in the data line in Figure 11.5 is the result of a ceiling effect imposed on the data by the Munsell chart: no matches above white are possible. Would the data line revert to a slope of +1 if we allowed observers to make matches in the zone of self-luminosity? The answer seems to be no. Cataliotti and I created an extended Munsell chart with samples of luminosity in 7 steps beyond white. Data produced by this chart were difficult to interpret. Indeed, two arguments show that the basic idea is misguided. First, as has been amply shown (Jacobsen & Gilchrist, 1988a,b), the ratio principle (with its characteristic +1 slope) does not apply to the zone of self-luminosity, only to the zone of opaque surface grays. Luminous surfaces produce luminance matching, not ratio matching. Second, the compression seen in Figure 11.5 is seen in the three darkest-gray squares, none of which appears self-luminous. If

the compression were the result of a ceiling effect, there should be a knee in the curve, with opaque targets, such as those on the left, falling along a +1 slope, and the luminous targets, such as those on the right, falling along a horizontal line. No such knee is obtained.

3. *Co-determination.* According to Kardos (1934), each of the squares will be seen both in relation to the neighboring group (the relevant framework) and in relation to the remainder of the laboratory (the foreign framework). This analysis is quite compelling when one views the display from the perspective of the observer. And it appears to account for the results, as we will see.

We seem to have here a dramatic example of what Kardos (1934) called co-determination by the relevant field of illumination and by the foreign field of illumination. This can be clarified by a thought experiment. Imagine we eliminate either the relevant field or the foreign field. To eliminate the foreign field, we would have to get rid of the laboratory scene. Merely turning off the lights would not be sufficient, however. We would have to enlarge the five squares so that they fill the entire visual field, say by painting them onto the interior of a dome. In that case they would be seen veridically. On the other hand, we could eliminate the relevant field containing the five squares. We could present each square by itself. We know that each square would be seen as white under such conditions.[6] The anchoring model described above is couched in terms of local and global frameworks rather than relevant and foreign, for reasons that are given later.

This analysis of the staircase Gelb phenomenon is illustrated in Figure 11.8. The x-axis gives the luminance of each square. The y-axis gives the predicted lightness value within each framework. Predictions from local anchoring are shown by the diagonal line (which coincides with veridicality). Predictions from global anchoring are shown by the horizontal line. The actual data obtained from observers who viewed the entire group of five squares are shown by the dashed line. One can readily see this line as a weighted average of the local and global lines. Even the error bars show a corresponding gradient, proportional in length to the discrepancy between local and global predictions for a given square.

If the compression is caused by local and global co-determination, it should be possible to move the data systematically between the local and global predictions by strengthening or weakening the competing frameworks.

Determinants of Framework Strength

Testing the hypothesis that greater articulation within a framework produces stronger anchoring within that framework, Cataliotti and I replaced the five squares in the spotlight with a 15-patch Mondrian using the same five shades of gray. This produced a dramatic decrease

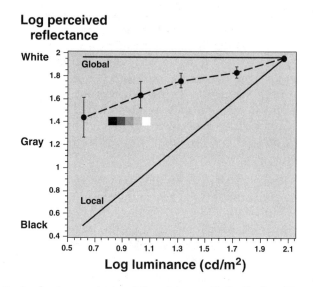

Figure 11.8. Anchoring analysis of the staircase Gelb display. The perceived values of the five squares represent a compromise between their computed values in their local framework and the values computed in the global framework. Adapted with permission from Gilchrist et al., 1999.

in the compression. The black patches, for example, appeared almost black as opposed to Munsell 6.0 in the five-square row.

This implies that the 15-patch Mondrian constitutes a stronger framework than the five-square linear array. What makes it stronger? There are three obvious differences between the five-square condition and the 15-patch Mondrian. First, there are 15 patches in one case and five in the other. Second, the 15-patch Mondrian constitutes a larger framework than the five squares in a row. And third, the squares in the five-square case are arranged in a graduated line from darkest to lightest, unlike in the Mondrian. In short, we found all three of these factors to play some role.

1. Testing the configurational factor, we compared the linear arrangement of the five squares to a five-patch Mondrian, holding both number of squares and total area constant. We also compared a 10-square linear array to a 10-patch Mondrian. The results are shown in Figure 11.9. In both comparisons, there is significantly less compression in the Mondrian configuration than in the linear configuration.

2. One can also begin to see from this figure that the number of patches plays a role. This is seen more clearly in Figure 11.9, in which the data are presented for Mondrians containing 2,

Log perceived reflectance

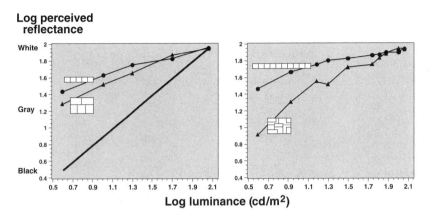

Figure 11.9. A collage of patches presented in a spotlight shows less compression than a line of patches. Adapted with permission from Gilchrist et al., 1999.

Log perceived reflectance

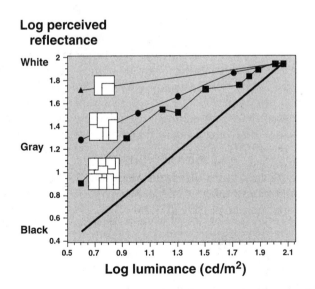

Figure 11.10. The greater the number of patches in a Mondrian under a spotlight, the less the compression. Adapted with permission from Gilchrist et al., 1999.

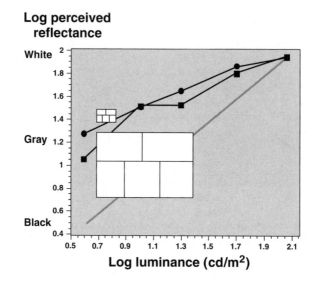

Figure 11.11. The larger the display under spotlight, the less the compression. Adapted with permission from Gilchrist et al., 1999.

5, or 10 patches. Here we see a strong effect of the number of patches.

3. We also made a test of the effect of area. Figure 11.11 presents a comparison between the five-patch Mondrian already mentioned and another five-patch Mondrian identical in every respect except its size, which was five times larger along each dimension (the area being 25 times larger). Here we found a small but systematic effect, with less compression for the larger framework. Recall that when we increased the retinal size of the display by reducing the viewing distance, this did not reduce the compression. Again, Katz's law of field size seems to work for perceived size but not for retinal size.

In a further experiment, we made everything in the observer's field of view totally dark except for the five-square display.[7] This produced a modest darkening of the five squares. This result, which is opposite to what would be predicted by contrast theories, might be explained by the reduced articulation in the surrounding framework.

APPLYING THE MODEL: ILLUMINATION-DEPENDENT ERRORS

In applying the anchoring model to the illumination-dependent errors listed in Chapter 10, keep in mind this helpful rule: local anchoring produces constancy,[8] while global anchoring produces failures of constancy. When the local framework is a separate field of illumination and when it contains a white surface, a veridical lightness value will be given by $L_t/L_h * 90\%$. Anchoring in the global framework is equivalent to luminance matching, which is the signature of zero constancy. The success of the model in accounting for illumination-dependent errors will hinge on the degree to which the strength of local anchoring correlates (negatively) with error size.

The Fundamental Illumination-Dependent Error

Because the anchor in the brighter field is necessarily higher than the anchor in the darker field, the lightness of any target in the darker field will be lower when computed globally than when computed locally. Thus, global anchoring darkens surfaces in lower illumination. Global anchoring lightens surfaces in higher illumination due to scale normalization. The global range typically exceeds the standard black–white range. Thus, values in the global framework are compressed upward toward white.

Illumination Difference: Larger Error with Larger Difference

The greater is the illumination difference between two frameworks, the greater is the difference between the anchors in the two. This means that for any given target, its value when anchored globally will differ from its value when anchored locally by a greater amount. The local/global compromise will thus deviate more from the local computation alone, meaning it will deviate more from veridicality.

Standard Gradient of Error: Error Size Depends on Target Reflectance

A white surface in the higher illumination will be computed as white in its local framework, but also white in the global framework. Thus, there will be no error for this surface. A black surface, however, will be black relative to its local framework but much lighter relative to the global framework. Thus, it will show a large error. Gray shades between these two poles will show a gradient of errors.

A similar logic applies to the darker field of illumination. A black will be computed as black in this field, but also as black relative to the global framework. A white surface, however, will be computed as white in this local field, but much darker gray relative to the global framework. Again, the intermediate shades show gradations of error.

Background Reflectance: Larger Errors with Darker Backgrounds

This fact follows from the asymmetry in anchoring: white is special, black is not. According to the anchoring model, a target will be computed as white in its local framework whenever it is the highest luminance, regardless of its actual shade of gray. Whenever both targets happen to be the highest luminance in their local frameworks, they will be computed as the same lightness value (white) even if they are actually very different. In this case local anchoring does not produce veridical perception.[9] The darker the backgrounds on the lighted and shadowed sides, the more likely it is that each target will be the highest luminance in its field. This is especially true when the two fields are poorly articulated.

Strictly speaking, this analysis implies that the lack of constancy is associated with incremental targets, not necessarily with dark backgrounds. Thus, anchoring theory predicts that decremental targets on dark backgrounds would produce better constancy than incremental targets on relatively light backgrounds. Indeed, this is exactly what Kozaki (1963, 1965) has reported to be the case. This may also explain why better constancy has often been found with targets of lower reflectance (Evans, 1948; Hsia, 1943; Oyama, 1968): they are more likely to be decrements.

Framework Size: Larger Errors with Smaller Frameworks

According to anchoring theory, the larger a local framework, the stronger the anchoring within that framework. This stronger local anchoring is held to be the reason that Katz obtained better constancy with larger field size. This is not merely a restatement of Katz's claim. Describing the result in terms of strength of local anchoring gives an account of why better constancy results from larger field size, an account that places the law of field size within a more comprehensive theory of errors.

Framework Articulation: Less Error with Greater Articulation

According to the anchoring model, the greater the articulation within a framework, the stronger the anchoring within that framework. Again, this explains Katz's observation that greater articulation is associated with greater constancy.

Thus, the basic model of local and global anchoring appears consistent with all six of the main features of illumination-dependent failures that turned up in our survey of errors. At least this should establish the model as a strong candidate for a theory of illumination-dependent constancy failures. But to constitute a theory of errors in general, the model must work for background-dependent errors as well.

Local and Global, or Relevant and Foreign?

The model given so far differs from the theory of Kardos in the definition of the interacting frameworks. While Kardos spoke of the relevant framework and the foreign framework, our model speaks of local and global frameworks. The difference is simply that the global framework includes the local framework (as in a nested hierarchy), while relevant and foreign frameworks exclude one another.

For the illumination-dependent errors we have just reviewed, we could use either the local/global construction or the relevant/foreign construction, although the latter works a bit better. But for background-dependent errors, such as simultaneous contrast, the local/global construction seems to work distinctly better.[10] Thus, to bridge the two classes of error, the model has been stated in terms of local and global frameworks.

This does, however, leave us with a problem in explaining the staircase Gelb display.

The Problem of the Horizontal Global Line

According to the local/global analysis of lightness given above, each of the five squares in the staircase Gelb display is computed to be white in the global framework. This shows up as a horizontal G-line in Figure 11.8. That would make more sense if we were using the relevant/foreign construction of Kardos (1934), because each of the squares would indeed appear white[11] relative to the foreign region outside the spotlight. But the model given here uses a local/global construction, which means that the local framework is part of the global.

This may seem puzzling. After all, the white square in the spotlight is the highest luminance in the global framework and each of the other four squares stands in a different ratio to the luminance of the white square. Why, then, is the G-line not sloping?

The short answer is that a horizontal G-line fits with plausible weighting values for the local and global framework. The empirical data shown in Figure 11.8 imply local and global weights that are roughly equal. This seems reasonable for a small field of only five elements. Adding some slope to the G-line can produce the slope of the empirical line only if global anchoring gets far more weight than local, and this doesn't seem intuitively reasonable.

In our prior paper (Gilchrist et al., 1999), the horizontal G-line was justified by the small area of the five squares relative to the area of the global framework. Thus, the five squares have little influence on the global anchor. This is consistent with the role of area we found in our anchoring experiments with domes. Each of the five squares is assigned a global value of white because each has a luminance equal to or higher than that of the global anchor (which is roughly that of a white surface in the normally illuminated laboratory). According to this analysis, if the group of five squares is made much larger, the G-line should acquire a slope and the compression should be reduced.

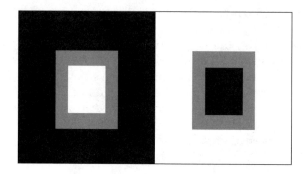

Figure 11.12. This contrast display (due to Elias Economou) suggests that figure belongs to ground more than ground belongs to figure.

Cataliotti and I did find a reduction in compression when we increased the total area of the five squares by a factor of 25, but this result was predicted based on the law of field size, and we have no clear evidence that it produced a sloping G-line.

Alternatively, the horizontal G-line might be justified by a kind of figure/ground asymmetry. There are some reasons to believe that figure belongs to ground more than ground belongs to figure. This asymmetry can be seen in Figure 11.12. The fact that the left-hand gray target appears lighter than the right-hand target shows that each gray region is seen relative to its surround, not to the region it encloses. This is closely related to the Kardos principle of the next deeper depth plane. In terms of fields of illumination, the spotlight containing the five squares constitutes a figural region of illumination, while the remainder of the laboratory constitutes a background region. If so, targets in the spotlight would be influenced by the surrounding framework, but not vice versa.

Depth and Lightness

The coplanarity principle of lightness fits happily within the anchoring model, but the idea of competing frameworks suggests that coplanarity should be viewed as a graded factor, as Koffka had suggested. Edge classification, by contrast, implies an all-or-none distinction, except in the case of compound edges.[12] Empirical evidence that coplanarity effects are indeed graded can be found in reports by Wishart et al. (1997) and Gogel and Mershon (1969).

APPLYING THE MODEL: BACKGROUND-DEPENDENT ERRORS

A crucial question now is how well the anchoring model performs on background-dependent failures, lightness errors produced by various configurations of regions that appear to differ only in reflectance. The model has proved its worth in accounting for the variety of illumination-dependent errors. If the same model could account for background-dependent errors as well, this would constitute an important theoretical development. The place to begin, of course, is with the simultaneous lightness contrast display.

McCann's Account of Simultaneous Contrast

Not only does the model work quite well for the simultaneous contrast display, but in fact just such an account has been already given by John McCann (1987, p. 280):

> If global normalization of the entire field of view were complete, we would expect that observers would report the two gray squares with identical reflectances would have the identical appearance. If local mechanisms were the only consideration, then the gray square in the black surround should mimic the results found in the Gelb experiment, and should appear a white, since it is the maximum intensity in the local area. Observer results give important information about the relative importance of global and local interactions. The gray square in the black surround is one lightness unit out of nine lighter than the same gray in the white surround. If local spatial calculations were the only consideration, the gray in black should appear a 9.0. If global spatial considerations were the only consideration, the gray in black should appear a 5.0. The observer matched the gray in black to a 6.0. In other words, the spatial normalization mechanism is an imperfect global mechanism. Alternatively, it is a local mechanism that is significantly influenced by information from the entire image.

(On the Munsell scale, 9.0 is white and 5.0 is middle gray.)

The data obtained for the staircase Gelb display require a larger weight for local anchoring than do the data McCann reports for the simultaneous contrast display. This is to be expected, however, because Cataliotti and I already found in the staircase Gelb experiments that weighting of the local framework varies with the number of elements in it (articulation). In the case of simultaneous contrast, the local framework contains two elements, compared to five elements in the staircase Gelb display; thus, its weight should be lower for the contrast display.

The Anchoring Model of Simultaneous Contrast

The application of the anchoring model is illustrated in Figure 11.13. Before applying the model, we must take a moment to reflect on the concept of the framework.

Definition of Framework

When Katz and the Gestaltists used terms like *field*, or *framework*, they meant a region of common illumination. But if we maintain this usage

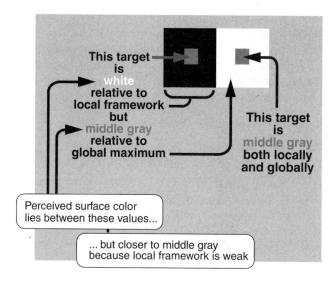

Figure 11.13. The anchoring explanation of simultaneous lightness contrast.

we cannot apply the model to simultaneous contrast, because the two backgrounds are not perceived to represent two fields of illumination.

Intuitively, however, the simultaneous contrast display lends itself readily to a frameworks analysis. The display can be seen as a single global framework composed of two local frameworks, one defined by the black background and one defined by the white, even though these local frameworks are not fields of illumination. This kind of perceptual structure, according to Gestalt theory, appears in our visual experience due to the operation of the grouping principles. This line of thinking leads to an alternative definition of framework in terms of the Gestalt concept of belongingness. Specifically, a framework can be defined as a group of surfaces that belong together, more or less. In the simultaneous contrast display, one target belongs to the black background while the other belongs to the white, due to factors of proximity and surroundedness.

Framework Segregation Factors

Of course, even in the domain of illumination-independent constancy, it is not sufficient to talk merely of fields of illumination. External fields of illumination must be represented internally, and this requires that fields be defined in proximal stimulus terms. I have, with Kardos, already emphasized the two strong factors by which fields are defined: penumbra and depth boundaries (corners and occlusions boundaries). I will assume that when these two factors are presented pictorially in an image, without oculomotor and stereo cues, they produce only weak frameworks. I will also assume that the traditional grouping factors produce weak but functional frameworks. And I will suggest two additional grouping factors: edge junctions (especially T, X, and Ψ) and luminance gradients.

Source of the Error: Local Anchoring

We noted earlier that for illumination-independent constancy, veridicality is associated with local anchoring while the errors come from global anchoring. For background-independent constancy these are reversed, at least when the display is uniformly illuminated. Global anchoring produces luminance matching (that is, veridicality), while the errors come from local anchoring. Thus, anything that strengthens the local frameworks will strengthen the contrast illusion.

Every theory of lightness accounts for the fundamental background-dependent error (dark backgrounds lighten, etc.) and the fact that increasing the background difference strengthens the illusion, and the anchoring theory is no exception. Thus I will not spend time on these points.

Simultaneous Contrast and Perceptual Grouping

A central claim of the anchoring account should be emphasized. The simultaneous contrast illusion is held to be the product of grouping processes, and the manipulation of grouping factors should be able to modulate the strength of the illusion and even reverse its direction. We have already seen grouping factors at work in the Benary effect and the Koffka ring.

Double Increments

The lack of a contrast effect in the double increments version of simultaneous contrast is a major clue to the source of the illusion. This fact is not obviously consistent with lateral inhibition accounts, but it flows directly from the highest luminance rule in the anchoring model. When both targets are increments, each will be the highest luminance in its local framework and receive a local assignment of white. Thus, the difference in local assignments that lies at the heart of the anchoring account is absent in the double increments version of the display, so no illusion is predicted.[13]

Modulating the Strength of the Illusion

In anchoring terms, the simultaneous contrast illusion is weak because the local frameworks are poorly articulated and weakly segregated from each other. When the local frameworks are articulated, the illusion is strengthened (Adelson, 2000; Bressan & Actis-Grosso, 2004;

Gilchrist et al., 1999). When the white and black backgrounds are better segregated by introducing a luminance ramp between them, the illusion is also strengthened (Agostini & Galmonte, 1997; Shapley, 1986). Agostini & Galmonte (1999) have reported a series of experiments in which they varied spatial articulation in the Benary effect. All these results are strongly consistent with the anchoring model.

Kingdom (2003, p. 37) claims that the contrast illusion is enhanced when the target boundaries are blurred. If true, this would contradict the anchoring model. But Kingdom offers no data, and his claim is inconsistent with data showing the opposite (MacLeod, 1947; Thomas & Kovar, 1965).

Grouping by Similarity

The Laurinen et al. variations shown in Figure 10.4 can be said to illustrate grouping by similarity. Laurinen et al. (1997) showed that when the target squares have texture of the same scale but different from the scale of texture on the backgrounds, as in the top and middle of Figure 10.4, the contrast illusion is almost eliminated. Bonato et al. (2003) also found this result varying type of texture rather than scale. Local frameworks are weakened because the grouping by similarity of each target and its background is weakened. In addition, the two targets tend to group with each other and the two backgrounds tend to group with each other. Inverting these grouping relationships, as I did in the bottom of Figure 10.4, strengthens the illusion. Bonato et al. (2003) also found this. Olkkonen et al. (2002) have used chromatic color to modulate illusion strength while holding relative luminances constant. When both targets share a common color and the two backgrounds share a different color, the illusion is reduced. These results follow directly from the anchoring model. And the model predicts that the illusion will be strengthened if the target and background on the left side share a common color and the target and background on the right side share a different color.

Common Fate

Agostini and Proffitt (1993) have shown that a simultaneous contrast effect can be created even using the unlikely grouping principle of common fate. They distributed a flock of large white dots randomly across a blue field and set all the dots into motion in the same direction. A separate flock of black dots was distributed across the same blue field and set into motion in a different direction. A single gray dot moved with the white dots appeared slightly darker than another gray dot that moved with the black dots. This result cannot be explained by lateral inhibition because the immediate background of both dots was the blue field. When the movement stopped, of course, the two gray dots appeared identical.

The finding by Agostini and Bruno (1996) that the illusion is twice as large when presented in a spotlight as when presented on paper is also consistent with the anchoring account. In the paper version, the global framework is very large and well articulated, including as it does much of the surrounding environment. The spotlight segregates a framework containing only the contrast pattern. Relative to this framework (which is weaker than the global framework) the two local frameworks have increased strength, causing a stronger illusion.

The same analysis applies to the contrast display when presented on a CRT screen. But Agostini and Bruno showed that even on a monitor, the strong illusion can be weakened by surrounding the contrast display with a Mondrian pattern that, in anchoring terms, strengthens the framework containing the whole SLC illusion.

Reversing the Illusion

White's illusion is consistent with the anchoring model because it shows that the direction of the illusion depends on inducing stripes with which the targets are perceptually grouped rather than those with which the targets share a greater border. Todorović (1997) has created a variation (see Fig. 10.7) in which the aspect ratio between black and white adjacency to the target is pushed to a greater extreme.

The T-Junction as a Grouping Factor

The key to grouping in the Benary effect, White's illusion, and the Todorovć illusion appears to be the T-junction. Thus, I want to suggest that a T-junction increases the belongingness across the stem of the T, and/or decreases the belongingness across the top edge of the T, as Figure 11.14 shows.[14] White's illusion is topologically equivalent to the

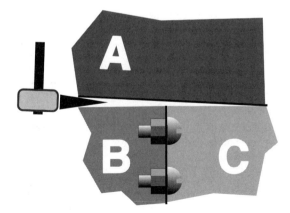

Figure 11.14. The role of T-junctions in anchoring.

Benary illusion, but stronger. The greater strength of the contrast effect in White's illusion is probably due to the relatively high articulation level in each framework[15] or, equivalently, to the large number of T-junctions.

Checkerboard Contrast

Checkerboard contrast can be attributed to the belongingness of one target square to the diagonal group of black squares and the belongingness of the other target to the group of white squares. Good continuation plays a role here. Now, of course, the targets might just as well be grouped with the horizontal rows or the vertical columns. These groupings would produce an equal appearance of the targets because each group would contain the same maximum luminance. Presumably grouping occurs in all of these directions, diagonal, vertical and horizontal, and the resulting compromise accounts for the weakness of the illusion. This analysis is illustrated in Figure 23 of Gilchrist et al. (1999).

Reverse Contrast Illusions

The displays by Agostini and Galmonte, Economou and Gilchrist, and Bressan (see Figs. 10.10, 10.11, 10.12) show dramatically that grouping factors can totally reverse the direction of the illusion.

Elias Economou and I varied the strength of each of the grouping factors in his reverse contrast display, including good continuation of the bar ends, similarity of the bars, orientation alignment of the bars, and number of bars. In each case we merely asked observers to match the lightness of each of the target bars, and from that obtained a measure of the strength of the illusion. We found that lightness is a direct function of the strength of grouping, as can be seen in Figure 11.15. As the grouping factors are weakened, the reverse contrast illusion also weakens. To our surprise, scrambling the orientation of the bars, as shown in the bottom left graph in Figure 11.15, did not weaken the illusion,[16] although rotating the target bars away from the orientation of the flanking bars did (bottom right graph in Fig. 11.15). These results provide strong evidence for the claim that simultaneous lightness contrast is fundamentally a phenomenon of perceptual grouping.

We also conducted stereo experiments that allowed us to place the target bars, flanking bars, and backgrounds in separate planes. As can be seen in Figure 11.16, the results are consistent with the anchoring model. The strength by which the target bars are anchored to either the flanking bars or the backgrounds is a direct function of the proximity in depth to those elements. This further confirms that the co-planar ratio principle is a graded function, not all or none, as I had originally believed (Gilchrist, 1980).

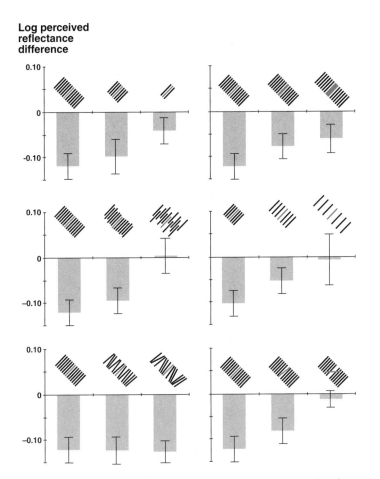

Figure 11.15. Reverse contrast illusion strength as various grouping factors are weakened.

Economou/Gilchrist Experiments

Elias Economou and I conducted a series of experiments further testing the anchoring model of simultaneous contrast.

Locus of Error

The anchoring model makes the very specific prediction that the bulk of the illusion is due to the lightening of the target on the black background caused by anchoring. A much smaller darkening of the other target is expected based on the scale normalization rule.[17] We tested this in three separate experiments (Gilchrist et al., 1999). Each time we found a much larger deviation from veridicality for the target on the

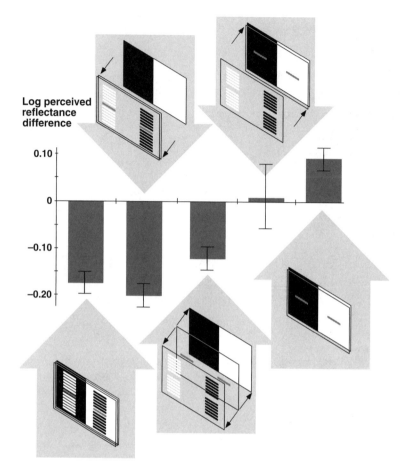

Figure 11.16. Reverse contrast illusion strength under various depth arrangements.

black background. Results consistent with ours have been reported by Adelson and Somers (2001), Bonato et al. (2001), and Logvinenko, Kane, and Ross (2002), who wrote, "the difference in lightness induction between Figs 1 and 2 arises from the dark surround." This prediction can be verified merely by inspection in versions of simultaneous contrast that are especially strong. For example, in Figure 10.3, inspired by an Adelson figure, the lower ellipse approaches white much more than the upper ellipse approaches black, even though both ellipses are middle gray.

Staircase Contrast

Staircase contrast displays presented by Hering (1874/1964, p. 125), Cornsweet (1970), and Shapley (1986, p. 51) are shown in Figure 11.17

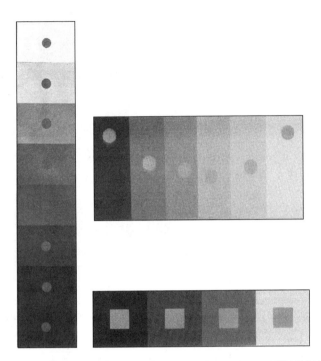

Figure 11.17. Staircase contrast displays. (Left) Hering, 1874/1964, p. 125. (Right top) Shapley, 1986, p. 51. (Bottom right) Cornsweet, 1970, p. 279. Reprinted with permission.

(see also McArthur & Moulden, 1999, p. 1212). The implication is that all of the targets appear different from each other, whether decrements or increments. But the anchoring model predicts that the curve of target lightness across these panels should show a knee, with a horizontal section for the increments. Economou and I tested this prediction and got exactly that result (Fig. 11.18). Notice that the theoretical curve, shown in white, was derived directly from the anchoring model. The 4:1 global/local weights were derived from the typical size of simultaneous contrast: a Munsell difference of 0.7. Factoring in the scale normalization effect would steepen the slope.

Target Luminance Variation

The anchoring model predicts a stronger illusion when darker targets are used. For the target on the black background (the main source of the illusion), the discrepancy between local and global values increases with darker targets. Testing this factor, we obtained just these results, as shown in Figure 11.19. Logvinenko and Ross (2005) obtained the same findings. It is not clear what a contrast theory would predict for this experiment.

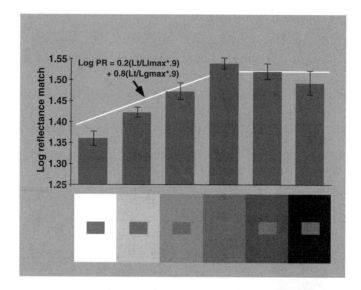

Figure 11.18. Perceived lightness of targets in a staircase contrast display. No contrast effect was obtained for increments. The white line represents predictions from the anchoring model, assuming a 4:1 global:local weighting, but without taking into account scale normalization. Reprinted with permission from Gilchrist and Economou, 2003.

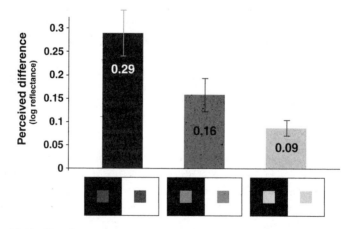

Figure 11.19. Simultaneous contrast is stronger with dark-gray targets, as predicted by the anchoring model.

Competing Groupings

The idea that a target is simultaneously part of more than one group and its lightness is a weighted average of its computed value in each of these is nicely illustrated in an experiment by Zaidi, Shy, and Spehar (1997). In their stimuli, shown in Figure 6.18, each gray target was grouped with one context region (either black or white) by coplanarity and with another context region by T-junctions. Mere inspection shows that for a restricted luminance range, the T-junction grouping is stronger than the coplanar grouping. However, by successively neutralizing each grouping, as shown in Figure 6.18b and 6.18c, Zaidi et al. also showed that both kinds of grouping separately influence target lightness, consistent with the principle of co-determination.

Adelson Illusions

Adelson's illusions lend themselves readily to an anchoring analysis. The regions that appear as transparent are perceptually segregated as separate frameworks. The various junction types discussed by Adelson (1993), Anderson (1997), Todorović (1997), and Watanabe and Cavanagh (1993) can be considered segmentation factors. In the corrugated plaid, perceived depth planes serve as frameworks. Todorović (1997) has shown that when the display is modified to create a staircase pattern, as in Figure 6.15b, the illusion persists. This fact supports an anchoring analysis over an intrinsic-image analysis, because in the staircase figure, although the targets do not appear to be differently illuminated, they do lie in different frameworks as defined by planarity. Wishart et al. (1997) varied the perceived angle in the folds of the corrugated plaid. They found that the strength of the illusion varied with the angle. In anchoring terms, this implies that the more two adjacent surfaces depart from coplanarity, the less they are treated as belonging to each other for purposes of anchoring.

The Luminance Gradient as a Grouping Factor

Luminance gradients are responsible for several delightful lightness illusions. It appears that these effects can be unified by the assumption that a luminance gradient functions to segregate (reduce their belongingness for anchoring) the luminance values on the two sides of the gradient. For instance, it has long been known that simultaneous lightness contrast is enhanced if the sharp border between the black and white backgrounds is replaced with a luminance gradient. If this gradient is thought to reduce the belongingness between the backgrounds, this would weaken the global framework, equivalent to strengthening the local frameworks. Because the model holds that the simultaneous contrast effect is caused by local anchoring, this should enhance the contrast effect.

The same analysis can be applied to the dramatically enhanced contrast effect presented by Agostini and Galmonte (1997), shown in Figure 10.3. The shallow luminance gradient surrounding each gray target square can be thought of as a barrier to anchoring. Thus, each target belongs strongly to its immediate surround, but much less to more remote regions. For example, if the segregating effect were total, the gray square with the black immediate surround would be equivalent to a gray square in a black dome, which we know appears white (Li & Gilchrist, 1999). Of course the segregation is not total. Some global anchoring occurs, and thus that target appears very light gray, but not white.

APPLYING THE MODEL: THE BRIGHTNESS INDUCTION LITERATURE

It might seem inappropriate to apply a model of lightness errors to the brightness induction experiments (described in Chapter 7). These experiments are about brightness, not lightness. However, lightness inevitably bleeds into brightness, presumably because the visual system struggles to interpret even such a highly reduced display as a set of surfaces. In any case, we have already found that the area rule, written for lightness, accounts very handily for the brightness data of those induction experiments in which area is varied. Thus, we will now proceed to apply the anchoring model to the other main brightness induction findings, to see whether anchoring or induction provides the better account.

Basic Finding: Highest Luminance Is Crucial

The fundamental study in brightness induction is that of Heinemann (1955). We have already seen that his results can be explained by the highest luminance rule plus the area rule (see p. 243).

The Role of Separation between Test and Inducing Fields

Experiments on the degree of separation, in the frontal plane, between inducing and test fields, reviewed in Chapter 5, have shown that the test field (of lower luminance) becomes darker as the separation is reduced. From the perspective of the lateral inhibition account, the closer the inducing field is to the test field, the greater the neural activation corresponding to the test field is inhibited by the inducing field.

From an anchoring standpoint, however, the perceived lightness of the test field will be some combination of its lightness relative to the dark surround and its lightness relative to the inducing field. Relative to the dark surround, the test field should appear white. Relative to the inducing field, the test field should appear as some shade of surface gray, the specific shade determined by the test/inducing field luminance ratio, according to the formula given earlier:

$$\text{Lightness} = (L_t/L_h * 90\%)$$

where L_t is the luminance of the test field, L_h is the highest luminance in the framework (the inducing field), and lightness is defined as perceived reflectance.[18]

Thus, target lightness should lie somewhere between white and the reflectance given by the above formula, depending on the degree to which the test field appears to belong to the inducing field. The greater the proximity between test and inducing field, the stronger the group formed by the two, and the more the lightness of the test field will be anchored by the inducing field. The greater the separation between test and inducing fields, the more the lightness of the test field is determined by its relationship to the dark surround.

Note that, according to anchoring theory, this separation effect applies only to test and inducing fields separated in space. When these fields are both part of an adjacent, coplanar group, the distance between them plays little or no role, as shown by Cataliotti and Gilchrist (1995), presumably because they are already strongly grouped together.

The anchoring account, unlike contrast/induction accounts, explains why the inducing field continues to appear white: because it is the highest luminance relative to both the test field and the dark surround. Thus, inducing field appearance becomes indifferent to local versus global weighting. This implies that separation between test and inducing fields should have no effect on inducing field appearance, and this is exactly what has been found.

Anchoring versus Induction

For the test field, however, anchoring and lateral inhibition appear to make the same qualitative predictions when separation is varied. Is it possible to find conditions under which anchoring and lateral inhibition make different predictions? The answer lies in depth separation. The test field can be separated from the inducing field in depth even as the two fields remain retinally adjacent. According to anchoring theory, this separation should reduce the perceived belongingness between the two fields. But from the induction perspective it should have no effect.

Gogel and Mershon (1969) have conducted such experiments in depth separation, and the results decisively favor the anchoring interpretation. Increasing the depth separation makes the test field appear lighter.

Strong Role of Surroundedness

One of the clearest findings to emerge from the brightness induction literature is that the degree of induction is much greater when the inducing field surrounds the test field than when the inducing field and test field are merely adjacent to one another. This is entirely plausible from a belongingness perspective because surroundedness (closely related to figure/ground) is a grouping principle that increases the belongingness of the two regions over and above the grouping principle of proximity.[19]

Thus, for the results of brightness induction experiments, the anchoring account compares favorably to the induction account, even explaining a variety of results not explained by induction.

SPECIAL PROBLEMS IN ANCHORING

Temporal Anchoring Effects

Cataliotti and Bonato (2003) have demonstrated that anchoring influences occur over time as well as across space. They found that while a relatively dim disk presented within a dark room appears white, it will appear light gray if it is preceded by a much brighter disk. Although these two disks were presented in the same spatial location, they were viewed with separate eyes, ruling out adaptation as a cause of the effect. The strength of this darkening, of course, depended on the time interval between the two disks. They found a strong effect with a 1-second delay. The effect got weaker as the delay was increased, with no effect left using a 32-second delay.

Cataliotti and Bonato also measured articulation effects acting both spatially and temporally. In a variation on the Gelb effect conducted in a normally illuminated room, they showed that a black paper square that appears white (Munsell 9.5) in a spotlight perceptually darkens to Munsell 7.7 when a white square is placed next to it. But it darkens further, to a Munsell 5.8, when the white square is replaced by a Mondrian pattern of the same size composed of six patches ranging from white to black. The fact that the average luminance of the Mondrian was much lower than that of the white paper shows that this effect is an anchoring effect. Were it a contrast effect, the white paper would have a stronger darkening effect than the Mondrian. In a further experiment they showed that this articulation effect works over time as well, finding that the dim disk presented in darkness appears to darken more (to Munsell 6.0 rather than 7.2) when preceded by a Mondrian-patterned disk than when preceded by a homogeneous white disk, even though the white disk was much brighter.

A Lightness Hangover

Earlier (p. 305) I described an experiment conducted in what we called the Mondrian world. The interior walls of a small room were completely covered with a Mondrian pattern containing nothing but rectilinear patches of different shades of dark gray and black. An observer's head is placed within the room so that the entire visual field is covered with the Mondrian pattern. Patches of the highest luminance (actually dark gray) duly appear white, and no blacks are seen. When several real white patches are introduced, by sliding a panel that constitutes the far wall of the room, all the patches in the room appear to darken, as one would expect, but this darkening occurs very slowly. Initially the real whites appear self-luminous, and it takes up to 3 full minutes before the darkening is complete.

How can this hangover be explained? After all, a black paper that appears white in a spotlight (the Gelb effect) instantly appears to darken when a real white is placed next to it. Vidal Annan and I conducted a series of experiments to answer this question (Annan & Gilchrist, 2004). Our results ruled out adaptation as an explanation and established that it is the anchor itself that resists the change, not the lightness of individual surfaces. We discovered that the strength of the hangover is directly related to the number of patches that remain constant in luminance and are continually visible from before the whites are added until after. When each wall contains only a single dark-gray surface, the hangover is hardly found; the walls darken almost immediately when the true whites are added. But the greater the articulation of the walls, the longer the hangover persists.

We interpret our results as follows. When the illumination in a room is increased, it produces several effects. First the highest luminance is increased. But in addition, most visible surfaces also increase dynamically in luminance. These effects suggest that the illumination has changed and the anchor, which can be thought of as a surrogate for the illumination level, must be recalibrated. But in our Mondrian world, only the first of these effects occurs: the highest luminance goes up. But all of the constantly visible surfaces remain constant in luminance. Apparently each such surface votes against changing the anchor, and the more such votes, the slower the new anchor is applied.

Multi-Lit Objects

According to the anchoring theory, lightness is computed within illumination frames of reference. But what about a surface that lies partly in one field of illumination and partly in another? Anchoring theory effectively predicts the lightness of each patch, or separately illuminated part of the object, but has not been able to predict the lightness of the multi-lit object as a whole. This is a serious problem because lightness is the property of an object, not the property of a patch. A patch is merely the intersection between a region of uniform illumination and a region of uniform reflectance. Whether appropriate or not, observers can readily assign lightness values to these patches, and they always assign a different value to the two patches (even as they insist that the object has only a single lightness). Experts do the same thing. Of course observers can also assign a single value to the object as a whole, and indeed this is more natural, as Kardos (1934) found many years ago.

Suncica Zdravković and I (Zdravković & Gilchrist, in press) reasoned that there must be some systematic relationship between the lightness of the separate patches and the lightness of the object as a whole, and we set out to determine that relationship. In a series of experiments we discovered that the lightness of the object as a whole is in agreement with the lightness assigned to the patch in the highest of the two regions of illumination, but also with the lightness of the patch in the larger of the two regions of illumination. Thus, if a shadow falls on half of an object, its lightness will be the same as the lightness assigned to the illuminated half, because that region of illumination is both the largest and the highest. On the other hand, if a spotlight falls on half of an object, its lightness will represent a compromise between the lightness values assigned to the two halves, because one half lies in the highest illumination while the other half lies within the largest region of illumination.

Why these two rules? Perhaps the visual system has implicit knowledge of the optimal conditions for perceiving lightness. Katz (1935) established his laws of field size, showing that lightness constancy is stronger in larger fields of illumination. It is also known that visual acuity increases with increasing levels of illumination.

These two rules—highest and largest—are strikingly reminiscent of the two basic rules of anchoring lightness within a framework: surface lightness is anchored by the highest luminance and the luminance with the largest area. Finding a similar pair of rules for multi-lit objects may not be a coincidence. Perhaps the multi-lit object also presents a kind of anchoring problem: anchoring with the domain of illumination. The visual system may be trying to determine which region of illumination should be considered normal.

SUMMARY

The decomposition story, it turns out, was too good to be true. Lightness constancy is not that good, and the representation of the external world is not that complete. Most lightness errors are not explained by the decomposition models, nor have efforts succeeded to explain those errors through failures of the various components of these models. Lightness now appears to be strongly influenced by factors that seem inconsistent with the logic of inverse optics. Take the strong influence of perceived area on lightness, for example. Such a function would mirror the process of image formation only if the physical reflectance of objects changed with a change in object size.

So it appears we must reject both the structure-blind approach of the contrast theories and the complete representation of the distal stimulus implicit in the decomposition theories. Lightness and perceived illumination represent their physical counterparts more crudely. The lightness system takes short cuts that presumably have turned out to be good enough for survival. This new look in lightness theory is sometimes called mid-level. In fact, it takes us back to Gestalt theory. Concepts like belongingness, grouping principles, and frames of reference are essential. The structure of the image is acknowledged, if not fully represented.

Fields of illumination exist in the external world. Without some representation of them, lightness constancy would not be possible. But to be represented internally, fields of illumination must be operationally defined in proximal terms. The two main factors by which the image is segregated into frameworks appear to be penumbra and depth boundaries, as Kardos said, with weaker frameworks spawned by virtually all the Gestalt grouping factors. For a given object, lightness is not computed exclusively within the framework to which the object primarily belongs. Rather, its lightness is computed partially in relation to that framework and partially in relation to a foreign, or global framework. This is the very important Kardos doctrine of co-determination.

So the framework that takes part in lightness computation is a surrogate for the field of illumination in the external world. These are not totally isomorphic. Segregation factors often appear in the image, without a corresponding external field. The obvious example is the black and white backgrounds of the simultaneous contrast display. These frameworks function as weak fields of illumination. Within each framework, the level of illumination is operationally defined in terms of the highest luminance (with largest area factored in). Again the correspondence between actual level of illumination and the functional level, by which lightness is computed, is rough. Mismatches occur.

12

Theories of Lightness

Having reviewed the history of developments in lightness theory, we turn now to a critical evaluation of the various theories.

HELMHOLTZ

One hundred and fifty years ago Helmholtz played a crucial role in drawing attention to the central challenge of lightness: visual experience correlates with the physical reflectance of the object, yet it is based on the luminance received by the eye. He proposed that the illumination level is unconsciously taken into account. This may be true, at least in some sense, but Helmholtz never explained just how. His theory, as MacLeod (1947, p. 140) has wryly observed, "possesses the advantage of being unassailable, except on logical grounds, since it involves a number of unverifiable postulates." As for the cognitive interpretation of raw sensations, both of these components appear flawed. There is really no evidence of raw sensations. And modern theories of lightness have rendered the notion of cognitive interpretation too vague to be useful. Lightness and color constancy have been demonstrated in a range of animals, including chickens and fish, not thought to be highly endowed with cognitive ability. The staircase version of Adelson's corrugated Mondrian (see Fig. 6.15) presents a serious challenge to Helmholtzian theory. This illusion, as well as other findings recently interpreted in terms of estimating the illumination (Boyaci et al., 2003; Ripamonti et al, 2004), can be understood in simpler, midlevel, terms (see p. 327).

PAST EXPERIENCE THEORIES

Earlier I described the flaw in Helmholtz's learning theory of color constancy. Helmholtz had proposed that through past experience, stimulation from a given surface under colored illumination came to be associated with stimulation from the same surface under white light. But as Land (1977) has shown, light of any wavelength can be associated with any color. To invoke the appropriate association, the color of the illuminant must be known. But ironically, if illuminant color is known, no associations are necessary, because the color of the reflected light plus the color of the illuminant provides enough information to solve for the actual color of the surface. The same logic applies to lightness. Helmholtz's learning model simply fails to provide any traction. Following Helmholtz, there had been little talk of a learning theory of lightness until very recently.

Past experience theories of vision have confronted formidable challenges, both logical and empirical. If we learn to see, how does seeing ever get started? The baby opens its eyes and gets a trapezoidal retinal image. Is it a trapezoid in the frontal plane or a slanted rectangle? This experience can be useful later on only if the correct answer can be found in this case. But how can this happen? What is the source of feedback? Berkeley argued that touch educates vision. This merely displaces the problem. Indeed, tactile stimuli are at least as ambiguous as visual stimuli. And the empirical evidence shows that, in general, vision educates touch (Rock & Victor, 1964), not vice versa.

How do we see novel or unlikely objects? If rectangular tables are so much more probable than trapezoidal tables, how do we ever perceive a trapezoidal table? Herein lies a crucial weakness of past experience theories, in my view. The sensory systems exist to give us new information, information about novelty and change. How useful is a visual system that has difficulty seeing novel objects and that functions best only when dealing with repeated inputs?

Infant habituation studies (Granrud, 1987; Slater, 1984, 1990) have shown that size and shape constancy are present in the first few days of life. The same is probably true for lightness.[1]

The empiricist theory requires that proximal stimuli be stored in memory. Yet the evidence from memory research shows that it is the percept that is stored in memory, not the raw stimulus. Little or no evidence exists that raw stimuli are stored in memory, whether conscious or not.

Efforts to demonstrate a role of memory color have produced only weak results, as noted in Chapter 5. The most interesting findings in this regard may be those in a recent study by Hurlbert and Ling (2005). Using an elegant method that allowed real 3D objects, both abstract and familiar, to be presented in arbitrary colors, they found that a yellow banana is more color constant than a purple or blue banana, and a yellow banana is more color constant than an abstract yellow dome. As usual in memory color work, these effects are relatively modest in size, and it remains to be seen whether they are truly visual, as opposed to cognitive effects on the observer's response.

The Wholly Empirical Theory of Purves

In the past few years, Purves and his colleagues (Purves & Lotto, 2003) have argued in a series of publications that the challenge of lightness perception is solved in a wholly empirical manner, based on probabilities derived from past experience. They refuse to specify whether they refer to the past experience of the organism or of the species. Either way, there are serious problems.

To the extent that they refer to the past experience of the organism, the claim is subject to the difficulties listed above, both logical and empirical.

On the other hand, attributing vision to the past experience of the species merely refers to the role of evolution in the development of vision. No one would disagree. The historical dispute concerns whether or not the ability to see is shaped by the past experience of the organism. Empiricism says yes. To the extent that vision was shaped by species past experience, it is inherited by each organism. This is called nativism, and it confuses the issue to call it empiricism.

Purves and Lotto argue that it doesn't matter whether the probabilities were learned by the organism or by the species; the main thing is that what we perceive reflects those probabilities. But just what role do these probabilities play? Finding an ambiguous proximal stimulus is not difficult. Every achromatic surface is ambiguous. (Remember, light of any luminance value can be perceived as any shade of gray.) Can this ambiguity be resolved by past probabilities? No. Given a target surface with a certain luminance value, I consult prior proximal stimuli with the same (or similar) values to discover what lightness they turned out to have in the majority of cases. This fails to return an answer because in my past experience, that luminance value has been associated with every shade of gray with roughly equal probabilities.

A more hopeful approach is to use the shape of the target surface. Surfaces in the shape of a leaf have turned out to be green in the majority of prior instances, and the memory of this could in principle aid constancy. This is called memory color. But, as we saw in Chapter 5, there is little convincing evidence that memory color exists.

And what about the effect of area on lightness? Reflectance does not depend on the size of a surface, but lightness does. How does this area–lightness linkage reflect the statistical probabilities of the world? Perhaps Purves and Lotto would claim that larger surfaces tend in fact to have higher reflectance values. No such evidence has been submitted. But even if it were, such statistics would tell us little about how lightness actually is computed. The visual system could not afford to assign more than a modest weight to this probability. Would the system assign the most likely reflectance to the target, ignoring information about its actual reflectance, such as luminance ratios? Of course not! How useful is the likely reflectance of a surface when there is information in the stimulus that specifies the actual reflectance?

Merely showing that lightness percepts are highly probable is not enough. As Chater (1996) has shown compellingly, likelihood and simplicity cannot be distinguished ultimately. Thus, evidence for likelihood may be equivalent to evidence for simplicity.

CONTRAST THEORIES

Contrast theories derive from Hering. His theory of lightness constancy has been completely undermined by the many countershaded backgrounds experiments (Gelb, 1932; Jaensch & Müller, 1920) that have shown robust constancy in the absence of every one of Hering's factors, both low and high level. The same critique applies to the contrast theories of the mid-20th century (Cornsweet, 1970; Jameson & Hurvich, 1966). Jameson and Hurvich (1961) have claimed that their empirical finding of diverging functions proves Hering's view that approximate lightness constancy results from the net change of excitation and inhibition when illumination varies. But the diverging functions pattern has never been replicated, and there are four published failures to replicate!

If anything, contrast theories should be able to account for simultaneous lightness contrast. But even here, the theory is seriously challenged. I have shown that logically, edge enhancement could explain simultaneous contrast only if some edges are enhanced more than others, but no tractable rule has been given for such differential enhancement.

Contrast in these models simply has no consistent strength. To explain lightness constancy in adjacent lighted and shadowed fields, contrast would have to be far stronger than needed to explain the much weaker effects found in the simultaneous contrast illusion, despite the structural similarity of the two displays. At their best, contrast theories get the direction of the effect right, but even this is unreliable. The many new examples of reverse contrast (Agostini & Galmonte, 2002; Bressan, 2001; Economou et al., 1998; White, 1981) are simply indigestible by contrast theories.

Contrast theories are far more flexible than has been realized. Like tools from a toolbox, components like disinhibition and remote inhibition can be engaged to explain the data, regardless of the direction. They are also more vague than has been realized. Economou and I simply could not obtain clear predictions from contrast models for many of our manipulations of simultaneous contrast.

BRIGHTNESS MODELS: MODERN CONTRAST THEORIES

Brightness models, reviewed in Chapter 7, offer several attractive features. First, they are simple and concrete. Second, they embrace the logic of lightness errors as the signature of the visual operations. And third, they attempt to accommodate both psychophysical data and physiological evidence in an actual computer-instantiated model. However, brightness models suffer from several serious, perhaps fatal, shortcomings.

First, they attempt to model the wrong thing. Brightness is perceived luminance. The goal should be to explain lightness, which is perceived reflectance. The human visual system evolved to determine object properties, like lightness, illumination level, and 3D form, which are adaptive for survival, not proximal qualities like brightness,[2] which are not. A model of brightness should have no more value than a model of perceived visual angle. Often these models make no distinction between lightness and brightness. How seriously would a model of size perception be taken if it failed to make a distinction between perceived size and visual angle?

Brightness modelers defend their approach in several ways. One argument is that when illumination is homogeneous, lightness and brightness collapse to the same thing. This is a weak defense because when illumination is homogeneous, the main challenges to lightness theory, including the central problem of lightness constancy, are excluded.

Brightness as the First Stage of Lightness Perception

Kingdom (2003) has argued that the many recent demonstrations challenging the lateral inhibition account of simultaneous contrast merely represent higher-level cognitive processes that modify the basic lightness errors produced by lateral inhibition. Likewise, Hurvich and Jameson (1966, p. 88) have argued that their opponent process model produces only brightness (and darkness) levels; turning these into lightness levels requires further interpretive processes.

The claim that lightness comes from brightness is pure theoretical prejudice. Its roots lie in the traditional conception of raw sensations that are subsequently interpreted by cognitive processes. No compelling evidence has been offered. Indeed, Schubert and I (1992) showed that relative luminance is detected 10 times faster than absolute luminance, a result that seriously challenges the primacy of brightness.

Even if brightness were the first stage, brightness models would be glaringly incomplete. None of them has even begun to specify the cognitive operations necessary to turn brightness values into lightness values, other than vague suggestions about the role of past experience. Under this defense, some of the brightness models are, ironically, more cognitive than the decomposition models. This defense also strikes at the heart of their vaunted concreteness. Is it fair to call these models simple and concrete just because they avoid discussion of the cognitive stages?

Finally, I would argue that the claim of brightness as the first stage is not falsifiable. Given that the lightness values presumably produced by lateral inhibition may be subsequently overridden by higher-level processes, one can never really be sure what the lateral inhibition stage produced. Results that are consistent with the direction of lateral inhibition are attributed to lateral inhibition, while results that are inconsistent are attributed to overriding cognitive operations. Bindman and Chubb (2004), who endorse this dualism, have noted the difficulty of falsifying such a position: "It is almost impossible . . . to definitively rule out lateral inhibition as a fundamental process underlying brightness perception. . . . image configuration may induce other (presumed to be higher order) processes that significantly augment or depress the effects of lateral inhibition."

While Bindman and Chubb find this a reason to retain the contrast account of lateral inhibition, I find it a reason to reject such an account (Gilchrist & Economou, 2003). All of this brings to mind an argument made by Köhler many years ago.

Unnoticed Sensations and Errors of Judgment

Köhler (1913) argued that the notion of a one-to-one relationship between the local stimulus and the resulting sensation (to which he gave the now-unfortunate name "constancy hypothesis"), despite its almost universal assumption, was merely a theoretical prejudice without supporting evidence. He noted that when the observer reports a percept that conforms to the distal object rather than the proximal stimulation, this is attributed to an unnoticed sensation, or an error of judgment. But when the observer's report fits the expected stimulus–sensation linkage: "Now, suddenly, the observation is considered correct without question, and the complicated events between sensation and report seem to be forgotten."

What the Brightness Models Cannot Explain

The brightness models are more sophisticated than the earlier simple contrast theories, but they fail on most of the same counts.

Lightness Constancy

At best, brightness models might be able to account for lightness constancy under a temporal change of illumination. But they cannot explain lightness constancy under spatially varying illumination. This is a major failing. Adjacent fields of different illumination within the same scene constitute the most important challenge to theories (Arend, 1994). Virtually every scene contains such variations. Brightness models are weak here because they refuse to incorporate the distinction between reflectance and illuminance edges.

Depth and Lightness

In general, brightness models do not provide for the role of depth perception in lightness. Empirical work (Gilchrist, 1977; Schirillo et al., 1990) has shown that depth manipulations can change perceived lightness essentially from one end of the gray scale to the other, with no significant change in the retinal image.

Background-Independent Constancy

Background-independent constancy has been shown to be just as important as illumination-dependent constancy. Because it goes in the opposite direction as contrast, it makes a difficult problem for contrast theories. Thus, it is not surprising that background-independent constancy has been regularly ignored by contrast theorists. Suggesting, as some writers (Cohen & Grossberg, 1984; Kingdom, 1997) have done, that the encoding of luminance ratios solves the problem of constancy is misleading because background-independent constancy is then left unexplained. It would be just as valid to claim that the encoding of luminance explains constancy, because that would explain background-independent constancy but not illumination-independent constancy.

Lightness Errors

The attempt of brightness models to achieve a systematic account of brightness/lightness errors is laudable. But how successful have they been? In Chapter 10, I argued that, first and foremost, a lightness model must provide a single account of the two major classes of error: illumination-dependent and background-dependent. The brightness models fail completely to account for the first class. They offer no explanation for why constancy fails when illumination varies. Indeed, they largely avoid this issue altogether.

Perhaps the reason lies in their implicit definition of errors. They seem more concerned with brightness errors than with lightness errors—that is, they attempt to explain why our brightness percepts deviate from luminance, rather than why our lightness percepts deviate from reflectance.

As serious as is the failure of brightness models on illumination-dependent errors, it might be forgiven if they could at least explain the range of background-dependent errors. But they cannot. As we have seen, each brightness model, including the ODOG model, has an associated list of failures. None of them can deal successfully with the kind of reverse contrast illusions produced in recent years (Agostini & Galmonte, 2002; Bressan, 2001a; Economou & Gilchrist, 1998). Even the ODOG model incurs a string of failures concerning both simultaneous contrast and grating induction (see p. 210).

DECOMPOSITION MODELS

The decomposition models have certainly been among the most effective models seen in recent decades. They offered a far better account of lightness constancy than the contrast theories that preceded them, especially for the important case of scenes that contain separate spatial fields of illumination. In their ability to produce veridical outcomes, they are unrivaled. They also acknowledge and accommodate background-independent constancy. And they handily accommodate the perception of illumination itself.

The biggest general weakness of decomposition models is their general failure to account for errors in lightness. And this is no small thing.

Intrinsic Image Models

The staircase Gelb effect provides a telling example. Consider the application of my intrinsic image model to the staircase Gelb display in which all five squares are present simultaneously. The luminance range in the observer's entire visual field is approximately 900:1 because we set the illumination on the five squares to be 30 times greater than the general room illumination. This large range tells the visual system that the image must be segmented into separate regions of illumination, each containing a range no greater than 30:1, the range between black and white (Gilchrist, 1980). But the range per se says nothing about where the illuminance borders lie within the image. The boundaries between adjacent squares are classified as reflectance borders because they are sharp and they divide coplanar regions (Gilchrist et al., 1983). The outer boundary of the entire group of five squares is an occlusion border. Thus, it is the obvious candidate for the illumination boundary.

Having classified the edges, the visual system integrates the reflectance edges within the group of five squares, discovering that the darkest square is 30 times darker than the lightest square. With the complete 30:1 range represented, anchoring is easy: the net lightest square is seen as white, the darkest as black, and the other three are distributed proportionately in between—in other words, veridical perception.

So my intrinsic image model totally fails to predict the dramatic illegitimate errors revealed by the staircase Gelb display. The failure is underscored by the additional fact that the retinal image produced by the staircase Gelb display, unlike other complex images, allows a very unambiguous application of the intrinsic image model.

Even though the model was not designed to explain errors, the initial hope was that some feature of the model necessary for achieving veridicality would in addition provide the key to errors. But this hope has not been fulfilled. Few errors can be explained by a failure of edge extraction. My partial edge classification scheme (Gilchrist, 1988) and the selective integration model of Ross and Pessoa (2000) achieve useful results and should be developed further. But although these ideas may contain important insights, they have not yet led to a general theory of errors.

Area and Articulation Effects

Another major challenge to such models involves recent findings that seem to defy the logic of inverse optics. Properties like reflectance and illumination are supposed to be recovered by inverting the process by which the retinal image is formed. Thus, if the absolute luminance of surfaces is lost in the initial encoding of edge ratios, then edge integration is postulated to recover at least the functional equivalent of absolute luminance. If reflectance and illuminance are confounded in the formation of the image, they are un-confounded by edge classification.

But the strong effects of area on lightness do not fit into this logic in any obvious way. If the world were such that an increase in the area of a surface increased its reflectance, then the area rule would allow the visual system to recover reflectance under a change of physical size. But surfaces do not change reflectance as their size changes. These dimensions are simply not coupled in the laws of physics. The fact that area and lightness are so strongly coupled in visual perception does not seem to reflect underlying physical principles.

Nor does the principle of articulation seem consistent with inverse optics. The physical reflectance of a patch is unaffected by the number of other contiguous, coplanar patches, but perceived lightness is. Thus, the dependence of lightness on articulation has no obvious counterpart in the structure of the physical world. And although an articulation factor can be added to the intrinsic image model, it does not fit comfortably.

The intrinsic image models are highly rational: a place for everything and everything in its place. The notion that illuminance and reflectance are overlapping layers that must be teased apart is very attractive and seems to agree very well with our phenomenal experience of the world. It may yet find a secure place in lightness theory.

The emphasis on edges is consistent not only with much psycho-physical data, but also with general principles of sensory functioning. But the challenges just described are too important to ignore. At present the intrinsic image approach and the anchoring approach seem fundamentally incompatible, but perhaps a synthesis will emerge.

The Response Paradox

When an obvious cast illuminance edge crosses a region of homogeneous reflectance, an intractable ambiguity is produced in the data, if not in the percept itself. Observers report that the lightness is the same on both sides of the illuminance edge, but when asked to make matches from a Munsell chart, all of the same observers assign different numbers to the two sides. This cannot be dismissed as confusion between lightness and brightness: expert observers show the same paradox. This paradox amounts to a measurement crisis in that it is not clear which should be accepted as a valid measure of perception, the same/different judgment or the Munsell matches. But if judging the two sides of the illuminance edge to have the same lightness is the equivalent of classifying the edge as an illuminance edge, then the very existence of this paradox presents a challenge to my earlier intrinsic image model. Given that edge classification leads to perceived lightness in that model, then edge classification and lightness matches should be tightly coupled, not in contradiction to one another.

Partial Integration and Partial Classification

The best hope for accounting for errors within the context of an intrinsic image model would appear to lie in the concepts of partial edge integration or partial edge classification. In 1988 I proposed a partial edge classification model as a common explanation for failures of illumination-independent and background-independent (simultaneous contrast) constancy. That work is described on page 290. The appeal of that proposal is that it bridges the two main types of errors. But it quickly runs into trouble. For example, it can explain only the first two of the six illumination-dependent errors given on page 275. Likewise, it can explain only several of the many background-dependent errors given on pages 277–287.

Ross and Pessoa: Selective Integration

Ross and Pessoa (2000) have recently proposed an interesting model based on the concept of selective, or partial, edge integration. The model encodes edges, then identifies context boundaries, then produces "a selective reduction of those retinal contrasts between scenic groupings, relative to those within context groupings" (p. 1164). They show that the model predicts, at least qualitatively, a range of phenomena, including White's effect, the Benary effect, Adelson illusions, Gelb effects, and others. The model employs concepts similar to those found in both intrinsic image models, like edge integration, as well as anchoring theory, such as frameworks, segmentation, and belongingness.

Ross and Pessoa did not attempt to solve the important problem of scene segmentation, but they recognize it as "perhaps the most outstanding problem in vision research" (p. 1166). In their simulation, they used only T-junctions, but they note that "context boundaries are indicated by any of a large number of scenic cues, such as motion and depth, as well as by configurational cues, such as T-junctions" (p. 1170).

Their model would encounter many of the same difficulties as my partial classification model. A key shortcoming in their model, which Ross and Pessoa acknowledge, concerns errors in predicting the magnitudes of phenomena. This problem and the segmentation problem are perhaps the biggest obstacles that must be overcome to make this approach viable as an overall theory of lightness errors. Meanwhile, Ross and Pessoa must be commended for the inclusion of a final section in their paper entitled "Shortcomings of the Model," setting a standard of scientific candor to be emulated.

The concept of partial integration can also be found in suggestions by Hurlbert (1986) that "weighting of nearby edges" (p. 1691) may partly explain simultaneous contrast and by Kingdom (1999) that simultaneous lightness contrast "results from a failure of integration" (p. 932). Rudd and Zemach (2004) have tested several variations on partial integration. Using stimuli consisting of a disk with two concentric annuli, they found the best support for a model of weighted edge integration in which the weight of a given edge depends on its distance from the target surface.

The challenge is that for such partial integration models to account for the general pattern of lightness errors, the models must be able to make the distinction between reflectance and illuminance edges.

Bergström Model

Bergström's analysis of light into common and relative components is a decomposition model but not an intrinsic image model. I find it a very impressive model. It is consistent with much of what we know about sensory functioning.

My intuition is that the Bergström model would face many of the same challenges as my intrinsic image model, although area and articulation effects might be more easily accommodated by it. I don't know whether the staircase Gelb results could be accommodated. But the bottom line is whether the pattern of lightness errors could be accommodated. No one has yet attempted a systematic account of lightness errors within the framework of the Bergström model.

Adelson's Atmospheres

As noted earlier, Adelson has produced some of the most interesting and revealing lightness illusions. In recent years his theoretical approach has undergone a shift similar to my own.[3] In his earlier work, Adelson took a Helmholtzian point of view. This can be seen in his corrugated plaid illusion. The lower target appears lighter because the visual system infers a lower level of illumination. Suggesting that "the Helmholtzian approach is overkill" (Adelson, 2000, p. 344), Adelson now speaks, in mid-level terms, about atmospheres and adaptive windows.

Atmosphere is a term he uses to describe "the combined effects of a multiplicative process (e.g., illuminance) and an additive process (e.g., haze)" (Adelson, 2000, p. 345). The concept is roughly equivalent to Katz's field of illumination or the Gestalt notion of an illumination frame of reference (Gilchrist et al., 1999; Kardos, 1934; Koffka, 1935). But it also refers to regions of veiling luminance as in fog or glare (Gilchrist & Jacobsen, 1983). For every atmosphere there is an atmospheric transfer function (ATF) describing the relationship between reflectance values in the distal stimulus and luminance values in the retinal image. For example, when the illumination level in an atmosphere is low, then the reflectance values corresponding to black, gray, and white will map onto relatively low luminance values in the image. With a higher level of illumination, these reflectance values will map onto higher luminance values. This is closely related to the anchoring problem. When a veiling luminance is present, reflectance values will map onto a more compressed set of luminance values. This is closely related to what I have called the scaling problem (see p. 224).

Lightness Transfer Function

These concepts clearly illustrate the problem facing the visual system. Luminance values in the image must be mapped onto lightness values. Conceptually, Adelson imagines that the atmospheric transfer function is inverted to produce what he calls a lightness transfer function. Of course this is easier said than done. It requires knowledge not only of the illumination level, but also of whether a veil component is present and its intensity.

Segmentation Problem

Complex images contain multiple atmospheres, and a critical question is how the visual system identifies atmosphere boundaries. Adelson has not offered a definitive answer to this question, but he has emphasized the role of junctions (T, X, and ψ) and depth boundaries.

Adaptive Windows

We know that the highest luminance plays a special role in anchoring lightness values. But how should this concept be applied to complex images? Highest luminance within what domain? The visual system cannot simply use the highest luminance in the entire visual field, especially when the image is composed of multiple fields of illumination. The result would be very poor constancy. Ideally, each field of illumination should have its own anchor, but this requires an effective means of segmenting such fields. Adelson suggests that the visual system might deploy an adaptive window. Within the adaptive window, lightness values would be assigned by taking the highest luminance as white and using that value to anchor lower values.

But finding the optimal size for the adaptive window is difficult. As Adelson notes, if the window is too small it will contain too few samples to assume that the highest is actually white, but if it is too large, it will include samples from different fields of illumination. Most of the problem could be solved if the adaptive window could be made congruent with an atmosphere. To this end, Adelson suggests that the size of the window might be adjustable, much as in the notion of a moving spotlight of attention. Moreover, to conform to a noncircular atmosphere, the window might also be adjustable in shape. Beyond these measures, Adelson would ascribe soft boundaries to the window, with surfaces close to a target getting more weight in the computation than those farther away from it.

Helson (1943, 1964) had earlier proposed a similar process by which the computed lightness of a target is based on statistics[4] from a cluster of surfaces weighted for proximity to the target. The difficult problems encountered by these ideas are discussed on page 80. Moreover, the idea of an adaptive window with soft boundaries does not seem consistent with the behavior of the probe disks shown in Figures 11.2 and 11.3. Lightness for a given probe luminance seems to be uniform throughout a given framework, but it shifts abruptly when crossing the framework boundary.

The issue here is whether the domain within which a highest luminance is taken should be defined by the structure of the retinal image or by the structure of the organism. Perhaps an adaptive window has more neural plausibility than an atmosphere, but like so many neurally inspired concepts, it corresponds poorly with the empirical findings. I find it premature to address the question of neural implementation before we have achieved greater consensus on the nature of the lightness algorithm in formal terms. In the meantime, I believe that the domain in which the highest luminance is taken is most fruitfully defined by the structure of the image, using segregative factors like edge and junction types, and cohesive factors like grouping principles.

Of course, even if the visual system were able to correctly identify framework boundaries, there would be a further problem. Empirical results have clearly shown that lightness is not computed exclusively within a single framework; rather, there is some kind of crosstalk between frameworks. According to the Kardos doctrine of co-determination, lightness reflects influences from both within the target's relevant framework and without. Kardos (1934) argues that such a compromise accounts for failures of lightness constancy and that it is necessary to avoid the larger errors that would otherwise occur in small, poorly articulated frameworks, however well segregated.

My sense is that neither soft boundaries nor the closely related idea of partial integration (Kingdom, 1999; Ross & Pessoa, 2000) can account for lightness errors as effectively as co-determination. But more work is needed here.

ANCHORING THEORY

The emergence of a rougher, mid-level, model of lightness coincides with a larger trend in cognitive psychology. Experiments on change blindness (Mack & Rock, 1998; Rensink et al., 1997) have revealed just how limited is our cognitive representation of the external world. Singh and Anderson (2002) have shown that a much cruder model of perceived transparency outperforms the decomposition approach of Metelli. Sedgwick (2004) talks about crosstalk between spatial frames of reference. And recently Chomsky, a key figure in the cognitive revolution, has embraced a new and less ratiomorphic view of psycholinguistics.

The anchoring model may not have the intuitive appeal of the decomposition models. Its main strength lies in its ability to explain an unprecedented range of data found in the literature. It was motivated by an attempt to model the pattern of lightness errors. As I have argued earlier, the error pattern provides a particularly strong form of constraint for models of lightness. Errors are the signature of the biological software.

There is skepticism in some quarters regarding the concept of frameworks. But it is difficult to avoid the conclusion that fields of illumination must be represented, however crudely, in the visual system. Otherwise constancy simply could not exist. Structure-blind attempts to explain lightness have consistently failed. The use of probe disks, as in Figure 11.2, provides compelling evidence that illumination frames of reference play a crucial role in lightness, however thorny the segmentation problem.

Co-determination, the interaction between frameworks first re-

vealed by Kardos (1934), is strongly supported both by empirical results and by a compelling logic. Co-determination offers the first coherent explanation for failures of lightness constancy. Equally
important, it draws both constancy failures and lightness illusions
such as simultaneous contrast together in a unified account of errors.

Intrinsic Image versus Anchoring Models: A Critical Test

Further support comes from a head-to-head test that my colleagues
and I (Annan et al., 1997) conducted between my older intrinsic image
model and the newer anchoring model. The stimulus we used is illustrated in Figure 12.1. A rectangular panel of matte black paper was
mounted in midair at approximate eye level. A smaller dark-gray target square was centered in the left half of the black rectangle and a
white square was centered in the right half. A bright beam of light
was projected across the left half of the black rectangle. The illumination resulting from this beam was approximately 30 times as bright
as the ambient illumination at that location. As a result, the luminance
of the dark-gray target in the bright light was approximately three
times higher than that of the white target in the dim light. The right-
hand boundary of the projected light contained a pronounced penumbra. There was no attempt to conceal the nature of this special illumination. To this end we jiggled the display so as to make it very
clear that the illuminance boundary did not belong to the paper display. All observers reported perceiving the penumbra as an illumi-

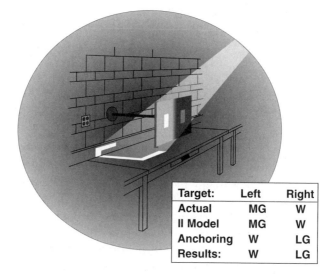

Target:	Left	Right
Actual	MG	W
II Model	MG	W
Anchoring	W	LG
Results:	W	LG

Figure 12.1. Test pitting anchoring theory against intrinsic image theory. Predictions and results are shown in the inset.

nance border. Observers viewed this display and made matches to each of the target squares using a Munsell scale under separate illumination.

The display was constructed so as to maximize the difference between these predictions made by the two models.

Classified Edge Integration

The concept that lies at the heart of the intrinsic image model is that of classified edge integration. This means that the visual system is able to integrate all the instances of a single type of edge that occur along a path between any two targets. For this display it means simply that the signal corresponding to the edge of the dark-gray target is integrated with the signal from the edge of the white target; the penumbra, being correctly perceived as an illuminance edge, is omitted from this integration. Such a classified integration reveals that the reflectance of the right-hand target is about 10 times higher than the reflectance of the left-hand target.

If the visual system calculates such an integral, it knows that while the left-hand target has the highest luminance, the right-hand target has a higher reflectance. According to the intrinsic image model, then, the right-hand target should be perceived as white and the left-hand target as dark gray.

Anchoring Predictions

The left-hand target has the highest luminance in the display. It also has the highest luminance in its local framework—the left half of the display. Thus, the anchoring model makes the clear prediction that the left target should appear completely white. The weighting of local and global assignments is of no importance because the local and global assignments are the same. The right-hand target is the highest luminance in its local framework; thus, its local assignment is white. But in the global framework, it is about three times darker than the highest luminance, making its global assignment light middle gray. The global framework is very weak, given that it is divided by a penumbra or luminance gradient, which plays a segregative role. Thus, the right-hand target should appear somewhere between white and middle gray, but closer to white.

The obtained results are shown in the inset of Figure 12.1, along with the predictions made by the two models. Given that the two models make opposite predictions, it is easy to see that the empirical results clearly favor the anchoring model.

Comparison of Anchoring and Intrinsic Image Models

It may be useful to point out several differences between these models that may not be immediately obvious.

1. A central difference, already discussed, is that the intrinsic image model was created to account for veridicality while the anchoring model was created to account for errors. The anchoring model does, of course, account for veridicality to the extent that it exists.

2. The intrinsic image models are fueled explicitly by relative luminance encoded at edges. The anchoring model, as currently formulated (Gilchrist et al., 1999), is couched in terms of luminance values rather than luminance ratios. But the model is somewhat indifferent on this point, and it would not be too difficult to revise the model to accept luminance ratios as an input.

3. Importantly, the retinal image is decomposed in different ways in the two models. Intrinsic images result from a horizontal slicing of the retinal image into layers. The anchoring model speaks of frameworks. Often these are arranged as adjacent regions, like states on a map, but not always. Frameworks can be arranged hierarchically, as in the local and global framework of simultaneous contrast. And they can interpenetrate one another, as in the horizontal, vertical, and diagonal groupings of checkerboard contrast.

Arend (1994) has emphasized that spatial variations in illumination constitute a far more difficult challenge to lightness models than do temporal variations. Intrinsic image models respond to this challenge with edge classification. The anchoring model employs that concept of illumination frames of reference. There is considerable resistance among lightness researchers to the framework idea. This is understandable, given the challenging problem of framework segmentation. But rather than avoiding the concept of frameworks because they are difficult to operationalize, I suggest that the problem needs to be tackled directly. I don't see how the problem can be avoided. I don't believe that any model that does not explicitly acknowledge the existence of frameworks can accommodate the appearance of probe disks in Figures 11.2 and 11.3.

The concept of frameworks goes back to the Gestaltists. More recently, Ikeda and colleagues (Ikeda, Shinoda & Mizokami, 1998; Mizokami, Ikeda & Shinoda, 1998) have reported a number of interesting experiments dealing with what they call the "recognized visual space of illumination" (RVSI), a construct that appears to be equivalent to the concept of framework[5] or field of illumination as used by Katz and Koffka, among others. In one interesting experiment (Mizokami, Ikeda & Shinoda, 1998) the observers looked into a miniature room, complete with furnishings. The far wall contained a large archway through which they saw a second room. The far room appeared more brightly illuminated than the near room, although this impression was created solely by the use of light-gray surfaces in the far room and dark-gray surfaces in the near room (as in Rutherford & Brainard, 2002). An actual paper target of fixed reflectance was placed at 14 locations along an imaginary line from the observer's eye to the far side of the far room. At each location, observers matched the target for lightness. When corrections were made for slight variations in illumination incident on the target, the results showed that even with the retinal image held constant, a target of constant luminance appeared darker in the far room than in the near, with a soft transition between the two levels. This suggests that there is an implicit level of perceived illumination at every location in perceived 3D space and that near the boundary between the rooms, the target is influenced by both levels of perceived illumination.

Anchoring and Perceived Illumination

The model of local and global anchoring evolved as a model of surface lightness (or more precisely, errors in surface lightness) and, unlike the intrinsic image models, it makes no reference to the perception of illumination. This may seem a bit strange, in light of much evidence showing a close relationship between lightness and perceived illumination. At the same time it may not be so difficult to bring perceived illumination into the picture. A number of studies (Beck, 1959, 1961; Kozaki, 1973; Noguchi & Masuda, 1971) have shown that the level of perceived illumination is determined by the region of the image with the highest luminance and the largest area. Of course, these are just the two factors that mainly determine the anchor for lightness. Thus, it appears that both lightness and perceived illumination are anchored to the same luminance value.

This gives us a good start in linking lightness to perceived illumination. But it is not clear that such a linkage will be consistent with Koffka's invariance theorem, despite the empirical evidence for that theorem reviewed in Chapter 8. The staircase Gelb display that inspired the anchoring model presents an immediate problem for the invariance hypothesis. To be sure, the Gelb effect on which it is based has often been cited as the prime example of a covariance of lightness errors and errors in perceived illumination. When a piece of black paper stands alone in the spotlight, it appears white. This is a huge error in perceived lightness. But it is complemented by an equally large error in perceived illumination. The white-appearing paper appears to stand in the same dim general illumination of the room, when in fact it is very brightly illuminated by the spotlight. Thus, we find large equal and opposite errors in perceived lightness and perceived illumination.

But in the staircase Gelb display, which is an incremental version of the Gelb effect, the size of the error is different for each of the five shades of gray. No single mistake in the perception of illumination on the five surfaces can account for the gradient of lightness errors shown by the different squares. The black square shows the largest error, appearing as a light middle gray. For this square the invariance hypothesis would be satisfied by perceiving the special illumination as approximately seven times dimmer than it really is. But the white square, on the other hand, shows no error in perceived lightness: it is perceived to be white. Thus, for the white square, the invariance hypothesis requires no error in perceived illumination. Likewise, each of the three intervening squares shows a different degree of lightness error, and therefore each of these squares requires a different degree of error in perceived illumination if the invariance hypothesis is to be satisfied. The invariance hypothesis could be salvaged by postulating a different level of perceived illumination for each of the five squares, but this approach is not consistent with the concept of illumination as a common component (Bergström, 1977).

The Aperture Problem for Lightness

Co-determination implies that the visual system accepts large errors that do not seem necessary. Why would it do this? To illustrate the problem, consider the following example, which could aptly be called the aperture problem for lightness perception.

Imagine you are sitting in a room that is highly articulated. The room is spatially complex, with objects of various sorts and lots of surface colors represented within the room. The retinal image you receive is rich with information for determining surface lightness. Somewhere in the room there is a hole in one wall. Through this hole you can see into a second room that, for all you know, might be more brightly or more dimly illuminated than the room in which you are sitting. But through this hole you can see only two surfaces, a lighter region and a darker region. How should your visual system go about determining the lightness of those two surfaces? Logically, there are two alternatives.

The visual system, finding too few statistics within the aperture, could simply anchor the two regions of the aperture using the highly articulated framework of the room in which you are sitting. But this strategy assumes that the room seen through the aperture has the same level of illumination as the room in which you are sitting, something that is not known. If that assumption is not correct, lightness errors for the two surfaces will result.

On the other hand, the visual system could treat the aperture containing the two surfaces as a world unto itself. The occlusion border that forms the boundary of the aperture could be considered a barrier to anchoring, across which no relationships can be taken with any degree of confidence. Computation within the aperture would proceed just as computation in one of our domes. The visual system would take the lighter region and call it white, and determine the lightness of the darker region relative to that, using the ratio principle. If the darker region is larger than the lighter region, the area effect would be engaged. This would be a logical approach, but notice that it comes with a different risk: it assumes that the lighter region seen within the aperture is actually a white surface, and this is not known. If it does not happen to be a white surface, then this algorithm would produce errors in the perceived lightness of the two regions.

So the visual system is caught between a rock and a hard place. What should it do? Note that an ideal observer could do no better. There is simply not enough information. Apparently the system chooses to hedge its bets and, for any given surface, strike a compromise between the two lightness values that would be derived from these two alternative strategies. Of course, logically the weights given to local anchoring and global anchoring should vary as a function of certain factors. For example, if there happen to be 10 surfaces visible within the aperture, then it makes sense to give a very strong weight to the local framework because it becomes more likely that the highest luminance among the 10 is in fact a white surface, or close to white.

But why doesn't the system get the answer right when there is enough information, using the hedging strategy only when the information is missing? Perhaps because it is more efficient to have a single system rather than two systems.

The aperture problem for lightness shows that the visual system cannot avoid errors because there will always be pockets of ambiguity in any image, no matter how complex. A pocket of ambiguity is a region of the image within which there is simply not enough information for a confident application of the intrinsic image model. Local anchoring risks an error to the extent that the local maximum is not in fact white, while global anchoring risks an error to the extent that the local illumination is different from the global. By compromising between local and global anchoring, the visual system guarantees that some error will occur in exchange for limits on the degree of any one kind of error.

Note for Machine Vision Modelers

During the 1970s, decomposition theorists and machine vision modelers made common cause because both were interested in modeling veridical perception. But the study of lightness errors, at least on the surface, poses little interest for people working in machine vision. Why would they care about the kind of mistakes made by the human system? Here is one reason. Computers seem to be able to outperform humans on any specific task. The great advantage of humans over machines involves the impressive human flexibility. Humans can perform adequately across a dramatically wide range of tasks. Errors, if they can be contained within limits, may simply be the price of this flexibility. Thus, it may be that machines will be able to simulate a fuller range of human abilities only by deliberately incorporating errors.

Shortcomings of the Anchoring Model

Several shortcomings simply represent the incomplete development of the anchoring model. A pressing matter that needs to be resolved concerns the reason for the horizontal G-line in the explanation of the staircase Gelb effect. A closely related question is whether the local/global construction should be replaced by the relevant/foreign construction of Kardos. This issue is discussed on page 315.

Choice of the Global Scaling Rule

Scaling in the global framework raises a problem because the global framework typically includes a luminance range much greater than the black/white range. There are several candidate rules for handling such a situation, and these will have to be determined by further research.

1. Wallach's ratio principle (1:1 scaling) is the general default rule. Starting with the highest luminance and scaling all lower luminances according to the ratio rule means that all target surfaces equal to or darker than 30 times darker than the maximum will be assigned the same value of black.
2. *Proportionate scaling.* A range normalization scaling rule might be used. The entire dynamic range of the global framework could be scaled down to fit the 30:1 range of the black/white scale. The highest luminance is taken as white and the lowest luminance as black, and all intermediate shades are determined by interpolation. This is equivalent to bipolar anchoring.
3. *Proportionate scaling, weighted by area.* Under this scheme, relative lightness distances between luminance values in the global framework would depend on the relative area of these regions. Thus, for example, if the highest luminance were relatively large, it would be taken as white, but if it were relatively small, it would be taken as above white.

Unintegrated Territory

Several important lines of research do not seem currently amenable to the anchoring analysis. One example is my earlier work on black rooms and white rooms (Gilchrist & Jacobsen, 1984). Another example

concerns lightness constancy in scenes with an overlay of veiling luminance (Gilchrist & Jacobsen, 1983). Here the question of scaling is
the issue. Perhaps a scaling rule can be found to solve this problem,
but given that a veiling luminance is discounted for some scenes but
not others, the scaling rule would have to depend on the contents of
the image covered by the veil. Manish Singh (2004) has presented a
transparency display that cannot be explained by anchoring theory
and appears to demand an explanation in terms of overlapping perceived layers.

Hypercompression

In the staircase Gelb effect, casting a spotlight on five adjacent squares
produces a dramatic compression of their lightnesses. The illumination level in the spotlight is 30 times higher than the ambient room
illumination. It is calibrated by raising the luminance of the black
square to equality with a white square outside the spotlight. If the
spotlight is made brighter than this, the compression becomes even
greater, and this should not happen, according to the anchoring
model. The equal lightness values assigned to each of the squares in
the global framework are thought to produce the compression. But if
so, the compression must be at its maximum under a 30x spotlight.
Further increases in spotlight intensity cannot make the G-line any
flatter, so the compression should not increase any further.

Insulation

If a white border completely surrounds a group of patches in a spotlight, the compression that would otherwise occur is prevented, as if
the border insulates the group from the global framework. There is
no special reason within the model why this should occur.

New Illusions

Figure 12.2 shows several recent configurations that pose minor problems for the anchoring model. Bindman and Chubb (2004) have observed that the cluster version of checkerboard contrast (top) and the
bull's-eye illusion (middle), which is similar to deWeert's pincushion
illusion, are not obviously consistent with the anchoring model. A
possible way to accommodate these effects is found in recent work by
Oh and Kim (2004). They presented observers with two displays, a
bull's-eye display, like that of Bindman and Chubb (2004), and a display consisting of alternating black and white squares, with a gray
square replacing one of the blacks and another replacing one of the
whites, similar to that shown at the bottom of Figure 12.2. Observers
judged the gray square replacing a black as lighter than the gray

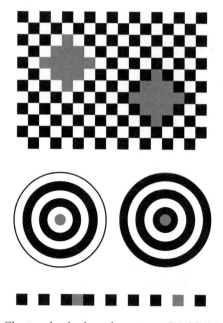

Figure 12.2. (Top) Cluster-checkerboard contrast. (Middle) Bull's-eye contrast. (Bottom) Alternation effect. Top and middle figures reprinted with permission from Bindman and Chub, 2004. Bottom figure reprinted with permission from Oh and Kim, 2004.

square replacing the white. Oh and Kim (2004) interpreted this effect within the context of anchoring theory, arguing that the display is perceptually segregated into two sets of alternating squares, much like the checkerboard contrast display can be segregated (Gilchrist et al., 1999). They apply the same logic to the bull's-eye illusion.

A further feature of the Bindman and Chubb results supports an anchoring interpretation. They found the bull's-eye illusion to be strongest with dark-gray targets, becoming weaker as the targets become lighter. This is just what Economou and I found for simultaneous contrast (see p. 326) and just what the anchoring model demands.

Both Oh and Kim (2004) and Bindman and Chubb (2004) measured the bull's-eye illusion using two methods: a forced-choice method and an adjustment method. Both found the same paradox: a strong illusion using forced choice, but a much weaker effect using adjustment. Indeed, both teams made the same interpretation of this paradox: that the adjustment method narrows the attentional window. Such alternation effects seem to present themselves most strongly when attention is more widely distributed. This suggests the pregnant idea that attention can modulate the size, and perhaps the strength, of a framework.

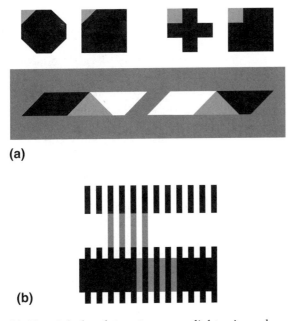

(a)

(b)

Figure 12.3. (a) The right-hand target appears lighter in each pair, showing grouping by global symmetry with T-junctions held constant. Reprinted with permission from Oh and Kim, 2004. (b) White's illusion is weakened or reversed because global T-junctions counteract local T-junctions. Reprinted with permission from Howe, 2001.

Figure 12.3 shows stimuli studied by Howe (2001) and by Oh and Kim (2004). These effects do not flow directly from grouping by local T-junctions, as suggested by the anchoring model, but they do seem amenable to grouping factors operating at a larger spatial scale. This suggests that grouping factors at a large spatial scale override or more likely combine with those at a smaller spatial scale.

Bressan's Double Anchoring Theory

Bressan (2006) has proposed an alternative to our anchoring theory. She replaces both the area rule and the scale normalization rule in the current anchoring theory with a surround-as-white rule. Her surround rule is similar to the one that Bonato and I (Gilchrist & Bonato, 1995) proposed and later rejected, but with one crucial difference. In the Bressan surround rule the surround need not appear white. It merely functions as a white standard for the object that it surrounds. Its own lightness depends on the application of the entire model. In a further departure, the Bressan model allows values above white in computing values within frameworks.

In a given framework, there are two anchoring steps: the highest luminance step and the surround step. The highest luminance is assigned the value of white and darker regions are computed relative to this value, as in the original anchoring model. In addition, the surround is assigned a value of white and darker regions are computed relative to this. These steps yield two lightness values for every surface in the framework. The weight of the surround step relative to the highest luminance step is a direct function of the size of the surround relative to the target, the articulation of the surround, and its absolute luminance.

Because not every framework is organized in a clear figure/ground manner, Bressan has been led to define surround in an unusual way, as any region that groups with the figure within a framework. The surround need not be strictly adjacent to the figure. For example, the functional surround for a window on the side of an office building would be both the wall of the building (one framework) and the matrix of other windows (another framework).

Once values within a framework are established by combining the highest luminance and surround steps, these values must be combined with those from frameworks at different scales, as in the Gilchrist et al. (1999) model. But these frameworks are somewhat different. Most importantly, Bressan substitutes a peripheral framework for our global framework. The peripheral framework, unlike the global framework, does not include the local framework. It appears to be the equivalent of the foreign framework proposed by Kardos. In short, Bressan's frameworks are not arranged in a nested hierarchy.

Final lightness values reflect a weighted average of values generated in local and peripheral frameworks. The weighting is a function of (1) the relative size, articulation, and absolute luminance of the framework and (2) the number and type of spatial and photometric grouping factors that make the target belong to it.

The double anchoring model was designed to address several of the failures of the original model. For example, the insulation effect obtained by Cataliotti and me (Gilchrist et al., 1999), and not currently explained by our model, follows directly from Bressan's surround rule. The surround rule also accommodates the double increments version of simultaneous contrast, although most studies have found no contrast effect for double increments. Evaluating this model is not easy, due mainly to its complexity. In addition to weighting the balance between local and peripheral frameworks, there is the question of weighting the balance between the highest luminance step and the surround step, within each framework, local and peripheral. The rules given for these weightings are complex.

In her model, Bressan has given up what I consider to be a major strength of both the original anchoring model and the Kardos theory of co-determination, namely the concept that failures of illumination-dependent constancy stem from global anchoring. In Bressan's model, the compression of the five squares in the spotlight follows not from global anchoring but primarily from the application of the surround rule within the group of five squares.

13 _____

Concluding Thoughts

AN OBSERVATION ON CREATIVE THINKING

Our review of the history of lightness perception has also revealed an insight concerning creative thinking. Each of the key players in the evolving story of lightness pushed the problem forward as far as he was able. Each got stuck at a certain point, and we can identify that point by a specific pattern of self-contradiction. So, for example, although Katz accepted uncritically the prevailing assumptions of raw sensations and their cognitive interpretations, he advanced the field by his emphasis on the role of fields of illumination, suggesting that the level of illumination within a field is represented by its average luminance. Moreover, his now-standard method of using adjacent regions of high and low illumination to study constancy highlighted the crucial problem of multiple spatial frameworks of illumination within a single scene. But at this point he made two mutually exclusive suggestions: that an average is taken of the luminances in the entire visual field, and that a separate average is taken within each field of illumination. He seemed at times on the verge of making a break with the traditional assumption of raw sensations but vacillated, making diametrically opposed statements concerning whether the color seen in the aperture of a reduction screen is a film color or not.

Koffka treated fields of illumination as frames of reference. The concept of the frame of reference, so important in motion and orientation, remains an indispensable tool in visual perception. But Koffka failed to directly confront the question of whether lightness computations are done exclusively within a framework or whether there is crosstalk between frameworks. He made contradictory statements as to whether belongingness is all-or-none or graded.

It was Kardos who advanced the important idea, which he called co-determination, that there are systematic influences across frameworks. This constitutes an important (though neglected) theory of failures of lightness constancy. But he seemed confused on whether co-determination could be extended to lightness illusions such as simultaneous contrast. Such an extension would have produced a general theory of lightness errors. He made contradictory statements on whether (illumination-independent) lightness constancy shows the same kind of faulty performance as seen in simultaneous contrast.

In each case the contradiction marks that person's high-water mark in thinking on lightness.

THE NETWORK OF TRADITIONAL ASSUMPTIONS

Looking back over the history of work on lightness, we can see that certain deeply rooted theoretical assumptions have hobbled progress. Koffka talked about the "network of traditional assumptions." Chief among these are the twin assumptions of raw sensations and cognitive interpretation of sensations. These go right back to the beginnings of the systematic study of perception. But these assumptions are still very much alive today, and they continue to prevent a coherent account of lightness computation.

Raw Sensations

In the era of Descartes, the concept of sensations represented an advance in thinking. It offered a way to begin to think in more concrete, less mystical terms about the relationship between physical forces impinging on receptor surfaces and the resulting experience. The doctrine of local determination (or constancy hypothesis, as the Gestaltists called it) postulates a one-to-one correspondence between local stimulation and visual experience. It was an obvious first guess, with an attractive simplicity. But the problematic nature of the concept soon emerged, as Helmholtz, Mach, and Hering realized that our visual experience correlates more closely with the distal stimulus than with the proximal.[1] Specifically, perceived lightness correlates more closely with the reflectance of the seen object than with the local stimulation produced at the receptors. Here these thinkers made a fateful decision. Instead of challenging the doctrine of local determination (apparently they saw no alternative), they added a second, cognitive layer to deal with this newly recognized objective reference in visual experience.

Cognitive Interpretation of Sensations

Helmholtz split the visual response into two parts, sensation and perception, one faithful to local stimulation and the other, following certain cognitive operations, faithful to the object. Hering argued for a more elaborate sensory stage, and he felt that Helmholtz gave too much emphasis to the cognitive stage, but he did not challenge the sensory/cognitive dualism. As MacLeod (1932, p. 22) has observed, "The distinction, however, between primary and secondary, between physiological and psychological, processes does not disappear with Hering. Essentially, perhaps, his position is only slightly different from that of Helmholtz; he has simply attributed more to peripheral and less to central factors. The constancy of colour is due primarily to conditions in the receptors; but central modification may take place, e.g., in the case of memory colour."

It is ironic that Helmholtz and Hering are so often taken to represent the poles of perceptual theory, because their views are strikingly similar. Both maintained a mind/body dualism implying that sensory processes are done by the body while cognitive operations are done by the mind.

Thus the doctrine of local determination was preserved, though at the cost of elegance, and despite the universal acknowledgement that raw sensations are very difficult to observe. Helmholtz (1866, p. 6) observed, "It might seem that nothing could be easier than to be conscious of one's own sensations; and yet experience shows that for the discovery of subjective sensations some special talent is needed." Helmholtz's point man von Kries (quoted in Gelb, 1929, translated by D. Todorović) admitted that it is difficult to observe raw sensations: "However, one must consider that these sensations can only be observed with difficulties and under special conditions. We do not doubt that they exist, but they are only in a limited way objects of our cognition, comparison, or conceptual apprehension."

Indeed, the introspectionists set up schools for training in the hunt for the elusive sensation. To aid in this hunt, stimuli were stripped of most of their complexity, but even then the effort to isolate the sensations failed to produce consensus.

So compelling was the doctrine of local determination that even a phenomenologist like David Katz failed to notice the absence of raw sensations in our direct experience of the world, although he did observe (1935, p. 141) that "The intensity of a retinal image, however, usually evades observation and can be compared with that of another only after reduction." But his loyalty to the network of traditional assumptions dulled his otherwise keen sense of phenomena. MacLeod (1932, p. 34) noted that "Phenomenological description furnishes no basis for the assumption of a primary, invariant, stimulus-conditioned sensation, which might act as raw material upon which experience could operate." Merleau-Ponty (1962, p. 5) would later write, "The alleged self-evidence of sensation is not based on any testimony of consciousness, but on widely held prejudice."

It is extremely difficult to make a brightness match for a dark gray in bright illumination and a light gray in dim illumination. Fred Bonato and I found that observers were completely unable to make a brightness match between a target that appeared self-luminous in a shadowed Mondrian and a gray target of the same luminance in an adjacent illuminated Mondrian. Under these and other conditions, it is virtually impossible to perceive that two targets have the same luminance, even though they are supposed to produce the same sensation.

The Gestalt psychologists rejected both raw sensations and cognitive interpretations. They argued that seeing is the product of a single visual process, in which the visual experience associated with a particular part of the visual field depends not simply on the stimulation at that point, but on an extended pattern of stimulation. They made dramatic headway in lightness until the events surrounding World War II threw them into exile and left the field of lightness in the hands of behaviorists who successfully suppressed the Gestalt history.

Now it might be argued that the behaviorists cannot be accused of maintaining the assumptions of raw sensations and cognitive interpretations. After all, they wanted to reject both cognitive operations and the phenomenology of sensation. But this view is too superficial. The S-R concept and the doctrine of local determination share the same kind of simplism. The main focus of those behaviorists working in lightness was brightness induction. And what is brightness if not a sensation? Is it not the experience of the intensity of light at a given point in the visual field? These contrast theorists accepted Hering's modification of the doctrine of local determination so as to accommodate the role of context in only the most minimal way. The brightness response at a given field location was now held to be a product not merely of the stimulation at that location, but also of the inhibitory effect produced by the immediately local surround. Ultimately the contrast theorists largely ignored the objective reference in perceptual experience, making little attempt to account for the surface lightness of real-world objects.

Hurvich and Jameson (1966, p. 88), like Hering before them, complemented their sensory mechanism with a cognitive stage, as we see in these comments on the Hering spot-shadow demonstration: "In the situations described by Hering, the areas in question are perceived as lighter or darker—be they seen as spots or shadows—not because of our interpretations of the situation but because of the way the visual system happens to work as a physiological mechanism that responds to patterns of stimulation. It is the significance alone of the lighter and darker perceptions—whether the areas are perceived as properties of the surfaces or as properties of the illumination—that depends on our interpretation of the total situation." In other words, the opponent process creates only the sensations of brightness and darkness. Turning these into percepts of surface lightness requires additional cognitive operations. Thus, if the Hurvich/Jameson model is to be considered a lightness theory, it is a cognitive theory, not that different from Helmholtz, ironically.

We don't know how long lightness theory would have languished in the grip of such failed ideas had it not been for certain influences from outside the field, namely the rise of machine vision driven by the Cold War.

Why did the cognitive revolution happen when it did—roughly at the end of the 1960s? After all, most of the crucial experiments (like response learning versus place learning) were done in the 1930s and 1940s, and the results favored the cognitive position. The answer probably lay in the arms race. Computing held out the possibility, attractive in the context of the Cold War, that weapons, having already become larger, could now become smarter. But mainstream psychology had little to say about intelligence; indeed, when the military asked how intelligence works, understandably psychology was brushed aside, and money was poured into the premier institutes of technology to create the new fields of artificial intelligence, information theory, and machine vision. For lightness theory, this meant escape from the Dark Ages.

Behaviorism had shown little interest in representing the objective properties of the external world. But machine vision was driven by just this problem; it had no interest in the arcane matter of sensations. This emphasis on veridicality resonated with the earlier Gestalt emphasis on constancy, bringing a burst of fresh air to the field of lightness. Little was heard about the cognitive interpretation of raw sensations among those concerned with veridicality.

But the traditional network of assumptions continues to thrive. McCann (2001, p. 111) writes that "lightnesses are sensations of lightness, that have been modified by past experience." Blakeslee and McCourt (2003, p. 48) write that "brightness is a primary sensation" and they speak of "higher-order effects on brightness" (p. 68).

The Photometer Metaphor

In lightness, the doctrine of local determination takes the form of what I have called the "photometer metaphor" (Gilchrist, 1994, p. 18): the assumption that the visual system initially encodes the intensity of light at each point in the visual field. Even when not explicitly acknowledged, this metaphor is exposed by a series of symptoms, including the neglect of illumination perception and the obsession with brightness.

The Strange Preoccupation with Brightness

The thriving brightness industry that we continue to witness is further evidence that the doctrine of sensations is alive and well.

Brightness is to lightness as perceived visual angle is to perceived size. According to current usage, as reflected in the glossary, brightness refers to the perception of luminance. Its equivalent in spatial perception is the perception of visual angle. But the parallel between these two proximal variables is not reflected in the empirical work of the two fields. In the lightness/brightness field, there has been a huge industry studying brightness. In the spatial domain, we find only several studies on the perception of visual angle. These are believed to establish that we do have some rough sense of visual angle. But the question is not a pressing one: there is a clear recognition that perceived object size is what matters, not visual angle. Why, then, such concern for the human sense of the brightness of light, as opposed to surface lightness? Why would the visual system want to compute the intensity of light reflected by a surface? Imagine a black surface in bright sunlight. It is useful to compute the low lightness of the surface and perhaps its level of illumination, but of what use is its brightness?

Confusing Energy with Information

I believe the obsession with brightness represents confusion between energy and information, between the medium and the message. As Barlow (1953, p. 373) has observed, "Light is the agent . . . but it is the detailed pattern of light that carries the information." Only rarely does light per se serve as information.[2] Of course, information about object size is also brought to our eyes on the vehicle of light, but no one would confuse spatial extent with light energy. Lightness is different: it is in fact quite easy to confuse surface lightness with light intensity. And in this confusion lies a modern extension of the doctrine of local determination.

Dualistic Thinking

Both raw sensations and the concept of their cognitive interpretation are problematic notions lacking in empirical support. They survive because together they are unassailable. Each depends on the other, and each protects the other from attack. Their mutual dependence was illustrated by Koffka (1935, p. 86) in this amusing anecdote:

> A man and his small son are viewing with great interest an acrobat walking on the tight rope and balancing himself with a long pole. The boy suddenly turns to his father and asks: "Father, why doesn't that man fall?" The father replies: "Don't you see that he is holding on to the pole?" The boy accepts the authority of his parent, but after a while he bursts out with a new question: "Father, why doesn't the pole fall?" Whereupon the father replies: "But don't you see that the man holds it!"

It is customary these days to talk about low-level, high-level, and mid-level theories of lightness. But in reality there are only two kinds of theories, because the low-level and high-level theories are really part of the same theory. If I'm not mistaken, every low-level theorist has a high-level theory simultaneously, and vice versa. With the possible exception of Cornsweet, all the well known low-level theorists (Hering, Mach, Jameson & Hurvich, Kingdom, and McCourt) have also embraced a role for cognitive influences in lightness. And all the well-known cognitive theorists (Helmholtz, Katz, and Beck) have also endorsed the role of low-level mechanisms. Low-level and high-level theories are just different parts of what Koffka called "the network of traditional hypotheses." The real distinction is between dualistic theories that include both low-level and high-level components, and monistic, mid-level theories.

Not only does the traditional dualistic approach fail the test of Ockham's razor, but, despite their almost universal assumption, neither the concept of raw sensations nor that of their cognitive interpretation is supported by evidence. As for sensations, virtually all of the principal students of lightness have noted that sensations are either very difficult or impossible to observe. As for cognitive influences on the percept, the fact that they are mainly obtained when stimuli are highly impoverished suggests that cognition is influencing the judgment rather than the percept. There is certainly no evidence of a major effect of past experience on lightness perception.

Proximal Mode

In rejecting the concept of raw sensations, I do not deny the subjective component in visual experience. Our visual experience includes, more or less, a sense of the impact of stimulation on our receptor surfaces. When the light entering our eyes becomes too bright we are moved to don sunglasses, regardless of whether we are standing in front of a brightly illuminated gray wall or a less brightly illuminated white wall. Koffka (1935, p. 113) spoke much about the representation of the ego in the proximal stimulus. Even when a dinner plate is perceived to have a round shape, its elliptical image tells of the observer's viewing angle. But none of this implies the existence of raw sensations.

Rock (1975) distinguishes between the constancy mode and the proximal mode, sometimes called the painter's mode. Evans (1964) calls them the object mode and the light mode. In the proximal mode of seeing, we attend to visual angle as opposed to objective size, and we attend to luminance as opposed to reflectance. Just because we have the ability to look at the world in this reduced way does not mean that the reduced way of seeing is prior to, and forms the basis of, visual perception in the constancy mode.

NEGLECT OF HISTORY

A key strength of modern science is it social nature. Science is a collective enterprise. We do not insist on giving credit where credit is due merely to be fair to other scientists. We do it because it allows us to keep track of ideas and to weigh those ideas against the evidence. Science, to be healthy, cannot be collective simply among contemporaries; it must be collective over time as well.

Our survey of the history of lightness has revealed something of the price that has been paid when history has been neglected. The worst period for this, of course, was the contrast period. But even today there is a growing tendency to cite only recent work.

The following three topics illustrate important but forgotten work that I believe remains essential to progress in lightness.

The Work of Lajos Kardos

The prevalence of adjacent fields of illumination within a single scene remains a crucial problem for lightness theory. It appears that the highest luminance is the fundamental anchor for relative luminance values. But if the highest luminance in the entire visual field is used to anchor everything in that field, constancy remains totally unexplained. Here the concept of frames of reference becomes indispensable. Veridicality requires that the highest luminance within each field of illumination be used to anchor the elements within that field. But empirical evidence shows that anchoring by highest luminance is neither entirely local nor entirely global. The visual system appears to use a weighted average of these, and the weighting depends mainly on the size and degree of articulation within the local framework. This is the Kardos concept of co-determination. It is hard to avoid logically, and it makes sense out of an enormous swath of empirical findings. It also constitutes a theory of failures of illumination-independent constancy and by extension a theory of failures of background-independent constancy, otherwise known as illusions. Yet the concept of co-determination was unavailable for further study as long as Kardos was forgotten.

There is much more of value in the extensive lightness work of Kardos, including his findings on the factors by which frameworks are segmented. Moreover, had his work been properly recognized, the crucial role of depth perception on lightness would have been established almost a half-century earlier than it was.

The Countershaded Background Experiment

The question of whether simultaneous lightness contrast depends on the physical luminance of the backgrounds or on their perceived lightness is raised on a regular basis, even though the issue was settled many years ago in a series of experiments using the countershading technique. But the more important application of this technique bears directly on the contrast theory of lightness constancy. Targets are placed within adjacent fields of high and low illumination. A background of high reflectance is used in the low illumination, and a background of low reflectance is used in the high illumination. By selecting the proper levels of background reflectance and illumination level, these backgrounds can be made equal in luminance. Despite this equality of luminance, substantial degrees of lightness constancy are found. In such an experiment, every one of the factors to which Hering attributed lightness constancy is absent. Hering's weak theory of lightness constancy could have been dismissed many years earlier had this important line of work not been forgotten.

Articulation and Field Size

In his early experiments that established the basic methods for studying lightness constancy, David Katz found that the degree of constancy obtained is strongly dependent on the degree of articulation (roughly the number of elements) within each field of illumination. This finding has important implications for lightness theories. For example, it is not at all clear how this finding can be accommodated to the decomposition models, not to mention several weaker models. For the greater part of the 20th century this concept languished in obscurity, even though its potent effects showed up in one publication after another (Arend & Goldstein, 1987; Gilchrist, et al, 1999; Kraft et al., 2002; Linnell & Foster, 2002; Schirillo et al., 1990; Schirillo & Arend, 1995; Wishart et al., 1997). Had I not brought this concept to the attention of the lightness community, it might have remained hidden for many more years.

DRIVING A THEORY OF LIGHTNESS

Theories of lightness have primarily been motivated in one of three ways: by physiology, by veridicality, and by error. All of these can be seen in the history.

Motivation by Physiology

The logic of the physiological approach is initially compelling. Because the problem of lightness computation has already been solved by human biology, we should look and see how it has been implemented. This should give us important clues. There is of course the hardware/software distinction. Computers based on different physical principles could be programmed to carry out the same algorithm. But in biological systems one would not expect the hardware (or wetware) and the software to be so distinct.

A further appeal of this approach lies in the quest for materialism. Breakthroughs in other sciences have been associated with the shift from mysticism to materialism, and there has long been an intuition that the same is needed in psychology. This was especially true in the 1950s and 1960s, when the behaviorists thought they could avoid idealism by talking strictly about bodily processes.

In principle, the notion that one should use the facts of physiology to constrain a theory of lightness is hard to challenge. Lightness perception, after all, in the end depends on underlying physiological processes. But although this approach is widely acclaimed today, it contains a hidden danger. We have, it is true, an enormous collection of physiological facts that have been gathered. The problem is that no one knows how to put this collection of facts together into a coherent story. We lack even a theory of how the brain works. We have only a metaphor: the computer.

Isolated physiological facts are of little use in constraining a theory of lightness, even when we know which facts to select. Currently this array of physiological facts can be organized in some coherent way only by invoking a collection of traditional, often unconscious, assumptions. The photometer metaphor is one of these assumptions. Another assumption is that the visual system works fundamentally on the order of a computer. Nerve fibers are treated like electrical wires. Ultimately what happens is that the lightness theory is constrained, not so much by the facts of physiology but by all these assumptions themselves.

The danger of using assumptions to constrain theories should be self-evident. This I believe is the reason why attempts to drive lightness theory by physiology have not led to the anticipated successes. Take the familiar example of lateral inhibition. There is nothing wrong with this concept; it is a physiological fact. But what does it imply about lightness perception? There are many ways to think about lateral inhibition. Initially people thought about it in terms of a pointwise encoding of the retinal image. But lurking beneath this concept was the old assumption of local determination—that is, the constancy hypothesis. This approach brings us to the problem of the missing scallops. The decomposition modelers took a different approach, treating lateral inhibition as a central part of the mechanism by which luminance ratios are encoded. With this approach, the problem of the missing scallops evaporates. Or consider the notion of edge enhancement. The concept of lateral inhibition does not necessarily mean edge enhancement; it could simply mean edge encoding. Lateral inhibition is surely a concrete neural mechanism. But if it can be interpreted in so many ways, how does it constrain a model of lightness?

It is premature to use physiological findings to guide lightness theory. But the results of psychophysical work can and must be used to guide the study of the brain. For a brief but excellent review of the current challenges for neuroscience posed by recent psychophysical findings, see Paradiso (2000).

Motivation by Veridicality

In the history of lightness, those periods of greatest advance have been driven by the quest for veridicality. Indeed, the field was launched by the challenge posed by the surprising veridicality of lightness perception, a veridicality that did not follow from the known physiology. Our basic psychophysical methods were created by Katz in an effort to measure and understand the achievement of veridicality. The Gestalt emphasis on constancy and veridicality as the core challenge of perception led to major advances. In the postwar years there was little concern for veridicality. Stimuli had little similarity to, or relevance for, complex natural images. Lightness theory languished. Finally, in the last third of the 20th century, we saw the development of more sophisticated models of lightness, driven by the challenge presented by machine vision. Uninterested in either physiology or errors, machine vision cares only about veridicality.

There are solid reasons for using veridicality to drive a model. As Marr (1982, p. 27) has noted, "an algorithm is likely to be understood more readily by understanding the nature of the problem being solved than by examining the mechanism (and the hardware) in which it is embodied."

Motivation by Error

One cannot deny the importance of veridicality or the inspiration it has provided to theory. Constancy, despite its imperfections, must be central to any theory. Yet I would argue that the pattern of lightness errors shown by humans constitutes a powerful, though largely neglected, constraint on theories. Lightness errors are everywhere, though often tiny. Crucially, they are systematic, not random! And they can come only from the visual system itself.

The use of errors is not new, but I argue that it has been applied to lightness only in fits and starts. Hering's theory was driven by a prominent error: simultaneous contrast. But it left him with a wholly inadequate account of constancy, predicting errors too large and errors that do not occur. Other errors, such as illumination-dependent failures of constancy, were completely left out. Modeling "brightness" errors has become a cottage industry, but the range of errors modeled is still pretty limited.[3] Lightness errors fall into two broad classes— essentially failures of illumination-dependent and background-dependent constancy. These two classes are quite different in character, and I argue that the primary test of a theory of lightness errors is whether it can explain, in principle, errors of both classes.

Frameworks versus Receptive Fields

Lightness theories are divided by a very important watershed concerning the units of analysis. While brightness models talk about receptive fields and spatial filtering, Gestalt theories talk about frames of reference, components, and intrinsic images. What is the relationship between these analytic tools? In the first case we are talking about units of analysis that belong to the organism itself; they are part of the neural anatomy. In the second case we are talking about units of analysis that belong to the image.

Contrast and brightness models are essentially structure-blind; the structure of the image is largely ignored. While an edge can be detected, the spatial filters are indifferent to the nature of the edge, whether it is a reflectance edge or an illuminance edge, for example. The structure they are concerned with is only the structure of the nervous system, and that mainly at the front end. This explains why these models fail to explain so many lightness phenomena, especially the central problem of lightness constancy.

Decomposition models and anchoring models, on the other hand, largely ignore the structure of the nervous system. They concentrate on determining the algorithms or processes that are logically required to derive the features of our visual experience from the retinal image, without concern for questions of implementation.

When anchoring theory talks about a local framework, "local" is not defined merely by retinal proximity. That would be structure-blind. Rather, elements that are part of a local framework are elements that belong together, according to the principles of grouping. Proximity is only one of those principles. Here perhaps the Kardos term "relevant framework" may be more apt.

Ultimately we must talk about both the structure of the nervous system and the structure of the image. More importantly, we must discover how the former can be used to parse the latter. We have touched upon this issue before, in relation to Helson's adaptation-level theory and Adelson's adaptive windows. If perception is to be at all veridical, there must be a rough match between the structure of the receptive mechanisms and the structure of the image/world.

Besides ignoring the structure of the image, brightness models, in my opinion, view the nervous system in too static a way. Several decades ago, receptive fields, mainly studied in unconscious animals, were treated as fixed. Now we know that they are much more flexible. Stimulus information from "outside" the receptive field also has an impact. Brain cells were said not to regenerate, but now we know that they do.

I once stood in the front hall of a house. At the end of the hall I saw the front door, which contained a transparent red window. I perceived the redness, but through the window I also saw the green grass and the white picket fence. Then I walked up to the door and pressed my face against the glass so that it filled my visual field. I still saw the green grass and the white fence, but the redness disappeared. This can be called adaptation. But my point is that in both cases, my visual system decomposed the image into its component colors, perhaps using adaptation in the second case and a Bergström-type analysis in the first case. It is important to consider the goal of the system, as Marr (1982, p. 25) has emphasized, which in this case is to decompose the layers. The visual system is flexible in its use of different mechanisms under different conditions. It is a mistake to become fixated on individual mechanisms.

One of the more striking recent discoveries comes from work in which the optic nerve of the ferret was detached from the visual cortex and attached to the auditory cortex (Roe, Pallas, Kwon & Sur, 1990). Not only did the behavioral evidence suggest that the ferret could see, but surprisingly, the auditory cortex acquired the functional architecture of the visual cortex, developing pinwheel stripes. This result shows that neural structure cannot be treated like some rigid machine into whose maw the image is blindly fed. There is an interchange between the nervous system and the optic array, and each can change the other.

The cost of ignoring the structure of the image is far greater than the cost of ignoring the structure of the nervous system. No model of lightness can succeed without an explicit recognition of the structure of the image. Nervous system structure, however, can be ignored, at least in the short run. The parallels between machine vision and human vision show that the problem of vision can be defined in formal terms, without being tied to particular mechanisms. Is the illumination taken into account or is it not? Are relative luminances anchored by the highest luminance or by the average? Are the ambiguities of the image resolved logically, probabilistically, or by a fundamental simplicity principle? What role does past experience play? These questions need not be held hostage to physiology. They can be answered without solving the mysteries of the brain. Indeed, the resulting answers will tell us much about what to look for in the brain.

The most effective in dealing with the structure of the image are the decomposition models and the anchoring models. The problem of segmenting frameworks, found in anchoring theory, is roughly equivalent to the problem of classifying edges, found in intrinsic image models. I recognize that many workers are skeptical about the concept of frameworks, and perhaps less so about the concept of edge classification. But something like these notions will have to be part of the final theory. After all, frameworks of illumination do exist in the external world, and their existence produces the central problem of lightness constancy. Ultimately this structure that exists in the world must be reflected in the visual software. Lightness constancy cannot be the accidental byproduct of a structure-blind visual system.

Of all the theories of lightness we have reviewed, I find the anchoring approach, including the Kardos co-determination principle, if not most elegant, the most compelling. This is because I find the logic of errors most compelling. The pattern of errors must be the signature of the visual software, and I find no other model capable of accounting for such an extensive portion of the by-now vast array of documented lightness errors. No other model can bridge the two main classes of error: background-dependent and illumination-dependent.

In terms of predicting veridicality, the decomposition models appear most adequate. Still, those models predict too much veridicality. The anchoring model predicts veridicality only to the extent that it exists. But the decomposition models effectively satisfy the constraints of phenomenology. We do experience a pattern of illumination projected onto a pattern of surface colors. And recent work involving perceived transparency (Anderson & Winawer, 2005; Singh, 2004) has produced results that appear to require a layered analysis and are not easily accommodated to the anchoring approach.

If the principle of co-determination, central to anchoring theory, can be translated into the language of partial decomposition (partial classification or partial integration), we could yet see an integration of these two kinds of models. Such an account could satisfy the twin constraints of veridicality and error.

Glossary

The following definitions apply mostly to the achromatic domain. "Nontechnical" means less precise description in ordinary language.

achromatic versus chromatic: In the case of surfaces, *achromatic* refers to colors along the scale of grays from black to white, whereas *chromatic* refers to colors that vary in hue, saturation, and lightness. In the case of lights, achromatic means neutral.

anchoring rule: a rule used for mapping relative luminance onto lightness. The rule identifies a measure of relative luminance (like highest luminance) with a specific lightness value (like white).

applicability assumption: A key assumption in anchoring theory that the rules of lightness computation found in very simple images also apply to frameworks embedded in complex images, subject to the principle of co-determination.

area rule: A function that describes the manner in which the lightness of a surface depends on its relative area, with relative luminance held constant.

articulation: Refers to Katz's finding that the degree of lightness constancy within a field of illumination is proportionate to the degree of complexity within that field. In this work, articulation is operationally defined as the number of elements within a framework.

assimilation: A lightness illusion in which the lightness of a target surface becomes more similar to that of neighboring regions. The outcome is opposite that of a contrast illusion.

background-independent constancy: Lightness constancy despite a change in the background surrounding a target surface.

brightness: Perceived luminance; the apparent amount of light coming to the eye from a region of the field

co-determination: The claim by Kardos (1934) that the lightness of a surface is partly determined by the value computed within its local framework and partly determined by the value computed relative to a neighboring framework (or in this work, the global framework).

coplanar ratio principle: The claim that lightness depends on the luminance ratio between retinally adjacent surfaces that are perceived to lie in the same plane in 3D space.

contrast: Use of the term *contrast* without modifiers has produced a great deal of confusion in the literature due to its several very different usages. In this book we have made an effort to minimize the use of the term *contrast* alone.

(a) *physical contrast:* relative luminance; common measures are Weber contrast ($\Delta L/L_b$) and Michelson contrast (Lmax − Lmin/Lmax + Lmin)
(b) *apparent contrast:* the perceived amount of a luminance transition
(c) a set of perceptual phenomena in which the color of a visual region is altered in a direction away from that of either an adjacent (simultaneous contrast) or a preceding (successive contrast) visual region
(d) a theoretical mechanism or process proposed to explain (c). Historically this use of the term has been associated with neural mechanisms like lateral inhibition.

Further discussion of these confusions can be found on page 8.

countershaded backgrounds: A technique used in asymmetric matching, lightness constancy experiments in which one target is placed in front of a highly illuminated dark gray background while the other target is placed in front of a dimly illuminated light gray background. The two backgrounds have equal luminance.

doctrine of local determination: The early belief that visual experience corresponds on a point-by-point basis to local stimulation. Called the constancy hypothesis by the Gestaltists.

edge classification: A hypothetical process by which each luminance edge in the image is determined to represent either a change of reflectance or a change of illumination.

edge integration: A method of calculating the luminance ratio between two remote patches of the image by mathematically integrating all luminance edges that lie along a path between the two patches.

ganzfeld: A simple image (typically completely homogeneous) that fills the observer's entire visual field.

global framework: A framework composed of the entire visual field.

highest luminance rule: The claim that the highest luminance within a framework is automatically computed to be white.

illegitimate errors: Lightness errors due to the particular method by which lightness is computed, despite sufficient stimulus information.

illuminance: In the technical definition, the illuminance at a point of a surface is the quotient of the luminous flux incident on an infinitesimal element of the surface containing the point under consideration, by the area of that surface element

$$E = K_m \int_\lambda E_{e,\lambda} V(\lambda) \, d\lambda$$

where K_m is a units constant, $E_{e,\lambda}$ is spectral irradiance, and $V(\lambda)$ is the CIE photopic luminous efficiency function (Wyszecki & Stiles, 1967).

illuminance edge: A luminance edge in the retinal image caused by a change of illumination in the distal stimulus.

illumination: the nontechnical word for illuminance.

illumination-independent constancy: Lightness constancy despite a change of illumination on the target surface.

intrinsic image: A hypothetical component image that represents the distribution of a particular property such as reflectance or illumination level across the visual field.

law of field size: Katz's claim that the degree of lightness constancy within a field of illumination is proportionate to the size of the field.

legitimate errors: Lightness errors due to insufficient stimulus information that would be made by an ideal observer.

lightness: perceived reflectance. Lightness is the dimension of perceived surface color that in the achromatic domain ranges from white to black. In the chromatic domain, lightness refers to the intensitive dimension.

lightness constancy: The stability of the perceived lightness of a surface despite changes in the proximal stimulus. These proximal changes are caused by factors such as changes in the level of illumination, changes in the background of a surface, and changes of orientation of the surface.

local framework: A collection of image patches that perceptually group with each other for purposes of lightness computation. The computational equivalent of a field of illumination.

luminance: In the technical definition, the luminance at a point of a surface and in a given direction is the quotient of the luminous intensity in the given direction of an infinitesimal element of the surface containing the point under consideration, by the orthogonally projected area of the surface element on a plane perpendicular to the given direction

$$L = K_m \int_\lambda L_{e,\lambda} V(\lambda) \, d\lambda$$

where K_m is a units constant, $L_{e,\lambda}$ is spectral radiance, and $V(\lambda)$ is the CIE photopic luminous efficiency function (Wyszecki & Stiles, 1967).
   The nontechnical definition is the physical amount of light reaching a viewpoint from a given region of the optic array; sometimes referred to as intensity. Note that intensity has a technical definition as a description of point sources (Wyszecki & Stiles, 1967).

luminance edge versus luminance gradient: in nontechnical usage, edge typically refers to an abrupt spatial transition from one luminance to another. Gradient refers to a gradual spatial change of luminance. Gradient also has a specific mathematical definition: the directional rate of change over space or time.

memory color: The hypothesis that the remembered color of a familiar object influences its perceived color.

reflectance: The technical definition is the ratio of the reflected radiant flux (or power) to incident radiant flux (or power) (Wyszecki & Stiles, 1967).
Spectral Reflectance:

$$\rho\ (\lambda) = \frac{P_\lambda}{P_{0\lambda}}$$

where P_λ is the reflected spectral power and $P_{0\lambda}$ is the incident spectral power.
Luminous Reflectance:

$$\rho = \frac{\int_\lambda \rho(\lambda)\ V(\lambda)\ P_{0\lambda}\ d\lambda}{\int_\lambda V(\lambda)\ P_{0\lambda}\ d\lambda}$$

where $P_{0\lambda}$ is the incident spectral power, $\rho(\lambda)$ is spectral reflectance, and $V(\lambda)$ is the CIE luminous efficiency function.

The nontechnical definition is the percentage of light a surface reflects; physical blackness or whiteness of a surface. Reflectance, unless otherwise specified, means luminous reflectance.

reflectance edge: A luminance edge in the retinal image caused by a change of reflectance in the distal stimulus.

self-luminosity: The visual property of a surface that appears to glow or emit light.

scale normalization: A hypothetical process by which the perceived range of grays in a framework shifts toward the standard white/black range (30:1), relative to the physical range in the stimulus.

Notes

Chapter 1

1. Other problems involve changes in the background of the object, and changes in the media intervening between the eye and the object.

2. For example, the question of whether simultaneous lightness contrast depends on the physical luminance of the backgrounds or on the perceived lightness of the backgrounds has been asked and answered over a dozen times. Each time the answer has been promptly forgotten.

Chapter 2

1. Köhler, 1947, p. 95.

2. Although my approach is historical, I will, where appropriate, include modern references to show the relevance of historical ideas to contemporary research.

3. Intensity of the illumination is inversely related to the square of the distance between the light source and the illuminated surface.

Chapter 3

1. A match between two adjacent regions that are indistinguishable.

2. The size of the white sector on the comparison disk indicates 100% constancy when equal to that of the standard disk, 0% constancy when disk luminances are equated using a reduction screen. The degree of constancy can then be determined by locating, between these two values, the value chosen by the subject as a perceptual match.

3. Keep in mind, of course, that if the surround illumination is changed,

special arrangements are necessary to prevent the target luminance from changing at the same time.

4. How ironic that terms like transformation and constancy could be synonyms!

5. Wolff may have overstated this claim (see Gibbs & Lawson, 1974).

Chapter 4

1. Indeed, had Gelb merely placed the observer in the abnormal illumination but allowed the reduction screen to remain in the normal illumination, he would not have gotten his paradoxical result.

2. In fact, lightness judgments are more faithful to reflectance values than are brightness judgments faithful to luminance values.

3. This supports the Gestalt claim that primitive vision is 3D, not 2D.

4. That is, a difference on the scale of log reflectance, which is equivalent to a reflectance ratio.

5. Koffka does not specify the color.

6. Katz may have been wrong on the facts here (König, 1897; Shlaer, 1937).

7. This idea continues to surface on a regular basis. See Helson (1964) and Buchsbaum (1980).

8. Katz argued that contrary to Gelb: (1) one can produce a change of perceived illumination without a change in the articulation of the scene and (2) one can change the articulation of the scene without producing a change in the perceived illumination. He demonstrated the first by showing that when a scene is viewed through the blades of an episcotister, the perceived illumination varies with the proportion of the opaque sector, even though this does not change the articulation of the scene. He demonstrated the second point by showing that objects can be added to or removed from a scene with no change in the perceived illumination.

9. Koffka (1932, p. 330) claimed that Katz had missed the point, although neither Koffka nor Gelb had made their position very clear. It is not clear whether Katz finally came to appreciate Gelb's emphasis on perceptual structure. To concede on this point would have been to relinquish the last component of his constancy theory.

10. Koffka uses 60:1 as the range between white paper and black paper, but the range of commercially available papers is more like 30:1.

11. Rock has shown that several grouping factors are defined not in retinal terms but in phenomenal terms, arguing that this presents a problem for Gestalt theory. But here we find Koffka using a phenomenal definition of coplanarity (it could scarcely be defined retinally). So rather than the exclusive choice posed by Rock, Koffka defines the grouping factors in both retinal and phenomenal terms, with the latter dependent on the former.

12. In fact, it turns only light middle gray (see p. 307).

13. The disk appears black only when the white paper totally surrounds it.

14. The Kardos illusion is very robust and simple to demonstrate to a class. In a darkened room, illuminate a large background wall using an overhead projector placed at a great enough distance. Within this beam, perhaps 5 to 10 feet in front of the wall, suspend a white paper by a rod that extends

horizontally behind the paper. Place a small piece of black paper on the overhead projector so that it casts a shadow just a bit larger than the suspended white paper. If the target does not appear black enough, it means there is too much secondary illumination reaching it. Make sure the projector beam does not illuminate surfaces that face the target and otherwise try to reduce any light reflected onto the target. Such sources can easily be identified by placing your head in the position of the target facing the projector.

15. Dark grays are predicted to appear darker as the illumination is increased, but in fact they become lighter. Results to the contrary by Hess and Pretori (1894) have been shown to be entirely due to an artifact of their method (see p. 96).

16. Of course, because the stimulus and the object lie in totally different universes, these poles can, at best, serve only as a heuristic.

Chapter 5

1. J.J. Gibson offered perhaps the most sophisticated S-R account of perception, and he did so by defining the stimulus in a much more sophisticated way. But Gibson said very little about lightness perception. What he did say was heavily influenced by his years with Koffka at Smith College.

2. For example, Wallach told me himself that he had been completely unaware of the Hess and Pretori experiments when he published his work in 1948.

3. This ratio is computed using log reflectance. If simple reflectance is used the ratio is 15:1, and in Munsell units the ratio is 6:1.

4. This ratio is computed using log reflectance. If simple reflectance is used the ratio is 3.5:1, and in Munsell units the ratio is 5.5:1.

5. This claim about the appearance of black finds no support in Katz. Katz distinguished three qualities in achromatic surface colors: brightness, insistence, and pronouncedness. In current terminology, these are lightness, brightness, and pronouncedness. But according to Katz, none of these drops in value when the illumination on a black surface increases. Lightness would increase some due to failure of constancy. Brightness would increase because the luminance has increased. And by Katz's definition, white surfaces are more "pronounced" under bright illumination while black surfaces are more "pronounced" under low illumination.

6. Even Wallach never claimed it applies to increments.

7. These conclusions apply to simple center/surround stimuli. They do not necessarily apply to more complex images, or to simple stimuli when edge integration is prevented (Whittle & Challands, 1969).

8. It inspired my work. When I saw a disk of constant luminance vary between white and black as the luminance of the surround was varied, I was hooked.

9. Indeed, they have been unable to assign any strength at all, in terms of either Munsell values or perceived reflectance values.

10. Wallach described these experiments to me in 1975, in discussions we had in relation to his role as a member of my dissertation committee.

11. Black = Munsell 2.0; White = Munsell 9.5.

Chapter 6

1. Metelli's (1970) model of transparency was an inverse optics model that predated the computational period. It held that color scission is the inverse of color fusion.

2. I have called this the photometer metaphor (Gilchrist, 1994).

3. In principle this could be done with both eyes, but given that the tremor movements of the two eyes are uncorrelated, the experiment is normally done with a single eye while the other eye is closed.

4. Wallach attributed this error to a compromise, not between relative and absolute luminance, but between a strong effect of the local luminance ratio and a weaker effect of more remote ratios.

5. "Brighter" and "more brightly illuminated" may sound like the same thing but can potentially be distinguished. The test is whether a dark-gray surface in high illumination can appear both less bright but more brightly illuminated than a light-gray surface in lower illumination.

6. They can be made visible, however. Look at a blank white surface through a pinhole placed very close to the pupil and oscillate the pinhole quickly within the area of the pupil.

7. A decrement can be seen as one part of a group of patches that together compose a self-luminous part of the scene—such as a TV image—but it may not be correct to say that the decrement itself appears self-luminous.

8. The possibility that our results could be due to changes in surrounding luminance caused by the reduction screen itself was ruled out in a control condition.

9. The opposite pattern is found for illumination-independent constancy: better constancy for decrements than increments.

10. For example, luminance matching in a contrast experiment means zero contrast, and luminance matching in a constancy experiment means zero constancy.

11. Under laboratory conditions, using a simple disk/annulus display seen within a dark field, at least for decremental centers, one obtains so-called contrast effects that are roughly equal to those in constancy experiments. But, as noted on page 8, this phenomenon is more aptly treated as constancy rather than contrast.

12. I don't believe that Rock had read the work of Kardos.

13. The vertical strip was necessary to make its location clear.

14. Total luminance range was 900:1 in one condition and 2,000:1 in another.

15. A within-group comparison showed less difference between conditions, consistent with the hysteresis effect I reported in 1980.

16. An additional control condition proved that these results could not have been due to inhibition from changes in the stimulus beyond the display itself.

Chapter 7

1. I am aware that Johansson called himself a Gibsonian, but I still maintain that his is more a Gestalt theory. For one thing, he postulates an internal algorithm for processing the stimulus.

2. Except as it sets the gain for the disk/annulus border.

3. When annulus luminance is less than disk luminance but not too much less, increases in annulus luminance paradoxically make the disk appear slightly brighter.

4. Both Kingdom and Todorović, authors of earlier models, have told me they now endorse the ODOG model.

Chapter 9

1. In fact we are making a statement that goes well beyond any surface in the scene. To see a surface as white means to see it as being as light as any surface we have ever seen in our entire visual experience. In this sense, of course, it is not strictly true that there is an absolute quality in our lightness percepts. Rather, we experience the lightness of a given surface in relationship to every other surface we have ever seen. It is this kind of comprehensive relationship that allows us, in practice, to speak of an absolute quality in the lightness percept.

2. Helson gave a clear anchoring rule (average luminance) but neglected the scaling question (mapping of luminance intervals onto lightness intervals). Wallach, on the other hand, gave a clear scaling rule (ratio principle) while he tended to gloss over the anchoring problem.

3. Heinemann (1972, p. 146) offered the disk/annulus as the simplest stimulus for studying the effects of relative luminance. But our split dome removes the complication of an outer background of darkness, and it avoids the geometric asymmetry of the disk/annulus.

4. Presumably an account of luminosity in terms of the average luminance rule would assign luminosity to a luminance value relatively far above the average. But Bonato and Gilchrist showed, using a pair of dihedral Mondrians, that luminosity can occur for a luminance value very close to the average luminance (see Chapter 9).

5. Heinemann and Chase (1995) use the terms *brightness depression* and *brightness enhancement*. Brightness depression is the same as what I have called downward induction. But while brightness enhancement and upward induction both result in a brightening of the lighter region, in upward induction this is caused by an increasing luminance difference, and in brightness enhancement it is caused by a decreasing luminance difference.

6. In coining the terms *upward* and *downward induction*, I make no assumption regarding physiological mechanism; I intend only the psychophysical sense of a transfer of effect.

7. Bressan (submitted) has proposed a surround rule in which the surround itself does not necessarily have to appear white, but merely function as white in the lightness computation for the surrounded figure.

8. This conflict helps to explain the qualitative effect of area. When the region of highest luminance also has the largest area, there is no conflict be-

tween highest luminance and largest area. The area rule describes how the conflict is managed by the visual system, and thus the rule applies only when the conflict exists, namely within the qualitative boundaries when the higher luminance has the lesser area.

9. Perceived gamut less than actual gamut.

10. This is true whether the area ratio is computed based on retinal area, as reported by Heinemann, or based on perceived area (Bonato & Cataliotti, 2000; Bonato & Gilchrist, 1999), which includes some portion of the amodal region of the larger disk (not annulus) perceived to lie behind the inner disk.

Chapter 10

1. Still, this error tells us something about the visual system. It tells us that the system does not have reflectance detectors, that lightness must be determined simply from the pattern of light in the retinal image. Stabilized images also produce legitimate errors. Retinally stabilizing edges prevents their encoding. Dramatic errors occur in a ganzfeld. When the surface of the ganzfeld can be seen at all (by virtue of visible microtexture), a ganzfeld painted black will appear white. Again, the image produced by a white ganzfeld is identical to that produced by a black ganzfeld with higher illumination.

2. Which is the case can be determined only with the use of a Munsell chart.

3. Over-constancy can be obtained. But it seems to occur only when the stimulus produces a strong background-dependent failure that opposes in direction a weaker illumination-dependent failure. Thus, a gray target on a black background standing in low illumination can appear lighter than a gray target on a light background standing in an adjacent region of high illumination.

4. Unfortunately, the term "simultaneous contrast" is also used for a very different stimulus usually involving two luminous regions within a totally dark (not black) surround (see, for instance, Heinemann, 1955). That phenomenon, which produces much larger effects, is treated separately under the topic of brightness induction.

5. The reverse contrast effect here may not be obvious but is consistently reported by naïve observers.

6. Although Adelson studies lightness, he has (reasonably) used a brightness task to probe pictorial displays like the corrugated plaid as a shorthand way to elicit judgments based on the apparent lightness of the target patches on the CRT screen (or on the paper), rather than on the lightness within the scene depicted in the display.

7. Ironically, however, Evans (1948, p. 166) concluded from the Hess and Pretori experiments that "normal brightness constancy is identical with simultaneous contrast."

Chapter 11

1. The name "staircase Gelb effect" was suggested by Bill Ross and Luiz Pessoa.

2. This mistake was later corrected by using steps equal in log reflectance. The Munsell scale is not a log scale.

3. A look at Figure 5 from Cataliotti and Gilchrist (1995) suggests that there might be a real but tiny effect of viewing distance. But even this effect might reflect a small failure of size constancy, as other work shows that perceived size does influence the amount of compression.

4. Again, the data hint at a slightly greater darkening for adjacent surfaces that might reach significance with greater power.

5. Diamond (1953) did not take Munsell matches, but his brightness matches show the same shallow drop that we obtained in our data.

6. Some would appear self-luminous as well. But, as other work we conducted made clear, that is a separate matter.

7. This was achieved by turning off the room lights and placing the observer in a closed booth so that the five squares were seen through an aperture.

8. An exception to this rule occurs when the local framework does not contain a white surface

9. Bringing in global anchoring doesn't help either, because the values so produced are likely to be even further in error.

10. The relevant/foreign construction cannot explain the simultaneous lightness contrast illusion without invoking some additional assumptions.

11. Possibly also self-luminous, but that is a different matter.

12. Virtually all occlusion edges are compound; they represent a change in both reflectance and illuminance.

13. This analysis is essentially the same as that given in Chapter 10 for why illumination-independent constancy is poor with dark backgrounds.

14. This is similar to proposals by Anderson (1997) and Todorović (1997), but Anderson's proposal involves transparency and Todorović's proposal is couched in terms of contrast.

15. If the strength is due to articulation it shows, as we have found elsewhere, that articulation is defined only by the number of distinct surfaces within a group, not by the number of different gray levels.

16. Gillam (1987) has shown that a stimulus very much like our scrambled group produces stronger subjective contour than a regular group (as long as the endpoint alignment is preserved). This suggests that the net effect of our manipulation did not weaken the group.

17. Scale normalization affects only the darker region in each local frame because locally the lighter region anchors on white.

18. The Munsell value equivalent for a given reflectance can be obtained from a table (Judd, 1966, p. 849) or by a formula (Wyszecki & Stiles, 1967, p. 478).

19. There are some good reasons to believe that the figure belongs much more strongly to the surrounding background than vice versa (see Fig. 11.11).

Chapter 12

1. It is apparently not true for color constancy, however, due to a maturational problem with the cones.

2. Brightness is not the same thing as perceived brightness of the illumination. Surfaces standing in the same region of illumination differ in brightness if they differ in luminance.

3. Though I never considered my approach to be Helmholtzian.

4. He used the average luminance rather than the highest.

5. Strangely, though, the brightness of the illumination within the framework is referred to as the "size of the RVSI."

Chapter 13

1. And after all, this objective reference in visual perception also represents another kind of advance for materialism. Visual experience is a product of the objective environment.

2. This might happen when we judge the brightness of a light bulb.

3. Indeed, they are more concerned with modeling brightness errors (deviations from luminance matching) than lightness errors (deviations from reflectance matching).

References

Adelson, E. H. (1993). Perceptual organization and the judgment of brightness. *Science, 262,* 2042–2044.

Adelson, E. H. (2000). Lightness perception and lightness illusions. In M. Gazzaniga (Ed.), *The New Cognitive Neuroscience* (2nd ed., pp. 339–351). Cambridge, MA: MIT Press.

Adelson, E. H., & Pentland, A. P. (1996). The perception of shading and reflectance. In D. Knill & W. Richards (Eds.), *Perception as Bayesian Inference* (pp. 409–423). New York: Cambridge University Press.

Adrian, E. (1928). *The Basis of Sensations.* London: Christophers.

Agostini, T., & Bruno, N. (1996). Lightness contrast in CRT and paper-and-illuminant displays. *Perception and Psychophysics, 58*(2), 250–258.

Agostini, T., & Galmonte, A. (1997). Luminance gradients, perceived illumination, and lightness perception. *Review of Psychology, 4*(1–2), 3–6.

Agostini, T., & Galmonte, A. (1999). Spatial articulation affects lightness. *Perception and Psychophysics, 61*(7), 1345–1355.

Agostini, T., & Galmonte, A. (2000). Contrast and assimilation: the belongingness paradox. *Review of Psychology, 7*(1–2), 3–7.

Agostini, T., & Galmonte, A. (2002). Perceptual organization overcomes the effect of local surround in determining simultaneous lightness contrast. *Psychological Science, 13*(1), 88–92.

Agostini, T., & Proffitt, D. R. (1993). Perceptual organization evokes simultaneous lightness contrast. *Perception, 22*(3), 263–272.

Alhazen, I. (1083/1989). Book of Optics (A. Sabra, Trans.). In *The Otics of Ibn al–Haytham* (Vol. II). London: Warburg Institute.

Anderson, B. (1997). A theory of illusory lightness and transparency in monocular and binocular images: the role of contour junctions. *Perception, 26,* 419–453.

Anderson, B., & Winawer, J. (2005). Image segmentation and lightness perception. *Nature, 434,* 79–83.

Anderson, B. L. (2001). Contrasting theories of White's illusion. *Perception, 30,* 1499–1501.

Annan, V., Economou, E., Bonato, F., & Gilchrist, A. (1996). A paradox in surface lightness perception. *Investigative Opthalmology and Visual Science, 38*(4), 895.

Annan, V., & Gilchrist, A. (2004). Lightness depends on immediately prior visual experience. *Perception and Psychophysics, 66,* 943–952.

Anstis, S. M. (1967). Visual adaptation to gradual change of luminance. *Science, 155,* 710–712.

Arend, L. (1994). Multidimensional models of surface color perception. In A. Gilchrist (Ed.), *Lightness, Brightness, and Transparency.* Hillsdale, NJ: Lawrence Erlbaum Assoc., Inc.

Arend, L., & Goldstein, R. (1987a). Lightness models, gradient illusions, and curl. *Perception and Psychophysics, 42,* 65–80.

Arend, L., & Goldstein, R. (1987b). Simultaneous constancy, lightness and brightness. *Journal of the Optical Society of America A, 4,* 2281–2285.

Arend, L., & Goldstein, R. (1990). Lightness and brightness over spatial illumination gradients. *Journal of the Optical Society of America A, 7*(10), 1929–1936.

Arend, L., & Spehar, B. (1993a). Lightness, brightness and brightness contrast. I. Illumination variation. *Perception and Psychophysics, 54*(10), 446–456.

Arend, L., & Spehar, B. (1993b). Lightness, brightness and brightness contrast. II. Reflectance variation. *Perception and Psychophysics, 54*(10), 457–468.

Arend, L. E. (1973). Spatial differential and integral operations in human vision: Implications of stabilized retinal image fading. *Psychological Review, 80,* 374–395.

Arend, L. E., Buehler, J. N., & Lockhead, G. R. (1971). Difference information in brightness perception. *Perception and Psychophysics, 9,* 367–370.

Arend, L. E., & Timberlake, G. T. (1986). What is psychophysically perfect image stabilization? Do perfectly stabilized images always disappear? *Journal of the Optical Society of America A, 3*(2), 235–241.

Baker, K., & Mackintosh, I. (1955). The influence of past associations upon attributive color judgments. *Journal of Experimental Psychology, 49*(4), 281–286.

Barlow, H. B. (1953). Summation and inhibition in the frog's retina. *Journal of Physiology, 119,* 69–88.

Barlow, H. B. (1963). Slippage of contact lenses and other artefacts in relation to fading and regeneration of supposedly stable retinal images. *Quarterly Journal of Experimental Psychology, 15,* 36–51.

Barlow, H. B. (1972). Dark and light adaptation: psychophysics. In D. Jameson & L. Hurvich (Eds.), *Handbook of Sensory Physiology* (Vol. VII, pp. 1–28). Berlin: Springer.

Barlow, H. B., & Levick, W. (1969). Three factors limiting the reliable detection of light by retinal ganglion cells of the cat. *Journal of Physiology, 200,* 1–24.

Barlow, R. B., & Verillo, R. T. (1976). Brightness sensation in a ganzfeld. *Vision Research, 16,* 1291–1297.

Barrow, H. G., & Tenenbaum, J. (1978). Recovering intrinsic scene characteristics from images. In A. R. Hanson & E. M. Riseman (Eds.), *Computer Vision Systems* (pp. 3–26). Orlando: Academic Press.

Bartleson, C. J., & Breneman, E. J. (1967). Brightness perception in complex fields. *Journal of the Optical Society of America, 57,* 95.

Beck, J. (1959). Stimulus correlates for the judged illumination of a surface. *Journal of Experimental Psychology, 58,* 267–274.

Beck, J. (1961). Judgments of surface illumination and lightness. *Journal of Experimental Psychology, 61,* 368–375.

Beck, J. (1965). Apparent spatial position and the perception of lightness. *Journal of Experimental Psychology, 69,* 170–179.

Beck, J. (1966). Contrast and assimilation in lightness judgements. *Perception and Psychophysics, 1,* 342–344.

Beck, J. (1972). *Surface Color Perception:* Cornell Univ. Press.

Benary, W. (1924). Beobachtungen zu einem Experiment über Helligkeitskontrast [Observations concerning an experiment on brightness contrast]. *Psychologische Forschung, 5,* 131–142.

Benussi, V. (1916). Versuche zur Analyse taktil erweckter Scheinbewegungen. *Archiv für die gesamte Psychologie, 36,* 59–135.

Bergström, S. (1970). Contour effects on a brightness paradox. *Vision Research, 10,* 1057–1064.

Bergström, S. (1994). Color constancy: arguments for a vector model for the perception of illumination, color, and depth. In A. Gilchrist (Ed.), *Lightness, Brightness, and Transparency* (pp. 257–286). Hillsdale, NJ: Erlbaum.

Bergström, S. S. (1977). Common and relative components of reflected light as information about the illumination, colour, and three-dimensional form of objects. *Scandinavian Journal of Psychology, 18,* 180–186.

Bergström, S. S. (1982). Illumination, color, and three-dimensional form. In J. Beck (Ed.), *Organization and Representation in Perception.* Hillsdale, NJ: Erlbaum.

Bergström, S. S., Gustafsson, K. A., & Jakobsson, T. (1993). Distinctness of perceived three-dimensional form induced by modulated illumination: Effects of certain display and modulation conditions. *Perception and Psychophysics, 53*(6), 648–657.

Bergstrom, S. S., Gustafsson, K. A., & Putaansuu, J. (1984). Information about three-dimensional shape and direction of illumination in a square-wave grating. *Perception, 13,* 129–140.

Bezold, W. v. (1874). *Die farbenlehrer im Hinblick auf Kunst und Kuntsgewerbe* (S. R. Koehler, Trans.). Brunswick: Westermann.

Bindman, D., & Chubb, C. (2004). Brightness assimilation in bull's-eye displays. *Vision Research, 44*(3), 309–319.

Blake, A. (1985). Boundary conditions for lightness computation in Mondrian world. *Computer Vision, Graphics, and Image Processing, 32,* 314–327.

Blake, A. (1985). On lightness computation in the Mondrian world. In D. Ottoson & S. Zeki (Eds.), *Central and Peripheral Mechanisms of Colour Vision* (pp. 45–59). New York: MacMillan.

Blakeslee, B., & McCourt, M. E. (1999). A multiscale spatial filtering account of the White effect, simultaneous brightness contrast and grating induction. *Vision Research, 39,* 4361–4377.

Blakeslee, B., & McCourt, M. E. (2003). A multiscale spatial filtering account of brightness phenomena. In L. Harris & M. Jenkin (Eds.), *Levels of Perception* (pp. 47–72). New York: Springer.

Bloj, M., Kersten, D., & Hurlbert, A. (1999). Perception of three-dimensional shape influences colour perception through mutual illumination. *Nature, 402*, 877–879.

Bloj, M., Ripamonti, C., Mitha, K., Hauk, R., Greenwald, S., & Brainard, D. (2004). An equivalent illuminant model for the effect of surface slant on perceived lightness. *Journal of Vision, 4*, 735–746.

Bocksch, H. (1927). Farbenkonstanz und Duplizitätstheorie. *Zeitschrift für Psychologie, 102*, 338–449.

Bolanowski, S. J., & Doty, R. (1987). Perceptual "blankout" of monocular homogeneous fields (ganzfelder) is prevented with binocular viewing. *Vision Research, 27*(6), 967–982.

Bolles, R., Hulicka, I., & Hanly, B. (1959). Color judgments as a function of stimulus conditions and memory color. *Canadian Journal of Psychology, 13*, 175–185.

Bonato, F., & Cataliotti, J. (2000). The effects of figure/ground, perceived area, and target saliency on the luminosity threshold. *Perception and Psychophysics, 62*(2), 341–349.

Bonato, F., Cataliotti, J., Manente, M., & Delnero, K. (2003). T-junctions, apparent depth, and perceived lightness contrast. *Perception and Psychophysics, 65*(1), 20–30.

Bonato, F., & Gilchrist, A. (1999). Perceived area and the luminosity threshold. *Perception and Psychophysics, 61*(5), 786–797.

Bonato, F., & Gilchrist, A. L. (1994). The perception of luminosity on different backgrounds and in different illuminations. *Perception, 23*, 991–1006.

Boring, E. (1942). *Sensation and Perception in the History of Experimental Psychology*. New York: Appleton Century Crofts.

Boulter, J. F. (1980). Recognition of reflection and illumination edges by the human visual system. *Applied Optics, 19*, 2077–2079.

Boyaci, H., Maloney, L., & Hersh, S. (2003). The effect of perceived surface orientation on perceived surface albedo in binocularly viewed scenes. *Journal of Vision, 3*, 541–553.

Brenner, E., & Cornelissen, F. (1991). Spatial interactions in colour vision depend on distances between boundaries. *Naturwissenschaften, 78*, 70–73.

Bressan, P. (2001). Explaining lightness illusions. *Perception, 30*, 1031–1046.

Bressan, P. (2006). The place of white in a world of greys: A double-anchoring theory of lightness perception. *Psychological Review.*

Bressan, P., & Actis-Grosso, R. (2001). Simultaneous lightness contrast with double increments. *Perception, 30*, 889–897.

Brown, R. O. (1994). The World is not grey. *Investigative Ophthalmology and Visual Science, 35*(4), 2165.

Brown, R. O., & MacLeod, D. I. A. (1997). Color appearance depends on the variance of surround colors. *Current Biology, 7*, 844–849.

Bruner, J., Postman, L., & Rodrigues, J. (1951). Expectation and the perception of color. *American Journal of Psychology, 64*, 216–227.

Bruno, N. (1992). Lightness, equivalent backgrounds and the spatial integration of luminance. *Perception Supplement, 21*, 80.

Bruno, N. (1994). Failures of lightness constancy, edge integration, and local edge enhancement. *Vision Research, 34*, 2205–2214.

Bruno, N., Bernardis, P., & Schirillo, J. (1997). Lightness, equivalent backgrounds, and anchoring. *Perception and Psychophysics, 59*(5), 634–654.

Brunswik, E. (1929). Zur Entwicklung der Albedowahrnehmung [On the development of the perception of albedo]. *Zeitschrift für Psychologie, 109*, 40–115.

Buchsbaum, G. (1980). A spatial processor model for object color perception. *Journal of the Franklin Institute, 310*, 1–26.

Buckley, D., Frisby, J., & Freeman, J. (1994). Lightness perception can be affected by surface curvature from stereopsis. *Perception, 23*, 869–881.

Bühler, K. (1922). *Handbuch der Psychologie. I Teil: Die Struktur der Wahrnehmungen. 1 Helft: Die Erscheinungsweisen der Farben.* Jena: Fischer.

Burgh, P., & Grindley, G. C. (1962). Size of test patch and simultaneous contrast. *Quarterly Journal of Experimental Psychology, 14*, 89–93.

Burkamp, W. (1923). Versuche über das Farbenwiedererkennen der Fische. *Zeitschrift für Sinnesphysiologie, 55*, 133–170.

Burnham, R. W. (1953). Bezold's color-mixture effect. *American Journal of Psychology, 66*, 377–385.

Burzlaff, W. (1931). Methodologische Beiträge zum Problem der Farbenkonstanz [Methodological notes on the problem of color constancy]. *Zeitschrift für Psychologie, 119*, 117–235.

Cataliotti, J., & Bonato, F. (2003). Spatial and temporal lightness anchoring. *Visual Cognition, 10*(5), 621–635.

Cataliotti, J., & Gilchrist, A. L. (1995). Local and global processes in lightness perception. *Perception and Psychophysics, 57*(2), 125–135.

Chater, N. (1996). Reconciling simplicity and likelihood principles in perceptual organization. *Psychological Review, 103*(3), 566–581.

Chevreul, M. E. (1839). *De la loi du contraste simultane des couleurs* (English translation: *The Principles of Harmony and Contrast of Colors.* Birren, F. van Nos Reinold, New York, 1967). Strasbourg.

Chomsky, N. (2000). *New Horizons in the Study of Language and Mind.* Cambridge, MA: Cambridge University Press.

Chubb, C., Sperling, G., & Solomon, J. (1989). Texture interactions determine perceived contrast. *Proceedings of the National Academy of Science, 86*, 9631–9635.

Cleland, B., & Enroth-Cugell, C. (1970). Quantitative aspects of gain and latency in the cat retina. *Journal of Physiology, 206*(73–91).

Cohen, M. A., & Grossberg, S. (1984). Neural dynamics of brightness perception: Features, boundaries, diffusion and resonance. *Perception and Psychophysics, 36*, 428–456.

Cole, R. E., & Diamond, A. L. (1971). Amount of surround and test inducing separation in simultaneous brightness contrast. *Perception and Psychophysics, 9*, 125–128.

Coren, S. (1969). Brightness contrast as a function of figure–ground relations. *Journal of Experimental Psychology, 80*(3), 517–524.

Coren, S., & Komoda, M. K. (1973). The effect of cues to illumination on apparent lightness. *American Journal of Psychology, 86*(2), 345–349.

Cornsweet, T. N. (1970). *Visual Perception.* New York: Academic Press.

Craik, K. J. W. (1966). *The Nature of Psychology. A Selection of Papers, Essays, and Other Writings of the Late K. J. W. Craik.* Cambridge: Cambridge University Press.

Dalby, T. A., Saillant, M. L., & Wooten, B. R. (1995). The relation of lightness and stereoscopic depth in a simple viewing situation. *Perception and Psychophysics, 57*(3), 318–332.

Davidson, M. L. (1968). Perturbation approach to spatial brightness interaction in human vision. *Journal of the Optical Society of America, 58,* 1300–1309.

De Valois, R. L., & De Valois, K. K. (1988). *Spatial Vision.* New York: Oxford University Press.

Delk, J., & Fillenbaum, S. (1965). Differences in perceived color as a function of characteristic color. *American Journal of Psychology, 78,* 290–293.

Dennett, D. C. (1991). *Consciousness Explained.* Boston: Little, Brown.

Derrington, A., & Lennie, P. (1982). The influence of temporal frequency and adaptation level on receptive field organization of retinal ganglion cells in cat. *Journal of Physiology, 333,* 343–366.

DeWeert, C. (1991). Assimilation and contrast. In A. Valberg & B. Lee (Eds.), *From Pigments to Perception* (pp. 305–311). New York: Plenum Press.

Diamond, A. (1953). Foveal simultaneous brightness contrast as a function of inducing- and test-field luminances. *Journal of Experimental Psychology, 45,* 304–314.

Diamond, A. (1955). Foveal simultaneous brightness contrast as a function of inducing-field area. *Journal of Experimental Psychology, 50,* 144–152.

Diamond, A. (1962). Brightness of a field as a function of its area. *Journal of the Optical Society of America, 52,* 700–706.

Diamond, A. (1962). Simultaneous contrast as a function of test-field area. *Journal of Experimental Psychology, 64,* 336–346.

Ditchburn, R., & Ginsborg, B. (1952). Vision with a stabilized retinal image. *Nature, 170,* 36–37.

Duncker, K. (1939). The influence of past experience upon perceptual properties. *American Journal of Psychology, 52,* 255–265.

Dunn, B., & Leibowitz, H. (1961). The effect of separation between test and inducing fields on brightness constancy. *Journal of Experimental Psychology, 61*(6), 505–507.

Economou, E., Annan, V., & Gilchrist, A. (1998). Contrast depends on anchoring in perceptual groups. *Investigative Ophthalmology & Visual Science, 39*(4), S857.

Ellis, W. E. (1938). *A Source Book of Gestalt Psychology.* New York: The Humanities Press.

Entroth-Cugell, C., & Robson, J. (1966). The contrast sensitivity of retinal ganglion cells of the cat. *Journal of Physiology, 187,* 517–552.

Epstein, W. (1961). Phenomenal orientation and perceived achromatic color. *Journal of Psychology, 52,* 51–53.

Epstein, W. (1982). Percept–percept couplings. *Perception, 11,* 75–83.

Evans, R. (1959). *Eye, Film, and Camera in Color Photography.* New York: Wiley.

Evans, R. M. (1948). *An Introduction to Color.* New York: Wiley.

Evans, R. M. (1974). *The Perception of Color.* New York: Wiley.

Fechner, G. (1860/1966). *Elemente der Psychophysik [Elements of Psychophysics]* (H. Adler, Trans.). New York: Henry Holt.

Festinger, L., Coren, S., & Rivers, G. (1970). The effect of attention on brightness contrast and assimilation. *American Journal of Psychology, 83,* 189–207.

Feyerabend, O. (1924). Der innere Farbensinn der Jugendlichen in seiner Beziehung zu der angenaeherten Farbenkonstanz der Sehdinge. *Zeitschrift für Psychologie, 94.*

Fisher, C., Hull, C., & Holtz, P. (1956). Past experience and perception: memory color. *American Journal of Psychology, 69,* 546–560.

Flock, H. R. (1974). Stimulus structure in lightness and brightness experiments. In R. MacLeod & H. Pick (Eds.), *Perception: Essays in Honor of James J. Gibson*. Ithaca: Cornell University Press.

Flock, H. R., & Freedberg, E. (1970). Perceived angle of incidence and achromatic surface color. *Perception and Psychophysics, 8*, 251–256.

Flock, H. R., & Noguchi, K. (1970). An experimental test of Jameson and Hurvich's theory of brightness contrast. *Perception and Psychophysics, 8*, 129–136.

Foster, D., & Nascimento, S. (1994). Relational colour constancy from invariant cone–excitation ratios. *Proceedings of the Royal Society London B, 257*, 115–121.

Freeman, R. B. (1967). Contrast interpretation of brightness constancy. *Psychological Bulletin, 67*, 165–187.

Friden, T. P. (1973). Whiteness constancy: Inference or insensitivity? *Perception and Psychophysics, 1*, 81–89.

Frisby, J. P. (1979). *Seeing: Illusion, Brain, and Mind*. Oxford: Oxford University Press.

Fry, G. A. (1948). Mechanisms subserving simultaneous brightness contrast. *American Journal of Optometry, 25*, 162–178.

Fry, G. A., & Alpern, M. (1953). The effect of a peripheral glare source upon the apparent brightness of an object. *Journal of the Optical Society of America, 43*, 189–195.

Fry, G. A., & Alpern, M. (1954). The effect of veiling luminance upon the apparent brightness of an object. *American Journal of Optometry Monograph 165*.

Fuchs, W. (1923). Experimentelle Untersuchungen über das simultane Hintereinandersehen auf derselben Sehrichtung. *Zietschrift für Psychologie Abt. I(91)*, 145–235.

Gelb, A. (1929). Die "Farbenkonstanz" der Sehdinge [The color of seen things]. In W. A. von Bethe (Ed.), *Handbuch der normalen und pathologischen Physiologie* (Vol. 12, pp. 594–678).

Gelb, A. (1932). Die Erscheinungen des simultanen Kontrastes und der Eindruck der Feldbeleuchtung. *Zeitschrift für Psychologie, 127*, 42–59.

Gerbino, W. (1994). Achromatic transparency. In A. Gilchrist (Ed.), *Lightness, Brightness, and Transparency* (pp. 215–255). Hillsdale: Erlbaum.

Gerrits, H. J. M., & Vendrik, A. J. H. (1970). Simultaneous contrast, filling-in process and information processing in man's visual system. *Experimental Brain Research, 11*, 411–430.

Gershon, R., Jepson, A. D., & Tsotsos, J. K. (1986). Ambient illumination and the determination of material changes. *Journal of the Optical Society of America A, 3*, 1700–1707.

Gibbs, T., & Lawson, R. B. (1974). Simultaneous brightness contrast in stereoscopic space. *Vision Research, 14*, 983–987.

Gibson, J. J. (1966). *The Senses Considered as Perceptual Systems*. Boston: Houghton Mifflin.

Gibson, J. J. (1971). The legacies of Koffka's principles. *Journal of the History of the Behavioral Sciences, 7(1)*, 3–9.

Gibson, J. J. (1979). *The Ecological Approach to Visual Perception*. Boston: Houghton Mifflin Co.

Gibson, J. J., & Waddell, D. (1952). Homogeneous retinal stimulation and visual perception. *American Journal of Psychology, 65*, 263–270.

Gilchrist, A. (1979). The perception of surface blacks and whites. *Scientific American, 240,* 112–123.

Gilchrist, A. (1988). Lightness contrast and failures of constancy: a common explanation. *Perception and Psychophysics, 43* (5), 415–424.

Gilchrist, A. (1994). Absolute versus relative theories of lightness perception. In A. Gilchrist (Ed.), *Lightness, Brightness, and Transparency* (pp. 1–33). Hillsdale, NJ: Erlbaum.

Gilchrist, A. (1996). The deeper lesson of Alhazen. *Perception, 25,* 1133–1136.

Gilchrist, A. (2003). The importance of errors in perception. In R. M. D. Heyer (Ed.), *Colour Perception: Mind and the Physical World* (pp. 437–452). Oxford: Oxford University Press.

Gilchrist, A., & Annan, V. (2002). Articulation effects in lightness: Historical background and theoretical implications. *Perception, 31,* 141–150.

Gilchrist, A., & Bonato, F. (1995). Anchoring of lightness values in center/surround displays. *Journal of Experimental Psychology: Human Perception and Performance, 21*(6), 1427–1440.

Gilchrist, A., Bonato, F., Annan, V., & Economou, E. (1998). Depth, lightness, (and memory). *Investigative Opthalmology and Visual Science, 39*(4), S671.

Gilchrist, A., Delman, S., & Jacobsen, A. (1983). The classification and integration of edges as critical to the perception of reflectance and illumination. *Perception and Psychophysics, 33,* 425–436.

Gilchrist, A., & Economou, E. (2003). Dualistic versus monistic accounts of lightness perception. In L. Harris and M, Jenkin (Eds.), *Levels of Perception* (pp. 11–22). New York: Springer.

Gilchrist, A., & Jacobsen, A. (1984). Perception of lightness and illumination in a world of one reflectance. *Perception, 13,* 5–19.

Gilchrist, A., Kossyfidis, C., Bonato, F., Agostini, T., Cataliotti, J., Li, X., et al. (1999). An anchoring theory of lightness perception. *Psychological Review, 106*(4), 795–834.

Gilchrist, A. L. (1977). Perceived lightness depends on perceived spatial arrangement. *Science, 195,* 185–187.

Gilchrist, A. L. (1980). When does perceived lightness depend on perceived spatial arrangement? *Perception and Psychophysics, 28*(6), 527–538.

Gilchrist, A. L., & Jacobsen, A. (1983). Lightness constancy through a veiling luminance. *Journal of Experimental Psychology: Human Perception and Performance, 9,* 936–944.

Gilchrist, A. L., & Jacobsen, A. (1989). Qualitative relationships are decisive. *Perception and Psychophysics, 45*(1), 92–94.

Gilchrist, A. L., & Ramachandran, V. S. (1992). Red rooms in white light look different than white rooms in red light. *Investigative Ophthalmology and Visual Science, 33,* 756.

Gillam, B. (1987). Perceptual grouping and subjective contours. In S. Petry & G. Meyers (Eds.), *The Perception of Illusory Contours* (pp. 268–273). New York: Springer Verlag.

Gogel, W. C., & Mershon, D. H. (1969). Depth adjacency in simultaneous contrast. *Perception and Psychophysics, 5*(1), 13–17.

Granrud, C. (1987). Size constancy in newborn human infants. *Investigative Ophthalmology & Visual Science, 28 (Suppl),* 5.

Gregory, R. L. (1997). Visual illusions classified. *Trends in Cognitive Sciences, 1*(5), 190–194.

Grossberg, S. (1983). The quantized geometry of visual space: The coherent computation of depth, form, and lightness. *Behavioral and Brain Sciences, 6*(4), 625–692.

Grossberg, S. (1987). Cortical dynamics of three-dimensional form, color, and brightness perception: I. Monocular theory. *Perception and Psychophysics, 41*(2), 87–116.

Grossberg, S., & Mingolla, E. (1987). Neural dynamics of surface perception: Boundary completion, illusory figures, and neon color spreading. *Computer Vision, Graphics, & Image Processing, 37,* 116–165.

Grossberg, S., & Todorović, D. (1988). Neural dynamics of 1D and 2D brightness perception: A unified model of classical and recent phenomena. *Perception and Psychophysics, 43,* 241–277.

Güçlü, B., & Farell, B. (2005). Influence of target size and luminance on the White–Todorović effect. *Vision Research, 45,* 1165–1176.

Haimson, B. R. (1974). The response criterion, the stimulus configuration, and the relationship between brightness contrast and brightness constancy. *Perception and Psychophysics, 16* (2), 347–354.

Hanawalt, H., & Post, B. (1942). Memory trace for color. *Journal of Experimental Psychology, 30,* 216–227.

Hano, A. (1955). The role of background in brightness constancy. *Japanese Journal of Experimental Social Psychology, 30,* 189–197.

Harper, R. S. (1953). The perceptual modification of colored figures. *American Journal of Psychology, 66,* 86–89.

Hartline, H., & Graham, C. (1932). Nerve impulses from single receptors in the eye. *Journal of Cellular and Comparative Physiology, 1,* 277–295.

Hartline, H., Wagner, H., & Ratliff, F. (1956). Inhibition in the eye of Limulus. *Journal of Genetic Physiology, 39,* 357–673.

Hatfield, G., & Epstein, W. (1985). The status of the minimum principle in the theoretical analysis of visual perception. *Psychological Bulletin, 97,* 155–186.

Heggelund, P. (1974). Achromatic color vision—I: Perceptive variables of achromatic colors. *Vision Research, 14,* 1071–1079.

Heinemann, E., & Chase, S. (1995). A quantitative model for simultaneous brightness induction. *Vision Research, 35*(14), 2007–2020.

Heinemann, E. G. (1955). Simultaneous brightness induction as a function of inducing- and test-field luminances. *Journal of Experimental Psychology, 50,* 89–96.

Heinemann, E. G. (1972). Simultaneous brightness induction. In D. Jameson & L. M. Hurvich (Eds.), *Handbook of Sensory Physiology* (Vol. VII/4, pp. 146–169). Berlin: Springer.

Heinemann, E. G. (1989). Brightness contrast, brightness constancy, and the ratio principle. *Perception and Psychophysics, 45,* 89–91.

Helmholtz, H. v. (1866/1924). *Helmholtz's Treatise on Physiological Optics.* New York: Optical Society of America.

Helmholtz, H. v. (1868/1962). The recent progress in the theory of vision. In M. Kline (Ed.), *Popular Scientific Lectures* (pp. 93–185). New York: Dover.

Helson, H. (1938). Fundamental problems in color vision. I. The principle governing changes in hue, saturation and lightness of nonselective samples in chromatic illumination. *Journal of Experimental Psychology, 23,* 439–436.

Helson, H. (1943). Some factors and implications of color constancy. *Journal of the Optical Society of America A, 33*(10), 555–567.

Helson, H. (1964). *Adaptation-Level Theory.* New York: Harper & Row.

Henneman, R. H. (1935). A photometric study of the perception of object color. *Archives of Psychology, No. 179,* 5–89.

Henry, R., Mahadev, S., Urquijo, S., & Chitwood, D. (2000). Color perception through atmospheric haze. *Journal of the Optical Society of America A, 17*(5), 831–835.

Hering, E. (1874/1964). *Outlines of a Theory of the Light Sense.* (L. M. H. D. Jameson, Trans.). Cambridge, MA: Harvard University Press.

Hess, C., & Pretori, H. (1894/1970). Quantitative investigation of the lawfulness of simultaneous brightness contrast. *Perceptual and Motor Skills, 31,* 947–969.

Hochberg, J. E., & Beck, J. (1954). Apparent spatial arrangement and perceived brightness. *Journal of Experimental Psychology, 47,* 263–266.

Hochberg, J. E., Triebel, W., & Seaman, G. (1951). Color adaptation under conditions of homogeneous visual stimulation (Ganzfeld). *Journal of Experimental Psychology, 41,* 153–159.

Hoekstra, J., van der Groot, D., van den Brink, G., & Bilsen, F. (1974). The influence of the number of cycles upon the visual contrast threshold for spatial sine wave patterns. *Vision Research, 14,* 365–368.

Horeman, H. W. (1963). Inductive brightness depression as influenced by configurational conditions. *Vision Research, 3,* 121–130.

Horn, B. K. P. (1974). Determining lightness from an image. *Computer Graphics and Image Processing, 3,* 277–299.

Horn, B. K. P. (1986). *Robot Vision.* Cambridge, MA: MIT Press.

Howard, I. P., Bergström, S. S., & Ohmi, M. (1990). Shape from shading in different frames of reference. *Perception, 19*(4), 523–530.

Howe, P. (2001). A comment on the Anderson (1997), and the Ross and Pessoa (2000) explanations of White's effect. *Perception, 30,* 1023–1026.

Hsia, Y. (1943). Whiteness constancy as a function of difference in illumination. *Archives of Psychology* (284).

Hurlbert, A. (1986). Formal connections between lightness algorithms. *Journal of the Optical Society of America A, 3,* 1684–1693.

Hurlbert, A., & Ling, Y. (2005). If it's a banana, it must be yellow: The role of memory colors in color constancy [abstract]. *Journal of Vision, 5*(8), 787a.

Hurlbert, A. C., & Poggio, T. A. (1988). Synthesizing a color algorithm from examples. *Science, 239,* 482–485.

Hurvich, L. (1966). *The Perception of Brightness and Darkness.* Boston: Allyn and Bacon.

Hurvich, L., & Jameson, D. (1957). An opponent-process theory of color vision. *Psychological Review, 64*(6), 384–404.

Ikeda, M., Shinoda, H., & Mizokami, Y. (1998). Phenomena of apparent lightness interpreted by the recognized visual space of illumination. *Optical Review, 5*(6), 380–386.

Ittelson, W., & Kilpatrick, F. (1951). Experiments in perception. *Scientific American, 185,* 50–55.

Jacobsen, A., & Gilchrist, A. (1988a). Hess and Pretori revisited: Resolution of some old contradictions. *Perception and Psychophysics, 43,* 7–14.

Jacobsen, A., & Gilchrist, A. (1988b). The ratio principle holds over a million-to-one range of illumination. *Perception and Psychophysics, 43,* 1–6.

Jaensch, E. (1919). Ueber Grundfragen der Farbenpsychologie. *Zeitschrift für Psychologie, 83,* 257–265.

Jaensch, E., & Müller, E. (1920). Über die Wahrnehmungen farbloser helligkeiten und den helligkeitskontrast. *Zeitschrift für Psychologie, 83.*

Jakobsson, T., Bergström, S. S., Gustafsson, K., & Fedorovskaya, E. (1997). Ambiguities in colour constancy and shape from shading. *Perception, 26,* 531–541.

Jameson, D., & Hurvich, L. M. (1961). Complexities of perceived brightness. *Science, 133,* 174–179.

Jameson, D., & Hurvich, L. M. (1964). Theory of brightness and color contrast in human vision. *Vision Research, 4,* 135–154.

Jameson, D., & Hurvich, L. M. (1989). Essay concerning color constancy. *Annual Review of Psychology, 40,* 1–22.

Johansson, G. (1950). *Configurations in Event Perception.* Uppsala: Almqvist & Wiksell.

Johansson, G. (1964). Perception of motion and changing form. *Scandinavian Journal of Psychology, 5,* 181–208.

Johansson, G. (1975). Visual motion perception. *Scandinavian Journal of Psychology* (June), 76–88.

Johansson, G. (1977). Spatial constancy and motion in visual perception. In W. Epstein (Ed.), *Stability and Constancy in Visual Perception. Mechanisms and Processes.* New York: John Wiley & Sons.

Judd, D. (1966). Basic correlates of the visual stimulus. In S. S. Stevens (Ed.), *Handbook of Experimental Psychology* (pp. 811–867). New York: Wiley.

Judd, D. B. (1940). Hue saturation and lightness of surface colors with chromatic illumination. *Journal of the Optical Society of America, 30,* 2–32.

Julesz, B. (1971). *Foundations of Cyclopean Perception.* Chicago: University of Chicago Press.

Kanizsa, G. (1954). Il gradiente marginale come fattore dell'aspetto fenomenico dei colori [Edge gradient as a factor of the phenomenal appearance of colors]. *Archivio Italiano di Psicologia, Neurologia, e Psichiatria, 3,* 251–264.

Kardos, L. (1928). *Zeitschrift für Psychologie, 108.*

Kardos, L. (1934). Ding und Schatten [Object and shadow]. *Zeitschrift für Psychologie, Erg. bd 23.*

Katona, G. (1929). Zur Analyse der Helligkeitskonstanz. *Psychologische Forschung, 12,* 94–126.

Katona, G. (1935). Color contrast and color constancy. *Journal of Experimental Psychology, 18,* 49–63.

Katz, D. (1906). Versuche über den Einfluss der 'Gedächtnisfarben' auf die Wahrnehmungen des Gesichtssinnes. *Zentralblatt für Physiologie, 20,* 518–530.

Katz, D. (1911). Die Erscheingsweisen der Farben und ihre Beeinflussung durch die individuelle Erfahrung. *Zeitschrift für Psychologie, 7.*

Katz, D. (1935). *The World of Colour.* London: Kegan Paul, Trench, Trubner & Co.

Katz, D., & Révész, G. (1921). Experimentelle Studien zur vergleichenden Psychologie. *Zeitschrift für angewandte Psychologie, 18,* 307–320.

Kaufman, L. (1974). *Sight and Mind: An Introduction to Visual Perception.* New York: Oxford University Press.

Kersten, D., & Yuille, A. (2003). Bayesian model of object perception. *Current Opinion in Neurobiology, 13*(2), 1–9.

Kingdom, F. (1997). Simultaneous contrast: the legacies of Hering and Helmholtz. *Perception, 26*(673–677).

Kingdom, F. (1999). Old wine in new bottles? Some thoughts on Logvinenko's "Lightness induction revisited." *Perception, 28.*

Kingdom, F. (2003). Levels of brightness perception. In L. Harris & M. Jenkin (Eds.), *Levels of Perception* (pp. 23–46). New York: Springer.

Kingdom, F., & Moulden, B. (1991). White's effect and assimilation. *Vision Research, 31*(1), 151–159.

Kingdom, F., & Moulden, B. (1992). A multichannel approach to brightness coding. *Vision Research, 32*(8), 1565–1582.

Kirschmann, A. (1892). Some effects of contrast. *American Journal of Psychology, 4,* 542–557.

Knau, H. (2000). Thresholds for detecting slowly changing Ganzfeld luminances. *Journal of the Optical Society of America A, 17*(8), 1382–1387.

Knill, D., & Kersten, D. (1991). Apparent surface curvature affects lightness perception. *Nature, 351*(May), 228–230.

Koffka, K. (1915). Zur Grundlegung der Wahrnehmungpsychologie. Ein Auseinandersetzung mit V. Benussi. *Zeitschrift für Psychologie, 73,* 11–90.

Koffka, K. (1932). Some remarks on the theory of colour constancy. *Psychologische Forschung, 16,* 329–354.

Koffka, K. (1935). *Principles of Gestalt Psychology.* New York: Harcourt, Brace, and World.

Koffka, K., & Harrower, M. (1932). Colour and organization II. *Psychologische Forschung, 15,* 193–275.

Köhler, W. (1913). On unnoticed sensations and errors of judgment. *Zeitschrift für Psychologie, 66,* 51–80.

Köhler, W. (1920). *Die physeschen Gestalten in Ruhe und im stationaeren Zustand, Eine naturphilosophische Untersuchung.* Braunschweig: Friedr. Vieweg & Sohn.

Köhler, W. (1929). *Gestalt Psychology.* New York: Horace Liveright.

Köhler, W. (1947). *Gestalt Psychology.* New York: Liveright.

König, A. (1897). Die Abhängigkeit der Sehschärfe von der Beleuchtungsintensität. *Sitzungsberichte Akademie der Wissenschaften, 35,* 559–575.

Kozaki, A. (1963). A further study in the relationship between brightness constancy and contrast. *Japanese Psychological Research, 5,* 129–136.

Kozaki, A. (1965). The effect of co-existent stimuli other than the test stimulus on brightness constancy. *Japanese Psychological Research, 7,* 138–147.

Kozaki, A. (1973). Perception of lightness and brightness of achromatic surface color and impression of illumination. *Japanese Psychological Research, 15,* 194–203.

Kozaki, A., & Noguchi, K. (1976). The relationship between perceived surface-lightness and perceived illumination. *Psychological Research, 39,* 1–16.

Kraft, J., Maloney, S., & Brainard, D. (2002). Surface-illuminant ambiguity and color constancy: Effects of scene complexity and depth cues. *Perception, 31*(2), 247–263.

Krauskopf, J. (1963). Effect of retinal image stabilization on the appearance of heterochromatic targets. *Journal of the Optical Society of America, 53,* 741–744.

Kravkov, S., & Paulsen-Baschmakova, W. (1929). Über die kontraster-regende Wirkung der transformierten Farben. *Psychologische Forschung, 12,* 88–93.

Kroh, O. (1921). Über Farbenkonstanz und Farbentransformation. *Zeitschrift für Sinnesphysiologie, 52,* 113–186.

Krüger, H. (1925). Über die Unterschiedsempfindlichkeit für Beleuchtungseindrücke. *Zeitschrift für Psychologie, 96,* 58–75.

Land, E. H. (1977). The retinex theory of color vision. *Scientific American, 237,* 108–128.

Land, E. H., & McCann, J. J. (1971). Lightness and retinex theory. *Journal of the Optical Society of America A, 61,* 1–11.

Landauer, A., & Rodger, R. (1964). Effect of "apparent" instructions on brightness judgments. *Journal of Experimental Psychology, 68,* 80–84.

Langer, M., & Gilchrist, A. (2000). Color perception in a 3D scene of one reflectance. *Investigative Ophthalmology & Visual Science, 41*(4), S239.

Laurinen, P. I., Olzak, L. A., & Peromaa, T. (1997). Early cortical influences in object segregation and the perception of surface lightness. *Psychological Science, 8,* 386–390.

Leeuwenberg, E. L. J., & Buffart, H. F. J. M. (1983). An outline of coding theory: A summary of related experiments. In H. Geissler, H. F. J. M. Buffart, E. L. J. Leeuwenberg & V. Sarris (Eds.), *Modern Issues in Perception.* Amsterdam: North Holland.

Leibowitz, H. (1965). *Visual Perception.* New York: MacMillan.

Leibowitz, H., Mote, F. A., & Thurlow, W. R. (1953). Simultaneous contrast as a function of separation between test and inducing fields. *Journal of Experimental Psychology, 46,* 453–456.

Leibowitz, H., Myers, N. A., & Chinetti, P. (1955). The role of simultaneous contrast in brightness constancy. *Journal of Experimental Psychology, 50,* 15–18.

Li, X., & Gilchrist, A. (1999). Relative area and relative luminance combine to anchor surface lightness values. *Perception and Psychophysics, 61*(5), 771–785.

Lie, I. (1969). Psychophysical invariants of achromatic colour vision. I. The multidimensionality of achromatic colour experience. *Scandinavian Journal of Psychology, 10,* 167–175.

Lie, I. (1969). Psychophysical invariants of achromatic colour vision. II. Albedo/illumination substitution. *Scandinavian Journal of Psychology, 10,* 176–184.

Lie, I. (1977). Perception of illumination. *Scandinavian Journal of Psychology, 18,* 251–255.

Linnell, K., & Foster, D. (2002). Scene articulation: dependence of illuminant estimates on number of surfaces. *Perception, 31*(2), 151–159.

Locke, N. M. (1935). Color constancy in the rhesus monkey and in man. *Archiv fur Psychologie, No. 193.*

Logvinenko, A., & Kane, J. (2003). Luminance gradient can break background-independent lightness constancy. *Perception, 32,* 263–268.

Logvinenko, A., & Menshikova, G. (1994). Trade-off between achromatic colour and perceived illumination as revealed by the use of pseudoscopic inversion of apparent depth. *Perception, 23*(9), 1007–1024.

Logvinenko, A., & Ross, D. A. (2005). Adelson's tile and snake illusions: A Helmholtzian type of simultaneous lightness contrast. *Spatial Vision, 18*(1), 25–72.

Logvinenko, A. D. (1999). Lightness induction revisited. *Perception, 28,* 803–816.

Logvinenko, A. D., Kane, J., & Ross, D. A. (2002). Is lightness induction a pictorial illusion? *Perception, 31,* 73–82.

Mach, E. (1865). Über die Wirkung der räumlichen Vertheilung des Lichtreizes auf die Netzhaut. *Sitzungsberichte der mathematisch-naturwissenschaftlichen Classe der kaiserlichen Akademic der Wissenschaften, 52*(2), 303–322.

Mach, E. (1922/1959). *The Analysis of Sensations* (English translation of *Die Analyse der Empfindungen,* 1922). New York: Dover.

Mack, A., & Rock, I. (1998). *Inattentional Blindness.* Cambridge, MA: MIT Press.

MacLeod, R. B. (1932). An experimental investigation of brightness constancy. *Archives of Psychology (No. 135),* 5–102.

MacLeod, R. B. (1940). Brightness constancy in unrecognized shadows. *Journal of Experimental Psychology, 27*(1), 1–22.

MacLeod, R. B. (1947). The effects of artificial penumbrae on the brightness of included areas. In *Miscellanea Psychologica Albert Michotte* (pp. 138–154). Louvain: Institut Superieur de Philosophie.

Marr, D. (1982). *Vision.* San Francisco: Freeman.

Marr, D., & Hildreth, E. (1980). A theory of edge detection. *Proceedings of the Royal Society London B, 207,* 187–217.

Marzinski, G. (1921). Studien zur zentralen Transformation der Farben. *Zeitschrift für Psychologie, 87,* 45–72.

McArthur, J., & Moulden, B. (1999). A two-dimensional model of brightness perception based on spatial filtering consistent with retinal processing. *Vision Research, 39,* 1199–1219.

McCann, J. J. (1987). Local/Global Mechanisms for Color Constancy. *Die Farbe, 34,* 275–283.

McCann, J. J. (1988). Image processing, analysis, measurement, and quality. *Proceedings of the SPIE, 901,* 205–214.

McCann, J. J. (2001). Calculating lightnesses in a single depth plane. *Journal of Electronic Imaging, 10*(1), 110–122.

McCann, J. J., & Savoy, R. L. (1991). Measurements of lightness: Dependence on the position of a white in the field of view. *Proceedings of the SPIE, 1453,* 402–411.

McCann, J. J., Savoy, R. L., Hall, J. A. J., & Scarpetti, J. J. (1974). Visibility of continuous luminance gradients. *Vision Research, 14,* 917–927.

McCourt, M. E. (1982). A spatial frequency dependent grating-induction effect. *Vision Research, 22*(1), 119–134.

Merleau-Ponty, M. (1945/1962). *Phenomenology of Perception* (C. Smith, Trans.). London: Kegan, Paul.

Mershon, D. H. (1972). Relative contributions of depth and directional adjacency to simultaneous whiteness contrast. *Vision Research, 12,* 969–979.

Metelli, F. (1970). An algebraic development of the theory of perceptual transparency. *Ergonomics, 13,* 59–66.

Metelli, F. (1974). The perception of transparency. *Scientific American, 230,* 90–98.

Metelli, F. (1975). Shadows without penumbra. In S. Ertel, L. Kemmler & M. Stadler (Eds.), *Gestalttheorie in der modernen Psychologie* (pp. 200–209). Darmstadt: Steinkopff.

Metzger, W. (1930). Optische Untersuchungen am Ganzfeld. II. Zur Zeitschrift für Psychologier Phanomenologie des homogenen Ganzfelds. *Zeitschrift für Psychologie, 13,* 6–29.

Mikesell, W. H., & Bentley, M. (1930). Configuration and contrast. *Journal of Experimental Psychology, 13,* 1–23.

Mizokami, Y., Ikeda, M., & Shinoda, H. (1998). Lightness change as perceived in relation to the size of recognized visual space of illumination. *Optical Review, 5*(5), 315–319.

Morrone, M. C., & Burr, D. C. (1988). Feature detection in human vision: A phase-dependent energy model. *Proceedings of the Royal Society London B, 235,* 221–245.

Müller, G. (1923). Ueber Jaenschs Zurückführung des Simultankontrastes auf zentrale Transformation. *Zietschrift für Psychologie, 93.*

Musatti, C. (1953). Luce e colore nei fenomeni del contrasto simultaneo, della costanza e dell'eguagliamento [Experimental research on chromatic perception: Light and color constancy, contrast, and illumination phenomena]. *Archivio di Psicologia, Neurologia e Psichiatria, 5,* 544–577.

Nakayama, K., He, Z., & Shimojo, S. (1995). Visual surface representation: a critical link between lower-level and higher-level vision. In S. M. Kosslyn & D. N. Osherson (Eds.), *Invitation to Cognitive Science* (pp. 1–70). Cambridge, MA: MIT Press.

Nakayama, K., & Shimojo, S. (1990). da Vinci stereopsis, depth and subjective occluding contours from unpaired image points. *Vision Research, 30,* 1811–1825.

Newson, L. J. (1958). Some principles governing changes in the apparent lightness of test surfaces isolated from their normal backgrounds. *Quarterly Journal of Experimental Psychology, 10,* 82–95.

Noguchi, K., & Kozaki, A. (1985). Perceptual scission of surface-lightness and illumination: An examination of the Gelb effect. *Psychological Research, 47,* 19–25.

Noguchi, K., & Masuda, N. (1971). Brightness changes in a complex field with changing illumination: A re-examination of Jameson and Hurvich's study of brightness constancy. *Japanese Psychological Research, 13,* 60–69.

O'Brien, V. (1958). Contour perception, illusion and reality. *Journal of the Optical Society of America, 48,* 112–119.

Oh, S., & Kim, J. (2004). The effects of global grouping laws on surface lightness perception. *Perception and Psychophysics, 66*(5), 792–799.

Olkkonen, K., Saarela, T., Peromaa, T., & Laurinen, P. (2002). Effects of chromatic contrast on brightness perception. *Perception, 31*(Supplement), 184d.

Osgood, C. (1953). *Method and Theory in Experimental Psychology.* New York: Oxford University Press.

Oyama, T. (1968). Stimulus determinants of brightness constancy and the perception of illumination. *Japanese Psychological Research, 10,* 146–155.

Paradiso, M. (2000). Visual neuroscience: Illuminating the dark corners. *Current Biology, 10,* R15–R18.

Pessoa, L., Mingolla, E., & Arend, L. (1996). The perception of lightness in 3D curved objects. *Perception and Psychophysics, 58,* 1293–1305.

Pessoa, L., Mingolla, E., & Neumann, H. (1995). A contrast- and luminance-driven multiscale network model of brightness perception. *Vision Research, 35*(15), 2201–2223.

Pritchard, R. M., Heron, W., & Hebb, D. (1960). Visual perception approached by the method of stabilized images. *Canadian Journal of Psychology, 14, 67–77.*

Purves, D., & Lotto, B. (2003). *Why We See What We Do: An Empirical Theory of Vision.* Sunderland: Sinauer.

Ramachandran, V. S. (1992). Blind spots. *Scientific American, 266*(5), 86–91.

Ratliff, F. (1965). *Mach Bands: Quantitative Studies on Neural Networks in the Retina.* San Francisco: Holden-Day.

Ratliff, F. (1972). Contour and contrast. *Scientific American, 226*(6), 90–101.

Rensink, R., O'Regan, J., & Clark, J. (1997). To see or not to see: the need for attention to perceive changes in scenes. *Psychological Science, 8,* 368–373.

Riggs, L., Ratliff, F., Cornsweet, J., & Cornsweet, T. (1953). The disappearance of steadily fixated visual test objects. *Journal of the Optical Society of America, 43,* 495–501.

Ripamonti, C., Bloj, M., Hauk, R., Mitha, K., Greenwald, S., Maloney, S., et al. (2004). Measurements of the effect of surface slant on perceived lightness. *Journal of Vision, 4,* 747–763.

Rock, I. (1975). *An Introduction to Perception.* New York: Macmillan.

Rock, I. (1977). In defense of unconscious inference. In W. Epstein (Ed.), *Stability and Constancy in Visual Perception: Mechanisms and Processes.* New York: Wiley.

Rock, I. (1983). *The Logic of Perception.* Cambridge, MA: MIT Press.

Rock, I. (1984). *Perception.* New York: Freeman.

Rock, I., & Brosgole, L. (1964). Grouping based on phenomenal proximity. *Journal of Experimental Psychology, 67*(6), 531–538.

Rock, I., & Ebenholtz, S. (1962). Stroboscopic movement based on change of phenomenal rather than retinal location. *American Journal of Psychology, 75,* 193–207.

Rock, I., Nijhawan, R., Palmer, S., & Tudor, L. (1992). Grouping based on phenomenal similarity of achromatic color. *Perception, 21*(6), 779–789.

Rock, I., & Victor, J. (1964). Vision and touch: An experimentally created conflict between the two senses. *Science, 143,* 594–596.

Roe, A., Pallas, S., Hahm, J., & Sur, M. (1990). A map of visual space induced into primary auditory cortex. *Science, 250,* 818–820.

Ross, J., Morrone, C. M., & Burr, D. C. (1989). The conditions under which Mach bands are visible. *Vision Research, 29,* 699–716.

Ross, W., & Pessoa, L. (2000). Lightness from contrast: A selective integration model. *Perception and Psychophysics, 62*(6), 1160–1181.

Rossi, A., Rittenhouse, C., & Paradiso, M. (1996). The representation of brightness in primary visual cortex. *Science, 273,* 1104–1107.

Rozhkova, G. I., Nickolayev, P. P., & Shchardrin, V. E. (1982). Perception of stabilized retinal stimuli in dichoptic viewing conditions. *Vision Research, 22,* 293–302.

Rubin, E. (1921). *Visuell wahrgenomenne Figuren.* Copenhagen: Gyldendalske.

Rubin, J., & Richards, W. (1982). Color vision and image intensities: when are changes material? *Biological Cybernetics, 45,* 215–226.

Rudd, M., & Zemach, I. (2004). Quantitative properties of achromatic color induction: An edge integration analysis. *Vision Research, 4,* 971–981.

Rudd, M., & Zemach, I. (2005). The highest luminance anchoring rule in achromatic color perception: Some counterexamples and an alternative theory. *Journal of Vision, 5*(11), 983–1003.

Rushton, W. A. H. (1969). Light and dark adaptation of the retina. In W. Reichardt (Ed.), *Processing of Optical Data by Organisms and Machines* (pp. 544–564). New York: Academic.

Rushton, W. A. H., & Gubisch, R. W. (1966). Glare: its measurement by cone thresholds and the bleaching of cone pigments. *Journal of the Optical Society of America, 56*, 104–110.

Rutherford, M., & Brainard, D. (2002). Lightness constancy: A direct test of the illumination-estimation hypothesis. *Psychological Science, 13*(2), 142–149.

Saunders, J. E. (1968). Adaptation, its effect on apparent brightness and contribution to the phenomenon of brightness constancy. *Vision Research, 8*, 451–468.

Schirillo, J., & Shevell, S. (1996). Brightness contrast from inhomogeneous surrounds. *Vision Research, 36*(12), 1783–1796.

Schirillo, J., & Shevell, S. (1997). An account of brightness in complex scenes based on inferred illumination. *Perception, 26*, 507–518.

Schirillo, J. A., & Arend, L. (1995). Illumination change at a depth edge can reduce constancy. *Perception and Psychophysics, 57*(2), 225–230.

Schirillo, J. A., Reeves, A., & Arend, L. (1990). Perceived lightness, but not brightness, of achromatic surfaces depends on perceived depth information. *Perception and Psychophysics, 48*(1), 82–90.

Schouten, J. F., & Ornstein, L. S. (1939). Measurements on direct and indirect adaptation by means of a binocular method. *Journal of the Optical Society of America, 29*, 168–182.

Schouten, S., & Blommaert, F. (1995a). Brightness constancy in a Ganzfeld environment. *Perception and Psychophysics, 57*(7), 1112–1122.

Schouten, S., & Blommaert, F. (1995b). Brightness indention: A novel compression mechanism in the luminance-brightness mapping. *Perception and Psychophysics, 57 (7)*, 1023–1031.

Schubert, J., & Gilchrist, A. L. (1992). Relative luminance is not derived from absolute luminance. *Investigative Ophthalmology and Visual Science, 33*(4), 1258.

Sedgwick, H. (2003). Relating direct and indirect perception of spatial layout. In H. Hecht, R. Schwartz, & M. Atherton (Eds.), *Looking into Pictures: An Interdisciplinary Approach to Pictorial Space*. Cambridge, MA: MIT Press.

Shapley, R. (1986). The importance of contrast for the activity of single neurons, the VEP and perception. *Vision Research, 26*(1), 45–61.

Shapley, R., & Enroth-Cugell, C. (1984). Visual adaptation and retinal gain controls. *Progress in Retinal Research, 3*, 263–343.

Shapley, R., & Reid, R. C. (1985). Contrast and assimilation in the perception of brightness. *Proceedings of the National Academy of Sciences of the USA, 82*, 5983–5986.

Shapley, R., & Tolhurst, D. (1973). Edge detectors in human vision. *Journal of Physiology, 229*, 165–183.

Shevell, S. K., Holliday, I., & Whittle, P. (1992). Two separate neural mechanisms of brightness induction. *Vision Research, 32*, 2331–2340.

Shimojo, S., & Nakayama, K. (1990). Amodal representation of occluded surfaces: role of invisible stimuli in apparent motion correspondence. *Perception, 19*(3), 285–299.

Shlaer, S. (1937). The relation between visual acuity and illumination. *Journal of Genetic Physiology, 21,* 165–188.

Singh, M. (2004). Lightness constancy through transparency: internal consistency in layered surface representations. *Vision Research, 44*(15), 1827–1842.

Singh, M., & Anderson, B. L. (2002). Toward a perceptual theory of transparency. *Psychological Review, 109,* 492–519.

Sinha, P., & Adelson, E. (1993). *Recovering Reflectance in a World of Painted Polyhedra.* Paper presented at the Fourth International Conference on Computer Vision, Berlin.

Slater, A., Mattock, A., & Brown, E. (1990). Size constancy at birth: newborn infants' responses to retinal and real sizes. *Journal of Experimental Child Psychology, 49,* 314–322.

Slater, A., & Morison, V. (1985). Shape constancy and slant perception at birth. *Perception, 14,* 337–344.

Spehar, B., Clifford, C., & Agostini, T. (2002). Induction in variants of White's effect: common or separate mechanisms? *Perception, 31,* 189–196.

Spehar, B., Gilchrist, A., & Arend, L. (1995). White's illusion and brightness induction: The critical role of luminance relations. *Vision Research, 35,* 2603–2614.

Speigle, J., & Brainard, D. (1996). The appearance of luminosity: effects of test chromaticity and ambient illumination. *Journal of the Optical Society of America A, 13,* 436–451.

Stevens, J. C. (1967). Brightness inhibition re size of surround. *Perception and Psychophysics, 2,* 189–192.

Stevens, S. (1961). To honor Fechner and repeal his law. *Science, 133,* 80–86.

Stevens, S., & Stevens, J. C. (1960). *The Dynamics of Visual Brightness* (No. PPR-246). Cambridge: Harvard University.

Stevens, S. S., & Diamond, A. L. (1965). Effect of glare angle on the brightness function for a small target. *Vision Research, 5,* 649–659.

Stewart, E. (1959). The Gelb effect. *Journal of Experimental Psychology, 57,* 235–242.

Takasaki, H. (1966). Lightness change of grays induced by change in reflectance of gray background. *Journal of the Optical Society of America A, 56,* 504.

Taubman, R. (1945). Apparent whiteness in relation to albedo and illumination. *Journal of Experimental Psychology, 35,* 235–241.

Taya, R., Ehrenstein, W., & Cavonius, C. (1995). Varying the strength of the Munker–White effect by stereoscopic viewing. *Perception, 24,* 685–694.

Thomas, J. P. (1966). Brightness variations in stimuli with ramp-like contours. *Journal of the Optical Society of America, 56*(2), 238–242.

Thomas, J. P., & Kovar, C. W. (1965). The effect of contour sharpness on perceived brightness. *Vision Research, 5,* 559–564.

Thouless, R. H. (1931). Phenomenal regression to the "real" object. *British Journal of Psychology, 22,* 1–30.

Todd, J., Norman, J., & Mingolla, E. (2004). Lightness constancy in the presence of specular highlights. *Psychological Science, 15*(1), 33–39.

Todorović, D. (1987). The Craik–O'Brien–Cornsweet effect: New varieties and their theoretical implications. *Perception and Psychophysics, 42*(6), 545–560.

Todorović, D. (1997). Lightness and junctions. *Perception, 26*(4), 379–394.

Todorović, D. (1998). In defense of neuro-perceptual isomorphism. *Behavioral and Brain Sciences, 21*, 774–775.

Torii, S., & Uemura, Y. (1965). Effects of inducing luminance and area upon the apparent brightness of a test field. *Japanese Psychological Research, 2*, 86–100.

Troy, J., & Enroth-Cugell, C. (1993). X and Y ganglion cells inform the cat's brain about contrast in the retinal image. *Experimental Brain Research, 93*, 383–390.

Turner, R. (1994). *In the Mind's Eye: Vision and the Helmholtz–Hering Controversy.* Princeton: Princeton University Press.

Ullman, S. (1976). On visual detection of light sources. *Biological Cybernetics, 21*, 205–212.

Valberg, A., & Lange Malecki, B. (1990). "Colour constancy" in Mondrian patterns: A partial cancellation of physical chromaticity shifts by simultaneous contrast. *Vision Research, 30*(3), 371–380.

von Bezold, W. (1874). *Die farbenlehrer im Hinblick auf Kunst und Kuntsgewerbe* (S. R. Koehler, Trans.). Brunswick: Westermann.

von Fieandt, K. (1966). *The World of Perception.* Homewood, IL: Dorsey Press.

von Fieandt, K., & Moustgaard, I. K. (1977). *The Perceptual World.* London: Academic Press.

Wallach, H. (1948). Brightness constancy and the nature of achromatic colors. *Journal of Experimental Psychology, 38*, 310–324.

Wallach, H. (1963). The perception of neutral colors. *Scientific American, 208*, 107–116.

Wallach, H. (1976). *On Perception.* New York: Quadrangle/The New York Times Book Co.

Walraven, J. (1973). Spatial characteristics of chromatic induction: The segregation of lateral effects from straylight artefacts. *Vision Research, 13*, 1739–1753.

Walraven, J. (1976). Discounting the background—the missing link in the explanation of chromatic induction. *Vision Research, 16*, 289–295.

Watanabe, T., & Cavanagh, P. (1993). Transparent surfaces defined by implicit X junctions. *Vision Research, 33*, 2339–2346.

Watanabe, I., Cavanagh, P., Anstis, S., & Shrira, I. (1995). *Shaded diamonds give an illusion of brightness.* Paper presented at the ARVO Annual Meeting, Fort Lauderdale, Florida.

Waygood, M. (1969). The visibility of rate of change of luminance in the presence or absence of a boundary. *Optica Acta, 16*, 61–64.

Weintraub, D. J. (1964). Successive contrast involving luminance and purity alterations of the Ganzfeld. *Journal of Experimental Psychology, 68*, 555–562.

Wertheimer, M. (1912). Experimentelle Studien über das Sehen von Bewegung. *Zeitschrift für Psychologie, 61*, 161–265.

Whipple, W., R., Wallach, H., & Marshall, F. J. (1988). The effect of area, separation, and dichoptic presentation on the perception of achromatic color. *Perception and Psychophysics, 43*(4), 367–372.

White, M. (1981). The effect of the nature of the surround on the perceived lightness of grey bars within square-wave test gratings. *Perception, 10*, 215–230.

Whittle, P. (1994). Contrast brightness and ordinary seeing. In A. Gilchrist (Ed.), *Lightness, Brightness, and Transparency* (pp. 111–158). Hillsdale, NJ: Erlbaum.

Whittle, P. (1994). The psychophysics of contrast brightness. In A. Gilchrist (Ed.), *Lightness, Brightness, and Transparency* (pp. 35–110). Hillsdale, NJ: Erlbaum.

Whittle, P., & Challands, P. D. C. (1969). The effect of background luminance on the brightness of flashes. *Vision Research, 9*, 1095–1110.

Wishart, K., Frisby, J., & Buckely, D. (1997). The role of 3D surface slope in a lightness/brightness effect. *Vision Research, 37*, 467–473.

Wist, E. R. (1974). Mach bands and depth adjacency. *Bulletin of the Psychonomic Society, 3*(2), 97–99.

Wist, E. R., & Susen, P. (1973). Evidence for the role of post-retinal process in simultaneous contrast. *Psychologische Forschung, 36*, 1–12.

Witkin, A. (1982). *Intensity-Based Edge Classification.* Paper presented at the Second National Conference on Artificial Intelligence, Menlo Park, CA.

Wolff, W. (1933). Concerning the contrast-causing effect of transformed colors. *Psychologische Forschung, 18*, 90–97.

Wolff, W. (1934). Induzierte Helligkeitsveränderung. *Psychologische Forschung, 20*, 159–194.

Woodworth, R. S. (1938). *Experimental Psychology.* New York: Holt.

Wyszecki, G. (1986). Color appearance. In K. R. Boff, L. Kaufman & J. P. Thomas (Eds.), *Handbook of Perception and Human Performance* (Chapter 9, pp. 1–57). New York: Wiley.

Wyszecki, G., & Stiles, W. S. (1967). *Color Science.* New York: John Wiley and Sons.

Yamauchi, Y., & Uchikawa, K. (2004). Limit of the surface-color mode perception under non-uniform illuminations. *Optical Review, 11*(4), 279–287.

Yarbus, A. L. (1956). Perception of the stationary retinal image. *Biofizika, 1*(5).

Yarbus, A. L. (1967). *Eye Movements and Vision.* New York: Plenum Press.

Yund, E. W., & Armington, J. C. (1975). Color and brightness contrast effects - as a function of spatial variables. *Vision Research, 15*, 917–929.

Zaidi, Q., Spehar, B., & Shy, M. (1997). Induced effects of backgrounds and foregrounds in three-dimensional configurations: the role of T junctions. *Perception, 26*, 395–408.

Zavagno, D. (1999). Some new luminance-gradient effects. *Perception, 28*, 835–838.

Zavagno, D., & Caputo, G. (2001). The glare effect and the perception of luminosity. *Perception, 30*, 209–222.

Zdravković, S., Economou, E., & Gilchrist, A. (2006). Lightness of an object under two illumination levels. *Perception.*

Author Index

Subject Index